These two photographic volumes depict Himmler's favourite unit in the *Waffen-SS*: the *III 'Germanic' SS Panzerkorps*, for it fulfilled Himmler's long-time political plans of recruiting 'Germanic' volunteers for the creation of a greater Germanic Reich in the future. As such, it consisted in part of SS volunteers from western and northern European countries. Although largely forgotten today, this elite SS unit fought on a variety of battlefields ranging from Croatia and Ingermanland's snow-covered forests near Leningrad to the historic Estonian city of Narva, where it defended the Baltic countries of Estonia and Latvia against the Red Army in 1944-45. The remnants of the *Panzerkorps* ended up in both the hopeless defence of Pomerania and the final apocalypse at the battle for Brandenburg and Berlin in April-May 1945, when the Third Reich went down in a storm of fire and steel.

Volume 1 covers the period from the creation of the *III SS Panzerkorps* in the summer of 1943 until the German evacuation of Estonia in September 1944. The coverage includes the unit's involvement in anti-partisan operations in Croatia (September- December 1943), the fighting at Oranienbaum-Leningrad and the battle for Ingria (January-February 1944); the defence of the Narva bridgehead and the battles for Dorpat and the Blue Hills, finishing with the German evacuation of Estonia (February-September 1944). On the Eastern Dront, a motley mix of nationalities and individuals fought under the Swastika and subsequently it was volunteers from various countries who served in the *III 'Germanic' SS Panzerkorps*, including Norwegians, Danes, Swedes, Swiss, Dutch, Flemings, Walloons, Estonians, Germans and ethnic Germans from Rumania. Even a handful of renegade British volunteers turned up in this unit during the final weeks of the Second World War. All of these soldiers had widely varying reasons for joining the *Waffen-SS*.

These volumes not only include a large number of photographs of the *III SS Panzerkorps* during 1943-45, many previously unpublished, but also a large number of previously unpublished personal battle descriptions by surviving officers and soldiers of this corps from the authors' archives of personal correspondence. The photographs are also accompanied by interesting unit histories, biographies, commentaries on weapons and vehicles, as well as analyses of battlefield tactics.

These volumes also destroy the myth that the *Waffen-SS* was purely a military phenomenon. The *Waffen-SS* was, and remained, in the world and in the long-term planning of Hitler, Himmler and the SS, primarily a political-ideological institution. The multinational *Waffen-SS* and its esprit de corps must be seen within the context of the European fascist movements of the time and of the polarization between fascism and communism during the years between the First and Second World War. This is especially true for the *III 'Germanic' SS Panzerkorps* as a future cadre providing SS functionaries for the creation and maintenance of a greater Germanic Reich in the West and the colonization of Lebensraum in the East. SS propaganda deliberately associated the character of the *III 'Germanic' SS Panzerkorps* with the medieval Teutonic Order in the East as an historic continuity. The dream of a Germanic empire and the Nazi war of extermination against Slavs and Jews were two sides of the same coin. Despite serious flaws during the hasty creation of the *III 'Germanic' SS Panzerkorps* in 1943, this unit achieved a remarkably successful military performance against a numerically superior opponent, the Red Army. The corps inflicted severe losses on Soviet units during all engagements. However, the losses of the *III SS Panzerkorps* in manpower and equipment were also extremely high. The personal battle descriptions included in the volumes provide a most powerful witness to the 'slaughterhouse' character of the Eastern Front in 1944-45.

Lennart Westberg is an elected memeber of the Swedish Military History Commission and co-author (with Lars Gyllenhaal) of the book *Swedes at War: Willing Warriors of a Neutral Nation, 1914-1945* (The Aberjona Press, US). He has written a number of articles on the Holocaust, the *Waffen- SS* and Sweden in the Second World War.

Petter Kjellander, a resident of Stockholm, Sweden, has researched the battles in the Baltic countries, Estonian and Latvian *Waffen-SS* volunteers, as well as Himmler's longterm pan-Germanic plans for the *Waffen-SS*, for a number of years. This is his first publication in English.

Geir Brenden was born in 1971. He has worked in the security industry for more than 21 years. Geir began researching the Norwegian volunteers in the *Waffen-SS* when he was 16 years old. He has 12 books, including co-authoring *Norwegian Volunteers of the Waffen-SS* with Tommy Natedal, published by Helion in 2016. He has also provided information and pictures for more than 60 books on the subject. Geir organises guided tours to the Eastern Front – where the Norwegians fought – and has led groups to Russia, Ukraina, Estonia, Latvia, Poland and Hungary.

III. GERMANIC SS-PANZER-KORPS

THE HISTORY OF HIMMLER'S FAVOURITE *SS-PANZER-KORPS*, 1943–1945

VOLUME 1: CREATION – SEPTEMBER 1944

Lennart Westberg, Petter Kjellander and Geir Brenden

with

Tommy Natedal and Martin Mansson

Helion & Company Ltd

Helion & Company Limited
Unit 8 Amherst Business Centre
Budbrooke Road
Warwick
CV34 5WE
England
Tel. 01926 499 619
Email: info@helion.co.uk
Website: www.helion.co.uk
Twitter: @helionbooks
Visit our blog http://blog.helion.co.uk/

Published by Helion & Company 2019. Reprinted in paperback 2023

Designed and typeset by Farr out Publications, Wokingham, Berkshire
Cover designed by Paul Hewitt, Battlefield Design (www.battlefield-design.co.uk)
Printed by Henry Ling Ltd, Dorchesster, Dorset

ISBN 978-1-804513-78-1

British Library Cataloguing-in-Publication Data.
A catalogue record for this book is available from the British Library.

For details of other military history titles published by Helion & Company Limited contact the above address, or visit our website: http://www.helion.co.uk.

We always welcome receiving book proposals from prospective authors.

Contents

LIST OF MAPS

LIST OF TERMS AND ABBREVIATIONS

Ia: Chief of Operations.
Ib: Chief of Supply/Maintenance.
Ic: Chief of Intellige.nce
IIa: Adjutant
AA: Anti-aircraft.
***Abteilung*:** Reinforced batallion or detachment. Aufklärungsabteilung was a reconnaissance battalion, often consisting of five companies.
***Abwehr*:** The central German military intelligence and counter-intelligence organization, headed by Admiral Wilhelm Canaris.
***APC*:** Armoured personnel carrier; see Schützenpanzerwagen (SPW).
***Armee (AOK, Armeeoberkommando)*:** Formation consisting of a number of Army and Panzer Corps.
***Armee-Abteilung*:** Army detachment, formation smaller than an army, containing, for example, one corps and a number of ad hoc units (Kampfgruppen).
***Armee-Korps*:** Army corps, normally a formation of two infantry divisions.
***Aufklärung*:** Recce or reconnaissance.
***Axis*:** The military alliance between Germany, Italy and Japan.
***Barbarossa*:** Operation code for the Nazi invasion of the Soviet Union in June 1941. Its name came from the Holy Roman Emperor Frederick I (1123–90).
***Batterie*:** The artillery equivalent of an infantry company.
***Begleitkompanie*:** Escort company.
***Bergepanzer*:** Vehicle that recovered tanks. In Narva the Waffen-SS used, for example, a T-34 without a turret as a Bergepanzer.
***Bewährungskompanie*:** Detention company.
Bolsheviks: Majority faction of the Russian main Marxist Party, founded in 1903.
***Brigade*:** Brigade, consisting of two or more regiments. For example: SS-Panzer-Brigade "Westfalen" (1945) or SS-Panzer-Brigade "Gross" (1944–45).
***Britisches Freikorps*:** British Free Corps.
***Brückenkopf*:** Bridgehead.
***Chef des Generalstabes*:** Chief of General Staff. The title and function normally used for Franz Halder, Kurt Zeitzler, Heinz Guderian and Hans Krebs, who held these positions 1938–45, in the Oberkommando des Heeres (OKH). The title was also used for the chief operations officer in an Army or Panzer Corps staff; for example, Joachim Ziegler and Helmut von Bockelberg as Chef des Generalstabes beim Generalkommando des III. (Germ.) SS-Panzerkorps 1943–45.
***Chef des Stabes*:** Chief of Staff.
***Comintern*:** Communist International Organization.
***Deutsches Kreuz in Gold (DKiG)*:** German Cross in Gold, a German military award.
***Dienststelle*:** Bureau or agency.
***Ehrenblattspange des deutschen Heeres*:** German military award.
***Einsatzgruppen*:** Battalion-sized, mobile armed units of Security Police and SD officials, Kriminalpolizei and Waffen-SS, mainly used for the mass murder of Soviet Jews, commissars, partisans and civilians behind the Eastern Front.
***Einsatzkommando*:** Company-sized component of the Einsatzgruppen.
***EK I*:** Iron Cross 1st Class.
***EK II*:** Iron Cross 2nd Class.
***Ersatzheer*:** Reserve Army.
***Ersatz- und Ausbildungstruppen (AuE)*:** Replacement troops, normally under training behind the Front (such as the SS-Panzer- und Ausbildungs-Regiment in Dondangen near Tukkums in Latvia) or in Germany (such as the SS-Panzergrenadier-Ersatz und Ausbildungs-Batallion 11 in Graz).
***Fallschirmjäger-Division*:** Parachute division.
***Feldgendarmerie or Feldpolizei*:** The field or army police; the feared "Chain Dogs".
Final Solution: Short version of the Nazi term, "Final Solution of the Jewish Question", a euphemism for the extermination of the European Jews.
***Flak (Flieger-Abwehr-Kanone)*:** Anti-aircraft gun.
***Freiwilligen*:** Volunteer.
***Führer Chancellery*:** Adolf Hitler's chancellery in central Berlin as Reichskanzler (head of government) and Führer des deutschen Reiches and of the NSDAP. Hitler's title as Reichskanzler was subordinate to that of Führer.
***Führerhauptquartier (FHQ)*:** Hitler's various command HQs where he resided with his closest military and political staff, the more well-known being the Wolfsschanze (Wolf's Lair) near the town of Rastenburg in East Prussia (where the attempted bomb plot against Hitler took place on 20 July 1944) and

Hitler's final command post in the Reich Chancellery in Berlin.

Funk: Radio communication.

***Generalkommando*:** The staff of an Army or Panzer Corps.

***Generalstab des Heeres*:** Army General Staff.

Gestapo: Geheime Staatspolizei (Secret State Police, also called Staatspolizei or Stapo; being a part of the Reichssicherheitshauptamt, RSHA).

***Gross-Deutschland (GD)*:** Originally an army elite regiment, later expanded to a Panzergrenadier-Division and Panzer Corps.

***Gulag*:** Glavnoe Upravlenie Lagerei (main camp administration); eventually in charge of Soviet concentration camps.

***Hauptkampflinie (HKL)*:** Main Defence Line.

***Heer*:** The German army.

***Heeresgruppe*:** Army Group, a formation consisting of two or more armies; the largest German formation at the Front with hundreds of thousands of men. For example the Heeresgruppe Nord (renamed on 26 January 1945 Heeresgruppe Courland) which held the northern Eastern Front. In early 1944 it retreated from the Leningrad area back to Narva, and later to the Courland pocket in Latvia.

***Hilfswillige (Hiwis)*:** Foreign auxiliary volunteers, often Soviet POWs doing supply or other secondary duties in the German Army.

***Hitler-Jugend (HJ)*:** Hitler Youth.

***Höherer SS- und Polizeiführer*:** Higher SS and Police Leader. Supreme territorial or regional commander for all SS and police functions within the territory or region.

Holocaust: Post-war term for the Nazi murder of the European Jews.

Jak 9: Soviet fighter plane.

Josef Stalin (JS): Heavy Soviet tank.

***Kampfgruppe*:** An improvised combat and battle group. Ad hoc task-forces formed to carry out a certain operational mission.

***Katyusha*:** The famous truck-mounted rocket artillery, nicknamed "Stalin's Organ", with a range between 2,500 meters and 8,400 meters. The low accuracy was compensated for by the large numbers of rockets, fast-firing sequence and their demoralizing effect. The German equivalent was the multi-barrelled Nebelwerfer.

***KPD*:** Communist Party of Germany.

***Kraftfahrzeug (Kfz)*:** Type (identification) of German military vehicle.

***Kriegsmarine*:** German Navy.

***KZ or Konzentrationslager*:** Concentration camp.

***Luftwaffe*:** German Air Force.

***Maschinengewehr (MG)*:** Machine gun.

***Nachrichtenabteilung*:** Signals battalion.

***Nahkampfspange*:** Close-combat award.

***Nationalkommittee Freies Deutschland*:** German Anti-Nazi organization, operating in the Soviet Union and founded on 12 July 1943 in Krasnogorsk, near Moscow. Its leadership consisted of 38 members, including 28 German POWs and 10 exiled German communists.

***Nebelwerfer*:** Rocket artillery.

***NKVD or Narodnyi Komissariat Vnutrennikh Del*:** The People's Commissariat for Internal Affairs. Often used as initials for the Soviet secret police when, from 1934, the GPU-OGPU was reorganized into the NKVD and named GUGB NKVD.

***NSDAP*:** National Socialist German Workers' Party, or the German Nazi Party.

***Oberkommando der Wehrmacht (OKW)*:** High Command of the German Armed Forces, including Heer, Luftwaffe and Kriegsmarine.

***Oberkommando des Heeres (OKH)*:** High Command of the German Army; the central operational staff of the OKH was normally close to Hitler's HQ (Rastenburg, Winniza etc). Other parts of the OKH were situated in Zossen, south of Berlin, while the commander of the Home Army (Generaloberst Friedrich Fromm) had his office in the Bendlerstrasse in Berlin.

***Ordnungspolizei (Order Police)*:** Separate from the Gestapo and Criminal Police. Included the city and rural police (Schutzpolizei and Gendarmerie). Battalions of Order Police functioned in the Soviet Union as the Einsatzgruppen and carried out mass killings.

OT or Organization Todt: Civil and military engineering group.

***Pak (Panzer-Abwehr-Kanone)*:** Anti-tank gun.

***Panzerfaust*:** Single-shot, hand-held anti-tank weapon.

***Panzergrenadiere*:** Mechanized or motorized armoured infantry.

***Panzergruppe*:** Armoured tank unit.

***Panzerkampfabzeichen*:** Armoured military award for conduct in tank warfare.

***Panzerkampfwagen*:** Battle tank.

***Pz IV (F)*:** Panzer IV tank with long-barreled 75mm/L 48 gun.

***Pz V*:** Panther tank

***Pz VI*:** Tiger I or Tiger II/King Tiger tank.

***Panzerkorps*:** A unit normally containing two Panzer divisions.

***Pionier*:** German Army engineer.

***Politbüro*:** Main committee of the Central Committee of the Soviet Communist Party.

***Quartiermeister*:** Quartermaster on a general staff, responsible for supply.

***Reichsarbeitsdienst (RAD)*:** Reich Labour Force.

***Reichsführer-SS*:** Reich Leader of the Schutzstaffel or SS, namely Heinrich Himmler. From 1936, Himmler also added the title "Chief of the German Police".

Rifle: Soviet designation for regular infantry formations.

Ritterkreuz: Knight's Cross, a military award.

RSHA or Reichicherheitshauptamt: Reich's Security Main Office, created in September 1939. A combined government-SS organization, incorporating major non-military offices responsible for intelligence work, security and criminal police work. Included the Sicherheitspolizei (Gestapo and Criminal Police) and the SS Security Service, or SD (Sicherheitsdienst) among other branches. Formally headed by Himmler, but run by Reinhard Heydrich (and his successor Dr Ernst Kaltenbrunner).

SA or Sturmabteilung: The Nazi Brownshirts.

Schützenpanzerwagen (SPW): Armoured half-track for carrying Panzer grenadiers and other infantry units. Every German Panzer or Panzer-grenadier division had normally at least one battalion of their infantry equipped with a number of SPW. The rifle companies within such a division's reconnaissance battalions were also equipped with half-tracks. There was a broad variety of SPWs due to their function; for example signals and communications, pioneering, ambulance or carrying staff officers at the Front.

Schwere: Heavy unit.

Schwimmwagen: Amphibious jeep.

SD or Sicherheitsdienst: Security Service of the Nazi Party.

Sipo or Sicherheitspolizei: Security Police. Founded in 1936 as the umbrella organization for the Gestapo and Kripo (German CID).

Sonderkraftfarhzeug (SdKfz): German identification for a type of motorized and often armoured military vehicle in the Wehrmacht, including the Waffen-SS.

SS: Schutzstaffel. Literally "Protection squadron", the Nazis' paramilitary organization.

SS-Führungshauptamt: SS command office for military training, affairs and organization.

SS-Hauptamt: SS central office for recruiting indigenous citizens and foreign volunteers.

SS-Junkerschule: SS-officers' candidate school (situated in Bad Tölz, Braunschweig and Prague).

SS-Kriegsberichter: War correspondent of the Waffen-SS.

Stalinorgel: Soviet multi-rocket launcher (see Katyusha).

Standarte: Regiment in the pre-war SS-Verfüngstruppe.

Stavka or Stavka Verkhovnogo Glavnokomandovaniya: Stavka is the term used to refer to the Headquarters of the Supreme Main Command of the Armed Forces of the USSR (since 8 August 1941). The term, sometimes in Western military literature falsely written in uppercase STAVKA, although it is not an acronym, refers both to its members as well as the location of the Headquarters.

Stuka (Sturzkampfflugzeug): Junkers Ju-87 dive bomber.

Stuka zu Fuss: "Stuka on foot", the nickname of the Wurfrahmen 40 mobile rocket launcher.

Sturmabteilung (SA): Storm Trooper detachment of the Nazi Party, the Brownshirts.

Sturmgeschütz (StuG): Assault gun, self-propelled artillery.

Sturmgewehr (StG): German automatic carbine.

T-34: Soviet medium/heavy tank.

Third Reich *(das Dritte Reich)*: Literally "Third Nation", or "Empire". Term for the Nazi Empire. The First Reich was the Holy Roman Empire from Charlemagne to Frederick II; the Second Reich was Germany under the Hohenzollern emperors Wilhelm I and II, 1871–1918.

Verteidigungsbereich: Defensive area.

Volkssturm: People's Army. Home defense militia, constituted by Hitler on 25 September 1944 and consisting of every male between 16 and 60 years old who had previously not been drafted. The creation of the Volkssturm was laid in the hands of the Gauleiters, while the responsibility for its military organization, training and armament was a task for Heinrich Himmler as new commander of the Home Army (Befehlshaber des Ersatzheeres). Hitler-Germany's last desperate call to arms of around six million men was badly trained and equipped. Their losses were horrible, especially on the Eastern Front. After the end of the war, 175,000 men from the Volkssturm were counted as missing in action. The number killed in action is not known.

Wache: Guard unit.

Waffen-SS: Literally, "Armed SS".

Wehrmacht: All German armed forces, including Heer, Luftwaffe and Kriegsmarine. Only in tactical terms was the Waffen-SS a part of the Wehrmacht.

Wehrmachtgefolge: Semi-military formations like the Reichsarbeitsdienst (RAD), Organization Todt (OT), etc.

Wunderwaffe: Wonder Weapons, like the V1 and V2 rockets and the Me-262 jet planes. SS-Obergruppenführer Hans Kammler was, from 8 August 1944, responsible for the development of the V1 rockets, and also for the V2 from January 1945. On 27 March 1945, Kammler was given overall command for the development of all jet planes; he was also in charge of the German nuclear research program.

Zitadelle: Citadel, the operational code name for the German offensive at Kursk in the summer of 1943. During the final battle of Berlin in April–May 1945, Zitadelle was the name for the inner defence circle, including the Reichskanzlei and the governmental blocks in the city of Berlin. The remnants of the SS Nordland division were part of the forces defending the Zitadelle up to 2 May 1945 and the German surrender of Berlin.

Zug (plural Züge): Platoon; a company's sub-divisions.

ACKNOWLEDGEMENTS

We have received invaluable help from several individuals, archives and other institutions during the process of writing and illustrating this book. We initially warmly thank Dr Jens Westemeier (Aachen), Associate Professor Sigurd Sørlie (Oslo), Professor Niels Bo Poulsen (Copenhagen) and Professor Lars Westerlund (Helsinki), all esteemed academic researchers in their fields, for contributing respectively to the two volumes on the Third "Germanic" *SS-Panzer* Corps with foreword and essays of the highest academic standards. This contributed substantially to the authors' and Helion's new concept of critically commented pictorial volumes on the *III. (Germ.) SS-Panzer-Korps*, emphasizing the *political and ideological* dimensions of Heinrich Himmler's favourite *SS-Panzer-Korps*.

New photographic material from private collections, archives and former volunteers in the *III. (Germ.) SS-Panzer-Korps* are in several cases published for the first time. In addition, there are a number of personal accounts from the various battlefields by former soldiers and officers in the *III. (Germ.) SS-Panzer-Korps*. The vast majority of those accounts are now published in English for the first time and give the readers a unique glimpse of the brutal reality on the Eastern Front: the 'Slaughterhouse'.[1]

We warmly thank our Norwegian friend, Tommy Natedal, for extremely valuable contributions from his private archives of correspondence with Norwegian former volunteers in the *Waffen-SS*. Petter Kjellander in Stockholm is not only a good friend and a specialist on the Estonian and Latvian units in the *Waffen-SS*, but has previously sacrified many hours to support our project. Petter has for many years also been a qualified partner for discussions on Himmler's long-term pan-Germanic plans for the *Waffen-SS*. Helion subsequently in December 2017 appointed Petter as a full co-writer for our project. Björn Leo has unselfishly assisted us with his profound knowledge about the history of the Estonian city of Narva, before and during the Second World War. Knut Sivertsen, Roland Pfeiffer and Uwe Kuppen have generously shared their solid knowledge of certain aspects of the *Waffen-SS*.

Lennart Westberg would like especially to thank Professor Gerald Fleming of the University of Guildford, for many conversations in London and via letters on the *SS* and the Holocaust. Special warm thanks to my late US-uncle Paul in California (Professor em. at UCLA), whose everlasting support and friendship will never be forgotten. Professor Stig Ekman of Stockholm University, the academic *doyen* about Sweden and the Third *Reich*, has always been a supportive friend. Many thanks to Hans Werner Neulen in Cologne, a friend since many years, and author of the pioneering book on the multinational *Waffen-SS: An deutscher Seite*.[2]

Lennart is also in debt to Professor Sven Ekdahl, Berlin, for his vast knowledge on the Teutonic Order, the Battle of Tannenberg 1410 and its effects on later Polish, German and National Socialist propaganda. Many thanks to Dr Adalbert Rueckerl, former Chief Prosecutor and Director for the German federal commission in Ludwigsburg (*Zentrale Stelle*) for indictment of National Socialist mass crimes, who for many years has shared his great knowledge about the *SS* and the post-war trials of *NS-Verbrechen* before German courts. For valuable seminar discussions in Oslo on Himmler's *gross-germanische* policies, etc., Lennart would like to thank Dr Terje Emberland and Dr Matthew Kott, Oslo, authors of the pioneering book *Himmler's Norge*. For 15 years, Rechtsanwalt a.D. Fritz Ulrich has always been kindly availabe for discussions and correspondence on the *Germanische Leitstelle* in Berlin and other issues regarding the *Waffen-SS*. Lennart is in debt to a long-time friend and Police colleague, the former *1. Polizei-Hauptkommissar* Harold Selowski in Berlin for his excellent knowledge on the Republic of Weimar, the *SS* and *NSDAP*. Warm thanks to Brigadier Einar Lyth for his valuable support during many years.

We also express our humble thanks to the following individuals who have helped us with information, photos, suggestions and valuable support: Jens Pank Bjerregaard, Predrag Blanusa, Alvin Carlsson, Andrew Found, Lars Gyllenhaal, Cees Kleijn, Ivar Kraglund, Lars Larsen, Lars T. Larsson, Michael Miller, John P. Moore, Aart Nömm, Marc Rikmenspoel, Bram van Straalen, Leo Tammiksaar, Charles Trang, Paul Turner and Andreas Vogt.

Finally, we wish to warmly thank Duncan Rogers and his qualified staff at Helion & Company Ltd for invaluable inspiration, deep knowledge and dedication to our book project.

Lennart Westberg, Geir Brenden, Petter Kjellander

1 The term appropriately used by the US military expert Keith E. Bonn of the Aberjona Press in *Slaughterhouse. The Handbook of the Eastern Front* (Bedford: 2005).

2 Hans Werrner Neulen, *An deutscher Seite. Internationale Freiwillige von Wehrmacht und Waffen-SS* (Munich, Universitas, 1985). His magnum opus is: *Feldgrau in Jerusalem. Das Levantekorps des Kaiserlichen Deutschlands* (Munich, Universitas, 1991).

FOREWORD

by Dr Jens Westemeier

In war, photography is one of the propaganda weapons of the warlords. Photographs are used to inspire the homeland and its war effort, and provide news of victories at the front. Additionally, by the use of images the observer is, as it were, drawn into the picture and can participate in the events portrayed. Photographs were regularly staged for their audience.

The photographs published in Nazi media regarding the *Waffen-SS* are no different. Material for this purpose was produced by the *SS*'s own propaganda companies. These propaganda images of the *SS* were intended to be seen as authentic, and as testimony of a reality which was, in fact, staged for the camera. The imagery itself should not be compared to other war photography, even that which attempted to reproduce scenes staged for the camera.[1]

Death and serious wounds, mutilations and facial injuries were masked out and the war is modelled in pictures as a clean and aseptic affair showing healthy and strong soldiers. The humane treatment of prisoners of war and the civilian population is another pattern. The German war of extermination against the Soviet Union, executions and massacres, as recorded by hundreds of thousands of *Wehrmacht* soldiers with their own cameras, cannot be found here. The contemporary publication of *SS* pictorial material was subject to a targeted and central selection as well as strict censorship. On the one hand, it was necessary to create a brand image and a form of cross-corporate identity through a uniformity of image material above all in the *Waffen-SS*, as a National Socialist and 'Aryan' organization, and military elite.[2] There were also privately held photographs of crimes of the *Waffen-SS*, which were destroyed in 1945, as was the case with units of the *4. SS-Polizei-Panzergrenadier-Division* and the *Ordnungspolizei*.[3]

Massacres in locations such as Mielec, Le Paradis, Wormhout, Pinsk and throughout the Pripyet Marshes, Boves, Lake Maggiore, Marzabotto, Sant' Anna di Stazzema, Ascq, Distomo, Oradour, Malmedy and Stavelot bore all the hallmarks of the *Waffen-SS*, which can be supplemented with an endless list of crimes throughout Europe, but especially in Eastern and South-eastern Europe. In the Nuremberg trials, the *Waffen-SS* was decreed a criminal organization, but in fact only a few perpetrators were brought to justice.

Photography has always been used as a weapon in the struggle for memory and the interpretation of history. This becomes clear in popular literature concerning, and justifying, the history and activities of the *Waffen SS*. In the battle for the whitewashing of the *Waffen-SS* after 1945, the images of the *SS* propaganda companies as well as selected images from the private collections of *SS* veterans were among the most effective means available, because these usually show only a purely soldierly environment. It was initially only organizations of *SS* veterans who reinterpreted their past with monumental illustrated volumes such as *Wenn alle Brüder schweigen* in the spirit of their group's policy, the *Waffen-SS* being portrayed as "*Soldaten wie andere auch*" (soldiers just like any others), as gurus and romantics, for the *SS* veterans were, in their view, following seamlessly in their footsteps as "objective and neutral historians void of political opinion".[4] With introductory phrases couched in unpolitical and unprejudiced objectivity, to this day they consciously detach the *Waffen-SS* from the context of the history of National Socialism, the Holocaust and the Nazi crimes in their publications, and agree with the grotesque eulogies on the *Waffen-SS*. Such an approach is unhistorical, but meets the self-presentation needs of *SS* veterans and their apologists as well as the desired images of their reading public.[5] The victims of the *Waffen-SS* remain faceless and nameless, while the "heroes of the *Waffen-SS*" are repeatedly put into the light and mutate their portraits to become icons of a fascist aesthetic.

In these icons, a sublime face, dashing *SS* uniforms and camouflage jackets, waxed leather boots, a fascist gun

1 See Gerhard Paul, "Kriegsbilder – Bilderkriege", in *Aus Politik und Zeitgeschehen*, No 31/2009, pp.39-46.

2 See Jochen Lehnhardt, *Die Inszenierung des nationalsozialistischen Soldaten: Die Waffen-SS in der NS-Propaganda*, as well as references to this topic by Lennart Westberg in the Introduction.

3 See Stefan Kühl, *Ganze normal Organisationen. Zur Soziologie des Holocaust* (Berlin: 2014), p.335. There is also the footage of the massacre in Minsk in the presence of Heinrich Himmler, or the slaughter in Ukraine with Max Täubner, which was documented in the personal staff of the *Reichsführer SS* and others, owned by *SS Obergruppenführer* Karl Wolff, who almost certainly destroyed it in 1945.

4 See Ronald Smelser and Edward J. Davies, *The Myth of the Eastern Front: the Nazi-Soviet War in American Popular Culture* (Cambridge: 2008).

5 See the Introduction by Bernd Wegner in Wolfgang Schneider, *Die Waffen-SS* (Hamburg: 2000).

design – the MG-42 or MP-40 – flashing Knight's Crosses, symbols of artificial *SS* mythology and phallic steel helmets, a sublime fetish is staged. In the cult of this worship of outward appearances, a sexualization of power also sets in. In the sexualization of National Socialist insignia, *Waffen-SS* photographs immediately turn into erotic material that satisfies a clear need of a particular clientele for these illustrated books.[6]

With a mostly unequivocal right-wing content, illustrated books about the *Waffen-SS* are regarded by historians as being disreputable and seem downright repugnant. This is likely to be a major reason why such analysis and its imagery are neglected in research, although photographs are an important source and can sometimes help to fill gaps in war diaries and *SS* personnel records as to location and affiliation.

Lennart Westberg, Geir Brenden and Martin Månsson face a difficult task with the illustrated book *Himmler's Favourite*.[7] Except for an essay by Bernd Wegner, the history of the *III. (Germanic) SS-Panzer-Korps*, which, for example, committed numerous war crimes in Croatia in 1943, possesses no academic or serious study. In addition to the usual *Waffen-SS* myths of the military elite, which had nothing to do with Nazi crimes, the authors see in this *SS*-formation in particular the stubborn post-war fairy tale of the *Waffen-SS* as the predecessor of NATO. This was just one example of numerous myths that *SS* veterans erected around the former commander of this *SS*-formation, Felix Steiner, after 1945. To this end, Western European *SS* members, as the "*avant-garde* of the West", are still seeing a transfiguration in right-wing populist and fascist movements in their countries of origin, in which they often continued to operate after 1945.

The authors of this critically commented illustrated book not only use the well-known material produced by the *SS* for their work, but supplement it with a wealth of previously unpublished photographs from archives and private collections. The authors also correctly classify the *Waffen-SS* as a predominantly political rather than military phenomenon. In critical accompanying texts, they point out Himmler's long-term goals of using the "Germanic" volunteers as a cadre for political functionaries of a "state protection corps" of the intended "Greater Germanic *Reich*" in the West or as administrators of the colonial *Lebensraum* in the East.[8]

The authors try to classify the material historically and critically in the history of the *Waffen-SS*, point out the origin of their traditions and also show new research on the *Waffen-SS*, because apologists like to ignore such research on the history of the *Waffen-SS*, which has presented significant work in recent years. Here one need mention only Jean-Luc Leleu's *La Waffen-SS*, Martin Cüppers' *Wegbereiter der Shoah*, Niels Weise' *Eicke*, Franz Josef Merkl's *Simon* or the anthology of Jan Erik Schulte, Peter Lieb and Bernd Wegner, *Die Waffen-SS*, which summarizes the results of two conferences on the *Waffen-SS*. Here, the essential contribution of Hitler's political soldiers as a pioneer of the Holocaust was demonstrated and the myth of a military elite deconstructed.

Only with critical editions of images can the frequently demanded "iconic turn" in humanities succeed in further exploring the history of the *Waffen-SS*. The present work contributes to this.

Jens Westemeier, PhD, University of Aachen
with the Institute for History, Theory and
Ethics in Medicine

6 See Marcus Stiglegger, *Nazi-Chic und Nazi-Trash. Faschistische Ästhetik in der populären Kultur* (Berlin: 2011).

7 After Dr Jens Westemeier wrote this foreword, Martin Månsson could unfortunately not contribute to this volume in more than a marginal way due to severe health problems.

8 See Lennart Westberg's analysis of Himmler's long-term goals for his "Germanic" policy in Lars Gyllenhaal & Lennart Westberg, *Swedes at War, Willing Warriors of a Neutral Nation, 1914-1945* (Bedford PA: 2010), pp.315ff.

PREFACE

One of our primary ambitions with two pictorial volumes at Helion & Company Ltd has been to emphasize the character of the Third "Germanic" *SS-Panzer* Corps as primarily a political-ideological phenomenon, alongside its military role during the fighting in Croatia, Ingria, the Baltic countries, Pomerania and Brandenburg-Berlin from 1943–45.[1]

Adding recent, partly fragmentary research on the various motives (or combination of motives) for volunteers from Northern and North-Western Europe to join the *Waffen-SS*, there is no doubt that these men, prior to joining the *SS*, in their absolute majority carried a solid National Socialist worldview. Domestic *SS* propaganda did not "shape" or "dupe" their minds, but acted generally as a "cosmetic" confirmation not only for their hatred of Eastern Bolshevism, but also of their consistent dissociation of their native countries' parliamentarism, and of the Liberal West.

The purpose of our project is also to present a critically commented, advanced pictorial study of the *III. (Germ.) SS-Panzer-Korps* from 1943–45, being one of the key multinational armoured units in understanding the long-term pan-Germanic visions of the *Reich* Leader of the *SS*, Heinrich Himmler, and his visions of a Greater Germanic *Reich* and *Lebensraum* (Life Space) in the East.

Not always, but in too many cases, traditional pictorial volumes on the *Waffen-SS* might be classified as uncritical, tending in a varying degree to be apologetic; not so much regarding what is actually described in such volumes, but due to what is *not* related in these publications. Instead, we hope to bring some of the latest academic research on the *Waffen-SS* to the interested reader's attention, thus putting the heterogenic and multinational *Waffen-SS* into its historical and ideological context.

We are very grateful to Dr Jens Westemeier of the UniKlinik RWTH of Aachen for his authoritative Foreword, and for analyzing many of the propagandist myths surrounding wartime National Socialist photography of the *Waffen-SS* within the Third *Reich*.

This volume is not a predominantly scientific work but it contains scientific contributions, written by highly qualified Scandinavian academic experts on the Second World War and the *Waffen-SS*. We would especially like to thank Professor Sigurd Sørlie, Associate Professor at the Norwegian Institute for Defence Studies in Oslo, and the foremost expert on Norwegian *SS*-volunteers, for his most valuable essay in this volume on the Norwegian volunteers in the *Waffen-SS* and the *III. (Germ.) SS-Panzer-Korps*. A warm thanks to Professor Niels Bo Poulsen, Director at the Danish Academy for Military Studies in Copenhagen, the academic *doyen* on Danish volunteers in the *Waffen-SS* and one of Scandinavia's leading experts on Nazism, Stalinism and the Second World War. (Dr Poulsen's essay on the Danish *Waffen-SS* will be published in Volume 2.) Dr Lars Westerlund of Helsinki, the esteemed expert on Finnish volunteers in the *Waffen-SS*, has contributed two extremely valuable essays in Volume 2.

Keeping the ideological aspects and institutional functions of the *Waffen-SS* in mind, we also have the ambition to complete the photographic material in this book with individual battle descriptions, extracted from private correspondence or archives. Strategic and tactical overviews will hopefully facilitate the reader to follow the actions of the *III. (Germ.) SS-Panzer-Korps* on various battlefields in Ingria, the Baltic countries, Pomerania and Brandenburg-Berlin in 1944–45. Also included are the important and characteristic so-called anti-partisan actions in Croatia, in the autumn of 1943, and the Holocaust in the Baltic countries. There are also minor biographies of German and Soviet commanders, as well as descriptions of armor, weapons and vehiclesused by both sides on the Eastern Front.to emphasize the political character of many *Waffen-SS* formations in the Northern and Western European countries occupied by Germany.

Comments on recent research on the Nazification and brutalization of the *Wehrmacht* and *Waffen-SS* in the East are also included on a wide scale, as well as insights into the harsh and brutal life of "Ivan", the Soviet infantry soldier at the Eastern Front: a person seldom depicted in the mass of books on the *Waffen-SS*. We have in this volume also added historic notes on, for example, the Dutch, Walloon, Norwegian and Danish fascist movements, which often served as catalysts for recruiting volunteers from these more or less pro-Nazi parties to the *III. (Germ.) SS-Panzer-Korps*. More extensive texts are signed by its respective co-author.

In the ranks of the *III. (Germ.) SS-Panzer-Korps* there fought volunteers from Denmark, Norway, Sweden, Switzerland, the Netherlands and Belgium (Walloons and

1 The Third Germanic *SS-Panzer* Corps is hereafter cited as *III. (Germ.) SS-Panzer-Korps*, corresponding to the official nomenclature of the *SS-Führungshauptamt*.

Flemish), but also to a major extent thousands of ethnic German recruits from Rumania: the *Volksdeutsche*. The ethnic character and history of this latter contingent has seldom been described and is therefore included in this volume.

Photographs illustrate the everyday life within a military unit. The reader should thereby be advised to keep in mind that the character of the photographic material differs. The official photos, taken by the war correspondents (the *Kriegsberichter*) from the *Waffen-SS* or the Army, were mainly for propagandistic purposes, while the snapshots taken by individual soldiers more often depict the realistic everyday life at the Front, although taboo atrocities and dead comrades were seldom photographed.

Except for Wilhelm Tieke's *Tragedy of the Faithful*, there are no available titles in English that cover the complete story of the *III. (Germ.) SS-Panzer-Korps*.[2] The offer from Duncan Rogers at Helion & Company Ltd to edit and publish a new concept of a critically commented pictorial study on this *Panzer* corps was indeed tempting, due to the large amount of photos, documents, interviews and other unique material on this unit which had never been published before.

After Duncan Rogers' proposal, the idea of editing this pictorial study on the *III. (Germ.) SS-Panzer Korps* and its function and transition into Himmler's visions of a Greater Germanic *Reich*, began to take form. The material was so extensive that instead of one volume, it was decided by Duncan Rogers to publish two. Geir Brenden from Norway now joined the team, being one of the leading authorities on Norwegian volunteers and owning a huge photo archive for this field. Another important contributor of material is his fellow Norwegian Tommy Natedal, who is an equally qualified expert on the Norwegian *Waffen-SS* and has conducted numerous interviews with former soldiers of the *SS-Panzer-Grenadier-Regiment 23 "Norge"*. We have also kindly profited from the knowledge of Petter Kjellander, the foremost expert on Estonians in the *Waffen-SS* and the decisive battles east of Narva, at the Tannenberg-line and around Dorpat, in July–August 1944.

Due to unfortunate reasons of health, Martin Månsson has not been able to participate in the present volume as planned, and the principal authors have been Lennart Westberg, Geir Brenden and Petter Kjellander. The majority of the photo captions have been written by Lennart Westberg and, whenever applicable, added and adjusted by Geir Brenden and Petter Kjellander. Björn Leo has been kind enough to share with us his expertise on the baroque city of Narva, mainly shaped and built during the reign of the Greater Swedish Empire during the 17th century.

The battles on the Eastern Front within the ranks of the *III. (Germ.) SS-Panzer-Korps* are the most fierce that volunteers from Scandinavia and North-West Europe participated in. The elements of the *III. (Germ.) SS-Panzer-Korps* – by strength and composition neither a *Panzer* corps nor especially "Germanic" – conducted during its existence some noteworthy military performances, and inflicted during its skillful rearguard actions in 1944–45 heavy casualties upon the opposing and vastly superior Red Army forces. This fact also adds to the overall picture of this *Panzer* corps.

Our Helion project on the *III. (Germ.) SS-Panzer-Korps* does not have the ambition to cover the complete military combat history of the corps. Such a book is still a *desiderata* for future academic publications. For an exemplary analysis of the German and Soviet strategic and tactical considerations during the final cataclysmic battle at the Oder Front in mid-April 1945, we recommend the brilliant study published at Helion by A. Stephan Hamilton, *The Oder Front 1945*.[3]

What long-term plans did Himmler have for the *SS* and the Scandinavian and Low Countries if the Germans had won the war? This question is essential to put into its military-historical and political context when writing about the Scandinavian and Dutch volunteers of the *Waffen-SS*, and it is important to keep this issue in mind when reading our book. Lennart Westberg has therefore written a lengthy introduction on the ideological and institutional phenomenon of the *Waffen-SS*, referring to the latest academic research.

The most comprehensive and in-depth study about Himmler's pan-Germanic politics in Norway is to be found in Sigurd Sørlie's brilliant recent dissertation *Solkors eller hakkors* (*Sun Cross or Swastika; Norwegians in the Waffen-SS 1941–45*) from 2015.[4] Sørlie's analyses are unsurpassable in their clarity and nuance. Closely followed in its broad perspectives on *SS* policies in wartime Norway is Matthew Kott and Terje Emberland's book *Himmlers Norge – Nordmenn i det Storgermanske Prosjekt* (*Himmler's Norway – Norwegians in the Greater Germanic Project*) from 2012.[5] Sigurd Sørlie's dissertation has recently been published in Germany by the renowned publishing company of Ferdinand Schöningh.

Regarding Himmler's pan-Germanic ambitions in wartime Denmark, the excellent volume *Under Hagekors og Dannebrog. Danskere i Waffen-SS* (*Under Swastika and Dannebrog. Danes in the Waffen-SS*) by Claus Bundgård Christensen, Niels Bo Poulsen and Peter Scharff Smith from 1998 provides a first-class insight into the Danish volunteer movement in the *Waffen-SS*.[6] The US-edition of Lennart Westberg and Lars Gyllenhaal's book *Swedes at War. Willing Warriors from a Neutral Nation, 1914–1945* contains Lennart Westberg's definitive account on the Swedish volunteers in

2 Wilhelm Tieke, *Tragedy of the Faithful* (New York: J.J. Fedorowicz Publishing, 2001).

3 A. Stephan Hamilton, *The Oder Front 1945. Generaloberst Gotthard Heinrici, Heeresgruppe Weichsel and Germany's Final Defense in the East, 20 March-3 May* (Solihull: Helion & Company Ltd, 2011). Hamilton's book also includes parts of the remaining units from the *III. (Germ.) SS-Panzer-Korps* in April 1945: the *11. SS-Freiwilligen-Panzergrenadier-Division "Nordland"* and the *23. SS-Freiwilligen-Panzergrenadier-Division "Nederland"*.

4 Sigurd Sørlie, *Solkors eller hakekors. Nordmenn i Waffen-SS 1941-45* (Oslo: Dreyers Forlag, 2015).

5 Matthew Kott & Terje Emberland, *Himmlers Norge. Nordmenn i det storgermanske prosjekt* (Oslo: Aschehoug, 2012).

6 Claus Bundgård Christensen, Niels Bo Paoulsen & Peter Scharff Smith, *Under hagekors og Dannebrog. Danskere i Waffen-SS 1940-45* (Copenhagen: Aschehoug, 1998).

the *Waffen-SS*, at the same time analyzing Himmler's and the SS's plans for Sweden's role in the Greater Germanic *Reich*.[7]

A refreshing new perspective on the relationship between Finland and the Third *Reich* in the Second World War appeared in late 2017 with Dr Lars Westerlund's new book on the Finnish Volunteer Battalion in the *Waffen-SS*.[8]

Still to be addressed in Volume 2 on the *III. (Germ.) SS-Panzer-Korps* is Martin R. Gutmann's pioneering, but somewhat confined, work *Fighting for the Nazi New Order. Himmler's Swiss, Swedish and Danish Volunteers and the Germanic Project of the SS*.[9]

A classic on the sociology and ideology of the *Waffen-SS* is Bernd Wegner's dissertation *Hitlers Politische Soldaten. Die Waffen-SS 1933–1945*.[10]

In 2018, Professor Niels Bo Poulsen of Copenhagen, one of Europe's leading military historians, published an enlarged and most welcome version of his already classic book on the fated struggle on the Eastern Front between the Third *Reich* and the Soviet Union: *Den store faedrelandskrig* (The Great Struggle for the Native Country, Gyldendal, Copenhagen 2018). This is a magnificent book that has all qualifications to become the standard work on the fighting at the Eastern Front 1941–45.

Lennart Westberg, Geir Brenden & Petter Kjellander
Sundsvall (Sweden), Oslo (Norway)
and Stockholm (Sweden), May 2019

7 Lars Gyllenhaal & Lennart Westberg, *Swedes at War. Willing Warriors from a Neutral Nation, 1914-1945* (Pennsylvania: Aberjona Press, 2010). Also in Swedish as: *Svenskar i krig 1914-1945* (Lund: Historiska Media, 2006).

8 Lars Westerlund, *Cirkus Collani. De finländska frivilliga 1941-43* (Norderstedt/Helsinki: Books on Demand, 2017).

9 Dissertation for Doctor of Philosophy degree in History at Syracuse University (US), 2011. For reasons of space, this publication could not be commented on in Volume I.

10 Bernd Wegner, *The Waffen-SS: Organization, Ideology and Function* (New Jersey: Blackwell, 1990).

INTRODUCTION – THE *WAFFEN-SS* AS A POLITICAL PHENOMENON

Lennart Westberg and Petter Kjellander

In the shape of the *Waffen-SS*, the front-line fellowship forges together young Teutons to unswerving loyalty, to political soldiers of the future. Hence the firestorm of the front creates an army of hardened men, who fight side by side in the struggle for the Germanic peoples' right to life, in the struggle for land that our ancestors acquired with blood in the grey twilight of time.
(Gösta Borg, Swedish *Untersturmführer* in the *III. (Germ.) SS-Panzer-Korps*)

We might go down, but we are taking a world with us.
(Adolf Hitler in January 1945 to his *Luftwaffe* adjutant Nicolaus von Below)

In war, national socialism came into its true existence. The National Socialist Party had developed out of a lost war. The British historian, Antony Beevor, has described the Battle of Berlin in 1945 as "The final funeral pyre of European right-wing extremism". Beevor is probably quite correct: Berlin was defended against the onslaught of the Red Army by remnants of several *Waffen-SS* units, consisting mainly of politically extreme-right-wing and ideologically still highly motivated French, Norwegian, Danish, Swedish and other European volunteers, who chose to fight on to the death for their *Führer* during this Apocalypse, other troops having become disillusioned. The majority of the Norwegian, Danish and Swedish volunteers in the *Waffen-SS* were organized or otherwise dedicated National Socialists long before their service in the *SS*.[1] "If I fall, my blood will have been shed for the Aryan fellowship and I will have died for my ideals," wrote Swedish *SS* rifleman Hans Lindén of the *SS-Division "Wiking"* in his diary during Hitler's campaign against the Soviet Union in the late summer of 1941.[2]

It is also time to abolish the myth that the *Waffen-SS* was predominantly a military phenomenon. Nothing could be more untrue. The *Waffen-SS* was, and remained, in the world and in the long-term planning of Heinrich Himmler, a political-ideological institution. The multinational *Waffen-SS* must be seen within the context of the European fascist movements of the time, and of the polarization between communism and fascism during the years between the First and Second World Wars.

The National Socialist War of Annihilation in the East (*der Vernichtungskrige im Osten*), i.e. the mass murder of Jews and Slavs, as well as the mobilization of Nordic-Germanic volunteers as "political soldiers" for the *III. (Germ.) SS-Panzer-Korps*, must be seen as two sides of the same coin. The Holocaust, the establishing of *Lebensraum* in the colonized East and the importance of the *III. (Germ.) SS-Panzer-Korps* as a political cadre hardware for functionaries within the future Greater Germanic *Reich*, constitute inseparable components in Himmler's long-term pan-Germanic policies.

The origins of the *Waffen-SS*

This critically commented pictorial book is focused on the *III. (Germ.) SS-Panzer-Korps*, dealing with part of perhaps the most debated and controversial military force of the Second World War: the *Waffen-SS*. This force originated not only from the hand-picked bodyguard, *Stabswache* Berlin, that protected Hitler as Nazi party leader during the time of violent street fighting in the Weimar Republic of Germany, but from various regional pre-war armed *SS* units, partly of heterogenic origin. The *Politische Bereitschaften* (political squads), the *Totenkopfverbände* (the concentration camp guards), the *Stabswachen* (staff guards), various *SS-Standarten* and auxiliary police units were all installed by the Nazis and constituted a nucleus for the future *Waffen-SS*. The *Stabswache* Berlin – acting as *primus inter pares* within the *SS* – was expanded after the Nazi takeover of power in 1933 to a Life Guard Regiment, the *Leibstandarte SS "Adolf Hitler"*.

The ideological roots of the *Waffen-SS* went back to certain phenomena of the First World War and Hitler's conception of an inseparable Trinity between the State, the Nation and its armed forces. Even before the takeover, the *Reichsführer-SS* (*Reich* Leader of the *SS*), Heinrich Himmler, had succeeded in expanding the SS mission as a bodyguard

The Apocalypse in Berlin: the Third *Reich* went down in a storm of fire and steel. An abandoned or destroyed German *Sturmgeschütz* (assault gun) stands in the Vosstrasse with the ruins of Adolf Hitler's *Reichskanzlei* (*Reich* Chancellary) in the background, May 1945. The remains of this building (then in East Berlin) were demolished in 1949 by orders of the Soviet occupation forces.

force to become "the Party Police" of national socialism. He thereby laid the foundation for a remarkable transformation of the *SS*. Between 1935 and 1938, Himmler also set up a *SS Junkerschule* for the training of officers and a further three infantry regiments, which together with the *Leibstandarte* formed the *SS-Verfügungstruppe*.

During the pre-war years, this *SS* force was an ideologically profiled paramilitary formation, with accordingly strong demands on its recruits for "racial" and ideological standards, and had both domestic, political functions and wartime tasks. This force also became the embryo for the future 38 field divisions of the *SS*. With the outbreak of the Second World War, the *SS-Verfügungstruppe* was continuously merged with personnel from the *SS* concentration camps, as well as from reserve police units. Hitler named this mixture *Waffen-SS*[5] and sent it both to the Front and behind the front lines, to perform "special tasks". When the war began, the *Waffen-SS* had 50,000 politically indoctrinated soldiers in its ranks, partly of an elite character and totally faithful to the Nazi Party and its ideology. The *Waffen-SS* participated in all of Hitler's campaigns, except in North Africa, and 253,000 of them were killed.[6]

However, the various recruiting sources of the pre-war *Waffen-SS* illustrate how socially and politically heterogeneous even Hitler's own praetorian, the *Leibstandarte SS "Adolf Hitler"*, was. The Belgian-German *SS*-recruit, Herbert Maeger, from the previously Prussian territory of Eupen-Malmedy (incorporated into Belgium in 1920 after the First World War), describes his personal impressions of the *Leibstandarte* in the summer of 1941, after reading his favourite literature, Ernst Jünger's *Storm of Steel*, during his train trip to Berlin as a volunteer recruit to the *Waffen-SS*:

Hans Lindén was a prototype for the few but ideologically highly motivated Swedish *SS* volunteers. Active in the Nazi Youth Movement in Stockholm from 1937, Lindén enlisted in the *Waffen-SS* prior to Operation "Barbarossa" in 1941. A survey made by the Swedish Security Police in 1953 found that at least 80 percent of the Swedes in the *Waffen-SS* were organized and dedicated National Socialists. This survey also confirms the profile given by later research of National Socialism as a predominantly youth phenomena: 60 percent of the Swedes in the *Waffen-SS* were 17–25 years old, and 23 percent between 26 and 30 years old.[3] The photo shows Lindén as a *Sturmann* in the anti-aircraft battalion of the *5. SS-Division "Wiking"* in the Ukraine, September 1941. He was also the first *SS*-Swede to be killed in action, at the age of 19, on the Eastern Front on 30 December 1941, near the village of Jusovka in the Ukraine. However, the low numbers of Swedish *SS*-volunteers (just 180 men from 1940–45) was an obvious disappointment for Berlin, and Hitler "voiced harsh criticism of the Swedes for the very meagre volunteer contingent they had provided for the struggles in the East".[4]

> Already, the first day in the *Leibstandarte* barracks in Berlin-Lichterfelde on 17 September 1941, brought the end for some of my illusions. The reality was hence a forceful sober-up: I did not arrive at an elite unit, as I had imagined it, but to a military force which due to its own conception was a "gang", whose mentality I recognized as a mixture between the Foreign Legion and mercenaries.[7]

In keeping with Himmler's efforts to implement a universal policy as a desired corporate identity for all *SS* personnel, there were several important common points of reference between the various branches of the *SS*, including the *Waffen-SS*. One important factor was the frequent rotation of personnel between the field units of the *Waffen-SS*, the *Totenkopfverbände* (the concentration guard units), the *Reichssicherheitshauptamt* (*Reich* Security Main Office), the police and the wartime *Einsatzgruppen* (murder squads). This deliberate personnel policy by Himmler, the incorporation of the *Totenkopfverbände* into the *Waffen-SS* and the political indoctrination in the *Waffen-SS* with its radical commitment to Nazi ideology, contributed to a destructive mentality and a culture of contempt for man.[8]

A pre-war photo of the *Feldherrnhalle* (Field Marshal's Hall), guarded by soldiers from the *Leibstandarte SS "Adolf Hitler"*, where the passing public were obligated to give the Nazi salute. Built on the Odeonsplatz in Munich between 1841 and 1844 as a monumental Florentine loggia, the Odeonsplatz was the site of the so-called Beer Hall Putsch on 9 November 1923. Here the Bavarian State Police, loyal to the democratic government, opened fire, ended the plot and killed 16 of Hitler's supporters. After Hitler seized power in 1933, he turned the *Feldherrnhalle* into a sacred memorial over his fallen comrades. The National Socialist memorial was demolished in June 1945.

SS-Brigadeführer Paul Hausser during an inspection of troops from the armed branch of the *SS* (by then known as the *Verfügungstruppe*) in 1936. Hausser is often mentioned as one of the most notable individuals for the training and development of the future *Waffen-SS*. As a retired army general, Hausser was appointed inspector of the *SS-Junkerschulen* (officers' training schools) in 1935, and from 1936 was inspector of the *Verfügungstruppe*. In the 1930s, Hausser experienced confrontations with the disparate regional power centres of the *SS*, who tried to maintain control over the nucleus of the armed *SS*. After 1945, Hausser went to a great deal of trouble in books and speeches, trying in a hardly convincing way to whitewash the *Waffen-SS* from any connection with the Death's Head units, war atrocities and the concentration camps, although his own units committed a number of war crimes.[11]

The Commander of the *Totenkopverbände* (Death's Head units), Theodor Eicke, shakes hand with Adolf Hiler in this pre-war photo. Behind Hitler is the "Blood Banner", the flag which was carried during the Munich Beer Hall Putsch in 1923. Next to Hitler stands Heinrich Himmler. Eicke is one of the most important and underestimated personalities in the *SS*, both during the war and since. His influence on and support for the institutionalized brutalities in the Third *Reich* remained threefold: firstly, Eicke created the "Model Dachau" as a concept for all *SS* concentration and extermination camps, which were so vital for upholding the terror and genocide in National Socialist Germany; secondly, he established the *SS* Death's Head units and personally selected many future camp commandants; and finally, Eicke went on to be one of the founders of the *Waffen-SS*, being the first commander of the *SS* Death's Head Division *"Totenkopf"* until he was killed on the Eastern Front in February 1943.

For quite some time, the pre-war *Verfügungstruppe* (VT) maintained the status of the "actual" forerunner of the *Waffen-SS* as "front soldiers", while the *Totenkopfverbände* (TV) remained "the criminals from the camp guards". In reality, recent research (Stefan Hördler) has shown that the *Totenkopfverbände* was not only a genuine part of, but also remained, an important personnel reservoir for the *Waffen-SS* from 1939 to 1942. Above all, due to the "transfer circus" between the concentration camps and the *Verfügungstruppe* with regard to the *Waffen-SS*, both the pre-war VT and TV must be looked upon as almost inseparable. In the Second World War, the personnel transfer between the concentrations camps and, above all, the units with a high degree of *Volksdeutsche* (ethnic Germans) and *Fremdvölkische* (non-Germanic recruits) would be frequent.[9] Stefan Hördler's pioneering research also clarified the intense pre-war regional networks between the TV and the VT, and in the Second World War between the *Waffen-SS* and the concentration camp system. Above all, the regional level of various, partly heterogeneous, pre-war armed units of the *SS* would serve as a personnel reservoir for the *Waffen-SS*: *Hilfspolizisten* (auxiliary police), *Politische Bereitschaften*, the various *Stabswachen* from the *SS-Oberabschnitte*, KZ guards units (*Wachmannschaften*) and *SS-Standarten* (regiments).[10]

The new *SS* officers' corps of the TV and VT, examined from the *SS-Junkerschulen* (officers' schools) at Bad Tölz and Braunschweig, would first serve either in the TV or VT, and be transferred between the two armed organizations. Among the young *SS* second lieutenants (*SS-Untersturmführer)* who in 1936 served in the concentration camp of Lichtenburg were Richard Schulze, the future adjutant to Hitler and Commander of the *SS-Junkerschule* Bad Tölz, and Werner Hoppe, who later served as adjutant to Theodor Eicke in the *SS-Division "Totenkopf"*. Other examples, who for various periods served in concentration camps and later became decorated commanders in *Waffen-SS* field units, were Rudolf Saalbach, Azelino de Masarié, Paul-Albert Kausch, Otto Reich and Hilmar Wäckerle.[12] Wäckerle was the first, and especially brutal, Commandant of the KZ Dachau, and both Kausch and Schulze served in KZ Buchenwald and were

A propaganda poster for joining the *Waffen-SS* as an officer. Being originally a pre-war, ideologically profiled paramilitary formation, the disparate factions of the armed *SS* were in 1940 merged with the personnel from the *Totenkopfverbände* (mainly concentration guards), as well as with reserve police units, and given the collective name "*Waffen-SS*". By 1945, nearly one million men had passed through the ranks of the *Waffen-SS*. One has to see the phenomena of the *Waffen-SS* within its context of the European fascist movements of the time. All major totalitarian systems during the 20th century – fascism, communism and national socialism – had one phenomena in common: the establishment of paramilitary elite bodies, outside the control of the ordinary army and police. That was the case with Mussolini's fascist black-shirts (*Milizia Volontaria*), Franco's *Falange Espanola*, the Soviets' *NKVD* elite security divisions and Himmler's *Waffen-SS*. These special formations also served as Praetorian Guards for respective nations' absolute party and state leaders.

later promoted to regimental commander of the *SS-Panzer-Regiment 11 "Nordland"* (Kausch) and divisional commander of the *38. SS-Grenadier-Division "Niebelungen"* (Schulze).

Especially frequent were the number of transfers of *SS* doctors and administrative personnel between the concentration camps, VT and the later *Waffen-SS* field units. In the period from October 1939 to March 1941, 77 *SS* doctors were transferred between concentration camps and the *SS-Division "Totenkopf"* alone, while many others commuted frequently between the task of murdering delinquents in the KZs and being field doctors in the *Waffen-SS*, especially in the *SS-Divisions "Totenkopf"*, *"Das Reich"* and *"Prinz Eugen"*.[13]

A previously unknown series of photographs shows the higher officers' corps from the *SS-Division "Das Reich"*, visiting the KZ Mauthausen and all its functions, on 31 May 1941, e.g. the notorious "*Todesstiege*" in the quarry "Wiener Graben", where numerous prisoners were murdered. Among the visitors were Paul Hausser, August Schmidhuber, Otto Kumm, August Zehender, Fritz Vogt, Peter Hansen and Wilhelm Bittrich. Besides the direct and deliberate "transfer of knowledge" about life and death in the concentration camps during this visit, the phenomena also illustrate the natural bonds between the *Waffen-SS* and the *Totenkopfverbände*.[14]

Especially significant and numerous were the transfers of liquidation specialists to certain field units of the *Waffen-SS*, above all to *SS* field units which were composed of ethnic Germans, Muslims and *Fremdvölkische* recruits, who were mainly engaged in so-called "anti-partisan" operations: the *SS-Divisions "Prinz Eugen"*, *"Kama"* and *"Handschar"*. As the "*Aktion T4*" (the murders of mentally ill and handicapped Germans)[15] and the "*Aktion 14 f 14*" (the murders of Soviet POWs) came to a preliminary end in 1942, personnel from these murder institutes were transferred to the *Waffen-SS*.[16] In March 1943, personnel from the *SS-Sonderkommando Kulmhof*, which had murdered at least 150,000 people in gas trucks, were transferred to the *SS-Division "Prinz Eugen"*. In 1943, essential parts of the personnel from the *Bataillon z.b.V. der Waffen-SS* (which had been deeply engaged in the mass murders of Soviet Jews as part of the *Einsatzgruppen*) were transferred to the Estonian Legion and its successor, the *3. Estonian SS-Brigade*, later incorporated into the *20. Waffen-Grenadier-Division der SS* (*Estnische Nr.1*). At the same time, personnel from the Estonian Security Police, who had actively participated in the mass murders of Estonian Jews, were transferred to Estonian *Waffen-SS* field units.[17] In 1941/42, Wilhelm Schäfer was responsible for the murders of 7,000 Soviet prisoners of war in KZ Buchenwald and was later transferred to the *20. Waffen-Grenadier-Division der SS* (*Estnische Nr.1*), with whom he took part in the murders of civilians and hostages in Estonia.[18]

A previously unknown key role in the transfer between concentration camps and the *Waffen-SS* was held by the ethnic Germans (*Volksdeutsche*). In January 1943, 1,200 ethnic German recruits from Slovakia were transferred as concentration camp guards, replacements for the German KZ personnel who in turn were transferred to field units of the *Waffen-SS*. In October 1943, 7,000 ethnic Germans served as KZ guards, while at the end of the war there were nearly 15,000. In October 1943, 3,100 ethnic German recruits from Rumania were placed as guards in the concentration camps of Lublin (850), Mathausen (510), Sachsenhausen (400) and Buchenwald (350).[19] New research (by Hördler) has also revealed that around 20,000 soldiers from the *Wehrmacht* were transferred as KZ guards during the Second World War.

The ideological roots of the *Waffen-SS*

In the *SS* concept of the world, the image of the enemy was fixed, regardless of whether it was at peace or war. The constant enemies were the Bolsheviks and the Jews, gypsies, homosexuals, mentally ill and Slavic people.

In 1918-19, at the end of the First World War and in its aftermath, two unique phenomena appeared which would come to have a deep impact on the ideology of the future *SS* and *Waffen-SS*; the *Stosstruppen* of the German Imperial Army and the *Freikorps* movement. In 1918, Germany's military dictator, General Erich von Ludendorff, employed entirely new tactics for infantry assault by creating elite battalions to spearhead the traditional and previously ineffective mass infantry attacks. These crack formations, *Stosstruppen* ("shock troops") trained to move in small groups across the battlefield, were recruited from among the fittest and most intelligent men and officers. They were specially armed and wore green uniforms with silver facings. Many sported the infamous *Totenkopf* ("Death's Head") symbol, which became the badge for some *Freikorps* and later the symbol for Himmler's *SS*. The soldiers in the *Stosstruppen* developed a unique *esprit de corps* based on their elite status.

The first *Freikorps* was established in December 1918 by General Ludwig von Maercker, with the twin tasks of fighting off the Bolshevik internal threat at home and securing Germany's crumbling borders. Maercker took the opportunity to learn from the previous *Stosstruppen* and created a flexible all-round unit, which even included training in street warfare.[20] On 4 January 1919, the Social Democratic Minister of Defense, Gustav Noske, invited the soon-to-be first president of the Weimar Republic, Friedrich Ebert, for a trip to the military training grounds of Zossen, just south of Berlin. There Noske presented to the astonished Ebert column after column of perfectly equipped and disciplined troops – rising like the Phoenix – personally presented to the two civilians as a perfectly loyal *Freikorps* to the government by its Commanding Officer, General von Maercker. The legal Social Democratic government thankfully "sponsored" this and other *Freikorps* to preserve its authority against rebelling communists, the Spartacus Movement.

However, after crushing the Bolsheviks, the *Freikorps*, with their paramilitary political violence, showed themselves equally hostile to the government as the extremists they had just destroyed. "A miserable socialist rabble" was how one *Freikorps* leader described the legitimate socialist government in Berlin. These forces now became "the breeding ground for a new elite that glorified war and was aristocratic in spirit but democratic in social origin".[21] Their mentality was a mixture of super-patriotism, nihilism, hostility to the political left and an appreciation for the "social equality of the fighting men from the trenches" (and therefore a law only to themselves). They were also anti-parliamentary, anti-Semitic and willing to build a new world, but also to smash the old, corrupt bourgeois one.

There was to be a clear line of development between the *Stosstruppen* and the *Freikorps* movement. The Nazis would in many ways look upon both phenomena as their immediate precursors. The German defeat in the First World War was the catalyst for these extreme forces, and the *Freikorps* became a significant factor for the growth of right-wing extremism in inter-war Germany, providing a nucleus around which the *SA* (*Sturmabteilung*, the "brownshirts") and the *SS* formed. This development reached its culmination during the Second World War with the *Waffen-SS*, the ethos of which harkened back to the *Freikorps* era.

The conservative revolution in 1919 Germany was in many ways a forerunner and catalyst for central components of *SS* ideology. Common for these ideological currents and the mentality of the *Freikorps* was that they in parts were conservative, but in their legitimacy were revolutionary, and propagandistically pointing towards the third way between conservatism and Marxism. Christian ideals were replaced with beliefs in heroism and faith, dreams of empires were camouflaged as historical vocation, the world was divided into friends and foes, the idea of the nation-state was replaced with the "Greater Germanic *Reich*" and the professional soldier was replaced by a political activist in military uniform.[22]

The Norwegian idea-historian Terje Emberland has pointed out that fascism is not by necessity an anti-modern phenomenon, but "is centred around a social reborn myth and therefore is anti-conservative as a racial-cultural revolution".[23]

A propaganda and recruiting poster for one of the many Free Corps (*Freikorps*) around 1919. Defeat in the Great War and a close escape from Communist revolution brought not true peace, but chaotic years between 1918 and 1923 of civil war, putsches and political murders in Germany. The conservative *völkische* German revolution from 1919 was in many aspects a forerunner and catalyst to the central contents of *SS* ideology. Common to these ideological currents and the mentality of the Free Corps was that they in certain parts were conservative, but in their identification, revolutionary and propagandistically pointed on the third way between Marxism and conservatism. Christian ideals were substituted with heroic beliefs in "destiny"; imperialistic dreams were camouflaged as "historic missions", the world was divided into friends and enemies, the idea of the traditional national state was replaced by racial overtunes and the soldier was no longer a professional but a political activist, and therefore a universal prototype. The right-wing writer and former officer in the paramilitary *Freikorps*, Ernst von Salomon, wrote in 1930 about the Free Corps generation: "War had taken hold of them and would never let them go. They would never really belong to their homes again. The war was over but the armies were still in being." The extreme *esprit de corps* of the Free Corps nurtured the seeds of the future *SS* and proved to be an omen for an even more shadowy world.

In contrast: Germany's democratic and liberal traditions

The horrible extent to which parliamentary democracy and liberal tolerance were deeply compromised during the Nazi terror regime from 1933–45 must not conceal Germany's unusual and strong democratic traditions already in existence before the First World War. The Holocaust was an unparalleled phenomena; its singular characterization being its murderous will to kill, without exception, everybody belonging to a specified ethnic group, i.e. every single Jew, thus separating Adolf Hitler from other mass-murderers like Josef Stalin.[24]

The British Professor Thomas Weber has, with his recent research on the political preferences within Hitler's Bavarian wartime *Regiment "List"*, stressed the fact, opposite to popular and long-lived myths, that Imperial pre-war German had developed a solid liberal and democratic tradition that easily could be compared with democracy in Britain and France. In 1912, 34 percent of the electorate in Catholic and agrarian Oberbayern voted for the Social Democratic Party, while 17 percent voted for Liberal. Right-extreme parties had few votes in Oberbayern at that time, and were marginalized. Bavarian anti-Semitism was concentrated on fragments of Bavarian society and, due to Weber and in contrast to historic clichés, German Jews had equal career opportunities as in Great Britain, above all in Bavaria and Württemberg. In 1910, the Bavarian Army commissioned proportionally more Jewish officers in their ranks than the far larger British Army. The fighting on the German-Russian Eastern Front did not develop any German anti-Semitism in its army of officers' corps. On the contrary, the German attitude was that its Army liberated Jewish-Russian population groups from the Tsar's Reich pogroms and the anti-Semitic Russian epidemic.

The horrible war experiences in the First World War had no measurable consequences on the political preferences for the soldiers in the *Regiment "List"*. Only eight of its soldiers joined the *Freikorps*, for example. The Bavarian electorate was not destabilized by extreme left and right forces in 1918, but retained its pre-war sympathies for Social Democratic or liberal parties. Hitler himself was in 1918 confused in his political beliefs, and expressed (like Heinrich Himmler) in this turbulent revolutionary and post-revolutionary period in Munich in 1918–1919, no anti-Semitic feelings (his Iron Cross First Class was awarded on the initiative of his Jewish regimental adjutant). Hitler was, during this revolutionary Munich period, on the payroll of the Soviet Räterepublic and was pictured in mourning and going behind the coffin of the murdered Munich communist leader Kurt Eisner in early 1919. His later fable-makings in *Mein Kampf* as a front-soldier and anti-Semite (neither of which he ever was) was explained by the fact that Hitler had much to hide.

The essential destructive catalysts that finally destabilized the German body of society, and enabled the development of fascism, were, according to Thomas Weber, as follows. First of all there was the extreme-left Bolshevik Republic in Munich in 1918–19 which partly legitimatized right-wing parties as a barrier against communism. Further, there was the economic crash of Wall Street in 1929, that had shaken the trust in democracy as capable of solving these deep financial wounds in society. Finally, there was the ill-fated Machiavellian conspiracy of the conservative government of von Papen in 1932, thereby overthrowing the legal Social Democratic Prussian government of Brüning. Germany's long-time and surprisingly strong democratic traditions and stable electorate were now destroyed and dissolved. The right-wing fanatics, the mass murderers and the gangsters were given free hand. The road into the abyss was a fact.

Expansion

Hitler, who anticipated a short war and a quick victory, opposed an expansion of the *Waffen-SS* up to the summer of 1942, viewing it mainly as the militarized elite of German National Socialists. The more visionary Himmler, however, searched for new ways to radically expand the *Waffen-SS*, both for expansionist and institutional purposes, as well as ideological, and he found two possibilities, one of which was to recruit *Volksdeutsche*, those of German ethnic stock abroad.[25] Another was to attract ideologically motivated volunteers from the parts of Northern and Western Europe that had been occupied by the Third *Reich* in 1940. Thus, beginning in the summer of 1940, the *Waffen-SS* actively began to recruit "Germanic volunteers of Nordic blood", meaning first and foremost, Norwegians, Danes, Swedes, Flemish and Dutch.[26] From the newly erected regiments "Nordland" and "Westland", together with the previous regiment "Germania" and an artillery regiment, Himmler established the new *SS-Infanterie-Division "Wiking"* in the latter part of 1940.

The strategic vision of Himmler, as demonstrated from 1938 and onwards, to recruit "Germanic" personnel long before the invasion of the Soviet Union in 1941, shows clearly that the *Reichsführer* had long-term plans to expand the *SS* on a multinational basis. Alas, these plans were not the product and effects alone of Operation "Barbarossa", but had both ideological and pragmatic origins, partly deriving from the *SS* concept that rather than the traditional national state, the *völkisch-raische* community of a superior race and its historical mission had priority.[27]

The "Germanic" strain within the *Waffen-SS* was, despite all of the recruiting propaganda, strikingly thin. The "*Wiking*" division, which was presented by the *SS* as an overwhelmingly multi-national "Germanic" unit, had in June 1941 only 631 Dutch, 294 Norwegians, 216 Danes, one Swede and one Swiss in its ranks of 19,000 men. The "*Wiking*" was in fact composed of up to 90 percent German personnel and only 10 percent of 'Germanic' stock at the time of the march into the Soviet Union in June 1941.

Recent research by the Norwegian scholar Dr Sigurd Sørlie on the motives of the 4,500 Norwegians in the *Waffen-SS* has revealed that while 2 percent of the Norwegian population were members of the pro-Nazi Quisling party, at least 80 percent of the Norwegians in the *Waffen-SS* were

SS-Brigadeführer Felix Steiner as commander of the motorized *SS* infantry division "*Wiking*" in January 1941, together with his divisional adjutant, *SS-Hauptsturmführer* Paul-Albert Kausch. Steiner, who had been an officer in the First World War and seen the mass slaughters on the Western Front, was innovative in training the men of his pre-war regiment "*Deutschland*" in new military tactics. Kausch had a long career in the *SS* Death's Head units, serving in *Totenkopf* regiments from 1936–40, as well in the concentration camp of Buchenwald. In 1944–45, Kausch served as a skilled *Panzer* commander in the *III. (Germ.) SS-Panzer Korps*. Under Steiner's command of "*Wiking*", the *SD* reported that 600 Jews were liquidated by the *Waffen-SS* around the Galician village of Zborow in July 1941 (being the operational area for "*Wiking*" at that time). A Swedish volunteer in "*Wiking*", Kurt Lundin, recorded in an interrogation by the Swedish Security Police in December 1943, that "the Division '*Wiking*' had for a long time [in 1941] taken no prisoners, but killed everyone that had gotten in the division's way".

If Paul Hausser and Felix Steiner to a great extent formed the military standards of the *Waffen-SS*, Gottlob Berger's organizational genius offered Himmler the personnel logistics for the rapid expansion of the armed *SS*, and hence Berger must be considered as the "Father of the *Waffen-SS*". Berger circumvented *Wehrmacht* control over conscription by extending recruitment to the *Waffen-SS* from the "Germanic" volunteer potentials in Scandinavia and Western Europe. Furthermore, Berger and Himmler went to exploit the *Volksdeutsche* (ethnic Germans from South-Eastern Europe) as recruits for the *Waffen-SS*. During the war, Berger upheld key roles in other departments and agencies, as the Reich Ministry for the Occupied Eastern Territories, the *Volkssturm* militia and the POW camps. In an interview with the author (LW), the former *SS-Sturmbannführer* and chief of the Political Department of the *Germanische Leitstelle* (Germanic Coordination Agency) in Berlin, Fritz Ulrich, declared: "Although Berger originally was only a school teacher, he possessed an impressive intellectual capacity and an extraordinary talent for organization. Coming from Swabia, Berger also possessed a shrewd tactical capacity, not seldom tending to be intriguing".

party members.[28] As is the case with recent research on the Danes in the *Waffen-SS* (Bundgard Christensen, Poulsen & Scharff Smith) and with regard to the Swedes in Himmler's formations in the East (Gyllenhaal & Westberg), Sørlie's results probably coincide with the following quotation from *Swedes at War* (while at the same time taking into consideration the different conditions between Sweden and Norway, the latter being an occupied nation with probably a broader variety of the volunteers' motives for joining the *Waffen-SS*):

> After the war many Scandinavian ex-volunteers in the *Waffen-SS* maintained that they served on the Eastern Front to "defend the Western countries against Bolshevism". What is lacking in their version of history is that many joined the Waffen-SS as much to obstruct or protest against, for example, Swedish democracy – a parliamentary system that they earlier had rejected or attacked during their active time as National Socialists in Sweden.[29]

Sigurd Sørlie also emphasizes that, although the majority of the Norwegian *SS*-volunteers were already

The turn of the tide: the major German summer 1942 offensive "Case Blue" (*Fall Blau*) has reached its maximum Eastern point in the all-absorbing High Mountains of the Eastern Caucasus near Malgobek. The attempt to open the road to Groznyj and the oil fields of the Caspian Sea has failed. Pictured are *SS* Grenadiers from the *SS-Division "Wiking"* on patrol, armed with MPi 40 sub-machine guns, in the interminable landscape. On the horizon are parts of the Caucasian mountain range. The *SS* field photographers in the Caucasus preferred to take images of Elbrus and the highest peaks of the range in order to maximize the propaganda effect back in Europe.

sympathetic towards Nazism, the ideological education and actual experiences in the *Waffen-SS* both confirmed and acknowledged their previous anti-democratic and anti-Jewish ideological comprehension.[30] In terms of pro-Germanic visions, a large proportion of the Norwegians in the *SS* identified themselves with the idea of a Greater Germanic *Reich*. Ultimately, however, most of them identified more strongly with the vision of their *Fører*, Vidkun Quisling: "In other words, they choose the *Sonnenrad* (sun wheel; symbol of the Quisling party) instead of the Swastika."[31]

Sigurd Sørlie's recent dissertation must be looked upon as generally the most brilliant and comprehensive work published on the *Waffen-SS*, regarding an occupied country's contribution to it in terms of volunteers and their various motivations.

In his nuanced way, Sørlie also points at permanent non-ideological factors for joining the *Waffen-SS*: longing for adventure, the choice of the *SS* by close comrades, materialistic advantages, prestige or domestic problems: "Male *NS* party members in draftee age were also [the] object of the party's enormous pressure to volunteer for the Eastern Front and many youngsters had a limited capacity to understand the consequences of their decision. It is also quite clear that individual personalities landed in the *Waffen-SS* against their will."[32]

Although nationalism, anti-communism and solidarity with the Finnish nation were partial motives for joining the *Waffen-SS* with, for example, Norwegian volunteers, these motives normally constituted mere elements in a more general sympathy for Vidkun Quisling's *NS* party. National Socialism and Nazi Germany were a sympathy which included notions of anti-Semitism and racism.[33]

Of the 6,000 Danes in the *Waffen-SS*, no less than 1,500 were ethnic Germans from the region of Schleswig. Equivalent with the Norwegians and the Swedes in the *Waffen-SS*, at least 75 percent of the 4,500 Danish *SS* volunteers were Nazi party members or otherwise dedicated Nazis. Between 100 and 200 Danes in the *Waffen-SS* served as guards in concentration camps.[34]

The expansion of the *Waffen-SS* in the Second World War was very fast and extensive. While the German Army between 1933 and 1942 was 60 times redoubled, the *Waffen-SS* had, at the end of the war in 1945, grown 100 times in 10 years. This pattern of dynamic expansion and constant reorganization was also typical for the dynamic and revolutionary nature of National Socialist Germany.[35] Up to 1938, Nazi Germany consisted of several different polarizations of power: the Nazi Party, the governmental offices, the *Reichswehr*, the leading capitalist industrialists and the police, with different, partly overlapping, interests. Their common denominator was their relationship to the *Führer*. It was in this complex world of powerful structures that Himmler and the *SS*, carrying the permanent radical dynamics of *NS*-ideology as a *corps d'élite*, could secure a substantial, although from time-to-time limited, influence.[36]

The identity crisis

Recent research (Jean-Luc Leleu) has shown that the latter phase of the expansion of the *Waffen-SS*, from mid-1943 onwards, was dominated by two factors: the German catastrophe at Stalingrad and Himmler's previous long-term argumentation before Hitler, that only the fanatical, ideologically founded and nourished *corps d'esprit* of the *Waffen-SS* could make up the inevitable gap between diminishing German manpower resources and the realities on the Eastern Front. In Hitler's and Himmler's eyes, the fanaticism of their troops was more important than their actual strength. Just a week after the defeat at the Volga, Hitler commissioned Himmler not only with the creation of a new *SS*-division, recruited mainly from the *Hitler-Jugend*, but also with the formation of a Latvian, Lithuanian and Bosnian *SS*-division.[37] On 15 July 1944, five days *before* Colonel von Stauffenberg's bomb plot, Hitler commissioned Himmler with the task of ideological indoctrination of the 15 brand new *Grenadier-Divisionen* that in 1944 were to be formed by the Army. Hitler looked upon the ideologically motivated *Waffen-SS* as a sort of "patent recipe", which idealistically could be used for the whole of the German Army, especially after the catastrophic destruction of the *Heeresgruppe Mitte* on the Eastern Front by the Red Army in June-July 1944, and the Anglo-American invasion in Normandy during the same period. Joseph Goebbels and his Propaganda Ministry had from January 1944 ecstatically praised Himmler and the *Waffen-SS* for their "heroic deeds" and "educational wonder".[38] An important fact remained that during the forming of new divisions for the *Waffen-SS* in 1943, the proportion of German recruits who all their lives had been socialized in the Third Reich and the *Hitler-Jugend* almost exploded.[39] As serious setbacks occurred at the front, combined with Hitler's mistrust in the Army after the 20 July bomb plot, the *SS* vanquished more and more responsibilities from the *Wehrmacht*: taking over the *Abwehr*, absorbing the Reserve Army, the new V-weapons and *Volkssturm*, etc. Ironically, the highlights of this new *SS* supremacy took place when the black clouds turned up on the horizon for the Third Reich. Several defeats for the *Waffen-SS* lay ahead during the next six months, and the final defeat for the Third Reich was inevitable.

As the troops of the *Waffen-SS* entered the Second World War, the "Guard of the *Führer*" rested on a monopolized Trinity: voluntary service, racial selection and political indoctrination. Soon, the *Waffen-SS* would lose control over its two first parameters, due to the general expansion of the *Waffen-SS* and the losses at the front. The "Germanic" profile of the *Waffen-SS* lost its image as soon as Baltic, French, Walloon, Bosnian and even recruits of Soviet origin entered its ranks. In certain cases, the *Waffen-SS* identified itself partly with the military traditions of the former Habsburg (Austrian-Hungarian) *Kaiserreich*, which had recruited, for example, Muslim Bosnians into its ranks.[40] Recent research (Toomas Hiio) on the Estonian *Waffen-SS* has estimated that around 25,000 Estonians served in units belonging to the *Waffen-SS*, and that 70,000 Estonians served in German uniform in the Second World War. Their motives were, little wonder after the brutal Soviet occupation and deportations from Estonia in 1940–41, mainly anti-communistic. The first phase of Estonian service in German armed units was dominated by volunteers, but these were soon replaced by mainly drafted, *nolens volens*, Estonians for the *Waffen-SS* or the *Wehrmacht*.[41]

However, the increasing "Nazification" of the German Army in 1944, with the *Waffen-SS* as a prototype, created an "identification problem" for the Black Order, as the *Waffen-SS* was threatened with losing its ideological supremacy to the *Heer*. No wonder, therefore, that during 1944, the *Waffen-SS* was described in propaganda as not so much the "shock troops" of the Nazi party but as a personification of a "people's community in arms" (*Volksgemeinschaft in Waffen*).[42] The *Waffen-SS* served from this social angle as an ideal example: its officer corps was much more representative for the average German people. At the same time, the commander of the *Leibstandarte "Adolf Hitler"*, *SS-Oberst-Gruppenführer* Sepp Dietrich, was stylized as *Volksmarshall* (People's Marshal). Not by coincidence, the Minister for Propaganda, Joseph Goebbels – who throughout the Nazi reign was the higher party functionary who used the word "socialism" most of all in his speeches – during the same period introduced the word *Volk* (People) in an almost inflationary way: *Volksgrenadier-Divisionen*, *Volkssturm*, *Volksjäger* (Heinkel 162), etc. Semantically, reminiscences could in this sense be made to the once revolutionary, and in 1934 liquidated, party wing of Ernst Röhm.[43] In the end, the *NSDAP* and the *Waffen-SS*, by mobilizing the last ideological resources of the Reich, destroyed the traditional military structures and demoted the German Army to a second place, thereby reconquering the threatened corporate identity of the *Waffen-SS* – not only as the *Führer*'s Guard but as the Guard for a "People in Arms".

The *Waffen-SS* and Operation "Barbarossa"

"Under Germany's leadership Europe is going into a war of the people against the Red Empire. On the flanks march Finland and Rumania. It has become Finland's great and noble mission to secure a bridgehead in the North against the Red Czarism" – so wrote the Swedish newspaper, *Aftonbladet*, following Hitler's surprise and massive attack on the Soviet Union on 22 June 1941.[44]

The European war had now received a new and radical dimension. The nearly two-year period of ideological abstinence of polemics between Nazi Berlin and Communist Moscow ended on 22 June 1941, and anti-communism regained its *rasion d'etre*. The Soviet opponent would now

The Swedish *SS-Panzer* Grenadiers, Karl-Olof Holm and Erik Wallin, near Jakobstadt in Latvia, July 1944. Their hard-hitting *Panzer* reconnaissance battalion, the *SS-Panzer-Aufklärungsabteilung 11 "Nordland"*, was part of the *Armee-Abteilung "Kleffel"*, acting as a blocking unit (*Sperrverband*) against Red Army *panzer* pincers through Latvia, after the disintegration of Army Group Center, following the massive Soviet offensive in June 1944, Operation "Bagration". Holm tried to desert from the *Waffen-SS* during the German evacuation of Estonia in the autumn of 1944, was condemned to serve in an *SS* punishment unit and was killed in action in Courland in October 1944. Wallin fought until the final battle of Berlin, survived, and made it back to Stockholm in the summer of 1945.

Adolf Hitler greets *panzer* generals Hasso von Manteuffel (shaking Hitler's hand) and Otto von Knobelsdorff in his *Wolfsschanze* (Wolf's Lair) military headquarters in East Prussia, September 1944. Third from right (in white tunic with the German Cross in Gold) is one of Hitler's adjutants, *SS-Sturmbannführer* Richard Schulze-Kossens, who in the 1930s served in the concentration camps of Lichtenburg and Dachau, as adjutant to Theodor Eicke. Schulze-Kossens ended the war as commander of the *SS-Junkerschule Bad Tölz* and the *38. SS-Division "Nibelungen"*. To the left stands Hermann Göring and Hitler's Chief Adjutant for the *Wehrmacht*, Colonel Erik von Amsberg (replacement for General Rudolf Schmundt from July to October 1944).

Recruiting poster from 1943 for the Norwegian *SS-Skijägerbatallion*. This unit had a strength of 700 Norwegians and saw action on the Finnish-Soviet Front in 1943–44, and is an example of an option other than the *III. (Germ.) SS-Panzer Korps* for Germanic SS-volunteers. Many Norwegians from the Legion, dissatisfied with the idea of a united Germanic *SS-Panzer* Corps, were transferred from the new *SS-Panzergrenadier-Regiment "Norge"* in the autumn of 1943 from Croatia to the *SS-Skijägerbatallion* in Finland. Around 500 Norwegians remained in the *III. (Germ.) SS-Panzer Korps*, their number being additionally reduced to 260 in the summer of 1944. During the final battle of Berlin in April 1945, around 50 surviving Norwegians took part in that final abyss. Himmler's plan was to create an *SS Skijäger-Brigade* (and later a *Skijäger-Division*). The *SS-Skijägerbatallion* in Finland was practically annihilated during the major Soviet offensive in Eastern Karelia on 25–27 June 1944, when 141 Norwegians were killed or counted as missing in action.

rank equal with the arch-enemy, *den jüdischen Bolschewismus* (the Jewish Bolshevism), whose "treacherous intrigues" were blamed for the German defeat in 1918. The Soviet Union was in many ways an ideologically cherished "dream opponent" for the *SS*, which now found its chief purpose and legitimacy acknowledged in the East. But Hitler's decision to invade the USSR also resulted in the destruction and death of the core of the pre-war *Waffen-SS*: the *Verfügungstruppe* and the *Totenkopfverbände*.

For many inhabitants in Europe, it appeared in the late summer of 1941 that Nazi Germany would have control of Europe, from Kirkenes in far northern Norway to the French-Spanish border, for a protracted period. The defeat of the Soviet Union was expected, even in London, to be only a matter of time. Rommel and his *Afrika Korps* would soon be in Cairo and the victorious German *Panzer* armies would then reach the Persian Gulf from the west and north, and Germany's oil supply would be secure.

Third Reich foreign policy had two major objectives. The first was to create a "Greater Germanic Empire", encompassing the major parts of Western and Northern Europe. The second goal was to expand to the East, achieving more *Lebensraum* (living space) by way of war and extermination of "subhuman" peoples. The *Waffen-SS* played an important role in support of both goals by recruiting and training non-Germans, making the eastern territories' military secure and, last but not least, by supplying Nazi-Germany's eastern colonies and the western "Germanic Reich" with a cadre of reliable administrators who had proved their loyalty and efficiency through front-line service in the *Waffen-SS*. The dream of a greater Germanic Reich and the war of extermination against the Jews and Slavonic people were two sides of the same coin. The Teutonic Order played a distinct role in the propaganda of the Third Reich and later the invasion of the USSR. In the words of Adolf Hitler: "Just as the German Military Order did not act with kid gloves, but employed both the Bible and the sword, so also our men sent to the east as fighters for the faith of the National Socialist world view must if necessary employ our national interest with brute force."[45] For Himmler, the *SS* acted as a reincarnation of the Teutonic Order, although the *SS*, due to its anti-aristocratic and anti-clerical nature, looked upon itself more as a new racially selected *Volksadel* (people's nobility).[46]

For Hitler and the *SS*, Operation "Barbarossa" – the attack on the Soviet Union – was not an ordinary war between two states, but rather a struggle to the death between two ideologies and races. The Soviet state was to be destroyed through the most brutal violence. The normal code of military honour, which for the most part was followed in the 1940 campaign against France, was not adequate on the Eastern Front. "All officers," emphasized Hitler in a speech before the German High Command, prior to the launch of the attack, "must free themselves from outdated conventions and ways of thinking."

As in occupied Poland, which in many ways served as an "experiment laboratory" for the genocide visions and plans of Hitler, Himmler and the *SS*, the Soviet leadership and elites were to be eliminated. Hitler was convinced that the Jews were at the heart of the Soviet-communist system, and his aim was subsequently also the elimination of the "Judeo-Bolshevik intelligentsia". In Russia, therefore, the campaign against the elites was also a campaign against the Jews.[47] It is apparent to what degree the German High Command (OKW) and Army now accepted anti-Jewish measures as an important part of the fight against the Soviet leadership, and obediently planned a new kind of war. The OKW made, for instance, no provision to feed the expected millions of Soviet prisoners of war, and the death toll among these POWs was extremely high, initially far higher than the number of Soviet Jews murdered.[48]

It should be kept in mind that the special brutalizing character of the Eastern Front was partly a consequence also of the *NKVD*'s, the Red Army's and the partisan movement's extremely brutal combat methods, revenge actions and mass deportations. The Germans and Soviets therefore prosecuted the battle with a new and unexpected brutality. With regard to the mass-murder of prisoners of war, Jews and other civilians, the scale of ruthlessness and barbarism practiced here extended beyond that experienced on all other fronts in Europe and the Far East. These atrocities were underpinned by the barbaric personalities and regimes of both Hitler and Stalin.

The non-German volunteers had widely varying reasons to join the *Waffen-SS*. Each individual was motivated by a mix of ideological, national and personal reasons. Hitler's campaign against the Soviet Union in the summer of 1941 was a major factor for the appeal of the *Waffen-SS* abroad. The campaign in the East was proclaimed as "a crusade against Asiatic-Jewish Bolshevism". The 1939 Hitler-Stalin Pact – which many Europeans had found incomprehensible – was suddenly thrown away. Recruiting into the *Waffen-SS* was enhanced and expanded by the anti-communist theme in the new campaign, amplified by very able German spin doctors. Thus a motley mix of nationalities and individuals fought on the Eastern Front under the Swastika: from Nazi collaborators in the occupied countries, to conscripted cannon fodder and pure adventurers. Joining this motley assortment were many East Europeans who mainly wanted to avoid a new Soviet occupation, or preferred German domination to that of the Soviets.

Hitler, in preparation for the attack, had assembled a gigantic multinational invasion force which recalled the *Grand Armeé* of Napoleon in 1812. Over three million German troops from the *Wehrmacht* and the *Waffen-SS* were augmented by a full Rumanian army group of 325,685 men, consisting of 12 divisions and six brigades; an Italian expeditionary corps (*Corpo di Spedizione in Russia*), consisting of three divisions with a strength of 62,000 men and 100 airplanes; three Hungarian brigades; as well as two Slovak divisions, all spread across the Eastern Front.[49] Later, these forces were to be augmented by the Spanish "Blue Division" and Croatian units, as well as some 18 Finnish divisions. Rumania, Hungary, Italy, Finland, Slovakia and Croatia additionally contributed to the German forces in the East with 980 aircraft of various types and standards, together with pilots and air support personnel.[50] Among this phalanx of invading German military power were 160,405 soldiers from the *Waffen-SS*.

In total, approximately 600,000 men participated in Operation "Barbarossa" from countries which came to be either "brothers-in-arms" or, for less ideological reasons, nonetheless German allies. Because many Soviet citizens turned against Stalin or joined independent nationalist guerrilla movements, the German-Soviet war also developed into a grim, Soviet civil war. According to both Western and Soviet researchers, at least one million Soviet citizens volunteered or were conscripted into the German armed forces or German police and security units on the Eastern Front.[51] Among Baltic and other East European volunteering personnel reservoirs, the Germans recruited security units, *Hilfsmannschaften* and *Selbstschutz*, that already from June-July 1941 played an essential part in the mass murders of their respective countries' Jewish populations, their motives being predominantly a combination of anti-Semitism and anti-Bolshevism.[52]

It remains remarkable to what great extent the regular German Army, *das Heer*, became actively involved in the mass murders of the Soviet Jewish population during Operation "Barbarossa". Army commanders at the top, such as Manstein, Reichenau and Hoth, demanded in their overall orders to their respective subordinate army units complete comprehension (*völliges Verständnis*) for the "hard but justifiable penance on the Jewish sub-humans" (*harte, aber gerechte Sühne am jüdischen Untermenschentun*).[53] As just one example, the *SS* reported that even before *Einsatzgruppe A* of the *SD* established their position in Eastern White Russia,

Heinrich Himmler inspects members of the Norwegian Hird, equivalent to the German *SA*, in January 1941. On the left is the Higher *SS* and Police Leader Wilhelm Rediess and *SS-Brigadeführer* Richard Hermann, and on Himmler's right is the leader of the Norwegian *NS*-party, Vidkun Quisling. The purpose of Himmler's visit to Norway was to encourage Norwegians to enlist for service in the *SS-Standarte "Nordland"*, and also to inspect the first 200 men who had been accepted as volunteers. During the war, Germany tried to establish a Norwegian *Allgemeine-SS*, first as *Norges-SS* and then as *Germanske-SS Norge*.

Young ethnic Germans (*Volksdeutsche*) from the Romanian town of Schässburg on 21 July 1943, being transported by train to Vienna after being mustered for service in the *Waffen-SS*. For some 900 years, 250,000 Germans had been living in the Romanian multicultural region of Siebenbürgen (Transylvania), which constituted the largest ethnic-German population outside the Third Reich. Due to Himmler's expansion of the *Waffen-SS*, 63,000 ethnic Germans from Romania served in the *Waffen-SS* from 1943–45. Within the *III. (Germ.) SS-Panzer-Korps*, these ethnic Germans were exposed to discrimination, as being second-class Germanic, by some of the Scandinavian volunteers in the corps. New research (Milata) shows that the majority of these men were actually volunteers. Not all *Voksdeutsche* opted for service in the *Waffen-SS* for ideological reasons, but as an alternative choice in their complex threefold minority situation between 1918 and 1940, involving aggressive Soviet communism, Romanian chauvinistic ethnic politics and pressure from Nazi Germany and the *SS*. Himmler's fatal decision to draft these *Volksdeutsche* to the *Waffen-SS en masse* in the end totally destroyed this rich century-old German culture and resulted in its final exodus from Siebenbürgen and Transylvania.

Civilian Jews being executed in the East by men from an *Einsatzkommando*. Between 1.5 and 2 million Jews fell victim to what is called "Holocaust by bullets", before the industrial mass gassings were introduced by the *SS*. The massive amount of murders in the field could not have been achieved in such a scale if the *Einsatzgruppen* were not supported, often by the German Army, *Waffen-SS* and police or local volunteers and militia, mainly Ukrainians, Latvians and Lithuanians. All branches from the German armed forces, including the *Waffen-SS*, participated in these mass killings, as well as members of the so called *Wehrmachtgefolge*, including *Organisation Todt* and the Reich Labour Service. Historians estimate that over 60,000 men participated in the mass murder of Jews on the Eastern Front.

Due to the loss of traditions in the *Waffen-SS*, its indifferent status and the heterogenous social structure of its officer corps, the *Waffen-SS* never had a clear *esprit de corps*. What left a stamp and influenced integration factors in the *Waffen-SS* was often the personality of the various *SS*-units' commanders. "The mentality of the officers' corps carried various accents ... partly conservative or national revolutionary and was only partially identical with the 'official' *SS*-ideology" (Wegner). The officer in the *Waffen-SS* was expected to act as a "political soldier", and these elitist *SS* ideals were no different between an *SS-Untersturmführer* from the *Verfungstruppe*, the *Allgemeine-SS* or the *Sicherheitsdienst* (Security Services); only their respective battlefields were different. This photo shows *SS-Panzer* grenadiers conferring with a Tiger commander from the Army, probably during the Kursk offensive in 1943.

the *Wehrmacht* had already annihilated 10,000 Jews in this area. No wonder that the commander of *Einsatzgruppe A*, *SS-Brigadeführer* Franz Stahlecker, wrote in his report to Berlin that the cooperation between his murder squads and *Generaloberst* Erich Hoepner, Commander of *Panzergruppe 4*, was close and "almost heartily" (*sehr enge, fast herzliche Zusammenarbeit*).[54]

Professor Omer Bartov has conducted an interesting analysis of the brutalization of the German Army during the Nazi campaign against Soviet Russia from 1941–45.[55] Bartov's thesis highlights a significant increasing Nazification – a "socialization" into Nazi education, ideology and propaganda – of Germany's soldiers on the Eastern Front during the campaign against the USSR:

> Was [the *Wehrmacht*] merely a military organization which carried out its orders with remarkable professional skill, or a highly politicized army? Was it a haven from the regime or an exceptionally effective school of National Socialism? Did it pose a threat to Hitler's rule or was it rather his most formidable instrument? ... The process [of Nazification] began long before the war and some of its roots predate the Nazi regime. Yet it was during the war, and most importantly on the Eastern front, that the *Wehrmacht* finally became Hitler's Army. I intentionally concentrate on the vast confrontation between Germany and the Soviet Union, where the *Wehrmacht* both won its greatest victories and was finally destroyed, and where the progressive ideological penetration of the Army reached its peak, motivating the troops to fight with extraordinary resilience, on the one hand, and to commit unprecedented crimes, on the other.

Nevertheless, it would be fair to mention the amount of surviving documents and testimonies of alienation and disgust from officers and soldiers of the German Army, at the Nazi massacres of Soviet Jews. This is even more remarkable, as the space for such protests was narrowing considerably during the war against the USSR, compared with the relatively few but honourable and intense protests to the German Army High Command given by, for instance, *Generaloberst* Johannes Blaskowitz, during and after the Polish campaign in 1939 against the mass murders of the *SS et consortes* in Poland. During the campaign against the Soviet Union, critics of mass shootings could no more count on the eventual support of the German Army High Command – which in the pre-"Barbarossa" planning had practically capitulated to Heydrich and Himmler in, for example, distributing the official orders to murder all captured Soviet Army Commissars. Critical voices had now also no protection from a former, in terms of ethical issues, relatively homogeneous German officers' corps, but stood instead under psychological pressure from numerous radical anti-Semites and pro-Hitler officers, whose reports could be fatal for any dissident, especially regarding such a central Nazi issue as the "Jewish question".

Notable examples of courageous, or at least non-conformist behaviour, include the report of 9 December 1941 from Major Rudolf Christoph Freiherr von Gersdorff, chief intelligence officer at the staff of *Heeresgruppe "Mitte"*, which he wrote after travelling along the front of the army group:

> During all lengthy conversations with officers, I was spontaneously asked about the mass shootings of Jews. I got the impression that the shootings of Jews, POWs and Commissars, nearly commonly are rejected within the officers' corps. The executions were described as tarnishing the honour of the German Army, especially its officers' corps. Also the issues of responsibility for these actions were raised. I could also establish, that these facts were common knowledge and the subject of frequent conversations within the officers' corps, as we had previously imagined.[56]

The memoirs of a German Army field doctor in the East, Dr Curt Emmrich, gives a probably polished, but essentially reasonable account of the mentality on the Eastern Front:

> Without hesitation, the disgust within the Army over the massacres was common. Everybody considered it shameful, that "the others" [the Nazis] misused the victories, won by brave soldiers, for their purposes. But it was not indignation of *Humanitas*, from the bottom of their hearts. The poison of Anti-Semitism had already advanced too deep into the [German] souls.[57]

No wonder, therefore, due to the various indifferent attitudes from Army officers, that *SS-Brigadeführer* Stahlecker praised "Papa Eicke", the previous commander of the Dachau concentration camp and during the Soviet campaign commander of the *SS-Division "Totenkopf"*, *SS-Gruppenführer* Theodor Eicke. In the Pripjet marshes, the *SS-Kavalleriebrigade* under *SS-Gruppenführer*[58] Hermann Fegelein murdered 17,388 Jews, while the *SS-Division "Das Reich"* assisted in September 1941 in killing 920 Jews in Lagoisk, near Minsk.[59] It is also highly probable that the *SS-Division "Wiking"* murdered 700 Galician Jews near Ternipil in July 1941.[60]

The outbreak of the Second World War, including the previous Sudetenland crisis, left the German people indifferent, negative and even depressed in their attitude to Hitler's war. The victory over France dispelled much of the gloom, mostly due to people's relief over the relatively low German casualties in the West. The invasion of the Soviet Union caught not only Stalin but also many Germans by surprise. However, the Red Army's determined resistance, the image of communist terror and the noticeable German losses in the East, filled the German people with anxiety: "Perceived as a struggle of all-or-nothing, the war in the East called for complete spiritual commitment, absolute obedience and unremitting destruction of the enemy ... The war had made the *Wehrmacht* into Hitler's army, the Germans into Hitler's people."[61] If Czechoslovakia was Hitler's first victim, it is reasonable to declare Germany as his last.

More than 30 years ago, on 8 May 1985, the newly elected West German *Bundespräsident* Richard von Weizsäcker reminded, in his speech in Bonn, that anyone who shut their eyes to the past will be blind for the age in which they live. Hence, von Weizsäcker pointed out, the Allied victory in 1945 was a liberation for the German people, and those horrors connected with the war's end and the time that followed – millions of Germans expelled from the present Poland, Rumania and the Balkans, and the death toll among German POWs in Soviet camps – were not to be connected with the German capitulation on 8 May 1945, but with Hitler's seizure of power on 30 January 1933.

Towards a Greater *Germanic Reich*

After a successful conclusion of the Second World War, Himmler – always not only a phantasm but also a strongly principled visionary – foresaw the complete fusion of the *SS* and the state's policing apparatus. This would lead to the creation of a *Staatssschutzkorps* (state protection corps) which would, in Himmler's mind, form the backbone of the pan-Germanic Reich and serve as the ultimate guarantor of its "Thousand Year" existence.[62]

A ghost always remained in Hitler's, Himmler's and other Nazi *coryphaei's* memory: the surprising and total breakdown of the German Imperial *Kaiserreich* in 1918–19 after the nation's defeat in the Great War. This phenomenon would not be permitted to repeat itself: the Nazi "Thousand Year Reich" would in the future be further strengthened by absolutely loyal administrative vassals.

Another central terminology in the *SS* was *die kämpfende Verwaltung* ("the fighting administration"), where the permanent Germanic mission and ideologization of the entire world would prove elastic, never in itself stiffening and degenerating bureaucracy. It was for Himmler unimportant whether this political cadre was of German, Walloon, Swedish, Norwegian, Dutch, Finnish, Flemish or Danish origin. Ideological loyalty and meritorious service at the front in the *Waffen-SS* were what would count in the *SS*.

The absolute majority of academic research on the phenomena of the *Waffen-SS* within the Nazi and *SS* hemisphere consists mainly of studies and monographs on separate West, North and East European nations' contributions in the form of volunteers to the *Waffen-SS* or the German Army, including these countries' collaborationists' pragmatic or ideological motives for cooperating with the *SS*. Other studies have focused solely on the German approach to and plans for the multinational *Waffen-SS* and the *SS* field of conduct in this area. The first two major academic works to give an overall view of and to cast light on the *SS* transnational "pan-Germanic" concept are the recent dissertation *Solkors eller Hakekors* (*Sun Cross or Swastica*) by Sigurd Sørlie from Oslo, and *Himmlers Norge* (*Himmler's Norway*) by the Norwegian-Swedish historians Terje Emberland and Matthew Kott.[63] These pioneering and comparative in-depth studies give new perspectives and reflections on Himmler's long-term and overall pan-Germanic plans, exemplified by the *SS* approach, versus the occupied "Aryan" Norway, both before and during the Second World War, illustrating the influence and importance of the *SS* in Norway, and above all placed it in its European context. Due to both Sørlie and Emberland & Kott, Norway was to become an experimental field as an "*SS* field laboratory" in terms of recruitment of ideologically motivated Norwegians to the *Waffen-SS*, to the *Germanske SS*, the establishment of the *Germanske Landtjenste* for the colonization of Eastern *Lebensraum* and the formation of a multinational *SS* elite political cadre (the *Staatschutzkorps*) for the administration of the Greater Germanic Reich and the colonial territories in the East.

An early photo of Rudolf Saalbach as *SS-Unterscharführer* and a member of *SS-Sonderkommando "Sachsen"*. He would later be transferred to *SS-Wachsturmbann "Elbe"*, which was eventually absorbed into *SS-Totenkopfstandarte 3 "Thüringen"*, guarding KZ Buchenwald. Rudolf Saalbach served from 1943 as commander of the *SS-Panzer-Aufklärungsabteilung 11 "Nordland"* during the battles in the Baltic countries, Pomerania and Brandenburg-Berlin in 1944–45. Saalbach's is a typical example of a pre-war career in the concentration camp system that then led to a front-line command in the *Waffen-SS*. An important element in Himmler's personnel policy was the deliberate rotation between field units of the *Waffen-SS*, *SS* security agencies and the concentration camps.

A propaganda poster for volunteer service in the *Legion Wallonie*. Following the swift occupation of Belgium in 1940, the *SS* and *Wehrmacht* profited from the historical national split between Dutch-speaking Flemings and French-speaking Walloons. Since the First World War, both ethnic camps contained large groups of right-wing extremists who strived for a *Neuordnung* (New Order) of Belgium in their respective interest. For ideological and political reasons, the "new masters" from the *SS* backed the Flemings while the "non-Germanic" Walloons were directed to the German Army for establishing volunteer military units, serving on the Eastern Front. Himmler, however, assumed management of the Walloon volunteers on 1 June 1943 and transferred them into the *Waffen-SS*, where they formed the *SS-Sturmbrigade* (Assault Brigade) *"Wallonien"*. The Belgian pre-war Fascist leader Leon Degrelle was to be a political favourite of both Hitler and Himmler. Consequently, Degrelle was catapulted from private to *SS-Standartenführer* and supported the idea of a Greater Germanic *Reich*, partly out of opportunism as Degrelle saw a way to political leadership over the Walloon part of Belgium via the *SS* and the *Reich*.

These facts coincide with earlier conclusions made in *Swedes at War 1914–1945* by Lars Gyllenhaal and Lennart Westberg, especially concerning the multinational *Waffen-SS* as a cadre force for politically reliable and battle-hardened functionaries for the administration of the future "Germanic *SS* Empire". Such motives emerge from a key document, quoted in *Swedes at War*: the interrogation in 1945 by British Intelligence of Karl Leib, former *SS-Obersturmbannführer* and chief of the *Waffen-SS* recruiting office in Oslo:

> The long term political goal was to obtain young Swedes for service in the *Waffen-SS*. After their front line experience and political schooling they would return to Sweden and help build a nucleus group that could be compared to

> the *SS-Junkerschulen* (*Waffen-SS* officers' schools). After two years in the *Waffen-SS* they would return to their land and act as a catalyst with the [Swedish] National Socialist Movement, on which the *Germanische Leitstelle* [*SS* central recruitment office in Berlin] placed so much faith and hope. These young men would not need to get involved in political action during the war, but their political influence would be expected to be of decisive importance after the end of war [in the East]. With this policy in mind, *SS-Obersturmbannführer* Riedweg was eager to recruit the largest possible number of Swedes to the *Waffen-SS*.[65]

What is more, the *SS* viewed Sweden as the most important component in the "Germanic tribe", as expressed in a speech in the autumn of 1943 at the *SS-Junkerschule* Bad Tölz by *SS-Obersturmbannführer* Dr Franz Riedweg: "[Sweden] is the most important Germanic human reservoir that there was."[66] Ironically, the Swedes in German uniform were quantitatively insignificant (200 men). Seen in relation to the great expectations that the *SS* originally had for a broad recruiting of "Nordic volunteers", the final result from the Nordic hemisphere was generally meagre and Hitler considered the recruiting from Sweden as a fiasco, as he himself expressed during a meeting at his *Führerhauptquartier* on 16 July 1941:

> The *Führer* voiced harsh criticism of the Swedes for the very meagre volunteer contingent they had provided for the struggle against Communism in the East, and even *Reichsmarschall* Göring described the Swedes as decadent. The Finns on the other hand earned broad praise for their pluck.[67]

Beside the number of volunteers to the *Waffen-SS* from Norway, Denmark and Sweden, Finland contributed with 1,400 men to a Finnish *SS* battalion in the East that became a chess piece in the Finnish-German wartime relationship, as quasi brothers-in-arms. An early academic work on the Finnish *SS* battalion was published in 1969 by the Finnish Professor Mauno Jokipii: *Panttipataljoona*.[68] A highly important academic work – including a radically new view on the ideological antecedent of the majority of the Finnish volunteers in the *Waffen-SS* from 1941–43 – is Dr Lars Westerlund's recent analysis of these volunteers' political affiliations, their motives for joining the battalion, the Finnish social democrats' engagement in the recruiting procedures and the semantic-propagandistic overtones surrounding the forming of the battalion. Lars Westerlund's accurate analyses of the existing sources shows that out of 1,088 finally accepted volunteers to the battalion, a clear majority (680 men, or 63 percent) represented right-wing or right-nationalist opinions and parties.[69] Westerlund's conclusions are at the same time an important correlative to Mauno Jokipii's previous results. While Jokipii admits only a percentage of one-fifth of Finnish right-wing volunteers in the battalion, Westerlund could prove that these were more than three times as frequent.[70] Other interesting results by Westerlund concern lucrative economic motives from the volunteers for serving in the *Waffen-SS*: during the period of June 1942 to October 1943, 20 million Finnish Marks were transferred from Germany to Finland and into the bank accounts of the battalion's serving volunteers. For internal political reasons, the Swedish-speaking Finns were mainly obstructed from serving in the *SS* battalion; also on this point, Westerlund disagrees with Jokipiis' previous assertions.[71]

Further expansion and the end

During the campaign against the Soviet Union, above all from 1942 onwards, the *Waffen-SS* was most rapidly expanded, and by the end of the war about one million men had passed through its ranks. By 1945 there were, or rather had been, nominally 38 field divisions in the *Waffen-SS* subordinated to Himmler, but they were ultimately led in the field by the regular German Army. By the end of the war, the *Waffen-SS* had, in fact, developed into a sort of unofficial branch of the *Wehrmacht*, alongside the three official branches of *Heer* (Army), *Luftwaffe* (Air Force) and *Kriegsmarine* (Navy).

The *Waffen-SS* ultimately encompassed a total of about 400,000 German citizens, as well as 300,000 *Volksdeutsche* (ethnic Germans from Eastern Europe) and 250,000 non-Germans: for example, 22,000 Dutchmen, 5,000 Norwegians, 4,500 Danes, 1,400 Finns, 150 Swedes and even 35–40 prisoners of war from Great Britain. It should be noted however, that up to 30 June 1943, 5,883 "Germanic" *SS* volunteers had resigned from the *Waffen-SS*.[72] During the campaign against the Soviet Union, many Eastern Europeans joined the *Waffen-SS*, both voluntarily and through conscription, including 60,000 Latvians, 50,000 Hungarians, 30,000 Estonians and 20,000 Ukrainians.

Recent research (Thomas Casagrande) on the creation of the *7. SS-Gebirgs-Division "Prinz Eugen"* in 1942 (mainly consisting of ethnic German recruits from Yugoslavia) also shows how historical ethnic conflicts, amalgamation with wartime ambitions of the Nazi occupations forces and internal interested regional *Volksdeutsche* parties finally ended in numerous atrocities, in terms of so-called anti-partisan actions, in the Balkans and, at the end, the destruction of a several hundred-year-old German culture in these regions.[73]

In opposition to the ethnic Germans in Yugoslavia (Banat) – with its more hostile connections to these neighbouring Yugoslav-Serbians – the 250,000 ethnic Germans in Rumania (Siebenbürgen) represented a 900-year-long tradition of a stable and non-feudalistic German culture in south-eastern Europe, whose unfortunate contribution to the *Waffen-SS* had other motives than preserving or taking power over other neighbouring ethnic groups. The Rumanian-Germans' mostly-volunteer decision to serve in German uniform must be seen in the threefold state of strain between Bucharest, Moscow and Berlin that existed for the ethnic Germans

The reality behind the suggestive recruiting brochures from the *Waffen-SS*: a long row of dead *SS* soldiers - German, ethnic-German, Dutch and Scandinavian - lie in the snow behind a wooden shed on the outskirts of the Estonian border city of Narva. The bodies await identification and a summary burial. The time is February 1944 after the great offensive of the Red Army through Ingria toward the Narva River, where entire companies and even battalions from the *III. (Germ.) SS-Panzer Korps* were wiped out.

Heinrich Himmler attends a mass meeting for Norwegian *SS*-volunteers in the Hippodrome in Oslo in January 1941. From the left are: *NS*-leader Vidkun Quisling, *Reichskommissar* for occupied Norway Josef Terboven, *Generaloberst* Nikolaus von Falkenhorst (Commanding Officer of the *Wehrmacht* in Norway) and the Higher *SS* and Police Leader in Norway, Wilhelm Rediess. Behind Himmler stands his adjutant, Werner Grothmann. Recent research (Sørlie) has clarified the contradictory interests between the *NS*-leader Quisling and the *SS* in terms of Norwegian volunteers for the *Waffen-SS*. While the *SS*'s ambition was to develop the volunteers as loyal exponents for pan-Germanic long-term goals within the future Greater Germanic *Reich*, Quisling looked upon these volunteers as an investment for a strengthened and partly independent Norway within the future German hemisphere. Sørlie's research has also abolished the myth that the volunteers, as supposedly mainly anti-communists or driven by non-ideological factors, were resistant to the Nazi and *SS* ideology. On the contrary, the majority volunteered out of sympathy for Nazi ideology.

The very first area of both war crimes and genocidical mass murder was not the German-Soviet front but Poland in 1939–40. *Wehrmacht* soldiers of the *8. Armee* are photographed after the killing of Polish civilians during the first days of war in September 1939. The man on the far left seems to be a Polish soldier, but the rest, including women, are civilians. All personnel from the *SS*, *SD* and *Verfügungstruppe* were taught to think in "wide spaces" and overcome traditional moral barriers. One of the first mass crimes committed took place in Poland: Lieutenant Colonel Helmut Grosscurth from the *Abwehr* noticed soldiers from Felix Steiner's *SS-Regiment "Deutschland"* murdering a number of Jews on 1 September 1939. Apart from the 15 percent of Poland's population that, according to the *SS*, were "of good race" and could be transformed into German (*eingedeutscht*), all Poles were to be "ethnically cleansed" to make way for Germanic colonizers.

between 1918 and 1939. Out of 63,500 *Volksdeutsche* from Rumania, 97 percent served in field units of the *Waffen-SS*, while 3 percent were transferred to "police duties" (largely as concentration camp guards). Recent research (Paul Milata) has shown that rather than ideological (pro-Nazi) opinions, pragmatic considerations played a key role; the catastrophic collapse of the allied Rumanian Army at Stalingrad was the catalyst for ethnic Germans to desert the Rumanian Army, where they traditionally had been mostly badly handled as Germans, and opt for service in the *Wehrmacht* instead.[74] Central decisions in Berlin between the *SS* and the *OKH* decided that these *Volksdeutsche* were primarily to serve in the *Waffen-SS*. The question of the *Volksdeutsche* in Rumania also illustrates the complex issue and relationship between the terms "State" and "Nation", a problem that has not vanished since the end of the Second World War in Europe.

The complex ambitions of Himmler to recruit Muslim volunteers to the *Waffen-SS* had been preceded by the German Army, the *Abwehr* and the *Sicherheitsdienst* (*SD*). From 1942 on, all these formations created large Muslim units in German uniform: the German-Arabic *Lehrabteilung*, the *Turkbatallion 450*, Krimtatarian *Selbstschutz* units (Home Guard) and numerous *Ostlegionen* from Soviet Oriental people (Turkmen, Turkestanis, Azerbaijanis/Azari, Chechens and Dagestanis). Examples of Himmler enrolling Muslims into the Waffen-SS included the *13. Waffen-Gebirgs-Division der SS "Handschar"* (*Kroatisches Nr.1*), the *21. Waffen-Gebirgs-Division der SS "Skanderberg"* (*Albanisches Nr.1*) and the *"Ost-Türkishe Waffenverband der SS"*.[75]

SS-Obergruppenführer Gottlob Berger, the dynamic head of *Waffen-SS* recruitment, understood how to win over Himmler to the idea of utilizing all possible reserves of personnel despite issues of race. After Himmler was appointed Chief of the German Reserve Army in mid-1944, many kinds of new non-Germans (who previously had fought in the ranks of the German Army) were transferred into the *Waffen-SS*, including Frenchmen, Italians, Cossacks, Indians, Russians, Spaniards, Tartars and other groups one would never have expected to see in *SS* uniform.

This *levée en masse* required, logically, a new qualitative (political) classification of all units in the *Waffen-SS*. This happened shortly after the turn of the year 1943–44. This happened during the spring of 1944 as Himmler implemented a new classification in three categories of the *Waffen-SS*: the

When the Third *Reich* emptied its last resources in 1943–45, never before in history had so many children been mobilized for war duty as in National Socialist Germany, like a destructive modern Children's Crusade. The *Moloch Waffen-SS* also contributed by, in practice, semi-conscription in 1943 of 16,000 German boys aged 16–17 to the *12. SS-Panzer-Division "Hitler-Jugend"*.[64] This unfortunate cooperation between the *Hitler-Jugend* leadership (Axmann) and the *Waffen-SS* resulted in thousands of juvenile deaths from the ranks of the *12. "Hitler-Jugend"* during this *SS*-division's actions in Normandy, the Ardennes and Hungary in 1944–45. Today, 43,500 German boy soldiers rest in cemeteries outside and inside the present Federal Republic of Germany.

first category became the classic *SS*-Divisions, in which ranks every man was fully qualified to be a member of the *SS*; the second was the *"SS -Freiwilligen-Divisionen"*, that consisted of either *Volksdeutsche* (ethnic Germans) or Germanic soldiers who were not individually qualified for membership in the *SS*; and the third category remained the *"Waffen-Divisionen der SS"*, which were recruited from non-Germanic (*fremdvölkische*) stock.

Significant is also the fact that the *SS* never parted from its severe standards of selection: although the *Waffen-SS* grew from 23,000 members on 1 September 1939 up to 501,000 on 31 December 1943, there were only 68,000 new members that were admitted into the *SS*. Those officers and soldiers in the *Waffen-SS* from all over Europe that did not qualify as "true" *SS* members wore the uniform of the *Waffen-SS*. Accurate corresponding notations were also made in their personnel files on their "*SS*-unworthiness", and in the case of a final Nazi victory in the Second World War, it would have been easy for Himmler and the *SS* to sift the wheat from the chaff.[76]

It was on the Eastern Front that the majority of Hitler's *Wehrmacht* and the *Waffen-SS* was mowed down and crushed – more than 70 percent of Germany's permanent loss of personnel occurred in the East.[77] Thus, by the end of the war, the *Waffen-SS* had lost much of its profile as Hitler's political-military Aryan *avant-garde*, not least due to the great losses, when many German volunteers were replaced by foreign ones and then even by ideologically indifferent conscripts, both foreign and German. In the *Waffen-SS*, there were consequently, from 1942, both elite troops and second or third-class units.[78]

The dark side: War crimes, genocide and "political soldiery"

As described above, the war between Germany and the Soviet Union from 1941-45 was more than the largest military-political conflict in history. In terms of mass murder of prisoners of war and civilians, the Eastern Front surpassed the other theatres of war in sheer brutality and barbarism. Out of a total of 5.7 million Soviet prisoners of war in German captivity, 3.3 million died by deliberate mistreatment, sickness or starvation, or were shot.[79] Where "traditional" war crimes are concerned – for example, the summary execution of prisoners of war at the front – the role of the *Waffen-SS* in such crimes has been much debated. The subject is complicated by the fact that common types of war crimes merged with Nazi politics of genocide, the slave worker system and reprisal actions in the anti-partisan war. The special status of the *Waffen-SS* as ideologically trained and indoctrinated political soldiers contributed in both large and small ways to give destructivity a free hand and to worsen the situation. Another important factor was the way some personnel were rotated between field units of the *Waffen-SS*, the concentration/extermination camps and *Einsatzgruppen* (murder squads), resulting in the implanting of a destructive mentality. That the soldiers of the *Waffen-SS* were therefore not quite "soldiers like any others" is apparent.

The fact has sometimes been neglected that numerous cases of war crimes were committed by units of the *SS-Verfügungstruppe* and other *SS* formations like the *SS-Totenkopfstandarten* (that in 1940 or later were incorporated into the *Waffen-SS*) during and shortly after Hitler's campaign against Poland in 1939. While the *Leibstandarte* and the regiments "*Deutschland*" and "*Germania*" fought within the German Army, the three *Totenkopfstandarten* were used as *Einsatzgruppen* behind the Tenth (Reichenau) and Eighth armies (Blaskowitz). It is therefore no wonder that the first mass crimes that were committed by the *Waffen-SS* were put down on the account of these *Totenkopfstandarten*.[80] The "*SS-Heimwehr Danzig*" was guilty of mass executions during and after the battle of Danzig,[81] the *SS-Artillerie-Regiment* of the *VT*, under *SS-Obersturmbannführer* Peter Hansen, committed atrocities against Polish Jews and other civilians in Siedlce and Modlin in September 1939, and there are many other cases to be mentioned.[82]

The first documented war crimes by a unit of the *Waffen-SS* during the French campaign of 1940 occurred when a company commander of the *SS-Division Totenkopf* used machine guns to murder 90 prisoners of war in the village of Le Paradis. On the same day, 27 May, Hitler's *Leibstandarte* murdered nearly 100 British prisoners of war in the Belgian town of Wormhoudt.[83] The *Totenkopf* were also guilty of mass executions of French colonial troops during the campaign in France.[84] Other examples of war crimes in Western and Southern Europe by *Waffen-SS* units are the massacres in Oradour (France), Marzobotto and Boves (Italy), and Klissura (Greece).[85]

The execution of the war against the Soviet Union was from the beginning criminal in nature. Hitler's general order to all units of the *Wehrmacht* and *Waffen-SS* on the handling of prisoners of war included, among other things, the liquidating of all Red Army political commissars. Recent research has shown that regular German Army units often complied and summarily executed political commissars in accordance with Hitler's order. Immediately after the war, a Swedish volunteer in the *SS-Infanterie-Division "Wiking"* reported to the Swedish Security Police: "Captured political commissars and *NKVD* soldiers normally did not become old." The location in August 1943 of the by then loosely composed *III. (germ.) SS-Panzer-Korps* to Croatia for final training included certain knowledge that these units probably would be engaged in anti-partisan warfare in the Western Balkans.

In Western European debate, focus lies often on war crimes committed by the *Waffen-SS* in the Western Europe theatre of war; e.g. Le Paradis in 1940, and Tulle, Oradour and, above all, Malmédy in 1944. The much more horrifying conditions on the Eastern Front are thereby too often neglected or misinterpreted. The British historian Max Hastings, however, quotes a conversation between two former German *Waffen-SS* officers who, after the war, discussed the

The propaganda purpose of this carefully posed photo is to show the international character of volunteers in the *Waffen-SS* reading "Germanic" *SS* newspapers. In the foreground, a Norwegian reads the March 1943 issue of *Germaneren*, the publication of *Germanske SS Norge*. A Fleming examines the back of *De SS Man*, while Luc Godderis, also Flemish, reads the Dutch *Storm SS*. The photo was taken at the facilities of the *SS*-camp in Sennheim. Formerly the French Saint Andre mental institution at Cernay, the *Waffen-SS* transformed the hospital into a military training base after the region of Alsace was incorporated into Germany in 1940. Ideological indoctrination in the *Waffen-SS* was intensive, to create a corporate identity. The desired fusion of national socialist ethos and military professionalism into political soldiery would amalgamate weapons and *Weltanschauung* (politics), tradition and a new beginning.

Soldiers from the Finnish *SS*-battalion in the Caucasus Mountains near Malgobek in October 1942. These men belonged to the *SS-Regiment "Nordland"* within the *SS-Division "Wiking"*. As the only one of its allies not occupied by the Third *Reich*, Finland recruited a battalion of 1,400 Finns in 1941 to serve in the *Waffen-SS* on the Eastern Front. The battalion was part of the military cooperation between Finland and Germany prior to Operation "Barbarossa". Within the framework of the *III. (Germ.) SS-Panzer Korps*, Himmler planned to establish a Finnish *SS-Jäger-Regiment "Kalevala"* in 1943, named after Finland's national literary epic. For political reasons (so as not to alienate the Western Allies), the Finnish government recalled and disbanded the Finnish *SS*-battalion in mid-1943.

massacre in Oradour. One officer (having served with the *SS-Division Totenkopf* in the East) said to the other: "In our circles, Herr Müller, this [Oradour] was *nothing*!"[86]

The behaviour of the unit was often dependent on the personality and character of their officers in charge.[87] The variation and freedom to act was often large, and the actions at or behind the front-lines are hard to reconstruct today. Recent research has also pointed out the *Wehrmacht* as an increasingly ideologically radicalized and streamlined war instrument of the Third *Reich*. One of the reasons was the input from 1943 by younger army officers from the so called *Hitlerjugend* generation, who during the 1930s and part of the 1940s were socialized into National Socialist ideology and thinking. But the clear political profile of the *Waffen-SS*, where mass murderers, idealists and indifferent conscripts were mixed together, contributes to the fact that its units too often left behind a bloody trail in the Second World War: "The dominant picture of the *Waffen-SS* is therefore neither white nor black, but rather grey."[88] Recent academic research in the US has pointed out that the *10.SS-Panzer-Division* "Frundsberg" lacked a political SS-profile as well as having committed no known or documented war crimes or other atrocities during its existence.[92]

The blind decade: The restorative Fifties in West Germany

The surviving veterans of the former *Waffen-SS* profited conveniently from the restorative forces in the newborn Federal Republic of Germany. In one of his election speeches in Hannover in 1955, the German Chancellor Konrad Adenauer declared: "The men of the *Waffen-SS* were soldiers as everyone else." Adenauer was forcibly backed up by the *Wehrmacht* lobbyist and former general Hasso von Manteuffel, who said that: "The soldiers of the *Waffen-SS* were decent persons.".[89] In 1951 and 1952, Adenauer had repeated his confidence in the *Waffen-SS* in declarations before the *Bundestag* (West German Parliament), and in the summer of 1954 Adenauer also visited the war criminal prison in Werl and shook hands with the former *SS-Obersturmbannführer* Kurt Meyer, condemned to death by Allied courts for war crimes in Normandy during his time as commander of the *12. SS-Panzer-Division "Hitler-Jugend"*. Such actions must be seen in the perspective of the restorative mentality in West Germany in the early and mid-Fifties.[90]

In the early Fifties, the lobby organization HIAG – which supported veterans of the former *Waffen-SS* and aimed to historically whitewash the Nazi formation – was frequently founded nationally and regionally in West Germany, no doubt nourished by Adenauer's declarations in favour of the *Waffen-SS*. In his cynicism, Adenauer no doubt looked upon the surviving hundreds of thousands of former members of the *Waffen-SS* as a potential electorate.

New perspectives

Recent research has shown the necessity of looking upon the phenomenon of the *Waffen-SS* from a broader, overview perspective: Volunteer service in the *Waffen-SS* was not only a goal but a means to realize a larger, more complex and long-term plan by Himmler and the *SS*. As Sigurd Sørlie, Terje Emberland and Matthew Kott have proved, the racial-military war in the East was intimately associated with, for example, security tasks back in Norway.[91] The *Staatsschutzkorps* (State Security Corps) – the administrative backbone of ruling the future and visionary Greater Germanic *Reich* – would consist of a political cadre of proven men from the *Waffen-SS* field units. The idealization by Himmler of Norway, Sweden and Denmark's Viking past was not just Germanic nostalgia but part of his plan to use Scandinavian *Waffen-SS* volunteers to colonize the "ethnically cleansed" territories in the East, for a greater *Lebensraum*.

Irrespective of the Third *Reich*'s diminishing fortunes of war, the *III. (Germ.) SS-Panzer-Korps* remained instrumental in Heinrich Himmler's long-term pan-Germanic policy. The war of annihiliation and genocide in the East and the mobilization of the Germanic potential from the Nordic countries for the *III. (Germ.) SS-Panzer-Korps* as a political-soldierly cadre for securing and exploiting Eastern *Lebensraum* would, according to Himmler, attain apocalyptic proportions.

Lennart Westberg & Petter Kjellander
Sundsvall (Sweden) and
Stockholm (Sweden) in May 2019

Notes

1 Lars Gyllenhaal & Lennart Westberg, *Swedes at War. Willing Warriors of a Neutral Nation, 1914-1945* (Pennsylvania: Aberjona Press, 2010), p.317. On the political background of the Danish *SS* volunteers: see Claus Bundgård Christensen, Niels Bo Poulsen & Peter Scharff Smith, *Under hagekors og Dannebrog. Danskere i Waffen-SS 1940-45* (Copenhagen: Aschehoug, 2000), p.39 (these authors' estimation is that 75 percent of the Danes in the *SS* were motivated Nazis). The Swedish Security Police analyzed in 1944 that similar percentages (80 percent) of Swedes in the *Waffen-SS* also were dedicated to National Socialism; Gyllenhaal & Westberg, *ibid.*, p.295. The recent book by the Norwegian scholar, Sigurd Sørlie, *Solkors eller hakekors. Nordmenn i Waffen-SS 1940-1945* (Oslo: Dreyer, 2015), comes to similar conclusions regarding the ideological motivation for Norwegians in the *Waffen-SS*. A recent study of the Finnish volunteers in the *Waffen-SS* and their political preferences comes to the conclusion that 80–90 percent of these Finns were extreme-right-wing and anti-parliamentarian; Lars Westerlund, *Cirkus Collani*, p.94.

2 Hans Lindén was killed in action at the Mius Front on 30 December 1941, and was buried in Stalino. At the time of his death he served in the *SS*-Anti-Aircraft-Battalion *"Wiking"*.

3 Riksarkivet Stockholm; Archives of the Swedish Security Police (*Säkerhetspolisen*); File 9.B.

4 Otto Bräutigam, army liaison officer for Alfred Rosenberg at Hitler's HQ, in his diary entry of 16 July 1941; Hoover Institution, Washington DC.

5 The term *Waffen-SS* appeared officially the first time in November 1939. Prior to that it was called *bewaffnete SS* (armed *SS*) or *bewaffneten Einheiten der SS und der Polizei* (armed units of the *Waffen-SS* and Police).

Felix Steiner as *SS-Oberführer*, probably after the Western campaign in 1940. After charges against Steiner in the Nuremberg trials had been dropped and he was released in 1948, Steiner became one of the founding members of the HIAG, the lobby group established in 1951 by former high-ranking commanders of the *Waffen-SS* in West Germany. The HIAG also founded social welfare to widows and children of fallen soldiers in the *Waffen-SS* and tried to clarify the fate of *SS* soldiers missing at the front. In 1958 and 1963, Steiner published two highly apologetic books, *The Volunteers of the Waffen-SS, Idea and Sacrifice* and *The Army of the Outlaws*. These publications tried to restore the reputation of the *Waffen-SS* as an apolitical, ordinary military force, rather than a part of Himmler's deeply ideological and partly criminal organization. The massive amounts of war- and mass crimes committed by the *Waffen-SS* were seldom or never mentioned by Steiner. New research (Wilke) has shown the dimension of the HIAG lobbying in West Germany as a success story on behalf of the former *Waffen-SS*. The West German *Bundeskanzler* Konrad Adenauer said in the early 1960s: "I am quite aware that the soldiers of the *Waffen-SS* were decent persons", probably with a cynical eye to a potential electorate.

6 In addition to those who were killed in action at the Front, one must also add those who died of wounds in hospitals and from sickness in POW camps, and those who were reported missing in action but were probably dead. The *Wehrmacht* had proportionally similar total losses as the *Waffen-SS*: 3,880,000 dead out of a total of over 12 million men.

7 Herbert Maeger: *Verlorene Ehre, verratene Treue. Zeitzeugenbericht eines Soldaten* (Rosenheim: Rosenheimer Verlagshaus, 2003), p.8. The quotation translated from the Swedish edition: *Ur askan i elden., 18 år, tysk och soldat i Waffen-SS* (Stockholm: Svenskt Militärhistoriskt Förlag, 2012), p.13. Herbert Maeger was resident in the former Prussian province of Eupen-Malmédy, which in 1920 became part of Belgium. After the annexation in 1940 of Eupen-Malmédy into the *Reich*, Herbert Maeger joined the *Leibstandarte SS "Adolf Hitler"* in mid-1941. His memoirs are worth reading and stand out favourably from the mass of apologetic recollections from former *Waffen-SS* soldiers.

8 The most compromising impact in the *SS* expansion probably came from the incorporation of the *Totenkopf* units into the *Waffen-SS*. These had served as guard personnel in concentration camps from 1933 under the notorious Theodor Eicke and were trained to treat prisoners in especially inhumane ways. Charles W Sydnor, Jr, *Soldiers of Destruction. The SS Death Head's Division 1933-1945* (Princeton, New Jersey: Princeton University Press, 1990), p.37.

9 Stefan Hördler, *KZ-System und Waffen-SS. Genese, Interpendenzen und Verbrechen*, in Schulte, Lieb & Wegner, *Die Waffen-SS. Neue Forschungen* (Paderborn: Schöningh, 2014), p.80.

10 Stefan Hördler, *KZ-System und Waffen-SS*, in Schulte, Lieb & Wegner, *ibid.*, p.85.

11 Smelser & Syring, *Die SS. Elite unter dem Totenkopf* (Schöning: 2000), p.203. Hausser was supported in this rehabilitation issue after 1945 by the former army general Hasso von Manteuffel (who knew about the involvement of both the *Wehrmacht* and the *Waffen-SS* in the Holocaust), who exclaimed that he "long-since knew that the soldiers of the *Waffen-SS* were decent persons who by the Allied powers were pointed out as guilty … and that the *Waffen-SS* did not shoot any Jews but were feared by the Soviet soldiers"; see: Jörg Friedrich, *Die Kalte Amnestie. NS-Täter in der Bundesrepublik* (List: 2007), p.292.

12 Hördler, *ibid.*, p.87. Hilmar Wäckerle was killed in action in Galicia in July 1941 as regimental commander with the *SS-Division "Wiking"*.

13 Hördler, *ibid.*, p.89.

14 Hördler, *ibid.*, p.92.

15 Later known as *Aktion 14 f 13*.

16 The chief organizer of the "T 4", from the *Kanzlei des Führers*, Viktor Brack, was transferred in 1943 to the *SS-Division "Prinz Eugen"*; Hördler, *ibid.*, p.95.

17 The 1st Company of the *Batallion z.b.V. der Waffen-SS (zbV = zu besonderer Verwendung*, "for special purposes") had in 1942 participated in the mass killings of at least 11,000 Jews near Minsk during May-July, under *SS-Brigadeführer* Walter Stahlecker. The company commander, *SS-Obersturmführer* Fritz Störtz, was installed as CO of the *SS* field-replacement battalion of the *20. Waffen-Grenadier-Division der SS (Estnische Nr.1)* in 1944, and was wounded in January 1945 in Silesia as CO of the *45. Waffen-Grenadier-Regiment*. One of the notorious people who were transferred to the Estonian *Waffen-SS* in 1942-43 was Ain-Ervin Mere, Chief of the Estonian Security Police under supervision of *SS-Sturmbannführer* Martin Sandberger, Chief of the German Security Police and SD in Estonia; Kjellander, *Undergången* (Stockholm: SMB, 2011), p.167.

18 Hördler, *ibid.*, p.98.

19 The ethnic Germans thereby formed nearly 50 percent of the KZ guards in 1945; Hördler, *ibid.*, p.96.

The Swede Hans-Gösta Pehrsson (here as *SS-Unterstürmführer* and platoon officer at Mummassare in Estonia) joined both the pre-war Danish National Socialist party and in 1941 the *Freikorps Danmark*. He became the most decorated Swede in the *Waffen-SS* (*Ehrenblattspange*, 1944) and advanced from private in 1941 to *SS-Obersturmführer* and company commander in the *11. SS-Panzer-Aufklärungsabteilung "Nordland"* in 1944. Pehrsson survived the fierce battles in the Baltic countries, Pomerania and Brandenburg-Berlin in 1944–45 and returned to Stockholm. In 1947, Pehrsson belonged to the former *SS* volunteers who were recruited by the Swedish General Staff to the highly secret, so-called "Stay-Behind" resistance groups, in the event of a Soviet occupation. The different European varieties of "Stay-Behind" groups, often recruited from circles of *SS*-veterans, were for many years the CIA's and NATO's best-protected secrets. Through "Stay-Behind" groups, veterans from the *Waffen-SS* (and also from the Gestapo, *SD* and *Abwehr*) found a new *raison d'etre* and a confirmation that their earlier activities in Hitler's War of Destruction were not only forgiven, but also appreciated by the new Western security elite. "Stay-Behind" groups also contributed to the long-lived post-war myth that the predominant motive for Western European volunteers to join the *Waffen-SS* was anti-communism. In reality, the dominant motives were anti-parliamentary, ultra-nationalism, anti-Semitism and corporate thinking.

20 Nigel Jones, *The Birth of the Nazis. How the Freikorps blazed a trail for Hitler* (New York: Carroll & Graf Publishers, 2004), p.54.
21 Jones, *ibid.*, p.9.
22 Terje Emberland & Matthew Kott, *Himmlers Norge. Nordmenn i det storgermanske prosjekt* (Oslo: Aschehoug, 2012), p.38.
23 Terje Emberland, *Religion og rase. Nyhedenskap og nazismen i Norge 1933-1945* (Oslo: Aschehoug, 2003), p.398 f.
24 On the discussion within the so-called *Historikerstreit* (between Ernst Nolte, Andreas Hillgruber *et cons.*), see: Rudolf Augstein, *"Historikerstreit", die Dokumentation der Kontroverse um die Einzigartigkeit der nationalsocialistischen Judenvernichtung* (Munich: Piper, 1987).
25 Peter Longerich, *Heinrich Himmler: A Life* (Oxford: Oxford University Press, 2011), p.530.
26 Bernd Wegner, *Hitlers politische Soldaten, die Waffen-SS 1933-1945; Leitbild. Struktur und Funktion einer nationalsozialistischen Elite* (Paderborn: Schöningh, 1982), p.295.
27 Bernd Wegner, "Auf dem Wege zur pangermanischen Armee. Dokumente zur Entstehungsgeschichte des *III. ('germanischen') SS-Panzer-Korps", Militärgeschichtliche Mitteilungen* 1980: 2 (March 1980), pp.101-04.
28 Sigurd Sørlie, *Sonnenrad oder Hakenkreuz. Norwegische Freiwillige in der Waffen-SS und die Herausforderungen der Integration*, in Schulte, Lieb & Wegner, *ibid*. Lennart Westberg is in debt to Sigurd Sørlie for his generous provision of the manuscript to his doctoral dissertation before publication in Norway.
29 Gyllenhaal & Westberg, *Swedes at War*, p.319.
30 Sørlie, *ibid.*, p.187.
31 Sørlie, *ibid.*, p.195. *Fører* (Leader) was the Norwegian NS equivalent for *Führer*.
32 Sørlie, *ibid.*, p.423.
33 Sørlie, *ibid.*, p.423f.
34 Bundgard Christensen, Poulsen & Scharff Smith, *Dänen in der Waffen-SS Ideologie, Integration und Kriegsverbrechen im Vergleich mit anderen 'germanischen' Soldaten*, in Schulte, Lieb & Wegner, *ibid.*, p.207.
35 A brilliant, today largely forgotten, publication on several aspects of the *Waffen-SS* remains John Keegan's *Waffen-SS, the asphalt soldiers* (London: Ballantine Books, 1970).
36 Ian Kershaw, *Hitlers Macht, Das Profil der NS-Herrschaft* (Munich: Deutscher Taschenbuchverlag, 2001), p.145.
37 Jean-Luc Leleu, *Gründe für die Expansion der Waffen-SS*, in Schulte, Lieb & Wegner, *ibid.*, p.27.
38 Leleu, *ibid.*, p.29.
39 René Rohrkamp, *Die Rekrutierungspraxis der Waffen-SS*, p.57, in Schulte, Lieb & Wegner.
40 As the *Waffen-SS* started to recruit manpower from Ukraine, they were adopted as 'Galicians'; this was a province in the former Habsburg Reich before 1918.
41 Toomas Hiio, *Estnische Einheiten der Waffen-SS. Vorgeschichte, Rekrutierung, Zusammensetzung*, in Schulte, Lieb & Wegner, *ibid.*, p.156.
42 Leleu, *ibid.*, p.31.
43 Leleu, *ibid.*, p.34.
44 Gyllenhaal & Westberg, *Swedes at War*, p.257.
45 Sven Ekdahl, *Crusades and Colonization in the Baltic: A Historiographic Analysis*, in Alan V. Murray (ed.), *The North-Eastern Frontiers of Medieval Europe. The Expansion of Latin Europe 1000-1500* (Farnham: Ashgate, 2014), p.14.
46 Ekdahl, *ibid.*, p.14.

Members of the *13. Waffen-Gebirgs-Division der SS "Handschar"* in 1944, wearing as special headgear the fez with a *Totenkopf.* The *SS*-mountain divisions "*Handschar*" and "*Kama*" attracted over 18,000 Bosnian Muslims to join these formations in the Balkan operations against Tito's partisans. Himmler looked upon the Bosnians as of "Germanic" race. German connections to Islam went back to the Russo-Turkish War of 1877–78 in the Balkans. The *SS* propagandist description of Hitler's War of Annihilation in the East as a "Crusade against Bolshevism" was not far from the truth in terms of its multinational composition. The Eastern Front saw Croatian and Slovac fighter pilots, Rumanian tank crews, Ukrainian militia, Russian Cossack troops and many other nationalities. Apart from 800,000 volunteering (or reluctant) Russians, 250,000 Ukrainians and 280,000 Caucasians served in or parallel to the *Wehrmacht*, together with 250,000 Italians, 1,400 Finns, 145,000 Croats and a handful of illustrious British volunteers in the abyss of 1945. The military importance of all these allied, volunteering or auxiliary non-German troops has mostly been underestimated, as offensive units, flank support or security troops in occupied territories (mainly in the Balkans), thereby freeing regular German units for front-line service.

47 Mark Roseman, *The Villa, the Lake, the Meeting. Wannsee and the Final Solution* (London: Penguin, 2002), p.29.
48 Roseman, *ibid.*, p.29.
49 The Italian corps was reconstructed on 10 July 1942 into the XXXV *Corpo d'Armata* when the Italian military engagement on the Eastern Front was expanded into an army, the *Armata Italiana* in Russia.
50 Hans Werner Neulen, *Am Himmel Europas. Luftstreitkräfte an deutscher Seite 1939-1945* (Munich: Universitas Verlag, 1998), p.211.
51 S.I. Drobjazko, *Vostochnye legiony i kazachi chasti* (Moscow: Izdatelstvo AST, 1999), p.4, states that the number is 1.2 million Soviet citizens.
52 Helmut Krausnick & Hans-Heinrich Wilhelm, *Die Truppe des Weltanschauungskrieges. Die Einsatzgruppen der Sicherheitspolizei und des SD 1938-1942* (Stuttgart: Deutsche Verlagsanstalt, 1981), p.597.
53 Krausnick & Wilhelm, *ibid.*, p.600. The background to these directives from such high-ranking commanders as Manstein *et al.*, could also be a lack of "understanding" among lower German commanders and their officers and troops for the physical extermination of the Soviet Jews.
54 Krausnick & Wilhelm, *ibid.*, p.599. Erich Hoepner was later executed for complicity in the 20 July 1944 plot against Hitler.
55 Omer Bartov, *Hitler's Army, Nazis and War in the Third Reich* (Oxford: Oxford University Press, 1992). See also Omer Bartov, *The Eastern Front 1941--5, German troops and the Barbarisation of Warfare* (London: MacMillan, 2001).
56 *Bericht über Frontreise vom 5.12.-8.12.1942 im Bereich der 4. Armee von Major i.G. Freiherr von Gersdorff*; cited in Krausnick & Wilhelm, *ibid.*, p.258.
57 Peter Bamm (*nome de plume* for Dr Curt Emmrich), *Die unsichtbare Flagge* (Stuttgart: 1952); cited in Krausnick & Wilhelm, *ibid.*, p.255.
58 The actual rank Fegelein held during those actions was *SS-Standartenführer*.
59 Krausnick & Wilhelm, *ibid.*, p.600. The *1. SS*-Cavalry Brigade noted from the same action its own casualties as being one dead and 15 wounded! On 20 April 1964, the former *SSS-turmbannführer* Franz Magill was convicted by the Braunschweig Court of Justice for taking part in these murders of the *1. SS*-Cavalry Brigade; Archives of the *Zentrale Stelle,* Ludwigsburg.
60 See my argument for the division's active part in these mass murders in Gyllenhaal & Westberg, *Swedes at War*, p.287, and the quotation of reports from the Swedish Military Attaché in Berlin to the Defence Staff in Stockholm, following interviews with Swedish *SS* volunteers from the "*Wiking*" division during the advance through Galicia in July-August 1941 and corresponding questionings by the Swedish Security Police, *Krigsarkivet* and *Riksarkivet*.
61 Bartov, *Hitler's Army*, p.182.
62 Gyllenhaal & Westberg, *Swedes at War*, p.316.
63 Sigurd Sørlie, *Solkors eller hakekors* (Oslo: Dreyer, 2015) and Terje Emberland & Matthew Kott, *Himmlers Norge* (Oslo: Aschehoug, 2012). The deliberate Nazification of the Norwegian Police is essential for understanding the *raison d'être* of *SS*-expansion in occupied Norway: in Himmler's eyes, the future Norwegian police was to be represented by police officials with *SS*-training and Front experience from the East, constituting a loyal instrument within the all- and pan-Germanic *Staatsschutzkorps*; Emberland & Kott, *Himmlers Norge*, p.493.
64 The Biblical *Moloch* was a Canaanite god, known for propitiatory child sacrifices by burning the children alive.
65 Gyllenhaal & Westberg, *Swedes at War*, p.315 f. The original interrogation is to be found in the archive of the Norwegian Resistance Museum (*Norges Hjemmefrontmuseum*) in Oslo; PWIS/(Norway)36.

Panzer grenadiers from the *Waffen-SS* observing a knocked-out IS-2 tank with its 122mm gun. During the last two years of the war, 1943–45, both the *Wehrmacht* and the *Waffen-SS* experienced how the Red Army distinctly improved their standards, weapons and tactics, mainly by learning from the Germans on the Eastern Front. For instance, the Swedish *SS-Untersturmführer* Gösta Borg experienced the decisive *panzer* battles at Radzymin, north-east of Warsaw, in August 1944: "The Soviet mass assault uses an enormous firepower and its qualification is a broad technical foundation. The techniques of the Red mass assaults were developed in 1944–1945. The fighting in 1941 was idyllic compared with the earthquakes of TNT and Panzer masses that during the fall of 1944 knocked the German Eastern Front to pieces." Borg, a dedicated National Socialist, graduated in 1943 as No. 1 from the Swedish War Academy, and in 1951 published (during the Korean War) a book on the Red Army: *The Red Mass Assault*.

66 BA-MA, RS 5/310 and letter to the author (LW) from Dr Franz Riedweg, Munich, 5 February 1985.

67 Gyllenhaal & Westberg, *Swedes at War*, p.257, as noted in the diary of Otto Bräutigam, Army liaison officer for Alfred Rosenberg at Hitler's HQ, entry of 16 July 1941.

68 Mauno Jokipii, *Panttipataljoona. Suomalaisen SS-pataljoonan historia*; Weilin+Göös, Helsinki, 1969.Unfortunately, Jokipii's dissertation has never been translated from Finnish. The Finnish Volunteer Battalion served until mid-1943 as a contingent within the *5. SS-Panzer-Grenadier-Division "Wiking"* in the Russian campaign, before it was dissolved and sent back to Finland.

69 Lars Westerlund, *Hörsamhet intill döden. Partipreferenser, socialdemokrater och språkpolitik bland de finländska SS-männen våren 1941*. LW is in great debt to Dr Westerlund for sending the first draft of his essay on certain issues connected with the Finnish *SS* volunteer battalion.

70 Lars Westerlund, *ibid*., p.5.

71 Westerlund, *ibid*., p.32. The reason being the over-representation of Swedish-speaking Finns in the German *Jägerbatallion 27* in the First World War, those Swedish-Finns receiving over-proportional influence in the free Finland's armed forces after 1918-19.

72 Jens Westemeier, *Jugend, Krieg und Internierung* (Universität Konstanz, 2015), p.58.

73 Thomas Casagrande, *"Unsere Gegner haben uns als Deutsche kennengelernt". Die 7. SS-Freiwilligen-Gebirgs-Division "Prinz Eugen" – eine volksdeutsche Kampfformation als nationalsozialistisches Herrschaftsinstrument*, in Schulte, Lieb & Wegner, *ibid*.

74 Paul Milata, *Motive rumäniendeutscher Freiwilliger zum Eintritt in die Waffen-SS*, in Lieb, Schulte & Wegner, *ibid*., p.228.

75 For recent research on the recruiting of Muslims to the *Waffen-SS*, see Franciska Zaugg, *Perfekte Kriger. Die deutsche Wahrnehmung muslimischer Albaner in der Waffen-SS zwischen 1943–1945*, and Stefan Petke, *Militärische Vergemeinschaftungsversuche muslimischer Soldaten in der Waffen-SS*, in Lieb, Schulte & Wegner, *ibid*.

76 Leleu, *ibid*., p.37.

77 Keith Bonn (ed.), *Slaughterhouse: The Encyclopaedia of the Eastern Front* (New York: Military Book Club, 2002), p.11.

78 On the reinforced ideological education in the latter phase of the war in 1943-44, due to e.g the recruitment of many Alsatians and young Germans born 1924-26, see Jörgen Förster, *Die weltanschauliche Erzieung in der Waffen-SS*, in Jürgen Matthäus (ed.), *Ausbildungsziel Judenmord?* (Frankfurt am Main: Fischer, 2003), pp.87-113.

79 Norman Davies, *Europe at War, 1939-1945. No simple victory* (London: MacMillan, 2006), p.259.

80 Charles W. Sydnor, *Soldiers of Destruction. The SS Death's Head Division, 1933-1945* (Princeton: University Press, 1977), p.39 ff.

81 Charles W. Sydnor, *ibid*., p.41.

82 Hördler, *ibid*., p.93. Hansen later advanced to corps artillery commander in the *III. "Germanic" SS-Panzer-Korps* during the fighting west of Narva in July-August 1944.

83 Most likely, a British Army unit committed war crimes at the same time as Le Paradis by murdering POWs from the *Waffen-SS*; see Angus Calder, *The Myth of the Blitz* (London: 1991), p.94.

84 Charles W. Sydnor, *ibid*., p.117.

85 Despite many detailed investigations, there is still a lack of modern, comprehensive research on the *Waffen-SS* and their role in "regular' war crimes; the latest attempt being Guido Knopp, *Die SS. Eine*

A knocked-out or abandoned German assault gun (*Sturmgeschütz*) in the Tiergarten after the final battle for Berlin in May 1945. In the background stands the Victory column, the *Siegessäule*, that commemorates the Prussian victory in the Danish-Prussian War of 1864. Inaugurated in 1873, the column is still a major tourist attraction in Berlin. The photographer has taken this photo looking directly to the east as we, in the distance, see the contoures of the Brandenburger Tor.

Warnung der Geschichte (Munich: Bertelsmann, 2002), p.284. On the anti-partisan actions of the *Waffen-SS* in Italy 1944,see Carlo Gentile,'*Politische Soldaten. Die 16. SS-Panzergrenadier-Division "Reichsführer-SS" in Italien 1944', Quellen und Forschungen aus italienischen Archiven und Biblioteheken 8* (2001), pp.529-61.

86 Max Hastings, *Das Reich. The March of the 2nd SS Panzer-Division through France 1944* (London: Pan Books, 2009). Another important issue, hitherto barely or vaguely researched, is the mass murder of French colonial soldiers by units from the *Waffen-SS* and the *Wehrmacht* during or shortly after the German campaign in the West in 1940.

87 Walter Görlitz wrote in 1960, in his short but reflecting study *Die Waffen-SS* (Berlin: Arani-Verlag, 1960): "The short history of these armed *Sonderverbände* of the *NSDAP* allows neither a collective judgement nor any general acquittal. Decisive remains in the end the attitude of the individual soldiers or officers and that of the specific units within the *Waffen-SS*."; Görlitz *ibid.*, p.31. Good examples of how a company commander by example and humanity apparently could leave his stamp on a unit and prevent an already merciless war from becoming unnecessary cruel are thosementioned in the memoirs of Herbert Maeger from his time as a young German-Belgian volunteer in the *Leibstandarte-SS "Adolf Hitler"* from 1941-44: Herbert Maeger, *Verlorene Ehre, verratene Treue*. Even with a sound scepticism against post-war memoirs, the reminiscences of Mager, who had grown up as an ethnic German in democratic Belgium, within a deeply religious Catholic family, urge confidence in his wartime recollections.

88 Colonel Marco Smedberg (Sweden), in *Pennan & Svärdet* (Stockholm: SMB), 4:2010.

89 Jörg Friedrich, *Die Kalte Amnestie. NS-Täter in der Bundesrepublik* (List, Frankfurt am Main: 2007), p.292.

90 E-mail to the authors (LW & MM) from Dr Jens Westemeier, 29 July 2016.

91 Matthew Kott & Terje Emberland, *Himmlers Norge. Nordmenn i det storgermanske prosjekt* (Oslo: Aschehoug, 2013), p.340.

82 Dieter Stenger, *SS-pansar i strid på öst- och västfronten. Historien om 10. SS-Panzer-Division 1943-1945* (Vaktel Forlag, Eskilstuna, 2017), p. 17 f.

1

FROM LEGIONS TO *SS-PANZERGRENADIER* REGIMENTS: HIMMLER'S PAN-GERMANIC VISIONS FOR THE *III. (GERM.) SS-PANZER-KORPS*

Lennart Westberg, Petter Kjellander and Geir Brenden

The Soviet Union was in many ways an ideologically cherished "dream opponent" for the *SS*. During the campaign in the East and the recruiting efforts of the *Waffen-SS* in Scandinavia and Western Europe, Himmler saw his most radical and extensive visions fulfilled. The *SS* had found its chief purpose and legitimacy acknowledged. The character of the *Waffen-SS* as an elite order was now associated with the medieval colonization of the Teutonic Order in the East as an historic continuity. The creation of the *III. ("Germanic") SS-Panzer-Korps* must be seen in this context. What makes this remarkable *SS* unit stand out in history is not its military performance – although the corps often achieved important defensive successes against the far more superior Red Army – but rather as a political crystallization point for decisive and long-term components of Himmler's pan-Germanic visions. Hence, the *III. (germ.) SS-Panzer-Korps* played an important role as Himmler's "experimental field" for building the personnel foundation for ruling the future "Germanic *Reich*" in Western Europe and in Nazi Teutonic colonies in the East.

In the philosophical world of Hitler and Himmler, the racial community was the fundamental basis for relations between people, not the traditional nation-state. The mobilization of the "Germanic" potential in Northern and Western Europe was in itself to create the necessary conditions for the exploitation of *Lebensraum* in the East.

In the summer of 1943, the Swedish volunteer and cadet at the *SS-Junkerschule* (Officers' School) Bad Tölz, Gösta Borg from Stockholm, wrote in the Swedish Nazi periodical *Den Svenske* (*The Swede*):

> In the *Waffen-SS* the unity of the front-line forges together young Teutonics into an unswerving loyalty, into future political combat soldiers. The Goths are still riding east. Thus the firestorm of the front-line creates an army of hardened men, who fight side by side in the struggle for the Teutonic people's right for life, in the struggle for that earth their ancestors bought with blood in the grey twilight of time.[1]

National Socialism's theory of the "historic mission of the Germanic race" and the *SS* plans for a "Greater Germanic Empire" made *SS-Reichsführer* Heinrich Himmler regard Northern and Western Europe as an essential recruiting potential for his *Waffen-SS*. That the *SS* favoured Scandinavia as a recruiting base depended on the especially dominant "Germanic" character there.[2] There was another reason for the recruitment of foreign volunteers to the *Waffen-SS*: the dynamic *SS* and the always visionary Himmler also wanted to create a politically powerful influence in the occupied European countries for their own future purposes.

The creation of the "Germanic" *Waffen-SS* was for Himmler not a purpose in itself, at least from a military point of view. Himmler's long-time strategic aim was, through selection and front-line duty in the ranks of the *Waffen-SS*, to create a political cadre of biologically chosen, ideologically motivated and politically indoctrinated functionaries to lead and administer the future Greater Germanic *Reich*, as well for the colonization of the Eastern territories and colonies. The selected *SS* officers were to form the cadre of future *Gauleiters* both in the West and East, while the NCOs and enlisted men were the potential *Wehrbauers*, future fighting and colonizing eastern peasants, in a true Viking spirit of the Germanic past. Himmler foresaw that the battles, even after a final German victory, would not stop at the boundaries of the Nazi colonial empire in the East but continue in partisan warfare etc. A permanent frontier battle against Asia would, in Himmler's eyes, keep the Germanic race pure and battle-worthy.

To build an empire, you need unswervingly loyal vassals. For Himmler it was unimportant if these functionaries were Norwegians, Swedes, Germans, Dutch, Finnish or Flemish. It was, however, essential that they had proved themselves worthy during active front-line duty in the *Waffen-SS* and had been influenced by their multinational comrades-in-arms. The *Waffen-SS* and its *Junker* schools were therefore not primarily military units, but an ideological nursery for a battle-hardened international cadre of the *SS*, which by nature must be restricted as an elite. Due to the *SS* terminology, this elite would also substitute a *Staatchutzkorps*, a mixture of political officers, administrators and colonizers, maintaining the Greater Germanic *Reich*.

After the opening of Operation "Barbarossa" in the summer of 1941, there was a parallel phenomenon alongside the recruitment of "Germanic" volunteers to the *SS-Division "Wiking"*: the formation by the *SS* of "national legions" of Dutch, Flemish, Norwegians and Danes for the Eastern Front. The *Wehrmacht* at the same time was permitted by Hitler to form national legions of Spanish, Croatian and French volunteers. The legions that were administered by the *SS* did not count as genuine *SS* formations. Their recruits did not fulfill the racial criteria for the *SS* and therefore did not wear the *SS*-runes on their uniforms. They symbolized merely their respective home country's symbolic support for the German "fateful struggle in the East". At the end of 1941, a total of 5,816 volunteers had been recruited to the legions under the supervision of the *SS*. Their number would, by the summer of 1943, rise to over 27,000.[3]

In a September 1942 letter to *SS-Obergruppenführer* Gottlob Berger, Chief of the *SS* Main Office (*SS-Hauptamt*), by the Chief of Staff of the *SS* Germanic Coordination Agency in Berlin (*Germanische Leitstelle*), *SS-Sturmbannführer* Dr Franz Riedweg, he described the legions as "double trails" and as the biggest problem with the Germanic ambitions of the *SS*. According to Dr Riedweg, the national Nazi leaders in the occupied countries (Mussert, Quisling, *et al.*) considered the legions as their own "Party Police", and even looked down on those fellow countrymen who had joined the *SS-Division "Wiking"* as "renegades".[4]

These legions had a limited military value on the Eastern Front and brought with them conflicts between the *SS* and the domestic collaborational Nazi leaders in the occupied Western and Northern European countries. Here we also find a clash between Himmler's pan-Germanic visions and Vidkun Quisling's pro-Nazi views, but also Quisling's national interests in Norway's future role in the "Greater Germanic *Reich*".[5] *SS-Obergruppenführer* Felix Steiner looked upon the legions as political rivals to his more "Germanic" *SS-Division "Wiking"*. The ambivalent status of the legions against the *SS* also contributed to, or even invited, conflicts of interest. In short, in March 1943, Hitler decided, upon Himmler's suggestion, to dissolve the legions and transfer them as *SS-Panzergrenadier* regiments in the proposed new *III. (germ.) SS-Panzer-Korps*. *SS-Obergruppenführer* Berger, Chief of the *SS-Hauptamt* and a close adviser to Himmler, wrote: "Only so, can the necessary unity between *Germanischer Schutzstaffel* in the various countries and the *Germanische Truppe* [i.e. the *Waffen-SS*] be guaranteed." With the creation of the *III. (germ.) SS-Panzer-Korps*, the pan-Germanic concept of the *SS* went into a new orientation, both politically and militarily.

Apart from political reasons, there were also tactical and military considerations for Felix Steiner to assemble the Germanic soldiers in an armoured, and therefore more effective and unified, *SS-Panzer-Korps*. One of the reasons for the fact that, by 1943, a third of the "classic" divisions of the *Waffen-SS* were buried in Russian soil, was the lack of their own *panzer* units. "Give us *Panzers*! Otherwise this wonderful troop will perish!" Steiner wrote to Himmler in the late autumn of 1942 from the Caucasus Front.

The original plan was that the new *III. (germ.) SS-Panzer-Korps* would consist of the old *5. SS-Panzergrenadier-Division "Wiking"* and a new German-Scandinavian division. Instead, the corps would eventually include the newly formed *11. SS-Freiwilligen-Panzergrenadier-Division "Nordland"* and the *4. SS-Freiwilligen-Panzer Grenadier Brigade "Nederland"* (from remnants of the Dutch Legion). Some 1,280 Danes from the *Freikorps Danmark* volunteered for further service in the *SS-Panzergrenadier-Regiment "Danmark"*, and 810 Norwegians did the same for the twin *Regiment "Norge"*. Scandinavian volunteers made up only ten percent of the "Nordland" division in the period from 1943 to 1944, with the remainder made up of German citizens (30 percent) and ethnic Germans (*Volksdeutsche*) from Rumania (60 percent). The III. (Germ.) SS-Panzer-Korps was, due to its structure and equipment, consequently neither a Panzer-Korps nor especially "Germanic".[6]

As news was spread about Himmler's plans to dissolve the legions and form a Germanic *SS-Panzer-Korps*, the leaders of various *NS*-parties in the occupied countries began to protest. The German press attaché at the *Reich* embassy in Copenhagen, Gustav Meissner, wrote in his memoirs about the reaction from the Danish *NS*-leader, Dr Fritz Clausen, in mid-1943:

> Recently, the *SS* focus on the creation of a Germanic Corps and has for this purpose already sent the Commander of the Danish Free Corps, *SS-Obersturmbannführer* Martinsen, to Denmark. The soldiers of this Germanic Corps will be sworn to loyalty directly to the *Reichsführer-SS* and will take orders from him. These plans have nourished the suspicion among Danish national socialists that the volunteers from the *DNSAP* [the Danish Nazi party] will not be of use for our own party but for other purposes. Dr Clausen looks upon this as a breach of the promise that the *SS* made in the spring of 1941.[7]

Ethnic Germans (*Volksdeutsche*) on 19 July 1943, minutes before they leave their home town of Hermannstadt in Rumania by train for service in the *Waffen-SS* and the *III. (Germ.) SS-Panzer-Korps*. In the middle stands Horst Borger with two friends. Himmler's ambitions to recruit all *Volksdeutsche* into the *Waffen-SS* – with subsequent Stalinist-communist deportations and oppressions after 1945 – completely destroyed the rich, up to 800-year-old ethnic-German culture in Rumania.

SS-Oberscharführer Walter Schwarck from Heidekrug (Memelland) with his men in Grafenwöhr troop training camp in Upper Palatine, Bavaria, during the summer of 1943. The Memelland was separated from Germany in 1919 under French control, annexed by Lithuania in 1923 and retaken by the Third *Reich* in 1939, thereby partly becoming the breeding-ground for aggressive German nationalism.

SS-Rottenführer Henrik Lundh wearing the second pattern cuff title (with German text *Frw. Legion Norwegen*) and the Sun Cross Patch, which indicates that he was a member of Quisling's *NS* party. Recent research (Sigurd Sørlie) shows that the majority of the Norwegian volunteers in the *Waffen-SS* from 1940–45 were not only anti-communist but at heart also pro-nationalsocialist. According to Sørlie, this fact, however, did not necessarily result in loyalty to German *SS* and national socialist ideals from the Norwegian volunteers. While a minority opted for a dissolution of the national states and the erection of a Germanic *SS Reich*, the majority dismissed such a political solution and supported Quisling's and the *NS*'s more nationalist ambition to "re-erect" Norway on the basis of *NS* ideology.

At the Leningrad Front in 1943 are, from the left, Legion *SS-Sturmbannführer* Artur Qvist (CO of the Norwegian Legion), SS-*Obersturmführer* Dieter Radbruch and Legion *SS-Obersturmführer* August Inger, the legion's medical officer. They are receiving the Iron Cross from the "herostratic famous SS-*Obergruppenführer* Friedrich Jeckeln" (Sørlie). The Norwegian Legion and other units were for a time attached to *Kampfgruppe Jeckeln*.

At the Leningrad Front in 1942, Legion SS-*Hauptscharführer* and platoon commander Björn Östring watches the result of German aerial and artillery attacks on Leningrad. Östring was born in 1917 in Gjövik. He became a member of the *NS* Youth organization in July 1933, and of the *NS* in 1935. In 1941–42, he fought as a volunteer NCO in the *Legion Norwegen* on the Leningrad Front and was, from 1942–45, a member of Vidkun Quisling's Life Guard (*Gjestene*). In 1945, Östring was sentenced to seven years in prison for treason, but was pardoned in 1949. After his retirement he was a key public figure for the Norwegian organization for former volunteers in the *Waffen-SS* (*Frontkjemper*), and died in 2012 in Hövik.

Legion SS-*Sturmbannführer*, Artur Qvist, on the Leningrad Front in 1942. Qvist, a former cavalry captain of the Norwegian Army, was appointed commander of the Norwegian Legion in December 1942, following the dismissal of Jörgen Bakke and the abolition of the Legion's Staff HQ in Oslo. Although initially widely unpopular among the rank and file, Qvist gradually won a reputation as a defender of 'Norwegian interests' *vis-á-vis* the Germans. Probably due to a surge in discharges among his men, Qvist fell into Himmler's disfavour in the winter of 1942-1943. When the Legion was dissolved and replaced by the *'Norge'* regiment in the spring of 1943, he returned to Norway to take up a position in the Quisling government's Ministry of Agriculture. (Sigurd Sørlie)

Three unknown Norwegian legionaries from *3./DNL* in the trenches before Leningrad in 1942. Weapons used are the MG 34, *Mauser* K98 with a mounted rifle grenade launcher and a 5cm *Granatwerfer* 36.

Protests from *NS*-circles in Denmark and from personnel within the *Freikorps Danmark* against the intended full incorporation into the *Waffen-SS* made the Danish envoy in Berlin, Carl Mohr, visit the Danish volunteer contingent in Grafenwöhr on 28–29 July 1943. There exist various statements on what Mohr actually expressed to his fellow Danes in Grafenwöhr, but the general impression was that he did not oppose their integration into the *SS-Panzergrenadier-Regiment 24 "Danmark"*.[8]

Himmler's political vision to chain together and unite the various "Germanic" units in the *Waffen-SS* into the *III. (germ.) SS-Panzer-Korps* was also only partly fulfilled in 1943: as before, the *SS-Panzer-Division "Wiking"*, with its essential share of West and North European volunteers, formed a second crystallization point outside the corps; the Flemish Legion (transformed into the *SS-Sturmbrigade "Langemarck"*) and the Norwegian *SS-Skijägerbatallion* in the *6. SS-Gebirgs-Division "Nord"* in Finland were also not integrated into Steiner's "Germanic" *Panzer-Korps*. As the corps was deployed for training and anti-partisan warfare in Croatia in the autumn of 1943 – and some Norwegians complained that they had volunteered to defend Europe on the Eastern Front and not to combat "bandits" in the Balkans – 100 Norwegians were permitted to voluntarily transfer from it to the Norwegian *SS-Skijägerbatallion* in Finland, indicating that former members of the Norwegian Legion and fresh recruits chose to fight "for Norway in Finland".[9] Swiss volunteers in the *Waffen-SS* were considered, due to the snowy and mountainous geography of Switzerland, to be especially qualified as mountain troops, *Jäger* or reconnaissance soldiers. Therefore, nearly 300 Swiss *SS* volunteers served in the *6. SS-Gebirgsdivision "Nord"* in northern Finland (Karelia) during the German-Finnish campaign against the USSR from 1941–44. In the staff of the *III. (germ.) SS-Panzer-Korps*, within the various units of the *11. SS-Freiwilligen-Panzergrenadier-Division "Nordland"* and the *4. SS-Freiwilligen-Panzergrenadier-Brigade "Nederland"*, served a total of 30–35 Swiss volunteers in 1944–45.[10] On 1 June 1944, Himmler ordered the creation of a separate Swiss unit within the *Waffen-SS*, but this proposal was never realized.

In 1943, when the Finnish *SS*-volunteer battalion within the ranks of the *SS-Division "Wiking"* were, for political reasons, called back to Finland by Marshal Mannerheim and dissolved, Himmler even speculated on forming a new Finnish *SS*-battalion, enlarging it to a regiment called "Kalevala" and integrating it into the Germanic *SS-Panzer-Korps*, but the reality brought an end to his plans.

In 1943, Himmler carried through an important classification of all *Waffen-SS* units and graded them for their future political and ideological usefulness: the "Germanic" volunteers in the *5. SS-Panzer-Division "Wiking"* counted as fully worthy *SS*-men, while the volunteers in the *III. (germ.) SS-Panzer-Korps* (heirs as they were to the national legions whose volunteers counted as second-class Germanics) were only under certain conditions looked upon as *SS*-worthy. Himmler probably planned the formation of a future pan-Germanic army that was to substitute or at least be a parallel to the *Wehrmacht*. On the other hand, the *SS* wanted to keep a more elite nucleus of first-class units in the *Waffen-SS* that would form a management cadre for recruitment and rotation within the future greater-Germanic *Reich* administration.

Behind the propagandistic façade for the *SS* to show a "Germanic *Panzer-Korps*" in the East and behind the high-flown regimental names of "*Norge*" and "*Danmark*", a trivial fact was hidden: the *III. (germ.) SS-Panzer-Korps*, by personnel and equipment, was neither especially Germanic nor a *Panzer-Korps*. Ninety percent of its personnel consisted of *Volksdeutsche* recruits from Rumania, its officer and NCO corps consisted of over 70 percent German citizens, and its equipment of *panzers* and *Sturmgeschütze* (assault guns) was negligible.

Despite these defaults, the *III. (germ.) SS-Panzer-Korps* achieved a remarkably successful military performance against a superior opponent, the Red Army, above all in the Baltic theatre of war in 1944, but also during the fighting in Pomerania and Brandenburg in 1945. The *III. (germ.) SS-Panzer-Korps* inflicted severe losses on the Red Army during all engagements of the corps units. A strong ideological motivation probably contributed to its remarkable *corps dé esprit*. As a consequence, the losses of the *III. (germ.) SS-Panzer-Korps* in manpower and equipment were extremely high. When the *11. SS-Freiwilligen-Panzergrenadier-Division "Nordland"* reached the River Oder-line in March 1945, its total losses in men from 1 September 1943 to 1 March 1945 were officially summarized: "*Nordland*" had during this period lost – in terms of dead, wounded and missing – 14,489 soldiers, NCOs and officers. In reality, it meant that the division was totally annihilated.

In the end, the significance of the "Germanic" *SS-Panzer-Korps* was not as a military, but as a political phenomenon; an important ideological crystallization point of a new programmatic pan-Germanic vision of Heinrich Himmler and the *SS*. During the time of the creation of the *III. (germ.) SS-Panzer-Korps*, Himmler and his entourage intensively speculated in establishing a future pan-Germanic Army, into which all Germans in the occupied territories could be conscripted. No doubt the *III. (germ.) SS-Panzer-Korps* was to be the nucleus of this future "*Germanic Wehrmacht*".

The Norwegian *Waffen-SS* volunteers and the *III. SS-Panzer-Korps*

Sigurd Sørlie

Associate Professor, Norwegian Institute for Defence Studies
Author of *Solkors eller hakekors. Nordmenn i* Waffen-SS *1941–1945* (Transl., *Sun wheel or swastika. Norwegians in the Waffen-SS 1941–1945*)

Convinced that the Norwegians belonged to the most valuable racial elements of the Nordic race, Heinrich Himmler had high hopes for the incorporation of this particular national group in the *Waffen-SS*. Yet despite Himmler's expectations, it soon became apparent that the recruitment and integration of Norwegians in the *Waffen-SS* would be highly challenging. Part of the rationale behind the *III. (germ.) SS-Panzer-Korps* was to reinvigorate recruitment efforts and amend integration problems among this group of non-German volunteers.

When the initial recruitment campaign was launched in Norway in January 1941, the *SS* had secured the active support of Vidkun Quisling and his collaborating party, the *Nasjonal Samling*. Quisling remained committed to the task of providing Nazi Germany with military manpower throughout the war. By supporting the German war effort with personnel, Quisling and his followers sought to convince Hitler of their loyalty and spirit of self-sacrifice, thereby hoping to be rewarded with political power in an independent and strong Norway when the war was over.[11]

Most of the approximately 650–800 Norwegians who chose to join the "*Nordland*" regiment in the winter and spring of 1941 seem to have been highly motivated at the time of admission. However, soon after their arrival in the training camps of the *Waffen-SS*, the first signs of discontent came to the fore. The decision to spread the Norwegians in the various units of the "*Wiking*" division rather than keeping them together in the "*Nordland*" regiment caused widespread disappointment. Many also reacted negatively to what they saw as disrespectful treatment by German officers and NCOs. In early 1942, after the "*Wiking*" division had been deployed to the front for several months, discontent once again flared up among the Norwegians. The immediate cause was signals that everyone had to serve for the duration of the war, despite the fact that many had time-limited contracts. This was considered a blatant breach of the agreed terms by the Norwegians, and seems to have brought about more or less universal resentment.[12] Himmler reluctantly decided to discharge those who insisted on leaving, and in the subsequent period a growing number of Norwegians left the *Waffen-SS*.[13]

In the meantime, the *SS* had decided to set up a new type of volunteer formation: the "Germanic" legions. The immediate background was the German invasion of the Soviet Union, which triggered a wave of enthusiasm among collaborationists in Nazi-occupied Europe. Quisling was among the first collaborationist leaders to offer Hitler a Norwegian contribution to the Barbarossa campaign. Himmler, in turn, ensured that this and other legions formed in the occupied "Germanic" countries were placed under *SS* control. Within days, the formation of a Norwegian Legion had been publicly announced in Norway, and the *Nasjonal Samling* now played the leading role. Quisling and his adherents envisioned a truly national unit that would take part in the "crusade in the East" and simultaneously form the nucleus of a new Norwegian Army. Potential recruits were told that the new unit would be trained in Norway, deployed under Norwegian leadership and guidelines, and equipped with Norwegian uniforms, symbols and insignia. In an attempt to utilize the widespread sympathy with the Finnish people during the Winter War against the Soviets, the propaganda also stressed that the legion would fight alongside the Finns on the Finnish Front. Shortly after their induction in the Norwegian Legion, the volunteers committed themselves to serve for a period of at least six months.[14]

However, step by step, all the original conditions were ignored or set aside. The unit was transferred to Germany, where it was equipped with German uniforms and insignia, trained according to German regulations and *de facto* incorporated into the *Waffen-SS*. In October, the legionnaires had to swear an oath of allegiance to Hitler, and in December they were forced to accept that the time-limited contracts were annulled. When the unit was finally deployed to the front, it was not sent to Finland as envisaged, but attached to the Eighteenth Army and used to fill in the gaps in the genocidal blockade of Leningrad. Consequently, the legionnaires were disillusioned even before they set foot in the trenches, and in the subsequent period soaring casualties and harsh front conditions exacerbated the problems.[15] In November 1942, Quisling called for the unification of all Norwegian volunteers in a more genuinely national unit.[16]

Himmler and the *SS* were increasingly dissatisfied with the *Nasjonal Samling*, the Norwegian Legion and the "Germanic" legions in general. Persistent grievances, mounting discharges and the inability to mobilize new

Christmas greetings to , *inter alia*, the Norwegian Legion.

Heinrich Himmler and Jonas Lie (recently promoted to SS-*Sturmbannführer*) in Mitau on 16 March 1943, at the dissolution of the Norwegian Legion. In 1940, Lie had been reinstated by Himmler as Chief of the Norwegian Police in occupied Norway, and was later Police Minister and commander of *Germanske SS Norge*. Lie was close to Himmler and the *SS*, and was designated by Himmler to "establish a politicized, militarized and ideologically reliable Norwegian Police apparatus that in the long term would be part of the Greater Germanic Reich's *Staatschutzkorps* (Sørlie). Lie belonged to a famous literary family in Norway and became renowned in pre-war Norway as an author of excellent crime novels.

The *Reich* Leader of the *SS*, Heinrich Himmler, gives a speech on 16 March 1943 in Mitau (Latvia) to the Norwegian volunteers, as the Norwegian Legion is disbanded. Himmler at the same time encouraged the legionnaires to join the new *SS-Panzergrenadier Division "Nordland".* In the end, most of the legionnaires chose to quit the *Waffen-SS*.

Norwegian *NS* propaganda posters for service in the Norwegian Legion or the *Waffen-SS*. "The threat from the Soviet Union constituted a common theme in the propaganda for volunteer war service. Other means were Norwegian symbols and uniforms, the Finnish flag and references to the heroes of the ancient sagas. The racist and antisemitic character of the National Socialist image of the enemy was also explicit in part of the propaganda." (Sørlie)

recruits threatened to undermine the "Germanic" project as a whole. According to the *SS*, the problems primarily emanated from the harmful influence of the collaborationist parties, above all their efforts to control the legions. It was against this background that the idea of dissolving the legions and transferring the personnel to a new "Germanic" corps evolved within the *SS* leadership in the course of 1942. With Hitler's formal approbation of the *III. (germ.) SS-Panzer-Korps* in March 1943, Himmler and his associates were confident that the problems would be solved.[17]

However, this proved to be far from the case with regards to the Norwegians. In Norway, Quisling was unable to mobilize a significant number of new recruits for the "*Norge*" regiment, and even though Himmler himself travelled to Jelgava (Mitau) in Latvia in March 1943 to persuade the legionnaires to join the new formation, the majority chose to leave the *Waffen-SS*. Similarly, it proved difficult to convince Norwegians in the regular *Waffen-SS* units to extend their time of service. Among those who did end up in the "*Norge*" regiment or other parts of the *III. (germ.) SS-Panzer-Korps*, discontent was rife from the beginning. Despite previous experiences, the *SS* left the impression that the regiment was going to be a "Norwegian unit". When the Norwegians realized that the unit was supplied with a large number of other nationalities, it caused massive unrest; in the course of the summer and autumn of 1943, hundreds of Norwegians asked to be discharged or transferred to the new *SS-Skijäger-Bataillon "Norwegen"*. By late 1943, probably less than 600 Norwegians served with the "*Norge*" regiment. Even among those remaining, the dissatisfaction continued in 1944 and 1945, leading to significant numbers being transferred to other units.[18]

To what extent did the recurring integration problems reflect a lack of commitment to the ideas and goals of the *SS*? There is little doubt that the bulk of the Norwegian volunteers were committed to some form of National Socialist ideology.[19] However, they saw their service in the *Waffen-SS* primarily as a means to promote Quisling's vision for an independent Norway within some sort of "Greater Germanic" confederation. Since they assumed that the national contribution would have a stronger impact if they were kept together in "national" units, this remained of utmost importance to the group.[20] The majority also preferred to commit themselves only for a limited period of time. When these and other conditions were ignored time and again, the Norwegians increasingly lost confidence in the *SS* and the Germans, manifested in growing resentment, discharges and transfers to what were perceived as more "national" units.

Sigurd Sørlie

The creation of the *III. (Germ.)* SS-Panzer-Korps

On the tenth anniversary of Hitler's assumption of power, 30 January 1943, Himmler sent a telegram from his field command post to the *SS-Hauptamt* and *SS-Führungshauptamt*, asking on Hitler's behalf for the numbers of volunteers serving in the Legions "*Nederland*", "*Norge*" (Norway), "*Flandern*" (Flanders), "*Estland*" (Estonia) and "*Freikorps Danmark*" (Denmark). All the legions were at the time engaged in battles on the Eastern Front. Besides the legions, a number of volunteers from Northern and Western Europe were also present in the *SS-Division "Wiking"*, along with Finnish and Swedish volunteers. Himmler also wanted to know how many volunteers were present in the various replacement units of the *Waffen-SS* and the legions, as well as the number of volunteers in the training camp at Sennheim.[21]

Despite the serious situation in Stalingrad in 1942–43, Himmler succeeded in obtaining Hitler's permission to form a new Germanic division consisting of volunteers. Himmler's intention with the formation of the *III. (germ.) SS-Panzer-Korps* was at least two-fold: he wanted to unite the Germanic volunteers under one *panzer-korps* instead of the national legions which were named after the countries of the respective volunteers; and the national legions in many ways were a little too nationalistic and patriotic, identifying themselves first and foremost as Norwegians, Danes and Dutch rather than being a part of the greater Germanic *Reich*. This caused Himmler trouble, both with individual volunteers but also with the occupied countries' national Nazi leaders causing political difficulties for himself and the *SS*. By dissolving the legions and creating brand new regiments, brigades and divisions directly on Himmler's orders, the *SS* tightened its grip on the volunteers and political issues from the occupied countries were sidestepped. Officers who held a strong patriotic profile, caring firstly for their fellow countrymen, were in several cases dismissed and replaced with far more convinced national-socialist soldiers who saw their future in a Nazi Germany and as a part of the Greater German *Reich*.

Himmler's plans to create an *SS-korps* began in 1942. In May 1942, Hitler sanctioned to Himmler the creation of a *SS-Generalkommando*, which was established on 9 July that year. Among the key figures who strongly agitated for this were *SS-Obergruppenführer* Paul Hausser and *SS-Gruppenführer* Felix Steiner. Even if the recapture of Kharkov in early 1943 appears to be the starting point for the creation of an *SS-Panzer-Korps*, this process had begun a year prior to Kharkov.[22] The previous restrictions regarding recruits were lifted and Himmler could finally expand the *Waffen-SS* in a way that he never had the possibility to do previously.[23]

By order of Adolf Hitler, as supreme commander of the *Wehrmacht*, the formation of the *III. (Germ.) SS Panzer-Korps* was activated on 30 March 1943. On 19 April 1943, the *SS-Führungshauptamt* ordered the formation of the *panzer-korps*, its general staff and various units to be located mainly at the Grafenwöhr troop training area in Upper

Franconia. Originally, the *SS-Panzergrenadier-Division "Wiking"* was planned to form the corps, together with a new German-Scandinavian *SS*-division. Already in February 1943, Heinrich Himmler had proposed the name "*Waräger*" for this new division, referring to the Swedish-Viking Varangian Guard which saw service in ancient Russia and in Byzantium.[24] Hitler, however, did not approve of the name, and renamed the division "*Nordland*" in March 1943.

Originally, the new *SS-Division "Waräger"* was planned to consist of three regiments: "*Danmark*", "*Norge*" and "*Nederland*". Each regiment would be based on the respective national legions from these countries, which since the summer of 1941 had been serving on the Eastern Front.[25] Due to protests from influential collaborating Dutch political forces in the Netherlands (Mussert), plans to integrate Dutch *SS* personnel from the Dutch *SS*-Legion into the "Scandinavian" Division "*Nordland*" were abandoned. Instead, the remaining Dutch *SS* soldiers were formed into a separate brigade: the *SS-Freiwilligen-Panzergrenadier-Brigade "Nederland"*, which was formed in Thuringia under its commander, *SS-Brigadeführer* Jürgen Wagner. The Dutch brigade consisted mainly of two regiments: the *SS-Panzergrenadier-Regiment 48 "General Seyffard"* (*SS-Sturmbannführer* Hans Collani) and the *SS-Panzergrenadier-Regiment 49 "de Ruyter"* (*SS-Obersturmbannführer* Fitzhum).

At the same time, the *Oberkommando des Heeres* decided that, for tactical reasons, the *SS-Division "Wiking"* could not be withdrawn from the Eastern Front, and the "*Wiking*" and "*Totenkopf*" divisions were later combined to form the new *IV. SS-Panzer-Korps*. The *III. (germ.) SS-Panzer-Korps* was therefore to consist of the *SS-Division "Nordland"* and the *SS-Brigade "Nederland"*, the new commander of the "*Nordland*" being *SS-Brigadeführer* Fritz von Scholz. Two infantry regiments were to be the backbone of the division: the *SS-Panzergrenadier-Regiment 23 "Norge"* (*SS-Obersturmbannführer* Wolfgang Jörchel) and the *SS-Panzergrenadier-Regiment 24 "Danmark"* (*SS-Obersturmbannführer* Hermenegild Graf von Westphalen zu Fürstenberg).

These combat units were principally made up of veterans from the Legion "*Norwegen*" and the *Freikorps "Danmark"*, and their ranks filled up with ethnic Germans from Rumania. Like was the case with the Dutch *SS*-legion, the Danish volunteers of the *Freikorps "Danmark"* and collaborating Danish political forces (Clausen) protested against their formally national unit being "kidnapped", dissolved and integrated into a *SS-panzergrenadier* regiment with a German commander. The *SS-Führungshauptamt* alarmed the Danish ambassador in Berlin, Mohr, who on 28 July 1943 visited the Grafenwöhr training camp and tried to settle the controversy. During this visit, Mohr encouraged the Danish volunteers from the *Freikorps "Danmark"* to "fight on" against Bolshevism in the new *SS-panzer-korps*. On 15 September 1943, there were 20 officers, 50 NCOs and 464 men from Norway in the "*Nordland*" Division, along with 33 officers, 162 NCOs and 1,191 men from Denmark.

Himmler had great hopes for further Swedish *SS* volunteers to the new *III. (Germ.) SS-Panzer-Korps*, but his affection for the Swedes "as the most important Germanic reservoir among all the Nordic countries" remained largely unanswered.[26] Already at the outbreak of the German-Soviet war in June 1941, Hitler himself was deeply disappointed about the meagre numbers of Swedes volunteering for the *Waffen-SS* in the Eastern campaign.[27] During the formation of the *III. (germ.) SS-Panzer-Korps*, Himmler ordered the centralization of all surviving Swedes in the *Waffen-SS* into the ranks of the new corps. This order was not always followed, and in December 1943, the corps HQ reported that only one officer, five NCOs and 31 men from Sweden served in the *SS-Division "Nordland"*. Additionally, 18 *SS* volunteers from the old ethnic Swedish folk group in Estonia, the Estonian-Swedes, served in the same unit of the "*Nordland*" as their fellow-countrymen.[28]

SS-Gruppenführer Felix Steiner, previously long-time commander of the *SS-Division "Wiking"* on the Eastern Front, was appointed corps commander of the *III. (germ.) SS-Panzer-Korps*, and on 1 July 1943 was promoted to *SS-Obergruppenführer*. Both the corps staff and the staff of the "*Nordland*" and the "*Nederland*" were strengthened with competent Army general staff officers as the *Waffen-SS* had no War Academy of their own. As Felix Steiner's Chief of Staff, the Army Personnel Department and *SS-Personalhauptamt* assigned Colonel Joachim Ziegler, with Major Jürgen von Bock (who in the summer of 1944 became operations officer of the Brigade "*Nederland*") as his operations officer, both transferring from the Army to the *Waffen-SS*. Operations officer in the Division "*Nordland*" was Major Helmut von Bockelberg (who succeeded Ziegler in August 1944 as corps Chief of Staff when the latter became divisional commander of "*Nordland*" after von Scholz was killed in action).

During the late summer of 1943, the organization of the corps units was completed at Grafenwöhr under the supervision of Joachim Ziegler. The various units belonging to the Division "*Nordland*" and the Brigade "*Nederland*" were formed and equipped under some difficulties. In the fourth year of the war, and after severe losses - such as the disaster of the Sixth Army at Stalingrad and the loss of the *Panzer-Armee "Afrika"* in Tunis - recruit depots and arms industries were under strain to provide the *Wehrmacht* with manpower reserves and weapons. As a result of an agreement between the German and Rumanian governments, Rumanian citizens of German ethnicity, the so-called *Volksdeutsche,* volunteered or were conscripted into the *Waffen-SS*, especially to the *III. (germ.) SS-Panzer-Korps*. While German and Scandinavian personnel remained in the minority, the Rumanian *Volksdeutsche* represented the majority in the various units of this "Germanic" *panzer-korps*: in its infantry, artillery, reconnaissance, engineering, anti-aircraft, signals, supply, administrative or medical units.

Norwegian volunteers being punished for minor offences by carrying their mattress on their back around the barracks in Grafenwöhr troop training camp, in the summer of 1943. While discipline was hard at Grafenwöhr, many Norwegians complained about the low standards of its military education. Lack of time seems also to have contributed to a faulty education. In December 1943, however, Steiner praised the good spirits among the recruits, but the division commander of "*Nordland*", von Scholz, stated in January 1944 that an additional 18 weeks of training were necessary to bring the division up to an acceptable standard.

Range training at Grafenwöhr, which was important for giving the correct coordinates for the artillery, etc. Far right on his knee is Siegfrid Lüngen, CO of *8. Kompanie, SS-Panzergrenadier-Regiment "Norge"*, who would later be decorated with the Knight's Cross.

A good view of parts of the vast training camp of Grafenwöhr in Franconia. The area served as a training ground for the Royal Bavarian Army from 1806-1919. After the First World War, the German High Command used Grafenwöhr for training the 100,000-man army allowed by the Treaty of Versailles. During the Third *Reich*, the area was expanded to its present size of 230 square kilometres. During the Cold War (1945–91), Grafenwöhr was an important combined arms training site for US and allied forces. Today, still operated by the US Army, the area houses the largest multinational military training area in Europe.

The Norwegian volunteer Oddvar Moss at Grafenwöhr in 1943, with his MG 34, which in the field would be replaced with the highly efficient MG 42. Oddvar fought in *10./ Norge*, was severely injured at Narva and lost an eye. He returned home to Norway and survived the war.

An unexpected encounter by Norwegian *SS* volunteers at Grafenwöhr with Hermann Göring, who had a hunting cabin in the neighbourhood and did not mind being photographed. On the left side of Göring stands the Norwegian volunteer Oddvar Halbostad, and the snapshot was taken by Knut Baardseth from Stange, Norway. Oddvar later transferred to the *Skijäger Bat Norge* in Karelia and survived the war.

SS-Obergruppenführer Felix Steiner (in white coat) visiting Grafenwöhr and the nucleus of his *SS-Panzer-Korps*, in the spring of 1943. To his left is the Norwegian minister Aksel Heiberg Stang, in black *NS* uniform. On the far right is Wolfgang Joerchel, CO of the *SS-Pz.Grenadier-Regiment 23 "Norge"*. "As Minister of Labour and Sports in Vidkun Quisling's collaborationist government, Stang was responsible for the Norwegian Labour Service and *Nasjonal Samling*'s youth organization, NSUF, both of which were considered key institutions by the SS. Stang served with the *SS-Kampfgruppe 'Nord'* at the Murmansk Front for a short period in 1941, and later got involved in the recruitment of Norwegians to the *Waffen-SS*. However, the evidence suggests that he never turned into a committed proponent of the *SS*, but rather sought to further the fascist agenda of Quisling's party." (Sørlie)

The *SS-Ausbildungslager Sennheim* (*SS*-Education Camp Sennheim) was established in 1941 in a former hospital in the former French town of Cernay in Elsass (today Department Haut-Rhin, Alsace). Incoming volunteers for the *Waffen-SS* were here given ideological and physical training before they were sent to more advanced military training camps of the *Waffen-SS*. The photo shows an obstacle course for Scandinavian and Dutch volunteers in 1942 at Sennheim, with the main building in the background.

SS-Untersturmführer Johan Peter Balstad from Koppang in Norway was only 19 years old when he took command of the *6. Kompanie* of the *SS-Regiment "Norge"* in May 1944. He was already a member of the *NS* Youth Organization when he volunteered for the *SS-Regiment "Nordland"* in July 1941, at the outbreak of "Barbarossa". By personally destroying three Soviet tanks in Estonia and Courland in 1944–45, Balstad earned the *Panzervernichtungsabzeichen*, which he bears on his right arm. Being severely wounded in October 1944 in Latvia, Balstad was transferred to the *Germanische Leitstelle* (Germanic Coordination Agency) in Oslo, took part in the final battles for the Third Reich in Germany in 1945 and escaped by hired boat with false papers, reaching Narvik in northern Norway in August 1945. Balstad was sentenced to two-and-a-half years in prison by a Norwegian court in 1946, educated himself to engineer, but took his own life in 1985 after being incapacitated from time to time at various mental institutions, probably due to his traumatic wartime experiences.

Hamburg, 5 August 1941: Danish volunteers for the Danish Legion swear the oath to Hitler at the premises of the *SS*-barracks at Hamburg-Langenhorn, after a speech by the Commander of the legion, Christian Peter Kryssing, a former lieutenant colonel in the Danish Army. Also present at the ceremony were the Danish vice-consul, Count Knuth, as representative for the Danish government, and higher dignitaries from the German Army, Navy, *NSDAP* and the *SS*, including the Chief of the *SS-Führungshauptamt*, *SS-Gruppenführer* Hans Jüttner. After the oath ceremony, Hans Jüttner made a speech in which he declared that the Danish Legion was about to participate in a struggle between "the Germanic race and the sub-humans and the Jews". The *SS*-barracks in Hamburg-Langenhorn were built in 1938 and housed a battalion of the *SS-Regiment "Germania"*, and later in the war the *SS-Panzergrenadier-Ausbildungs-Batallion 18*. Since 1945, and until today, the *SS*-barracks in Langenhorn have functioned as medical clinics.

Knud Börge Martinsen (photographed as SS-*Sturmbannführer* at Lake Ilmen in the summer of 1942) served from 1928–40 as a soldier in the Danish defence forces, and had in 1940 advanced to General Staff officer, rated first in his class. Martinsen had early on showed Nazi sympathies, partly affected by his time as international control officer during the Spanish Civil War. After the German attack on Denmark in 1940, he joined the Danish Nazi party *DNSAP* and also the *Waffen-SS*, becoming a company commander in the *Freikorps Danmark* in September 1941. In June 1942, Martinsen took charge of the *Freikorps* in the Demjansk pocket until the unit's dissolution in early 1943. He was a corrupt alcoholic who misbehaved gravely. Martinsen focused more on Nazi ideology than anti-Bolshevism, and in 1943 founded the so-called *Schalburg-Korps*, the domestic Danish Germanic *SS*, which also fought the Danish Resistance Movement for the rest of the war. Convicted of murder in this capacity, Martinsen was tried and executed in 1949 in Copenhagen.

Part of the vehicle park used by the *Freikorps Danmark* in 1941. The Danish legal collaborationist government sponsored the *Freikorps* with 60 trucks, 60 cars and 70 motorcycles. (Courtesy of Lars Larsen)

Two Danes from the *Freikorps* on the North-Eastern Front in 1942 at Demjansk. Sitting to the right is Leon Langebeck (with the sub-machine gun MP-40), who later served in the 1st battalion of the *SS-Panzergrenadier-Regiment 24 "Danmark"* in the Germanic Corps. Langebeck went missing in action in 1945 during the fighting in Hungary with the *I./"Danmark"* as part of the *SS-Panzer Division "Wiking"*. (Courtesy of Lars Larsen)

In the Demjansk pocket on 4 August 1942, preparations are made to transport the *Freikorps Danmark* back to Germany by train. To the left stands the CO of the *1. Kompanie, SS-Hauptsturmführer* Per Sörensen, who before 1940 served as a Danish regular officer. He is wearing the army eagle on his sleeve instead of the *SS* eagle. Sörensen was shot dead by a Soviet sniper on 24 April in 1945 in Berlin, as CO of the *SS-Panzergrendier-Regiment "Danmark".* (Courtesy of Lars Larsen)

A row of JU52s at an airfield at Heiligenberg are ready to take the *Freikorps Danmark* to the Demjansk pocket on 7–8 May 1942, where 90,000 German soldiers were encircled by Soviet troops. In Demjansk, the *Freikorps* was subordinated to the *SS-Division "Totenkopf"*. The CO of *Freikorps Danmark*, the Dänish Christian Frederik Schalburg, had previously served with Felix Steiner in the *SS-Division "Wiking"* and was a true believer of pan-Germanic ideas in the *SS*. Schalburg was killed in action in June 1942 in Demjansk and was posthumously promoted to *SS-Obersturmbannführer* by Himmler. (Courtesy of Lars Larsen)

A photo taken inside a JU52, with Danish *SS* soldiers and their equipment en route for the Demjansk pocket. (Courtesy of Lars Larsen)

SS-Obergruppenführer Felix Steiner greeting Danish volunteers of the *SS-Panzergrenadier-Regiment "Danmark"* in July 1943 in Grafenwöhr-Kulmbach. During his posting in Kulmbach, he took quarters at the medieval castle of Plassenburg, overlooking the town. In Steiner's view, the opportunity to gather all Germanic volunteers in a *SS-Panzer-Korps* was an event of historic proportions. In a guidance to all officers from the corps, dated 25 May 1943, Steiner wrote: "The essence of this war lies in the gathering of the Germanic elements of *Ordnung* against the Eastern storm of the culture-destroying Bolshevistic-Asiatic flood." Steiner was already thought visionary about the end of the war: "The young *SS*-leaders, that we have won over from the Nordic countries will some time solve important issues in the Nordic Raum."

SS-Obergruppenführer Felix Steiner (in white coat) greets soldiers from the *SS-Feld-Ersatz-Bataillon (FEB) "Nordland"* in Grafenwöhr. In the middle stands *SS-Sturmbannführer* Lang, CO of the FEB.

The Danish ambassador in Berlin, Carl Otto Mohr (in dark suit), with SS-*Obersturmbannführer* Count Hermenegild von Westphalen in Grafenwöhr troop training camp on 28 July 1943. The purpose of this visit was to convince the majority of the Danish in the dissolved *Freikorps Danmark* to continue their service within the *Waffen-SS* in the new *SS-Panzergrenadier-Regiment "Danmark"*. In a speech before the assembled Danes, ambassador Mohr praised their previous efforts in the East against Stalin's forces and reassured them of the Danish government's continued support. This resulted in the majority of the Danes from the legion volunteering for the new Germanic *panzer* corps. The *SS*-officer standing to the left behind Mohr is *SS-Obersturmbannfuhrer* Helmut von Bockelberg, Chief Operational Officer (I a) of the *11. SS-Freiwilligen-Panzergrenadier-Division* "Nordland".

SS-Obergruppenführer Felix Steiner greets Danish volunteers in Grafenwöhr-Kulmbach, July 1943.

SS-Obegruppenführer Felix Steiner greets Danish volunteers in Auerbach, in the summer of 1943. To the right stands SS-*Obersturmbannführer* Count Hermenegild von Westphalen, Commanding Officer of the *SS-Panzergrenadier-Regiment 24 "Danmark"*.

Inspection by *SS-Obergruppenführer* Steiner of part of the *SS-Panzer-Grenadier Regiment 24 "Danmark"* in Petrinja, Croatia, in August 1943. In accordance with Himmler's intentions, Steiner put the soldierly virtues in concordance with National Socialistic understanding: "The soldiers must be convicted of the fact that our struggle against Bolshevism and materialism's destructive mental activity serves our own race and origin." (Courtesy of Uwe Kuppen)

SS-Obersturmführer Georg Erichsen, an ethnic German with Danish citizenship from Schleswig, as SS-*Untersturmführer* and Adjutant to the CO of the *SS-Panzer-Aufklärungsabteilung 11*, SS-*Sturmbannführer* Rudolf Saalbach. Erichsen was appointed chief of the *4. Kompanie* of this battalion in December 1944, and was killed in action on 23 January 1945 in Courland. He was posthumously awarded the Honor Roll Clasp of the German Army. He was a representative for the large German minority in southern Denmark (Schleswig) (*ca.* 30,000 in 1940), and 1,500 ethnic Germans in Denmark served as volunteers in the *Waffen-SS* between 1940 and 1945.

SS-Oberführer Jürgen Wagner (third from left), the future CO of the *SS-Freiwilligen-Panzergrenadier-Brigade "Nederland"* from 1943–45, here still with the *Division "Wiking"* in the East after having decorated Walter Iden (second from right) with the German Cross in Gold. Wagner, born in 1901 as a general's son in Strasbourg, Alsace, did not participate in the First World War, studied to be an engineer, lost his job due to the Depression in 1929–30 and joined the *NSDAP* in 1931. Joining the *SS* in 1931 at the age of 30, he became SS-*Sturmbannführer* and battalion commander in the forerunner to the *Leibstandarte "Adolf Hitler"* in Berlin.

Gerardus Mooyman was raised in a Catholic middle-class family, with National Socialistic sympathies, in Apeldoorn. He joined the *Frewilligen-Legion "Nederland"*, destroyed 13 Soviet tanks in February 1943 at Lake Ladoga and was decorated at 19 years old. As the very first European volunteer in the *Waffen-SS*, he was decorated with the Knight's Cross. Mooyman trained to be an officer at the *Junkerschule* and served from the spring of 1944 as commandant of a *Sturmgeschütz* in the *4. SS-Panzergrenadier-Brigade "Nederland"* until 4 May 1945, when he was taken as a POW by the US Army. After the war, Mooyman lived quietly in Gröningen as a businessman and family man. In 1967, he gave a sole interview in the newspaper *Revue*, where he condemned the crimes of the Third *Reich* and described his option for the *Waffen-SS* in the Second World War as a mistake. Mooyman gave away his Knight's Cross to a collector.

Dutch propaganda poster urging Dutchmen to enlist in the *Waffen-SS*. The *SS* was, of course, positive to the idea of recruiting Dutch *SS* volunteers. However, like the Norwegian Legion, the Dutch leaders felt that the *Legion "Niederlande"* was more or less hijacked into the *Waffen-SS*. This caused tensions between the Dutch politicans, who often served their own fascist ideals, and the German administration. (Courtesy of Charles Trang)

The sleeve band for *"Freiwilligen-Legion Niederlande"* with Latin text. During 1943, the sources for recruitment to the *Waffen-SS* from the Netherlands had stagnated: the German policy of occupation had hardened, and in May a general strike against the Germans broke out in the country. Plans to start a separate *SS*-division of Dutch recruits had to be abandoned. Instead, a weak *SS-Panzergrenadier-Brigade "Nederland"* was formed, with the help of substantial numbers of ethnic Germans from Rumania. These human resources were, however, also insufficiant, and the brigade's size was cut down to only two battalions per regiment, and four companies per battalion.

Sitting to the left is Jürgen Wagner, here probably still as *SS-Oberführer* and Commander of the *SS-Panzergrenadier-Regiment "Germania"* in the summer of 1943. Wagner was promoted in 1943 to command the *4. SS-Freiwilligen-Panzergrenadier-Brigade "Nederland"*, in which capacity he continued until May 1945. In 1947, Wagner was extradited to Yugoslavia, where he was put on trial before a military tribunal, probably facing charges over mass executions of civilians in Yugoslavia in 1941, when Wagner served in the *SS-Division "Das Reich"*. Condemned to death, Wagner was executed by firing squad on 27 June 1947.

The Dutch *NS*-leader Anton Mussert, in black coat and cap, greets the first Dutch volunteers. Next to Mussert is *SS-Obergruppenführer* Hanns-Albin Rauter, Higher *SS* and Police Leader *"Nordwest"*, who had his seat in Den Haag. Behind them, on the left, are *SS-Brigadeführer* Kurt Knoblauch and *SS-Oberführer* Otto Reich. By the 1920s, Mussert was already active in far-right organizations, like the *Dietsche Bond*, which advocated a Greater Netherlands including Flanders (Dutch-speaking Belgium). In 1931, Mussert was one of the founders of the *Nationaal-Socialistische Beweging* (*NSB*). (Courtesy of Charles Trang)

Hanns-Albin Rauter receives his death sentence in the court in Den Haag on 4 May 1948. He was responsible for sending over 100,000 Jews to the extermination camps, and reported to Himmler in March 1944 that the Netherlands was *Judenfrei* (free of Jews). The Netherlands had the highest death-rate of all countries occupied by the Third *Reich* in the Second World War: 2.36 percent. Rauter was hanged on 25 March 1949. (Courtesy of Charles Trang)

Third from the left is *SS-Hauptsturmführer* Heinrich Heckmüller from the "*Nordland*" reconnaissance batallion, together with other officers and NCOs, delivering a speech to his men from the *2. Kompanie* at Grafenwöhr in June 1943. Due to flaws in his leadership during the battles for Ingria in January 1944, and after being wounded, Heckmüller never returned to his battalion again. "It was agreed among the battalion CO, adjutant and the platoon leaders that his return was not wanted" (Langendorf).

Ceremony for the oath-taking by the *SS-Pioneer Bataillon "Nordland"* and *SS-Pioneer Bataillon 54 "Nederland"*. This unit was only partly trained in Grafenwöhr (Westlager-Auerbach), being mainly in Dresden and Beneschau-Hradischko in Bohemia, and spent a longer time in training than the other units. It thus did not take part in, for example, the anti-partisan actions in Croatia. The commander of the battalion, *SS-Sturmbannführer* Fritz Bunse, is shown giving a speech to the men. In front of Bunse stands the Norwegian *SS-Hauptsturmführer* Egil Hoel, and to the left (with the German Cross in Gold) is *SS-Hauptsturmführer* Günther Wanhöfer. Bunse ended the war as *SS-Korpspionierführer* in the *IV. SS-Freiwilligen-Gebirgs-Korps* and died in 1970. Hoel's wife was Jewish and he was forced back to Norway from the *III. (Germ.) SS-Panzer-Korps*. Hoel ended the war as *SS-Obersturmbannführer* and CO of *SS-Polizei-Skijäger-Bataillon 506*, and in 1945 was sentenced by a Norwegian court to 12 years in prison. He passed away in 1971. In 1944, Wanhöfer took command of the *SS-Pioneer Bataillon "Nederland"*, and was decorated with the Knight's Cross in autumn 1944. After the war, Wanhöfer published his memoirs and died in 2015 in Bavaria.

The Swedish *SS-Untersturmführer*, Gösta Borg, in 1944 as a *SS* war correspondent in the *Standarte "Kurt Eggers"*. Borg was top of his class at the Royal War Academy of Karlberg in Stockholm in April 1943 and joined the *Waffen-SS* in the summer of 1941 and 1943. He graduated from the *Junkerschule* in Bad Tölz in April 1944. Borg had been an old-time Nazi in Sweden since the early Thirties and remained faithful to this ideology after the Second World War. As a war correspondent in 1944, Borg covered the fighting at the Narva Front, at Ihantaala in Finland, Dünaburg in Latvia, Modlin north of Warsaw and East Prussia. In 1945, he covered the battles for the Ardennes. He returned to Sweden in the summer of 1945, via Oslo, and became a businessman in Stockholm, but also lectured at officers' courses about his war experiences in the *Waffen-SS*. In 1951 (during the Korean War), Borg wrote a brilliant military book about the tactics of the Red Army: *The Red Mass Assault*. Gösta Borg died in Stockholm in 2000.

From 1942–43, *SS-Sturmbannführer* Fritz Klingenberg was an instructor and teaching group commander at the *SS-Junkerschule* Bad Tölz. During his time at Bad Tölz, the first course for Germanic officers in the *Waffen-SS* was founded on 8 June 1942, of which Klingenberg was in charge. Some 154 cadets were examined from this course. During his service at Bad Tölz, Klingenberg also visited the Fortress Kongsvinger in Norway, the HQ for *Germanske SS Norge*, in company with the Chief of the *SS* Personnel Main Office, *SS-Gruppenführer* Maximilian von Herff. On 24 August 1942, *SS-Sturmbannführer* Dr Franz Riedweg, Chief of Staff for the *Germanische Leitstelle* in Berlin, wrote a letter to Himmler, praising Klingenberg for his dedicated work at Bad Tölz by "establishing a Germanic-Political officers' corps" in the *Waffen-SS*. Klingenberg was killed in action on 23 March 1945, fighting against the US Army near Herzheim in Rhineland-Palatinate as commander of the *17. SS-Panzergrenadier-Division "Götz von Berlichingen"*.

The commander of the *SS-Standarte "Kurt Eggers"*, the propaganda regiment of the *Waffen-SS*, *SS-Sturmbannführer* Gunter d'Alquen. The activities of the war correspondents in the *Waffen-SS* were firm components of the Nazi regime and the *SS* ideology, being highly praised by those such as Joseph Goebbels. The great variety and impact of the *"Kurt Eggers"* productions in photographs, words and sound did not only forcefully catapult the supposed elite character of the *Waffen-SS* units at the front within the hemisphere of German-occupied Europe (and its neutral countries), but also the image of the *Waffen-SS* within the Third *Reich* itself. Towards the end of the war, d'Alquen and the *SS* consequently also absorbed the war propaganda machine of the *Wehrmacht*.

This *Schützenpanzerwagen* (*SPW*), probably a forward artillery observing vehicle, from the *5. SS-Panzer-Division "Wiking"* advances through a cornfield outside Warzaw-Modlin in August 1944.

Part of the vast complex that constituted the troop training camp Grafenwöhr in Upper Franconia for the units to be formed into the *III. (Germ.) SS-Panzer-Korps*. It was here that political implications and other internal problems came to the surface and complicated the amalgamation of the Germanic *SS-Panzer-Corps*. The practically dried-out recruiting sources for *SS*-volunteers from Scandinavia and the Netherlands, in combination with the fact that the *SS-Division "Wiking"* had to remain on the Eastern Front and not join the *Panzer-Korps*, made it necessary for the *SS* to reinforce the corps with 13,000 ethnic Germans from Rumania. This led to protests from Scandinavian *SS*-contingents, who feared for the "true Nordic" character of the corps.

Notes

1 Gösta Borg (1915-2000) served as NCO with the Royal Lifeguard Regiment in Stockholm and was active in various Swedish Nazi parties throughout the Thirties. From July to October 1941, Borg served as a volunteer in the *SS-Division "Wiking"* in the Russian campaign. In April 1943, he came top in the examination at the Swedish officers' school Karlberg in Stockholm. As Borg refused to dissociate himself from further Nazi activities, he left the regiment and served another period with the *Waffen-SS*, graduating from the *Junkerschule* Bad Tölz as *SS* war correspondent on various battle fronts until May 1945; Gyllenhaal & Westberg, *Swedes at War*, p.269.

2 In a speech at the *SS Junkerschule* Bad Tölz in the autumn of 1943, *SS-Obersturmbannführer* Dr Franz Riedweg, the Chief of Staff of the *Germanische Leitstelle* (the central *SS* recruiting bureau in Berlin), stated that Sweden "was the most important Germanic human reservoir that there is"; undated manuscript in RS 5/310, *Bundesarchiv-Militärarchiv (*hereafter BA-MA); RS 5/310, and Dr Franz Riedweg, Munich, in letter to author (LW), 5 February 1985.

3 Wegner, *Hitlers Politische Soldaten*, p.103.

4 Riedweg to Berger, 2.9.1942, NARA, SSO Riedweg.

5 Emberland & Kott, *Himmlers Norge*, p.431. For the discussions between Himmler and Vidkun Quisling (the leader of the Norwegian collaborationist party *Nasjonal Samling*) to form a Norwegian *SS*-Volunteer Mountain Brigade for the Finnish Front against the USSR and the transfer of Swiss *SS* volunteers from the Norwegian *SS-Skijäger-Batallion* to the new *"Nordland"* division, see Rolf Michaelis, *Die 11. SS-Freiwilligen-Panzergrenadier-Division "Nordland"* (Berlin: Michaelis Verlag, 2001), p.19.

6 In December 1943, shortly before the Germanic *SS-Panzer-Korps* was transported from Croatia to Ingria, its total strength consisted of 19,000 soldiers, i.e. the normal strength of a division, with a weak tank battalion. The officers and NCO personnel consisted of 75 percent of Germans from the *Reich*; BA-MA: RS 2-3/2.

7 Gustav Meissner, *Dänemark unterm Hakenkreuz* (*Denmark under the Swastica*) (Frankfurt: 1990). Meissner (1910-95) was a German journalist, fluent in Danish as he was born in Sönderjylland, and served as a press attaché at the German Embassy in Copenhagen from 1939-43.

8 For an analysis of Mohr's visit to Grafenwöhr, see Bundgård Christensen, Poulsen & Smith, *Under hagekors og Dannebrog*, p.374. A memo of 1 July 1943 from the Danish War Ministry encouraged volunteer service in the German or Finnish armed forces, including the *Waffen-SS*, and secured pensions, etc., for such service. Although the Danish government resigned on 29 August 1943, until the end of the war the Danish Foreign Office supported propaganda posters in public places for Danish volunteering to the *Waffen-SS*; *ibid.* p.376.

9 Emberland & Kott, *Himmles Norge*, p.441. It was also decided and approved by Steiner in Croatia, that Norwegians in the *Waffen-SS* who were brought up in coastal areas would have the opportunity

ties up with previously reported evidence of a close connection between the Corps and 162 Div; the Div. is definitely under 1 S.S. Pz. Army. (Cf. also para. 18, below).

(b) On 27/10, an administrative report went from the Corps to Pz. Army 2.

Again, one is forced to conjecture that the Corps is for the moment operating under 1 S.S. Army, but is still administered by Pz. Army 2.

16. Corps H.Q. was still in AGRAM on 23/10.

17. (a) On 20/10 it reported on 15 Assault Guns L/48, including 4 undergoing short-term repairs.

(b) 38 Italian tanks (38) were sent to the Corps on 23/10.

(c) On 24/10, it mentioned that it had been allotted 80 Italian tanks. It was not clear from the context whether this number included the 38 mentioned above.

18. On 24/10, the Corps reported its Ration Strength on 20/10.

This comprised:

S.S. Div. NORDLAND	9,129
162 Turken Div.	21,755 (apparently with another unit).
S.S. Div. NEDERLAND	4,222
Corps troops, with Pol. Regt. 14.	7,780

This raises three points (a) The appellation "Div. NEDERLAND". This is in accord with previous information; but hitherto the unit under III S.S. Corps in the BALKANS has only been called a Brigade. (b) The relatively small strength of NORDLAND and NEDERLAND, suggesting that much of those units have yet to arrive. (c) The large number of Corps troops, coupled with the fact that no return is made for the elements of Div. Wiking known to be operating with III S.S. Corps confirms the supposition that these elements are acting as Corps troops.

19. Two new units are operating under the Corps: S.S. Pz. Regt. 11, which may just possibly be part of NEDERLAND, and part at least of S.S. Assault Gun Abt. 5; this latter is part of S.S. Div. Wiking.

20. On 27/10, the Corps mentioned forthcoming operations on a comprehensive scale by tanks and "many motorised Battle Groups". This last explains to a certain extent the way in which the Corps' Divisions, etc. are at the moment split up into smaller units

V S.S. Mtn. Corps

1. The H.Q. of the Corps was in MOSTAR on 28/10.

2. Its operational areas are apparently to include CROATIA, MONTENEGRO and the South ADRIATIC coast.

A unique document on the *III. (Germ.) SS-Panzer-Korps* from the National Archives in London: The far-reaching British decryption project "Ultra" (deciphering the German "Enigma" code machine) has decrypted documents relating to the Germanic *SS-Panzer-Korps* in Croatia in October 1943. The *SS-Division "Nordland"* had at that time 9,129 men in its ranks, and the *SS-Brigade "Nederland"* 4,222 soldiers.

to volunteer from the *panzer* corps to the German *Kriegsmarine*, a possibility that some Norwegians in "*Nordland*" made use of.

10 Vincenz Oertle, *"Sollte ich aus Russland nicht zurückkehren ... " Schweizer Freiwillige an deutscher Seite 1939-1945* (*Swiss volunteers in German uniform 1939-1945*) (Zürich: 1997), p.237.

11 For a brief overview of the motives and policies of Quisling and the *Nasjonal Samling*, see S. Sørlie, "Norway", in D. Stahel (ed.), *Joining Hitler's Crusade: European Nations and the Invasion of the Soviet Union, 1941* (Cambridge: Cambridge University Press, 2017), pp.321-23.

12 Report from *SS-Schütze* Per Imerslund, not dated [December/January 1941/1942], Bundesarchiv Berlin (BAB), NS 19/3519/88-89.

13 S. Sørlie, *Solkors eller hakekors. Nordmenn i Waffen-SS* (Oslo: Dreyers forlag, 2015), pp.380-83.

14 Sørlie, "Norway", pp.326-30, 334-35.

15 *Ibid.*, pp.335-39.

16 Quisling to Himmler, 17 November 1942, BAB, NS 19/3451/13.

17 Bernd Wegner, "*Auf dem Wege zur pangermanischen Armee. Dokumente zur Entstehungsgeschichte des III. ('germanischen') SS-Panzerkorps*", *Militärgeschichtliche Mitteilungen* 2 (1980).

18 Sørlie, *Solkors*, pp.400-10.

19 *Ibid.*, Ch.6.

20 See e.g. Berger to Himmler, 5 July 1944, BAB NS19/1000/30-31.

21 NARA, T-175/59/574755.

22 George Nipe Jr, *Last victory in Russia. The SS-Panzer-Korps and Manstein's Kharkov Counteroffensive February-March 1943* (Pennsylvania:Schiffer Publishing, 2000), p.34 f. Robert L. Koehl, *The Structure and Power Struggles of the Nazi SS* (Madison, Wisconsin: University of Wisconsin Press, 1983), p.209.

23 René Rohrkamp, *"Weltanschaulich gefestigte Kämpfer" – Die Soldaten der Waffen-SS 1933-1945* (Ferdinand Schöning, 2010).

24 The name "*Waräger*" also referred and was associated in Himmler's world to the ancient "Germanic-Viking" *Lebensraum* in the East. "*Waräger*" would also, due to a memo by Himmler in early 1943, serve as a collective name for Danish, Flemish, Dutch, Norwegian, Swedish and Swiss volunteers. Interestingly, Himmler also mentioned at this time that the *III. (Germ.) SS-Panzer-Korps* would in the future have the capacity to receive and train thousands of Germanic recruits, when conscription had been enforced within the future "Germanic *Reich*"; Emberland & Kott, *Himmlers Norge*, p.430.

25 The "*Norge*" would be a light regiment, or *Voraus-Regiment*, which reflected Himmler's opinion of the Norwegians as especially suited as *Jäger* or *Skijäger*; Emberland & Kott, *Himmlers Norge*, p.430.

26 In a speech at the *Waffen-SS* officers' school at Bad Tölz in the autumn of 1943, *SS-Obersturmbannführer* Dr Franz Riedweg, chief-of-staff of the *Germanische Leitstelle* (the central *SS* recruiting and coordinating bureau for "Germanic" issues, etc.), stated that Sweden "was the most important Germanic human reservoir there was"; undated manuscript in RS 5/310, Bundesarchiv-Militärarchiv; cited in Gyllenhaal & Westberg, *Swedes at War*, pp.315, 364.

27 Gyllenhaal & Westberg, *Swedes at War*, p.315. A maximum of 180 Swedes volunteered for the *Waffen-SS* from 1940-45, and only around 100 men arrived at the front with weapons in hand. In various formations of the *Waffen-SS*, a total of 28 Swedes were killed in action, according to the registration of the Swedish Security Police.

28 These Swedish and Estonian-Swedes formed a platoon within the *3. Company* of the *SS-Panzer-Aufklärungsabteilung 11 "Nordland"* (an armoured reconnaissance battalion) from Croatia until the final battle in Berlin in 1945. Nicknamed "the Swedish platoon", it consisted generally of 30-40 volunteers of Swedish origin, sustaining heavy losses during the battles in Latvia in the summer of 1944 and above all during the campaigns against the Red Army in Courland, Pomerania and Brandenburg-Berlin in 1944-45; Gyllenhaal & Westberg, *Swedes at War*, p.257.

2

TRAINING AND ANTI-PARTISAN ACTIONS IN CROATIA (SEPTEMBER 1943–DECEMBER 1943)

THE STRATEGIC SITUATION FOR GERMANY IN 1943

Despite the setback at the approaches to Moscow during the winter of 1941–42, the Germans fought back with a large summer offensive in the East in 1942, pressing on almost as far as to the oilfields of the Caucasus. During the autumn and winter of 1942–43, the Battle of the Atlantic developed into a severe crisis for the Allies. In March 1943 alone, the Germans managed to sink 108 merchant ships and had more than than 100 U-boats simultaneously operating at sea.

During 1943, however, the German fortunes of war took a turn for the worst in the East, West and South as the Red Army struck back with massive waves of tanks and infantry. First, the Sixth Army was annihilated at Stalingrad in January 1943, with German losses of up to a quarter of a million men. The Red Army had by then successfully adopted German *panzer* and artillery tactics, the Soviets holding out in the ruins of Stalingrad and in the meantime preparing counter-attacks in the open terrain on the southern German flank. *Fremde Heere Ost*, the German military intelligence, had once again delivered faulty intelligence and underestimated the Red Army, above all ignoring the threat against the southern flank.[1] Thereafter, Hitler was forced to order retreat from the Caucasus. The conquests which the *Wehrmacht* had made in the East during the summer offensive of 1942 were hastily lost.

Albert Speer, the successor of Fritz Todt as Minister of Armament and War Productions in February 1942, revolutionized the previous inefficiency and lack of central coordination for the armament of the fighting services. Speer centralized planning, priorities and production on the *Wehrmacht*'s behalf and its three arms. Above all, Speer introduced armament industrial responsibility, far from the chaos and inefficiency of the Four Year plan under Göring. On 1 March 1943, the *panzer* pioneer General Heinz Guderian was reinstated by Hitler, on advice from the chief of the personnel department of the German Army, Rudolf Schmundt, and became Inspector General of Armoured Troops in order to reorganize and revitalize the German *Panzerwaffe* – at that time, the German *panzer* divisions on average had only 32 tanks at their disposal – supplying it with a new doctrine and working closely with Speer. Guderian's influence and authority, however, was undermined not only by Hitler, but above all by the artillery branch of the *Oberkommando des Herees* (*OKH*).[2]

Field Marshal Erich von Manstein's brilliant counter-attack, recapture of Kharkov and his following exploits in crushing the Soviet Sixth Army and its Third Tank Army in February-March 1943, is looked upon by military historians as a masterpiece in manoeuvre warfare. Soviet losses in this sector were 46,000 dead and 14,000 prisoners, with 600 tanks and 1,200 pieces of artillery destroyed.[3]

In May 1943, *Panzer-Armee "Afrika"*, the German forces in Tunisia, surrendered, very soon followed by the Anglo-American invasion of Sicily on 10 July 1943. The Western Allies now stood at the southern footsteps of Europe.The catastrophies at Stalingrad and Tunis reduced the German Army and the *Luftwaffe* considerably. Continued rivalry and lack of coordination between the *Oberkommando der Wehrmacht* and the *Oberkommando des Heeres*, combined with the reinforced deterioration of Hitler's judgement and intuition, did not improve the German situation.[4]

Although in 1939 the *Luftwaffe* was considered the world's best air force, there were in its structure severe faults: of these, the *Luftwaffe*'s high command was perhaps the greatest, combined with an under-dimensioned educational organization, a weak transport air force and an exaggerated focus on dive bombers, which handicapped the development of new bomber types. As late as 1936, the Germans had established a central air force staff, but as the *Luftwaffe* lacked air force officers with general staff education, many had to be transferred from the Army. One of Göring's most serious mistakes was in February 1940, interrupting all plans for new planes that could not be finished within one year. This decision seriously disrupted new and important projects, most seriously concerning jet planes, where the Germans were far ahead. Already early in the war, instructors and technical personnel from air training schools had been transferred to the front to compensate for losses in battle. Not even after the Battle of Britain was the production of planes and the training of new pilots increased. Compared to the campaign in the West in 1940, where 2,890 German planes were at their disposal, the far larger attack on the Soviet Union in the summer of 1941 saw only 2,775 planes in action.[5]

The U-boat war, the Battle of the Atlantic, being Gemany's fifth front, was definitively lost by the Germans in the autumn of 1943, primarily due to the reinforced air protection for Allied convoys and the successful British decoding of the German Navy's encrypted radio traffic to and from the U-boats ("Ultra"). German ignorance that their codes were not unbreakable, combined with the pioneering genius of the British mathematician Alan Turing and the dedicated work at Bletchley Park (GCHQ), was decisive for the Allied war effort and no doubt considerably shortened the war.[6]

The German heartland, as of the end of 1943, lay under continuous British and American bomb attacks since the American Air Force had established bases in both England and Italy. When the new American Mustang fighter was introduced as a fighter escort in the winter of 1943–44, the heavy losses which the *Luftwaffe* had been inflicting on American daylight bombers ceased. Hamburg was almost completely destroyed by massive bombing attacks in July 1943. Beginning in the spring of 1944, prior to the planned invasion of Normandy; the Allies redirected their bombing strategy towards Germany's oil refineries and synthetic oil factories.

After the great *panzer* battles at Kursk in July 1943, the German summer initiative on the Eastern Front was lost forever to the Red Army. The Soviet losses at Kursk were as high as 177,000 men (including 40,000 dead), with 1,600–1,900 tanks and self-propelled artillery guns destroyed, while German losses were recorded at 56,000 men (including 9,400 dead) and 280 armoured combat-vehicles. However, Hitler's losses, in contrast to those of the Soviets, could only be partially replaced, and the scale weighing personnel and materiel now definitively began to tip in favour of the Soviets. After the repulse of Operation "*Zitadelle*" around Kursk, the course of the war fundamentally changed for the Germans: apart from the Allied misjudging of Hitler's offensive in the Ardennes in December 1944, a constant retreat now ensued.

At the end of August 1943, after completing basic training, orders came from Berlin to the *Generalkommando* of the *III. (germ.) SS-Panzer-Korps* that its units were to be transferred to Croatia for further training and securing the area against partisan forces in the former Yugoslavia. The *OKH* had initially proposed that the corps be deployed for training on the Atlantic coast, which Felix Steiner opposed as the corps' western and northern European recruits had volunteered for the Eastern Front. The Germans anticipated in 1943 that the post-Mussolini government under Pietro Badoglio would defect from the Axis pact, and on 2 August 1943, Hitler ordered reinforcements from Germany to the Balkans. These German preventive measures were parallel to the planning of Operation "Alaric", the later occupation of northern Italy and the installment of the fascist Saló Republic. At the end of the month, the corps staff and almost all units of the *Division "Nordland"* had been redeployed into Croatia, while the *Brigade "Nederland"* would follow somewhat later from its training depot in Thuringia. In Croatia, the corps was subordinated to *Armeegruppe von Weichs* and attached to the *2. Panzer-Armee-Oberkommando* (Dr Lothar Rendulic).[7] The *OKH* and Steiner's corps staff deliberately looked upon the anti-partisan war as an opportunity to educate the fresh troops and recruits in the corps for the coming conditions and fighting on the Eastern Front, including the education of these new units in the ideological *SS* approach of looking upon the partisans as "sub-humans" from the inferior Slavic race.[8]

On 8 September, Steiner's corps staff received news of the Italian capitulation and was assigned the task of disarming the Italian units in Croatia. The *Division "Nordland"* was mainly billeted in the Sisak-Glina area, while *SS-Panzer-Abteilung 11* was located at Samobor. The *Brigade "Nederland"* was in the area north of Agram.

Three groups controlled Croatia: the German troops, the pro-German Ustascha native police with its security troops, and the communist partisans. Very soon the partisan war began, with ambushes against various parts of the *III. (germ.) SS-Panzer-Korps*. Throughout the autumn of 1943, many troops from the corps were engaged in anti-partisan warfare in Croatia. In late November, the partisans annihilated a whole company of the *Regiment "Danmark"* in Hrastovica. Serious war crimes were committed by both sides in these operations: racial indoctrination and the general brutalization of war becoming a murderous combination for some, although not all, units of the *Waffen-SS*. The communist partisans' torture and killing of captured *Wehrmacht* and *SS* soldiers also contributed to a threatening escalation of brutality in Croatia.

During an interrogation on 13 November 1943 by the Swedish Security Police, the former *Unterscharführer* Karl Martin Agrahn stated: "Agrahn's section of '*Nordland*' was based at Sisak. Combat with the partisans had thereafter continued until the beginning of the month of August. Combat took place daily between the division and the partisans."[9] During the *"Nordland" Division*'s presence in Croatia, two major anti-partisan actions were carried through by the *Wehrmacht* under the codename "Armin" and "Wildsau" (neither with units from the Germanic Corps participating, probably due to inadequate motorization of these *SS* units). On 16 October 1943, during "Wildsau", the death of 207 partisans was reported (German losses were one dead and two wounded).[10] There are numerous accounts of anti-partisan activities by all-Danish units from the *SS-Panzergrenadier-Regiment "Danmark"*, supported by wartime letters from and post-war interviews with Danish former *SS*-men on the situation in Croatia in the autumn of 1943:

> Most likely the Ustasha had hanged alleged partisans on every telegraph pole from Sisak to Perinja. I cannot remember which town was in the south. But then we drove through an espalier of hanged Tito-partisans.[11]

The Danes, together with other members of the *III. (germ.) SS-Panzer-Korps*, also took part in the brutal practice of burning down villages and shooting alleged partisans among the civilians. The CO of the *1. Kompanie* in the *Regiment "Danmark"*, Per Sörensen, wrote home that on a Sunday he had killed "200 Reds, without having one wounded of my own". Interviews with Danish former soldiers in the *Regiment "Danmark"* confirmed that suspected partisans who were found not in regular uniform but in civilian clothes, were shot.[12] Recent research in Norway also confirms the participation of Norwegians from the *SS-Panzergrenadier-Regiment "Norge"* in such actions, although available sources states that the *Regiment "Danmark"*, for various reasons, participated in far more anti-partisan actions than the Norwegians in Croatia during this time.[13]

As always, and especially during signs of brutalization in, for example, the complex anti-partisan warfare, the character, authority and morals of the commanding officers in the *Waffen-SS*, right down to platoon level, were probably decisive for their respective military unit's approach towards alleged partisans and the civilian population. Especially during the anti-partisan actions in Croatia, Steiner and the corps staff reacted against desertions to the communist partisans from the *"Nordland"* recruits, among them five Swedes from the *SS-Panzer-Aufklärungsabteilung 11*.[14] A Norwegian volunteer who in the autumn of 1943 was transferred from the *Regiment "Norge"* in Croatia to the SS-Skijägerbatallion in Finland, expressed his opinion that "the war in the Balkans was not the type of warfare I had volunteered for".[15] LW

Karl Balint, former *SS-Unterscharführer* in the *SS recce batallion 11* (Lennart Westberg's archives)

In my home region, Schässburg in Rumania, I had already received a basic education in becoming a vehicle mechanic. During my training I worked with various autos and trucks of certain models. The German Sixth Army was deployed in 1941 in and around Schässburg and we made repairs on their vehicles during this time. I took this knowledge with me to Grafenwöhr, Croatia and the Baltic countries. After being put into the 5th company of the *SS*-reconnaissance battalion 11, and successfully completing a military driver's licence course in Spielfeld in Steiermark, I was then sent directly to Croatia. In Sisak, the mechanics got their first vehicles, among them the amphibious VW *Schwimmwagen*. I was the youngest one when I joined the mechanical and repair platoon in the battalion, a portion of my comrades old enough to be my father. The supply of reserve parts was inadequate and we had to improvise, a practice that continued until the war's end. One day, *SS-Obersturmführer* Georg Langendorf from the 5th company came to our repair platoon with his mortar-launcher. He suggested that the steel base-plate of the launcher should be mounted on the half-track, thereby removing the machine-guns from the *SPW*. It was no problem to mount the 8cm mortars with bolts but the more powerful 12cm mortars would destroy the bolts after two or three rounds of fire, so we let that specific idea go. Later, the 28cm rocket launchers, the *"Stuka zu Fuss"*, had to be mounted on the heavy half-tracks of the 5th company, three to each side. Günter Kloos, our electrician in the platoon, fashioned an ignition device from the rockets in the driver's location in the half-track. Each pair of rockets were pre-installed to fire at three different distances. The first rocket launchers used wooden frames on the half-track but this solution was quickly abandoned and angle irons were used which gave more stability when firing the rockets and during transport.

Notes

1 The German intelligence information on the USSR prior to Hitler's attack on the Soviet Union in 1941 had already been notoriously unreliable. Germany had, due to the Rapallo Pact of 1922, better relations with the Soviet Union than other countries, but Stalin's Russia was practically closed to German intelligence (the German section leader in *Fremde Heeres Ost*, Lieutenant Colonel Eberhardt Kinzel, did not even speak Russian). "Dominated by the thoughtless theory that the campaign against the UdSSR would last only ten weeks and with only fuel reserves of the Reich for three months, the planning of the campaign was a product of teutonic arrogance and stupidity"; Kenneth Macksey, *Why the Germans lose at War – The Myth of German Military Superiority* (London: Greenhill Books, 1996), p.139. One can also recall the comment by Carl von Clausewitz (1780-1831): "A great part of the information one gets in war is contradictory, an even larger part is default and the absolute majority of the information is of dubious character."

2 Above all, one of the eternal points of controversy was organizational responsibility for German assault gun units (*Sturmgeschütze*) between the *panzer* and artillery arms of the *OKH*.

3 Manstein's reputation has in later years been diminished by his obvious involvement in the Holocaust, and by his post-1945 cover-up of his responsibility for giving Hitler the advice not to permit the encircled Sixth Army to break out from Stalingrad in time.

4 In terms of the education of capable military staff personnel and commanders, the Germans in September 1939 made the same mistake as in August 1914, by closing down the *Kriegsakademie* in Berlin. It was reopened in 1942 with courses for operative personnel on divisional and corps level.

5 Smedberg, *Militär ledning. Från Napoleonkrigen till fredsbevarande insatser*, p.104. Both the Inspector General of the *Luftwaffe*, Ernst Udet, and its chief of staff, Hans Jeschonneck, committed suicide during the Second World War.

6 Alan Turing (1912-54) has been compared to the Swedish Professor of Mathematics in Uppsala, Arne Beurling (1905-86), who in the summer of 1940, in two weeks, singlehandedly and with just pen and paper broke the even more sophisticated *Geheimschreiber*, the coded teletypewriter (*Siemens and Halske T52*) used for Nazi Germany's highest level of communications, thus enabling the Swedish authorities to read Germany's most secret messages between 1940 and 1943. Sweden's discreet warning to the Soviet Union of the imminent attack by the Nazis in June 1941, as decoded by the Swedes, was ignored by Stalin.

7 The *SS-Division "Nordland"* was upgraded to the status of a *SS-Panzergrenadier-Division* on 12 November 1943. Unlike the *SS-Division "Wiking"*, the *"Nordland"* was however named as *"SS-Freiwilligen-Division"*. This meant that *"Nordland"* consisted of men who were qualified to the standards for German armed services, but not necessarily living up to the higher demands of being *SS*-men. In-line with the reconstruction of the *SS-Division "Wiking"* (which had to give up its infantry-regiment *"Nordland"* to form the core of the new division with the same name), the *SS*-infantry regiment *"Germania"* within the *SS-Division "Wiking"* was to be the unit for all "*SS*-worthy Germans"; Emberland & Kott, *Himmlers Norge*, p.430.

8 Emberland & Kott, *Himmlers Norge*, pp.434-40.

9 Cited in Gyllenhaal & Westberg, *Swedes at War*, p.287.

10 Bundgard Christensen, Poulsen & Scharff Smith, *Under hagekors och Dannebrog*, p.203.

11 Bundgard Christensen, Poulsen & Scharff Smith, *Under hagekors och Dannebrog*, p.204.

12 Bundgard Christensen, Poulsen & Scharff Smith, *Under hagekors och Dannebrog*, pp.199-209.

13 Emberland & Kott, *Himmlers Norge*, pp.438-40. On participation of Swedish *SS* soldiers in such actions, see Gyllenhaal & Westberg, *Swedes at War*, p.287.

14 Gyllenhaal & Westberg, *Swedes at War*, p.293.

15 Emberland & Kott, *Himmlers Norge*, p.440.

Soldiers from the *5. Kompanie* of *SS-Pz.Aufklärungsabteilung 11* digging bunkers just outside the Croatian village of Sisak, September 1943. (Courtesy of Predrag Blanusa & Björn Leo)

An *SS-Rottenführer* from the *11. SS Aufklärungsabteilung "Nordland"* is testing a recently delivered *Schwimmwagen* (Volkswagen Type 166), in the Croatian River Save in October 1943. It was far from a homogenous division *"Nordland"* that arrived in Croatia at the end of August 1943. The soldiers came from different countries and a great part of them were recruits from different training depots. At the time of their arrival in Croatia, *"Nordland"* could only muster 32 percent of its planned vehicles, and a subsequent report to superior staff stated: "The division is immobile." (Courtesy of Predrag Blanusa & Björn Leo)

Officers conferring in Croatia, September-October 1943, near the River Save. From the left: *SS-Hauptsturmführer* Rudolf Saalbach, CO *SS-Pz.Aufklärungsabteilung 11*; *SS-Untersturmführer* Siegfried Lorenz, CO *1. Kompanie*; and two unknown officers from the same battalion. (Courtesy of Predrag Blanusa & Björn Leo)

Ethnic Germans (*Volksdeutsche*) from Rumania in the Croatian village of Hrastelnica on 4 October 1943, before or shortly after swearing the oath to Hitler. (Courtesy of Predrag Blanusa & Björn Leo)

The company commander for *5./SS-Pz.Aufklärungsabteilung 11*, Hans Schmidt, leads the oath to Hitler on 4 October 1943 in Hrastelnica, Croatia. Behind him stands the platoon leader, *SS-Untersturmführer* Georg Langendorf. (Courtesy of Predrag Blanusa & Björn Leo)

The oath to Hitler in Hrastelnica on 4 October 1943 with the *5. Kompanie*, in the presence of *SS-Obersturmführer* Hans Schmidt and *SS-Untersturmführer* Langendorf. (Courtesy of Predrag Blanusa & Björn Leo)

Units from the *SS-Panzergrenadier-Regiment 23 "Norge"* embark on one of the trains from Grafenwöhr to Croatia at the end of August 1943. The *"Norge"* battalions were located in the Croatian villages of Generals-Kistol (*I./23*), Bosn.-Nowi (*II./23*) and Kostanica (*III./23*).

From the left: *SS-Unterscharführer* Andreas Nilsson and *SS-Unterscharführer* Tor Svenneby, who later attended *Junkerschule* Tölz and was killed in action in March 1945 in Krepcewo, Poland. (Courtesy of Alf Johannesen and Tor Strömsnes)

The *SS*-railway guard in Sisak, Croatia, in September 1943. To the left is *SS- Unterscharführer* Fritz Ihle from "*Nordland*", a German with Danish citizenship from the Danish province of Schleswig.

The dull train journey, which lasted for several days, was enlightened by the scenery in Austria and the Balkans.

The village of Kostanica, the garrison location in Croatia for *I./"Norge"*. After Yugoslavia's capitulation on 10 April 1941, the Croatian fascist movement of Ustascha proclaimed the independent state of Croatia (NDH – *Nezavisna Drzava Hrvatska*) with its capital in Agram (modern Zagreb). The so-called NDH state, in contrast to Serbia and Montenegro, was not an occupied alien state but a privileged nation, allied with the Third *Reich* and fascist Italy. Croatia's *poglavnik* (regent) was Ante Pavelic (1889–1959) and the Ustascha counted more than 75,000 militia troops in their ranks.

A number of vehicles, mostly VW *Schwimmwagen*, having arrived at the *Regiment "Norge"* in Croatia. Some half-tracks were delivered to the corps as late as December 1943, barely giving time to install the necessary radio equipment in these *Schützenpanzerwagen* (*SPW*).

Norwegians taking a pause and a meal during anti-partisan actions. From the left: *SS-Unterscharführer* Andreas Nilsson, *SS-Oberscharführer* Alf Lie and *Sturmmann* Bjarne Borgersen. Norwegian losses due to partisan activities in Croatia were few, with six dead from *Regiment "Norge"*, while the number of Danish soldiers illed in Croatia was substantially higher: until 27 November 1943, *Regiment "Danmark"* lost 145 men, including 49 killed in action, with the rest wounded or missing. Total Norwegian losses from units serving in the *III. (Germ.) SS-Panzer-Korps* during the period from August 1943 until 2 May 1945 was 212 men. During the fighting of *"Nordland"* in Croatia in the autumn of 1943, five Swedish *SS*-volunteers deserted collectively to the Croatian partisans. One Swede, Karl Ograhn, was shot in the chest by Croatian militia during this attempt and was saved from court-martial (and a sure conviction to death) by the personal intervention of Heinrich Himmler.

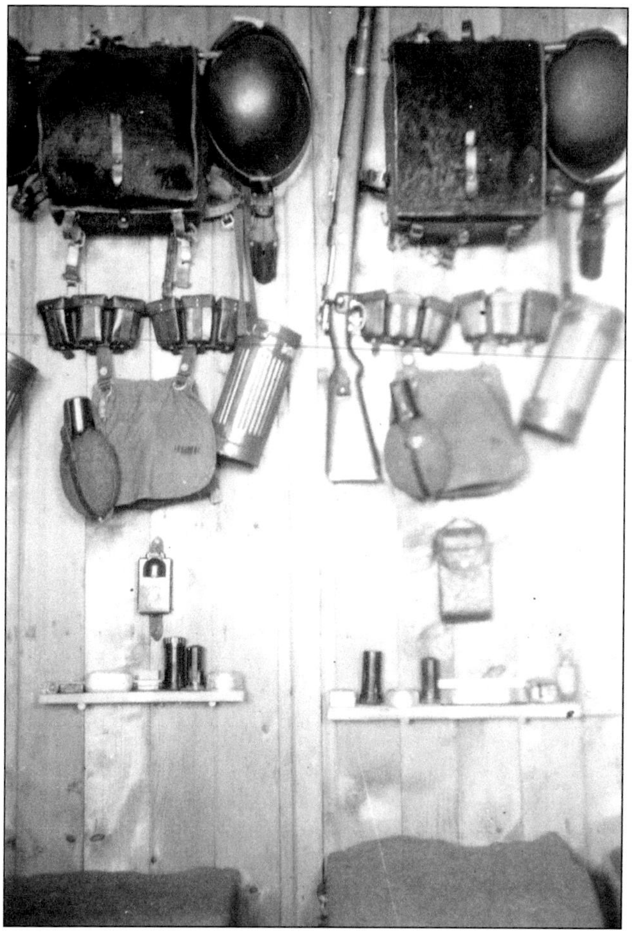

Sturmmann Horst Borger's own caption to this photo was: "My equipment in Camp Sisak, 2 September 1943".

Soldiers and officers from the *3. Kompanie* of the *SS-Aufklärungsabteilung "Nordland"* in Sisak, on their way to swear the oath to Hitler (not all units had done this in Grafenwöhr). To the far right in the front row is the Swedish *SS-Untersturmführer* Hans-Gösta Pehrsson, who previously had served in the *Freikorps Danmark* at the Leningrad Front in 1941–42.

VW *Schwimmwagen* of the "Nordland" in the River Save, Croatia, in September 1943. The CO of the SS-*Aufklärungsabteilung "Nordland"*, *SS-Hauptsturmführer* Saalbach, wanted to test the water-worthiness of this vehicle and, without the responsible officer's permission, Saalbach took a tour on the Save, without knowing that the *Schwimmwagen* had no propeller. It took 200-300 metres until Saalbach managed to manoeuvre with the paddle that every *Schwimmwagen* was equipped with.

A musical joke by officers and NCOs from the ranks of the *SS-Panzer-Abteilung "Hermann von Salza"*, which was stationed in Samobor, Croatia. From the left: Prendka, Willi Fleck, Paul-Albert "Peter" Kausch, Richard Stübben, Casper and unknown.

Officers from the *SS-Panzer-Abteilung "Hermann von Salza"* in Samobor, Croatia, in the autumn of 1943. From the left: Rudolf Rott (Adjutant) and Paul-Albert Kausch (CO) giving orders to their company commanders, with their backs to the camera. While the *III. (Germ.) SS-Panzer-Korps* arrived in Oranienbaum from Croatia on 12 December 1943, the *"Hermann von Salza"* remained in Croatia, where they were still waiting to be equipped with *Sturmgeschütze* (assault guns) that never arrived.

Soldiers from the *2./SS-Panzer-Aufklärungsabteilung "Nordland"* in Croatia with their company commander, *SS-Hauptsturmführer* Heinrich Heckmüller, in the middle in black *panzer* uniform. The cannon in the middle belongs to a *Sd Kfz. 250/9 Panzer-Spähwagen* with a 2cm KwK 38 L/55.

Soldiers from the *SS-Panzer-Abteilung "Hermann von Salza"* during an anti-partisan action in the mountains around Samobor, Croatia, in the autumn of 1943. The *panzer* soldiers, in this action used as infantry, are armed with the MG 42, MPi 40 and the Walther P38 pistol. The intensive anti-partisan engagement by various units from *"Nordland"* made many Scandinavian volunteers quit service in Croatia and opt for serving on the Finnish-Soviet Front instead, in the Norwegian *SS-Skijägerabteilung*.

Armoured vehicles (*Sd Kfz 251/9* with towed 7.5cm anti-tank cannons) from the *5./ SS-Panzer-Aufklärungsabteilung "Nordland"* in Ingria, 1944.

A *Sturmgeschütz* from the *Panzerjäger-Abteilung "Nordland"* fires against Croatian partisans, September 1943. After the creation of the fascist Croatian state, the Ustasja arrested all suspected communists, mainly intellectuals but also farmers. The result was that many of the male population escaped into the remote mountainous areas. The first partisan groups were organized in the spring of 1942. The Ustasja responded with harsh reprisals against the civilian population. In 1943, however, the situation had been destabilized, to the disadvantage of the Ustasja, and the German High Command began to send reinforcements to Croatia and the Balkans generally. However, these were mainly second-class troops or not yet fully trained units, like the *III. (Germ.) SS-Panzer-Korps*. (Westemeier)

Soldiers from the *SS-Panzerjäger-Abteilung "Nederland"* on a *Sturmgeschütz* in Croatia, before an anti-partisan action. The Brigade *"Nederland"* was located around Zabok, west of Agram, in the area called Hrvatsko Zagorje, characterized by high mountains and remote small villages with a mainly poor and Catholic population.

The back of the platoon commander-*SPW* of the *5./SS-Panzeraufklärungs-Abteilung "Nordland"* in Hrastovica, Croatia, in September 1943. In the *SPW* stands *SS-Oberscharführer* (later *Standarten-Oberjunker d.R.*) Walter Schwarck.

SS-Unterscharführer Herbert Poller in the Croatian village of Topolovac, in November 1943, standing in the turret of a *Sd Kfz 250/9*. Poller was engaged in the Nazi Party's school and educational branches in the early 1930s, and made study tours to the Scandinavian countries. "By touring Sweden, we were rejected by the Swedish school system: they did not want anything to do with us Nazis" (Poller to LW). Poller was wounded in Ingria in January 1944, was top of his course at the *Junkerschule* Bad Tölz in 1945 and served as platoon leader in the *38. SS-Grenadier-Division "Nibelungen"*, which in March 1945 was formed *ad hoc* by the staff and trainees of the *SS Junkerschule* Bad Tölz. The division was named after the medieval poem, the "Nibelungenlied" of epic German mythology, made famous by Richard Wagner in his opera *Ring des Nibelungen*.

A burning Croatian farm during an anti-partisan action in September 1943. On the far right, with a MPi 40 at his shoulder, stands *SS-Hauptsturmführer* Walter Nieft, chief of the mechanical reparations platoon from the *SS-Panzer-Aukflärungsabteilung 11 "Nordland"*, among other soldiers from "*Nordland*". At this time, it was obvious that Italy would soon defect from its ally Germany, and on 14 September 1943, an armistice was signed between Italy and the Allies. Units from the *III. (Germ.) SS-Panzer-Korps* disarmed Italian troops in Italy and participated in reinforced actions against the flourishing partisan movements (partly rearmed with Italian weapons). *SS-Obergrupenführer* Steiner wrote in an order from the corps staff: "Armed resistance is to break ruthlessly and with all means possible." To units from the *Waffen-SS*, such formulations often meant an invitation for excessive use of violence against the civilian population. (Westemeier)

Anti-partisan action in Croatia on 26 November 1943. From the left are *Sturmmann* Hoffmann (with MG 42) and *SS-Unterscharführer* Berthold Behnke in their *SPW*, carrying the typical *Waffen-SS* camouflage smock.

The *3. bataillon* of *SS-Pz.Grenadier Regiment 24 "Danmark"* is drawn up for inspection by *SS-Obergruppenführer* Steiner in Petrinja, Croatia, in August 1943. In contrast to the overoptimistic German High Command in Berlin, Steiner was realistic about the inadequate standards of education and training of the various units in his *SS-Panzer-Korps*. Experienced instructors had been too few, coordination of units from battalion size upwards was non-existent, equipment and vehicles had not been delivered and coordination was lacking between the artillery and infantry. (Courtesy of Uwe Kuppen)

Norwegians and other soldiers of the *SS-Panzergrenadier-Regiment 23 "Norge"* swearing the oath at Bos. Novi, October 1943. Note that the soldiers (Norwegians, Germans and ethnic Germans) are swearing the oath towards the Norwegian flag and not the *SS*-flag!

A *"Badoglio-Panzer"* (Fiat M 42 tank) used by the *"Hermann von Salza"* in Samobor. Originally captured from Italian stocks within the German Army Group South, 65 were delivered to the *III. (Germ.) SS-Panzer-Korps* in Croatia for training purposes. The staff and personnel of the *SS-Panzer-Abteilung "Hermann von Salza"* in Samobor also used them for anti-partisan actions. There were several changes to the organization and equipment of the *"Hermann von Salza"* during 1943. The intention was originally to establish a *panzer-regiment*, partly equipped with tanks, for the *Division "Nordland"*. As it became obvious that the German armaments industry was barely able to produce Panthers in sufficient numbers for both the Army and the *Waffen-SS*, a new order of 30 October 1943 stated the *Panzer-Regiment "Nordland"* would be downsized to a *Panzer-(Sturmgeschütz) Abteilung*.

Gerhard Zühlke and Toni Diefenthaler from *SS-Panzer-Grenadierregiment "Norge"* in Bosn.-Novi, Croatia, in the autumn of 1943.

SS-Untersturmführer Robert L. Hansen, *SS-Zugführer 6./SS-Panzergrenadier-Regiment 24 "Danmark"*, from Odense, Denmark, sitting on the front of a VW *Schwimmwagen*, returning from an anti-partisan action in Croatia.

Recruiting poster in occupied Norway for service in the *SS-Panzer-Grenadier-Regiment 23 "Norge"* ("Your place: *SS*").

Recruiting poster in occupied Norway for service in the *Waffen-SS*. The drawing is made by the Swedish-Norwegian artist, Finn Wifgorss, whose father was a cousin to the Minister of Finance in wartime Sweden, Ernst Wigforss. The text reads: " … and where are YOU?"

Personnel from the *SS-Sturmgeschützabteilung 11* assembled in Sisak, Croatia.With his back to the camera is *SS-Hauptsturmführer* Karlheinz Schulz Streeck, and to his right is *SS-Obersturmführer* Helmut Krohmer (commanding officer, *3. Kompanie*). Schulz Streeck served from 1943 as adviser to the CO of this assault gun battalion (*SS-Haupsturmführer* Ernst Roentsch) and was previously an artillery captain in the German Army. Schulz Streeck took command of the battalion after Röntsch was killed in action on 21 January 1944. Next to him in the photo is Helmut Krohmer, CO of the battalion's *3. Kompanie*.

Exercise near Sisak, Croatia, with personnel from the *SS-Sturmgeschützabteilung 11*. The vehicles are a VW *Kübelwagen* (left) and *StuG III Ausführung D*.

Maintenance of a *StuG III* at the edge of a river. The bridge in the background is the Kupa bridge and sitting to the right on the *StuG* is *SS-Unterscharführer* Müller, with his driver Kupka to the left.

SS-Gruppenführer Fritz von Scholtz (left) visits personnel from the *SS-Sturmgeschützabteilung "Nordland"* in Croatia.

Recruits from the SS-*Sturmgeschützabteilung 11* standing beside a VW *Schwimmwagen* after an anti-partisan action near Glina in September 1943.

Panzer soldiers from the *SS-Panzer-Abteilung "Hermann von Salza"* in a lorry during anti-partisan actions around Samobor, Croatia, in the autumn of 1943.

Panzer recruits from "*Hermann von Salza*" during anti-partisan actions around Samobor in Croatia, in September 1943.

An Italian *"Badoglio-Panzer"* used by *"Hermann von Salza"* crews in Croatia, Samobor, in September 1943.

NCOs and soldiers from *"Hermann von Salza"* in the terrain around Samobor, Croatia, in autumn 1943. The men seem to be wearing the camouflage one-piece overall for tank crews (pea-dot pattern).

Two NCOs from the *"Hermann von Salza"*, probably in Croatia during training. They both wear the camouflage one-piece overall for tank crews (pea-dot pattern).

Unknown *panzer* soldier from the *"Hermann von Salza"* in 1943.

3

IN THE FRONT-LINE AT ORANIENBAUM-LENINGRAD AND THE BATTLE FOR INGRIA (JANUARY–FEBRUARY 1944)

THE STRATEGICAL AND TACTICAL SITUATION, 1943–44

During the Winter Campaign of 1942–43, the German Army's back had practically been broken: the *Wehrmacht* had lost their most powerful army (the Sixth) at Stalingrad, together with the Romanian Second and Third Armies. At the Don River, the German Second Army was severely mauled, and on top of that, the Italian Eighth and Hungarian Second Armies were annihilated. After the Battle of Kursk, the Soviet forces plunged deep into the Ukraine in November–December 1943 and cleared the Crimea, damaging the German First Panzer Army and the new Sixth Army.

In late November 1943, the *Oberkommando der Heeres* issued orders that the *11.SS-Freiwilligen-Panzergrenadier-Division "Nordland"* was to be transferred to the Leningrad Front. The battalions and companies of the "*Norge*" and "*Danmark*" were successively, beginning on 25 November 1943, relieved of their anti-partisan activities by pro-German Cossack units. The *Brigade "Nederland"* remained in Croatia to complete its training. Some units, like the *SS* engineer battalion, were never sent to Croatia, but were instead transferred to the training depot at Beneschau in Bohemia, while the *SS-Flak-Abteilung 11* was trained at the Arys military grounds in East Prussia, and from there directly arrived at the Leningrad Front.

The *SS-Panzer-Abteilung 11* and the *Brigade "Nederland"* were the last units to leave Croatia, arriving at the Oranienbaum sector of the Leningrad Front on 22 December 1943. The *III.SS-Panzer- Korps* was put under the command of *SS-Generaloberst* Georg Lindemann's Eighteenth Army within *Heeresgruppe Nord* (Field Marshal Georg von Küchler). On 30 December, the total troop strength of "*Nordland*" was 11,393 (304 officers, 1,734 NCOs and 9,355 enlisted ranks). The *III. (germ.) SS-Panzer-Korps* had a total strength of about 19,000 men, which normally constituted the strength of a division. Proportionally, the personnel of the corps consisted at the end of 1943 of 29.6 percent Germans, 44.5 percent ethnic Germans and 25.9 percent "Germanic" volunteers from Western and Northern Europe.[1]

All signs pointed to an imminent Soviet offensive to relieve Leningrad. In early December 1943, the *Stavka* had expressed their strategic plans for a third winter campaign. This demanded the Red Army to drive von Küchler's *Heeresgruppe Nord* from the Leningrad region. In this area, combat had stabilized since late 1941 with the siege of Leningrad. On 14 January 1944, the Soviet offensive to relieve the besieged city broke loose, with support from heavy naval guns at the Kronstadt naval base. The Soviet attacking force consisted of the 2nd Baltic Front, composed of six armies which outnumbered the opposing German forces four-to-one. The weakest point in the German lines, two inexperienced *Luftwaffe Feld-Divisionen*, were quickly penetrated by the Second Assault Army with two corps, nine guards divisions, three tank brigades and a coastal brigade. The Red Arm, broke through the weak *9.Luftwaffe Feld-Division* and crushed it.

The southerly German units were ordered to retreat by Field Marshal von Küchler and the backbone of the German *Heeresgruppe Nord*, the newly arrived *III. (germ.) SS-Panzer-Korps* and reliable *Wehrmacht* divisions, had to act as blocking forces and cover the German retreat westwards through Ingria. On 25 January 1944, the Soviets achieved a new decisive breakthrough: the front cracked, and the first battalion of the *SS-Panzergrenadier-Regiment "Danmark"* was nearly annihilated at the village of Vitino. On 30 January, the units of the *III. (germ.) SS-Panzer-Korps* had regrouped around the town of Yamburg and pulled back across the Luga River with all bridges blown behind them. In the course of February 1944, the *III. (germ.) SS-Panzer-Korps* withdrew to the strategically important city of Narva in Estonia, holding its bridgehead.

After von Küchler had ordered a general retreat to the Luga River, a furious Hitler replaced him with "Hitler's fireman", *Generaloberst* Walter Model.[2] It is to Küchler's credit, however, that he succeeded in performing an orderly

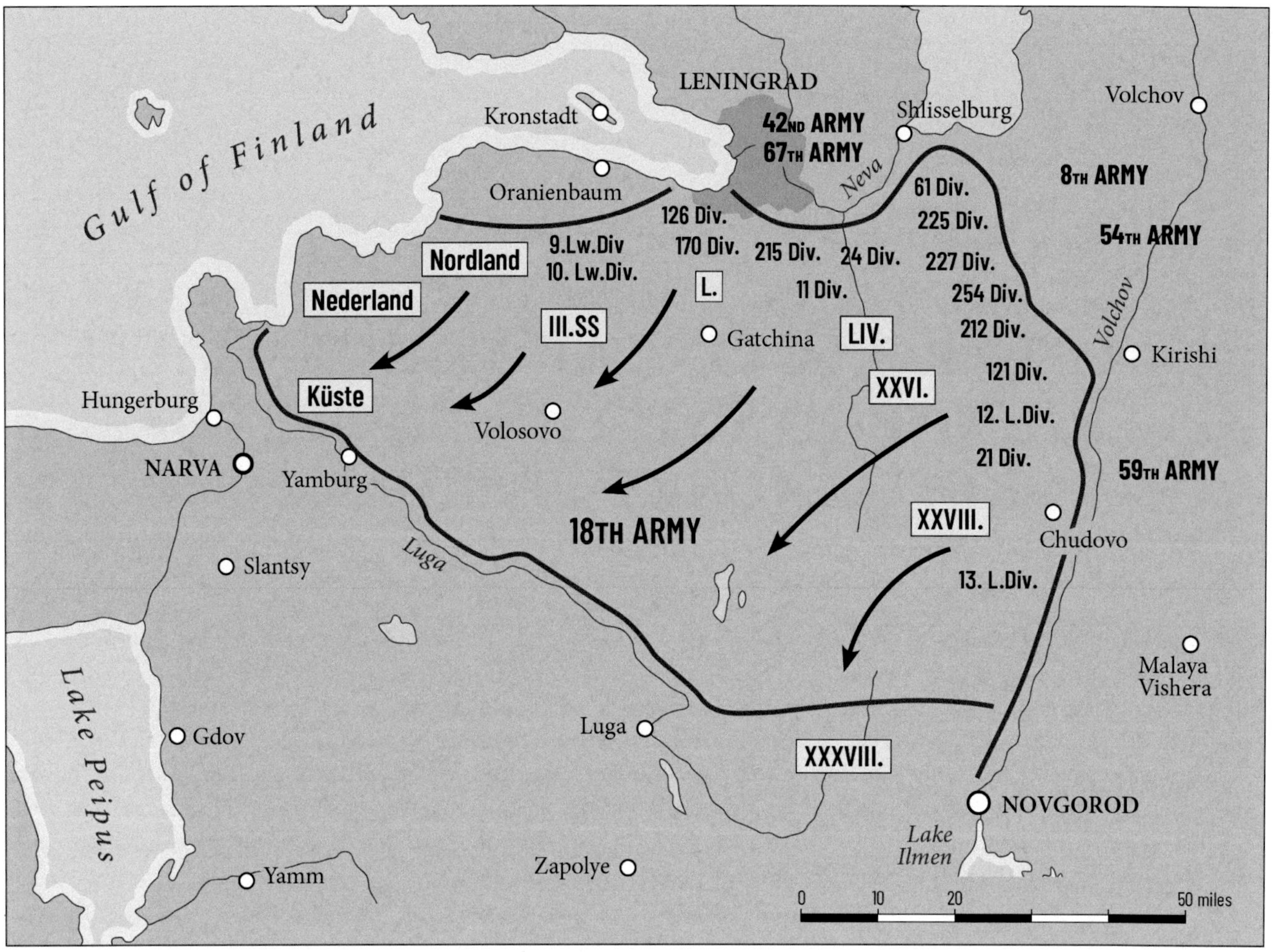

The retreat from Leningrad.

retreat of his army group through Ingria, reaching the Narva River in relatively good order. Model was successful in getting additional army divisions as reinforcement to the new Narva Front and miraculously stabilized a bridgehead around the city of Narva along the Narva River for the following six months. The Red Army was troubled with difficult terrain, bad intelligence and outdated tactics. For Model's defensive merits at Narva – where his formula for success was a variation of Manstein's tactical "*Schild und Schwert*" ("Shield and Sword") doctrine, by retreating within the framework of a planned counter-offensive – Hitler promoted Model to *Generalfeldmarschall*. LW

Walter Schwark, commander of the 5th Company's Cannon *SPW* platoon in the *SS recce battalion "Nordland"* (Lennart Westberg's archives).

Christmas is carried out here, it would be irresponsible to say "is celebrated". I still remember my thoughts in the company of these splendid young companions singing Christmas carols together: Who among us will survive into the coming year? As for the rest, the Germans from Siebenbürgen and Banat taught us one and another German folksong that we hadn't heard before. Those who have survived undoubtedly remember those few peaceful days before the battle with longing.

Erling Schiötz, Norwegian Soldier in the *SS-Panzergrenadier-Regiment "Norge"* (Tommy Natedal's archives)

On January 13, 1944, our mortar group, consisting of 10–15 men, arrived at the divisional *Panzer* school at Kirova. There we would be taught the new anti-tank weapon *Panzerfaust*. Our battalion was among the first that would be equipped with this weapon in the field and we would be instructors. But this did not happen. The next day we were told that the Soviets had started a major offensive and we were forced to return to our battalion immediately. The whole *Panzer* school left and there we were without vehicles and maps. We marched the whole day towards the front and got the message from passing motorcycle messengers that we were on the right track. In the evening, we arrived at one of the Tsar's hunting castles and we two NCOs gained access to the chief of staff, a colonel in spotless uniform whose office consisted of one of the grand rooms in the castle including its shining furniture. It was as grand as when the Tsar resided there. The colonel was most obliging and told us that our battalion from the "*Norge*" was under heavy fighting and had performed

Sverre Larsen

Olav Sandstad

Erling Schiötz

extremely well south of Ropsja, but we must be prepared for the fact that we probably have lost quite a lot of comrades in the battalion. We were promised transport and early the next morning we arrived with a lorry to the front line and our battalion. I got the impression that they had looked forward to reinforcement from the *Panzer* school, but we ten to fifteen men with infantry weapons did not constitute any major asset.

We soon came under fire from *Stalin organs* [Katyusha rocket launchers] but due to the heavy snow nobody was wounded. After this, all impressions of time and space left me. When we were later assembled in a wood with our battalion commander, Fritz Vogt, our first battalion had ceased to exist. All that remained was the battle group Vogt, with perhaps 200 men from various units. Of the officers, only Vogt, the battalion doctor, Böresen, and a second lieutenant, were left. We formed ourselves to an "all-around-defence" as the Russians were everywhere. During a scout patrol in the woods, we discovered a Soviet sniper who was shot down by one of our soldiers. Early next morning we started a thirteen-hour-long march. At the top of the column Vogt marched with a group, then doctor Böresen and five to ten reindeer sleighs with the wounded. Then came an *SS* officer who was to keep a watch on those soldiers who were not from the *Waffen-SS*, and organize the replacement for those pulling the sledges with the wounded. I marched last with a group that made sure nobody was left, and that no one threw away his weapon. We also served as a rearguard.

After passing a small hill, we came under machine-gun fire from behind. We responded with a rapid fire. I remember that Herstad Halvorsen was especially fast in getting his machine gun ready for firing while I and some others ran to the side to out-flank the Russian patrol. But they were quicker and got away. During the latter part of our march, many soldiers lay down in the snow and did not want to go any further, but no *SS* men were among these. I have never before made so many kicks in the back, and I have never uttered so many oaths and encouraging words to get these soldiers out of the snowy ground. Böresen was forced to draw his pistol to persuade the soldiers to replace those drawing the sledges with the wounded. Finally, we arrived at a village that was being held by *Luftwaffe* soldiers. We paused for the first time in fifteen hours to clean our weapons, for food and to sleep. After just one hour there was alarm again and we manned the positions, as the *Luftwaffe* had left them and retreated. Then we marched in the direction of Kingisepp (Jamburg). The whole way from Vitino was crammed with civilian refugees and soldiers, a depressing sight. Soviet planes attacked the columns from behind with machine guns and hit some civilians. From then on, with some fighting, we retreated during the nights until we reached the Narva river.

Björn Heisholdt, Norwegian volunteer in the *SS-Panzergrenadier Regiment "Norge"* (Tommy Natedal's archives)

Something has awakened me. It is January 14th 1944, 07:30 hours at the Oranienbaum Front. Is it the steps of the cook on the stairs? Remarkable, because he usually goes very carefully in the mornings on his way to the kitchen. Slowly, my brain awakens and I register an unusual sound in the distance as of distant thunder. Suddenly I am wide awake. I have heard that sound before, but not so intensive since all our artillery was put in action before the storming of the bridgehead of Kamenka in 1941. Now I hear running steps on the stair and boots in the corridor. The door slams open and the NCO on watch calls out: "Alarm! All men out!" The door closes and he runs to the next house. I am up in a second and dressed. I hasten the men. For myself I want to be at the company HQ as soon as possible. When I enter the fresh air, I hear the cannon thunder even more clearly, like a doomsday sound. Our own artillery has also responded now, and is sharper in its sound, like individual weak voices, trying to be heard in a choir.

I tumble to the company staff. The last reports on the phone told about a veritable drum fire from the Soviet batteries at Oranienbaum. Attacks on our positions could be expected any time. Our first battalion in the regiment "*Norge*" was a reserve unit in our *Panzer-Korps*. We could expect to be put into action in the worst turmoil. The corps staff had ordered us to get into the highest alert. We had been stationed in the vincinity no more than a month. Previously, this area had been seen as the calmest section of the whole Eastern Front. Since 1942, battles had been restricted to patrol duty and minor skirmishes but otherwise, a long period of calm had reigned at this Front. The company commander gave a brief orientation: Soviet artillery had focussed on crossroads and staff locations plus other vital parts of our defence system. Prisoners had told about a major Soviet offensive.

A couple of weeks ago, we had got our skiing equipment. From our Norwegian perspective, these skis were heavy and clumsy. The ethnic Germans from Rumania, the *Volksdeutsche*, were unused to skiing and we Scandinavians [had to] teach them. Some ethnic Germans were eager to learn skiing while others did not want to touch the thing. The only advantage with these skis was that reindeer sleighs went with them, which were handy to pack the ammunition on, so we did not have to carry it. The company commander gave orders that everyone should equip themselves with ammunition from the store under *SS-Unterscharführer* Wilhelm König. If we were to get something from this store, we had literally to take it from the hands of König. It seemed to us that he wanted to save both weapon and ammunition for the next war. But now other conditions ruled, we carried away boxes with ammunition for the machine guns and mortars, plus a number of hand grenades. We had supplied ourselves with ammunition for our pistols and sub-machine gun earlier. The men went to work gladly. When the order for action came, we had polished our weapons, oiled the mechanisms, packed our storm carriage and relieved ourselves of things we did not need. Some of the men had had time to write letters, but for most of the company there was no time for writing.

Norwegians in the *Waffen-SS*

The leading fascist party in Norway, the *Nasjonal Samling* or *NS* (National Gathering), was founded on 13 May 1933 by the former minister of defence, Vidkun Quisling (1887–1945), and other supporters. Its ideology was dominated by national romanticism, Norse paganism, anti-Semitism and corporative-authoritarian ideas. Gravely affected by internal conflicts, the *NS* was, at the time of the Nazi occupation of Norway in April 1940, reduced to a political sect of minor importance. Vidkun Quisling, who in a fashion of a *coup d'état* established a short-lived cabinet in the early phase of the German invasion in 1940, was quickly thrown aside by the Germans. Already dismissed by Heinrich Himmler in the late Thirties, Quisling gained support only from Alfred Rosenberg, leader of the Nazi party's foreign political office, and Erich Raeder, chief of the German Navy. Josef Terboven, Hitler's new *Reichskommissar* for occupied Norway, also mistrusted Quisling. In late 1940, however, Quisling was assured of Hitler's support and appointed acting Prime Minister, later Minister-President, in a collaborationist government, dominated by the *NS*. Although partly opposed to the *SS*, and vice-versa, Quisling approved the recruitment of Norwegian volunteers to the *Waffen-SS* in late 1940. In February 1941, the first 300 Norwegians left Oslo to join the *Waffen-SS*; around 1,000 Norwegians joined the *SS-Regiment "Nordland"* in 1941 as part of the *SS-Division "Wiking"*. After Hitler's attack on the USSR, a Norwegian "national" Legion was established for the Eastern Front, following the pattern of other occupied Western European countries. After being engaged on the Eastern Front in the Leningrad area, the *Legion Norwegen* (which in January 1942 had a strength of 1,218 men) was dissolved in May 1943 and re-formed into the *SS-Panzergrenadier-Regiment "Norge"* of the new *III. (germ.) SS-Panzer-Korps*. On 30 January 1944, the total number of Norwegians in the *Waffen-SS* was 3,878. Quisling's *Hird*, a copy of the German *SA*, and the more independent *SS* formation *Germanske SS Norge*, were recruiting potentials for Himmler's *Waffen-SS* and other German uniformed units: Quisling's *NS* naval detachment, the *Hirdmarine*, recruited 500 Norwegian sailors to the German *Kriegsmarine* (navy); the *NS* flying corps, *Flyhirden*, supported the *Luftwaffe* with 75 Norwegian volunteers; and the *Waffen-SS* recruited 350–400 Norwegian nurses for the Eastern Front. For domestic guard service, the *SS-Wachbatallion 6*, was formed in Oslo in 1942 with 500 Norwegians, and in the late summer of that year, a *SS-Skijäger* company for the Finnish Front was established, consisting of 200 Norwegians. Bolstered by Norwegian Police companies, this unit was expanded in 1943 to the *SS-Skijäger-Batallion*, operating in Finland and assigned to the *6. SS-Gebirgsjäger-Division "Nord"*.[3]

In the period 1940–45, around 15,000 Norwegians applied to the *Waffen-SS* and 7,000 were accepted (10 percent being killed in action). The majority of the Norwegians in the *Waffen-SS* were quite young (16–25 years old) and were primarily politically motivated.[4] LW

Björn Heisholdt, Norwegian volunteer in the *SS-Panzergrenadier Regiment "Norge"* (Tommy Natedal's archives)

The lorries stood ready to transport us up to the Front and the awaiting Soviet assault. We were soon on the move. We passed four *Sturmgeschuetze* at the side of the road. It was mentioned that they were to accompany us. The closer we came near the Front, the more the clamour increased. The most intense drum fire had decreased and was replaced with more regular artillery salvoes. Traffic coming in the other direction increased and we saw more and more wounded, both on lorries and on foot.

Björn Heisholdt

The Norwegian SS-*Untersturmfüher* Borger Dahl "Bobbo" Larssen belonged to the new officers' corps in the *SS-Regiment "Norge"* from Bad Tölz, which completed its training in July 1943. During the retreat from Ingria, Larssen took over the *10. Kompanie* of *"Norge"* on 30 January 1944, but was killed three days later at Dubrowka, hit in his head while trying to replace a fallen crewman of an MG 42. Larssen's body could not be recovered from the battlefield.

During a pause I spoke to one of the wounded, who did not seem as apathetic as the others. His right arm was badly mangled and his snow camouflage-wear was stained with blood. He belonged to a heavy artillery battery, placed some kilometres behind the frontline. The Soviet artillery assault had caught them napping. In the early morning, the battery had been hit by one salvo after another right into their positions. Before they themselves could open fire, three of their *haubitz* [howitzers] had been destroyed. The whole position was an inferno of detonating shells, splinters and the shouting of the wounded. All over was a layer of smoke and the smell of cordite. Some of the men and the *SS-Obersturmführer* could save the only artillery piece left, but the problem was to get the frightened horses into position to transport the heavy gun away. The soldier himself had been wounded when a salvo hit their firing control board. He had been bandaged by a comrade and was now on his way to the field hospital. Their ammunition supply had also gone up in smoke and most of the battery crews were either dead or wounded. And all this had happened before they themselves had had the time to fire one single round.

Our column now was on the move again. At the next crossroad we took to the left and drove up along a row of grey, abandoned houses. We took a short pause and the opportunity to make a fire in the stoves in these houses to make a meal. I tried to put butter on the bread but it was so frozen that I had to cut the butter in slices. Halvdan, our company staff sergeant, appeared and we asked him about the situation. "We shall wait here, for the moment. No one has the notion of what is happening," he said. Halvdan asked if he could share the bread with me, but added: "Better to fight with an empty stomach, to avoid infections." Perhaps he had a sense of what was going to happen. Twelve hours later Halvdan got a shot in the stomach and died. This happened when he tried to salvage his wounded company commander, Olaf Lindvig.

SS-Obersturmbannführer Dr Franz Riedweg

Franz Riedweg (1907–2005) was born in Lucerne, Switzerland. He grew up in a wealthy family, and by the age of 16 was, as a young idealist, a supporter of the Coudenhove-Calergi Movement, which called for a united and federal Christian Europe, opposing communism. In 1934, he was introduced to circles of the Prussian aristocracy in Berlin. As a medical student in 1937, he was a co-founder of the Swiss National Action against Communism (*Action Suisse contre le Communisme*) and chief of the secretariat to the former Swiss *Bundespräsident* Jean-Marie Musy, thereby successively

SS-Obersturmbannführer Dr Franz Riedweg

This Danish *Waffen-SS* recruitment poster from 1944 makes a symbolic historic parallel. In the foreground "Germanic" *SS* soldiers from the *III. (germ.) SS-Panzer-Korps* and its *SS-Panzergrenadier-Regiment "Danmark"*, are marching east to Narva in 1944. The background depicts the Danish medieval King Valdemar II, with his army of crusaders, during the battle of Lyndanise (today´s Tallinn) castle in 1219 as the Danish flag *Dannebrogen* emerges in the sky and, according to the tale, made the Danish victorious over the Estonian tribes. In mid-1944, the German bridgehead at Narva constituted the most eastern part of the German front in the Soviet Union. This, combined with the fact that large contingents of "Germanic" soldiers from the *Waffen-SS* defended Narva, made the bridgehead highly important to Hitler and Himmler.

The symbolism in this Dutch *Waffem-SS* recruiting poster derives from the Boer War in South Africa between the Dutch-related Boer colonists in Transvaal and the British Imperial forces. The portrait shows Paul Krueger (1825-1904), the President of the South African Republic 1883-1900. The poster appeals to Dutch sentiments about the Boer War as a historic parallel to the ongoing war between the Third *Reich* and the Soviet Union, encouraging the Dutch to join the *III. (germ.) SS-Panzer-Korps* as SS recruits. The Dutch text above Krueger appeals to duty and faithfulness.

An *SS* lorry from the Germanic Corps during the retreat from Oranienbaum, passing an Ingria village and the Luga River towards the Narva River. The *III. (germ.) SS-Panzer-Korps* acted as rearguard in Ingria while the roughly manhandled 9th and 10th *Luftwaffe* Field Divisions – whose existence since 1942 (initiated by Hermann Göring) was a grave tactical mistake by the German High Command and consequently proved worthless at the front – and other units were given the opportunity to retreat. Excellent Army divisions – like the legendary 11th and 227th Infantry Divisions also proved reliable in this chaos. Colonel Maximiliian Wengler's battlegroup from the 227th, together with a small number of Tiger tanks, held the village of Wolosovo for several days, which proved essential for the shattered German front. To honour the steadiness of their Colonel, Wengler's grenadier nicknamed the village "Wenglerovo".

A *SPW* (*Sd.Kfz. 251/9*) with towed 7.5cm anti-tank cannon in Ingria, in January 1944.

A photo of a *SPW Sd.Kfz. 250/9* from *"Nordland"*, in winter camouflage, with 2cm *KwK 38 L/55*, Ingria, January 1944. Sitting at the front is the ethnic German company cook, Saschek, from Rumania, in the *2./SS-Pz.AA 11*. Within the *SS-Panzer-Aufklärungsabteilung "Nordland"*, six soldiers belonged to the German minority in the Danish province of Schleswig (Georg Erichsen, Hans Jakob Andresen, Werner Ladiges, Eduard Thomsen, Fritz Scheel and Fritz Krämer). "True" Danish volunteers were Mogens Schwarz, Kaj Feilberg and Erik Larsen.

positioning him as a far-right activist. He finished his medical studies in Bern, Rostock and Berlin.

In 1938, Riedweg co-produced the film *Die Rote Pest* (*The Red Plague*) in Munich, at that time the most expensive Swiss film in history. After the filming was finished (it was banned in Switzerland), Riedweg remained in the Third *Reich* and left Switzerland for ever. In 1938, he joined the *SS* and married the daughter of Field Marshal Werner Blomberg (War Minister, who the same year removed from his post) and acquired German citizenship. In 1939, Riedweg served as a doctor in the *Waffen-SS* during the invasion of Poland as part of Hitler's life guard regiment, *Leibstandarte SS "Adolf Hitler"*. In 1940, Riedweg was a staff physician at *SS-Hauptamt* in Berlin and was co-founder of the *"Panorama-Heim"* in Stuttgart, which in the Second World War served as a coordinating camp for Swiss volunteers who wanted to serve the Third *Reich*, mainly in the *SS* and *Waffen-SS*.

Dr Riedweg also served in the *Waffen-SS* during the campaign against France in 1940, thereafter returning to Berlin. In 1940, Himmler entrusted him as Chief of Staff for the newly created office of *Germanische Freiwilligen-Leitstelle* in Berlin. With his ideological dedication to "Germanic" issues, combined with a considerable talent for organization and influence in the highest circles of the Nazi-German elite, Riedweg proved initially successful in recruiting volunteers for the *Waffen-SS* from Western and Northern Europe. Together with Felix Steiner, Riedweg was also the architect for dissolving the semi-national *SS*-Legions on the Eastern Front and amalgamating them into the new *III. (Germanic) SS-Panzer Korps*, stressing the overall pan-Germanic political influence and purpose of the "Germanic" *Waffen-SS* as a future personnel cadre for the administration of the future Greater Germanic *Reich*, and the colonization of the East as *Lebensraum*.

The surprisingly fast career as Heinrich Himmler's and *SS-Obergruppenführer* Gottlob Berger's protegé in the *SS* was probably founded on Riedweg's deep and firm convictions in the "Germanic mission" of the *Waffen-SS*, together with his good manners and excellent connections within various circles of the Third *Reich*'s political and social elite.

In the autumn of 1943, Dr Riedweg made a speech at the *SS-Junkerschule* (one of the officers' schools for the *Waffen-SS*) at Bad Tölz, where he emphasized the prerogative of the *SS*, not the National Socialist Party, in leading a united Europe, based on "Germanic" virtues from the *Waffen-SS* and not relying on force. When Riedweg's speech was reported to Martin Bormann, head of the Nazi Party Chancellery, Himmler was forced to sack Riedweg as Chief of Staff of the *Germanische Leitstelle* and send him to the front, where he first served as a physician in the *III. (germ.) SS-Panzer-Korps* and from the summer of 1944 as Chief-Adjutant to SS-*Obergruppenführer* Steiner at his corps staff for the remainder of the war.[5]

On 3 May 1945, Riedweg was taken prisoner in Mecklenburg by the US Army, but released due to false statements. In 1946, he was again arrested by the British, appeared as a witness before the Nuremberg War Crimes Court but was, after denazification, released in 1948 after paying a fine of 2,000 Marks. In December 1947, Riedweg was sentenced *in absentia* by the Swiss Federal Criminal Court to 16 years in prison for treason. Remarkably, Swiss authorities never tried to extradite him from Germany for trial. The Swiss historian, Marco Wyss, who has written a biography on Franz Riedweg, is of the opinion that Swiss politicians, civil servants in Bern and envoys in Berlin, "had certain interests that Riedweg did not appear before a Swiss court, which could prove problematic for them and others in Switzerland".[6]

Regarding the issue of what Franz Riedweg knew about the Holocaust, Wyss comments:

> He probably didn't know everything, but he must have known about 99 percent of what was happening. First, he moved in the highest *SS* circles. Second, he received regular reports from his headquarters in occupied countries, reports which included, among other things, details of the persecution and deportation of Jews from Western Europe to the East. Moreover, the concentration camps were guarded by units which were partially integrated in the *Waffen-SS*. Riedweg also visited *SS* troops fighting in the East. He must have known about the Holocaust, from Himmler either mentioning it directly or indirectly. He was clearly in the know. These and other Nazi atrocities seem not to have disturbed him.[7]

After the war, Franz Riedweg resided in Munich as a physician. He remained politically active in the Pan-European *Liga* and founded the German *Gesellschaft für Wehrkunde* with Felix Steiner and Ewald-Heinrich von Kleist-Schmenzin. He passed away in 2005 in Munich. LW

Ethnic Germans: the *Volksdeutsche*

Volksdeutsche were, in Nazi terminology, Germans living beyond the borders of the *Reich*, in contrast to Imperial Germans (*Reichsdeutsche*) who were Germans living within the borders of Germany. The term *Auslandsdeutsche* referred to German citizens living abroad. By German estimates, some 30 million *Volksdeutsche* and *Auslandsdeutsche* were living outside the *Reich*. Many *Volksdeutsche* had been living in Central Europe since the 18th century, when foreign governments invited Germans to settle in Rumania (Transylvania), Hungary, Serbia (Western Banat), Slovakia, Russia, Bessarabia, Poland, the Baltic States and the later Yugoslavia, in order to repopulate regions whose numbers were reduced by the Ottoman Empire or by disease. German craftsmen, tradesman and settlers were especially attractive to invite to these countries. Peter the Great brought many Germans into Russian government service, and also German engineers to construct his new capital, St Petersburg.

Ethnic Germans (*Volksdeutsche*) from Rumania, belonging to a crew of a *SPW* 215/9 *"Stummel"* with 7.5cm cannon, from the *5./SS-Pz.Aufklärungsabteilung "Nordland"* in Ingria, January 1944.

Officers and men from the *Regiment "Norge"* looking out over the flat, marshy and wooded winter landscape of Ingria in January 1944. The trenches are protected by logs and camouflaged by spruce-twigs. The officers are wearing the new reversible winter camouflage suit, introduced by the *SS-Führungshauptamt* on 1 October 1943. The marshy Ingrian terrain between the Estonian border and Leningrad favoured defensive warfare, but any major Soviet armed breakthrough could not reasonably be intercepted by Army Group North as it had very few reserves.

A *"Nordland"* artillery crew photographed in Ingria beside their heavy 15cm *Feldhaubitze 18*. Due to its limited range, this howitzer was supplied with a rocket-driven type of shell that increased the range up to 18.2km. After initial use by the Soviets, grenade-firing weapons (artillery and mortars) often became the backbone in every act of warfare. Access to experienced fire controllers with radio or telephone in the forward lines was vital.

A typical view of the Oranienbaum Front with its wooded, snowy scenery in January 1944. The static German-Soviet front in the Baltic States had not changed much from 194244, with the exception of the steady stream of reinforcements that reached the Soviet forces. Additionally, the *Luftwaffe* had lost control of the skies over the entire Eastern Front. While the ordinary German infantry divisions normally lacked both mobility and anti-tank firepower, the Soviet rifle divisions had been increasingly mechanized, mainly due to the deliverance of equipment such as Studebaker lorries from the US.

A heavy 15cm *Feldhaubitze 18* from *"Nordland"* at the Oranienbaum Front in January 1944. During the subsequent battle of Narva, the artilllery of the *III. (germ.) SS-Panzer-Korps*, due to the German inferiority against the Red Army in manpower and fire strength, developed an effective and flexible barrage fire from one sector to another.

A grenadier group from the *11. Kompanie* of *Regiment "Norge"* in the village of Sinkowitzy at the Oranienbaum Front. Commander of the *11. Kompanie* was *SS-Hauptsturmführer* Karl-Heinz Reinecke.

Two *"Nordland"* officers are stuck in the snow behind the Oranienbaum Front, with their VW *Kübelwagen* behind, in December 1943.

Catherine the Great (herself of German extraction) also invited Germans to settle along the Volga River.

The treaty of Versailles separated *Volksdeutsche* in former Prussian provinces from Germany, and other large German ethnic groups within the former Austro-Hungarian Empire now found themselves as citizens in newly erected Slavic or Magyar national states, and Rumania. After the Nazis came to power in Germany in 1933, they erected a party organ, the *Volksdeutsche Mittelstelle* (Ethnic German Liason Agency) under the *SS*, to coordinate all issues connected with the *Volksdeutsche*. Nazi propaganda deliberately and aggressively depicted the *Volksdeutsche* as being harassed and suffering oppression from their national governments (a classic example being the Czech Sudetenland) to help legitimize Nazi aggression.

About 300,000 ethnic Germans from German-occupied or satellite countries in Eastern Europe, categorized by the Nazis as *Volksdeutsche*, joined the *Waffen-SS*. They were especially frequent in the *7. SS-Freiwilligen-Gebirgsdivision "Prinz Eugen"* (with ethnic Germans from Serbia) and in the *III. (germ.) SS-Panzer-Korps*, the majority being conscripted involuntarily after an initial volunteer movement for *Volksdeutsche* to join the *Waffen-SS*. From September 1942, Himmler did not only succeed in recruiting younger *Volksdeutsche* from the Banat in Serbia, but also conscript all male *Volksdeutsche* in the so-called *Deutsche Mannschaft*, a paramilitary militia for domestic security missions. Other groups of *Volksdeutsche* served in the German *Wehrmacht* or remained in the Rumanian Army. During the German disaster at Stalingrad, thousands of *Volksdeutsche* who, still serving as soldiers in the Rumanian front units that were crushed by the Red Army during the encirclement of Stalingrad, spontaneously left their Rumanian Army units and joined the *Wehrmacht*. They remained there, although the Rumanian General Staff protested vividly to the *OKW* on the matter. The Rumanian Army had for years been notorious for, in many cases, treating their *Volksdeutsche* recruits in a badgering way, which of course simplified matters for Himmler's recruiting parties to make the alternative service for *Volksdeutsche* in the *Waffen-SS* more attractive.

After Second World War, the 19-year old Rumanian *Volksdeutsche*, Hans Hedrich, described his situation:

> Born in 1924 in Mediasch (Siebenbürgen), I volunteered for the *Waffen-SS* in 1943. I wanted to contribute to the German people's struggle for existence, as the war was described for us at that time. There was also pressure against us from the organization "*Deutsche Volksgruppe* in Rumania" and also from our local social context. I was attached to the *SS-Panzer-Aufklärungsabteilung "Nordland"* after being trained in Grafenwöhr. My personal opinion was that the training was unnecessary and exaggeratedly harsh. But generally, there existed no problems between the *Reichsdeutsche*, us *Volksdeutsche* and the Scandinavian volunteers.

Himmler's fanatically racial, chaotic and contradictory ethnic politics in the traditional *Volksdeutsche* regions of the Balkans and South-Eastern Europe did not only catastrophically drain the century-old multiculture of German settlements in these areas by conscription to the *Waffen-SS*, but also culturally destroyed them.

After the German defeat, the *Volksdeutsche* in the *Waffen-SS* who were captured by the Red Army or were still living in countries with their new brutal communist regimes, were harshly punished and sent for compulsory labour in the Soviet Union (including tens of thousands of women capable of labour) or exiled to the Baragan Steppes. Those who were, by communist ethnic cleansing, expelled from Eastern European countries were naturalized by the West German state. Although major parts of former *Volksdeutsche* emigrated from, for example, Rumania, in the 1980s, remnants of the ethnic German community still survive today in the Rumanian province of Siebenbürgen (Transylavania) or in Upper Silesia (Poland). LW

Franz Bereznyak, ethnic German from Rumania and later *SS-Unterscharführer* in the "Swedish Company" (Lennart Westberg's archive).

With tenfold superiority, the Soviets broke through the positions of the *Luftwaffen-Feld-Divisionen* and threatened the positions of "*Nordland*". *SS-Panzer-Aufklärungsabteilung 11* was employed everywhere as a fire brigade, wherever things got too hot. We attacked at Kostalitzi. It was our first baptism of fire. For many it was also their last. But we succeeded in stopping the Russians. Thanks to that, our comrades from *SS-Panzergrenadier-Regiment "Norge"* and the *4. SS-Freiwilligen-Panzergrenadier-Brigade "Nederland"* could withdraw. We suffered great losses and almost every one of the survivors was slightly or severely wounded. We were only able to break our way through at night.

Fritz Höpfinger, *SS-Oberscharführer* and platoon commander in the *SS-Panzer-Aufklärungsabteilung 11 "Nordland"*, 1943–44 (Lennart Westberg's archives)

We were grouped into our first firing positions in the Alt-Bor area. Snow covered the ground and there was a winter chill. I, myself, dragged the power line out to the battery location, drawing it through very thinly forested terrain. My radio operator, who was with me, carried the equipment. We had just barely established the battery position in the snow on the edge of the woods and located the target, when contact with the firing position was broken. My radio-operator, *SS-Panzergrenadier* Heber, had to follow the line and find the break which had probably been caused by mortar fire. Some considerable time passed without my having contact with him. Finally, I followed the line back. It passed through bushes and sparse forest. After a short while, I found Heber on his knees with the line in his hand. He had been shot in the head and was dead. This meant that there were hidden snipers nearby. Shortly afterwards, a shot passed through my hat, but it only left a surface wound. Finally, the communication-connection was again in working order and we could finally begin our first firing mission.

Danes in the *Waffen-SS*

Contrary to other Nazi-occupied European countries, Denmark was able to keep its federal institutions, army and parliament intact from 1940 to August 1943, when the Germans dissolved them.[8] Out of 144 members of parliament, only eight could be considered as reliable collaborationists with the Germans, the most cooperative political faction being the *DNSAP* (*Dansk Nationalsocialistisk Arbejderparti*), the strongest out of 24 right-wing and Nazi Danish parties from 1930–45. It was founded in 1930 and its party leader (*Förer*) between 1930 and 1945 was Dr Fritz Clausen (1893–1947). The main ideology of the *DNSAP* and that of Clausen was practically identical with the German *NSDAP* and Adolf Hitler.[9] Although German support for Clausen was, for various reasons, somewhat restricted (the *Reich* plenipotentiary *Gruppenführer* Dr Werner Best described Clausen as an "incalculable alcoholic"), the *DNSAP* administrated two important organized potentials for the *SS* (this being a pattern in other collaborationist Nazi parties in occupied Europe as well, indicating the Nazi movement as primarily a phenomenon of the youth): its paramilitary party troop, the *SA* (*Storm Afdelinger*), and the *DNSAP* Youth organization (*Nationalsocialistiske Ungdom*), both of which served as a recruiting source for the *Waffen-SS* from 1940–45.

SS propaganda for Danish volunteers to join the *SS-Standarte "Nordland"* started in May 1940. The response was, however, weak, with only 216 Danes serving in the *SS-Division "Wiking"* (the *SS-Standarte "Nordland"* being integrated into that division in late 1940) at the beginning of the Nazi military campaign against the Soviet Union in June 1941. As the *SS*, the *DNSAP* and also the Danish government supported and recruited Danish volunteers (among them 115 Danish officers) to a "national" legion for the Eastern Front (the *Freikorps Danmark*), the number of Danes in German uniform rose: 1,066 Danes serving in the *Freikorps* in December 1941, the majority being members of, or sympathizers with, the *DNSAP*. Those Danes who did not sympathize with the *DNSAP* volunteered instead for the Finnish Army against the USSR.[10] In May 1943, the *Freikorps Danmark* was dissolved and used as a nucleus for the new *SS-Panzergrenadier-Regiment "Danmark"* within the *III. (germ.) SS-Panzer-Korps*.[11] Apart from this new *SS-Panzer-Korps*, several Danes served in various other *Waffen-SS* units, mainly in the *SS-Panzer-Division "Wiking"* (177 Danes in the summer of 1944). In total, around 16,000 Danes applied to serve in the *Waffen-SS* and 8,000 were selected and actually served as *SS* volunteers on the Eastern Front between 1940 and 1944, among them 2,000 men from the German minority in North Schleswig. Of these Danes, 3,890 were killed in action against the Red Army. Consequently, the Danes in the *SS* had a higher causalty rate compared with Danish losses in the war against Prussia in 1864. LW

Björn Heisholdt, Norwegian volunteer in the *SS-Panzergrenadier Regiment "Norge"* (Tommy Natedal's archive)

After a while there came orders that we should equip ourselves. We took down skis, sleighs and weapons from the lorries. Under command of *Untersturmführer* Eirik Mytting, our heavy platoon soon was under ski-march. We took a forest road, pretty narrow but easy to advance on. We had orders to reach a small depression in the terrain near a village a couple of kilometres ahead. There we met soldiers from the *Luftwaffe* that had been attacked by the Russians and separated from their unit, one of the *Luftwaffen-Feld-Divisionen*. At the same time, we heard salvoes from machine guns and submachine guns nearby, from the sound it was German weapons. Behind us, where we had left our lorries, our divisional artillery had regrouped and shot salvoes over our heads. The answer was sporadic Soviet artillery which indicated that they had not installed any artillery observers or were uncertain where we were. The company commander had been called to a meeting with the battalion commander and meanwhile we secured our flanks under experienced NCOs. In the edge of a wood we found an abandoned German anti-tank gun with destroyed optical sights and cartridges around, probably abandoned by the *Luftwaffe* soldiers. It began to darken and among some villages in the distance we could see dark silhouettes, probably Russians. At the same time we heard the noice of motors from tanks, the screech of treads in the woods and darkness ahead; it seemed to be stuck. As so often your spine chilled when one heard tank motors, especially as our platoon had no anti-tank weapons. After New Year's Eve we had heard about such a weapon, the *Panzerfaust*, which was effective up to 30 metres. The day before, some men from the platoon had been sent to the divisional staff to learn how to use that weapon, but we had no use of that in our situation. We had heard that a bundle of hand grenades could knock out a tank but it demanded of course that you came quite close to the colossus.

After a short while the company commander came back. He had orders from Vogt to advance against the village ahead and retake it from the Russians with an assault attack. The village was situated at an important crossroad. We were promised support from the heavy weapons from the 4 Company during the attack. Vogt's idea of our first position to start the attack did not coincide with my own ideas, as we then could have reached our objective unseen and come much closer before the assault. But we began to advance. Two hundred metres ahead we approached

Long columns of retreating German troops in Ingria from various units of Army Group North, heading for the new defensive line at the Narva River. Despite Adolf Hitler's strict "no retreat" order to the CO of Army Group North, Georg von Küchler, his Chief of Staff, Eberhard Kinzel, took the initiative to advise the CO of Eighteenth Army, Georg Lindemann, to begin a withdrawal on 27 January 1944. The retreating German units made for the strategically important Ingrian town of Kingisepp (Jamburg) and the crossings over the River Luga. Luckily, the Sixteenth German Army in the south could make an orderly withdrawal, thanks to a lack of aggressive initiative from the Soviet Volkhov Front. Thereby, the Sixteenth Army could even support the hard-pressed

Eighteenth Army, whose infantry strength by now had shrunk by two-thirds, with substantial units, like the 8th *Jäger* Division, *Sturmgeschütz-Abteilung 303* and the 58th Infantry Division. Note the horses among the retreating German troops. During the war, the German Army fully occupied its engineering industry by manufacturing *panzers*, aeroplanes and U-boats, and therefore lacked motor vehicles for transports. It thus took more horses into service than the German Army had done between 1914 and 1918. The Americans and the British were the only war participants that were able to supply their troops at the front alone by motorized transports, and this thanks to the enormous production capacity of the USA's oil and car corporations.

On 29 January 1944, General Walter Model (shown here as field marshal), succeeded Georg von Küchler as CO of Army Group North. Adolf Hitler sacked von Küchler after the Soviets had successfully reached the Luga River at the end of January. Model had shown great talent and capacity in defensive warfare in command of Ninth Army in 1942–43, and was now dispatched to rescue the situation in the north. Model handled Hitler's stubbornness well and, like General Ferdinand Schörner, had his respect. Interested in defensive theories during his sevice in the *Reichswehr* between the wars, Model became a pioneer on the Eastern Front with his concept of a "shield and sword" defence. On 23 February 1944, Model concentrated all German forces in and along the Narva bridgehead under the newly formed Army Detachment Narva (*Armee-Abteilung Narva*) under General Johannes Friessner. He subsequently became the direct superior commander for *SS-Obergruppenführer* Felix Steiner and the Germanic *SS-Panzer-Korps*.

Two SS soldiers from the *Brigade "Nederland"* has reached the city of Narva. They are wearing the new 1943 reversible winter camouflage suit. The city proved a strategical key to hinder the Red Army in its advance along the Estonian coast to Tallinn, thereby capturing the oil shale plant on the Estonian shore of the Gulf of Finland. Aware of Finland's peace negotiations with the USSR, Hitler was, for political reasons, forced to keep Estonia under German control. (NARA)

Two photos of truly anonymous victims of war: driven out of their homes and village in mid-winter to face an uncertain fate.

The MG 42 machine gun

The Red Army nicknamed the MG 42 "Hitler's electrical gun" due to its high rate of fire. The British called it the "Spandau" after the metal stamp on some machine guns (from the city district in Berlin). The 7.92x57mm caibre gun weighed 10.6kg and had a practical fire-rate of 1,200 rounds per minute (the British, Soviet and US equivalents could only manage around 600rpm). The long barrel and the straight visor contributed to a high accuracy of aim: the effective range of fire was 1,000 metres. The weapon was well adapted to mass production and cheap to manufacture. Fabricated out of stamped metal, the new MG 42 required 50 percent less man hours and cost 25 percent less (250 Reichsmark) to manufacture than its predecessor, the MG 34 (312 Reichsmark) general purpose machine gun that was manufactured by *Rheinmetall* and *Mauser-Werke* between 1936 and 1945, with 354,000 examples. The constructor of the MG 42, the engineer Werner Gruner from the *Metall- und Lackwarenfabrik Johannes Grossfuss*, was an expert in punching metal and mass production but had no previous experience in weapon construction. Gruner participated in a six-week *Wehrmacht* course in machine-gunning, where he also experienced what the common soldier expected and thought was essential about a new machine gun. Gruner also minimized the number of costly precision parts in the MG 42, simplified the punching metal process and thereby economized its mass production. The unique quick-change barrel system (for when the gun overheated after 250 rounds or around 12 seconds of fire) permitted an unusually consistent and prolonged firing. Experienced gunners shifted barrels in just five to seven seconds. However, the method of barrel change made the MG 42 unsuitable for mounting in German *panzers*, with exception of the *Jagdpanzer IV*. After replacing the MG 34, over 414,964 examples of the MG 42 were produced by the *Mauser-Werke* from 1942–45. German officers were not entirely in favour of the new MG 42, believing that it would result in waste of ammunition. For the grenadiers using the MG 42, the high rate of fire was invaluable as it permitted the soldiers to fire a deluge of bullets during those fragments of seconds that targets are usually in sight, before quickly taking cover. US Army authorities were so impressed by the MG 42 that they developed their own version of it, the T 24; this, however, was abandoned due to ammunition problems. After the Second World War, the MG 42 was in use during various conflicts in the Middle East and Africa. When West Germany was elected a member of NATO in 1955, the German *Bundeswehr* commissioned *Rheinmetall* to update the MG 42 to the standardized NATO-ammunition calibre 7.62x51mm. The result was the MG1, which two years later became the MG3, which, in various forms, is still in use by the *Bundeswehr*.

Unterscharführer Helmut Seidel, who commanded an *SPW Sd.Kfz. 231*. On 26 January 1944, northwest of the village of Gubanizy in Ingria, he managed, at a distance of 100 metres, with his crew and the vehicle's tiny 2cm cannon, to destroy a Soviet tank which was attacking the regimental HQ of Colonel Paul Wengler of the 227th Infantry Division.

something of a stone wall under the snow. At the same time we saw a column of Russians, marching in the snow against a hill, probably to dig out new trenches. We put in order one heavy machine gun and two other machine guns to respond to any enemy fire. The platoon leader gave the orders to open fire and the Russian group tumbled down, dead or wounded. I gave the orders for my men to take off the skis. Many of the ethnic Germans had difficulties advancing on ski without noise. Now came the first rounds of enemy fire from the Russians, and the first wounded on our side were carried back. Russian machine guns took part in the game while we waited for support from the heavy weapons in the 4 Company of "*Norge*", but we heard nothing of the sort. We had not seen any of our artillery observers. At the same time we heard that our company commander had been wounded and his staff sergeant had been killed. We fired upon a Soviet machine gun nest with tracers and observed that our bullets were in the right direction; the target was destroyed. Some of our wounded called for help in the wood and out in the field. Two of our strongest men sacrified themselves and fetched the wounded with sleighs. One of them got a shot in the back that hit his rucksack but did not go through it. The Russians tried to perform an assault attack over a field in the wood and both our machine guns fired all they could. We could see the Russian bayonets when they came running. While parts of our platoon were destroyed by

SS-Sturmbannführer Fritz Vogt was CO of the first battalion of *Regiment "Norge"* during the rearguard fighting in Ingria in January 1944, where his battalion was pracically annihilated. Vogt died on 3 April 1945 from wounds durng the final battles in Austria as CO of the reconnaissance battalion *5. "Wiking"*. Vogt often went ahead of his men during the most severe fighting, but was also known as an officer who did not care for the losses of his own unit. Norwegians in his unit characterized him, both during and after the war, as a psychopath. Vogt was a typical exponent for the ideal type of *SS* officer: daring, ruthless and aggressive, coming from simple and uneducated backgrounds and being catapulted through the *Waffen-SS* hierarchy to his sole career by military abilities and absolute loyalty to the Nazi ideology. Those ideologically influenced German recruits or aspirants without an undergraduate exam often went to the *Waffen-SS*, as they would be allowed an officer's exam due to other informal qualifications (leadership of men, ideology etc), while those with a university exam often went to the *SD*.

the Russians, the rest of us succeeded in stopping up their attacks with machine-gun fire, and finally we got a pause.

Dutch in the *Waffen-SS*

In 1931, the *Nationaal-Socialistische-Beweging* (*NSB*), the Dutch counterpart to the German Nazi Party, was founded. Among the founders were the future Dutch right-wing and Nazi leader Adrian Mussert (1894–1946), who before the war advocated a Greater *Niederländisches Reich* (*Groot-Nederland*), uniting Dutch and Flemings, the Belgian-Congo, the Dutch colonies and even South Africa (Dutch descendants speaking *Afrikaans*). After the German occupation of the Netherlands in 1940, Mussert was confirmed leader (Dutch: *Leider*) of the *NSB* as the only permitted political party in the country. Mussert was, however, treated with contempt by the *Reichskommissar* Arthur Seyss-Inquart and also by the *SS* as being too critical of the "Greater Germanic" ideal. Instead, Himmler favoured the leading *NSB*-functionary Rost van Tonningen, who uncompromisingly voted for the Netherlands being incorporated into the *Gross Germanisches Reich*. The membership of the *NSB* during the war rose to a figure of around 100,000. As described in the chapter "From Legions to *SS-Panzergrenadier-Regiments*", the *SS* actively recruited Dutch volunteers to the *Waffen-SS* in 1940 and enrolled these into the *SS-Standarte "Nordwest"*. After the Nazi attack on the USSR in the summer of 1941, Dutch volunteers formed the *SS-Legion Niederlande*, which in 1943 was dissolved and partly reconstructed into the *4. SS-Freiwilligen-Panzergrenadier-Brigade "Nederland"* (later nominally upgraded to the *23. SS-Freiwilligen-Panzergrenadier-Division "Nederland"*). Some 25,000 Dutch served in the *Waffen-SS* in the Second World War, while 4,000 served in the *Germaansche SS en Nederland*, 800 in the German Army, 1,500 in the *Kriegsmarine* and 10,000 in the Organisation Todt, *SS-Postschutz* etc.[12] LW

Alfred Weiss, *SS-Unterscharführer* in the anti-tank platoon of the *SS-Panzer-Aufklärungsabteilung 11 "Nordland"* (Lennart Westberg's archives)

I heard the warning cry: "Tanks!" ... and immediately gave the order to ready the guns for firing ... We did not need to wait long before it was time. Four tanks came at high speed along the left road into the village, with only a short space between them, down the hillside toward us. The first vehicle began shooting its gun wildly and managed to hit my unmanned *SPW* which was parked unprotected on the right-hand side of the road. It was apparently the last audacious act of this tank gunner. An instant later, as he was about to pass us and enter the village, I gave the command, "Fire!" which marked his end. The salvo hit along the left side of his tank, opening up a large hole. It stopped immediately, blocking our field of fire. This allowed tank number two to go around it on the right-hand side and escape. The third and fourth vehicles met the same fate as the first. After a couple of minutes, the battle was over, or so we thought, since there was no sign of any other tank as far the eye could see. This however, was a major mistake on our part. It never occurred to us that this may merely have been an advance patrol. After approximately 10 to 15 minutes, this possibility became abundantly clear: halfway over to the right, roughly level with the village, just behind the crown of a hill, a widely spread formation of heavy tanks thundered towards the village. They were undoubtedly not prepared for the waiting anti-tank platoon's three other anti-tank guns. As soon as the heavy tanks went over the crown and onto the hill's front slope, they were fired on by all four of our 7.5cm anti-tank guns. The distance was well within our range and every shot hit its target. The tank formation was immediately thrown into enormous confusion. When the command tank, apparent by the profusion of antennas on its turret, was hit, the enemy was reduced to panic. No one dared to continue the advance. They drove back and forth, from right to left again. This tactic eventually caused them to ram into each other and crash.

Fritz Höpfinger, platoon commander in the *SS-Panzer-Aufklärungsabteilung 11 "Nordland"* (Lennart Westberg's archive)

A lot happened before the infantry-gun platoon experienced new operations in the area of Gubanitzy. I had redeployed the platoon in the terrain. The weather was overcast and snow lay on the ground. Accompanied by the messenger, Maier, I reconnoitred the terrain and looked to choose our next location. An explosion put a stop to my endeavours: I never heard the blast from the detonating shell. But a piece of shrapnel from the right struck me in my throat, pressed through my gullet and lodged in my tonsils, just a millimetre from its base. My white snowsuit became dyed in red. Maier came crawling, I was expecting to lose consciousness and therefore asked him to tell my wife what had happened. My voice was not very strong, because one of my vocal chords had also been hit. But nothing happened and Maier retrieved a tank that was nearby. I asked the driver to take me back to the platoon combat position. I handed over command to *Sturmmann* Krämer. Taking leave of the troops was difficult: I was around 10 years older then they were and something of a father-figure to these young men. They stood there, arms hanging, and I was forced to leave them. That moment will remain with me forever.

Anton Ging, ethnic German in the *SS-Panzer-Aufklärungsabteilung "Nordland"* (Lennart Westberg's archive)

After the arrival of the third company, *SS-Panzer-Aufklärungsabteilung "Nordland"*, in the middle of December 1943, we were stationed in a minor village. There we were equipped with new, semi-tracked armoured vehicles, but also with armoured vehicles that were armed with 20mm cannons and an MG 34 in a movable turret. I was the driver in such a vehicle, the commander was a *SS-Rottenführer* and the gunner was a Swede. We stood near a 7.5cm PaK vehicle and an anti-tank cannon from the 5th Company. Through the turret I saw how *SS-Untersturmführer* Langendorf gave orders to his men during the battle. In the evening, we and some other *SPW*s from the 3rd Company acted as rearguard. Our *SPW* was the last to leave Gubanitsy. During the motorized march back, I saw how our Swedish platoon chief, *SS-Oberscharführer* Walter Nilsson, walked aside the column in the snow. In the morning, I heard that he was killed during the night.

On 27 January, we had reached Volosovo and we got the mission to go for a scouting patrol if the Russians had reached the next village. We got cover from another *SPW* with *Panzer* grenadiers. We went along a narrow road and around100 metres before the village, I drove aside the road to give supporting fire. The other half-track went further. Until now everything was calm and quite. The other *SPW* returned to us when suddenly "Ivan" hammered against us with everything he had. Luckily for us, the Russians had only infantry weapons. I turned our half-track and was about to give full gas away, when the vehicle did not move an inch! Our half-track had stuck on a big rock. The infantry fire became more disturbing and we had to abandon the half-track. First the commander in the turret, then the Swedish gunner and then me. We ran, crouching for the other *SPW* that waited for us. The Swede was hit in the back and fell. We two others went back for him and pulled him with us, got him into the other *SPW* through the rear door and took cover in the half-track. After driving 300 metres, having reached a covering wood, we saw how our *SPW* suddenly exploded. We left the Swedish gunner at a field hospital but he died shortly afterwards from severe wounds in the lungs. After the battle at Volosovo, the 3rd Company had only 25 men who were not wounded or dead.

> **The Soviet Mosin-Nagant rifle**
>
> The standard service rifle of the Red Army was the Mosin-Nagant Model 1891/30. The rifle fired a 7.62x54mm rimmed cartridge in a five-round magazine. The rifle, introduced in 1891 to the Tsar's Army, was developed by the Russian Colonel Sergei Mosin and, with small adjustments in the magazine, designed by the Belgian weapons manufacturer Leon Nagan. It has in Western literature usually been named "Mosin-Nagant". In the Thirties, the rifle was standardized and modernized to the Red Army Model 91/30.

Mass starvation in the besieged Leningrad

Leningrad (today's St Petersburg) was, next to Moscow, the largest and most important city in the USSR, housing three million inhabitants. During the German offensive through the Baltics, the German *Heeresgruppe Nord* reached the outskirts of Leningrad in early September 1941, but never succeeded in conquering the city. In coordination with Finnish troops, the Germans could cut off the Tsars' old capital from all connections by land. The supply of Leningrad was only possible by water and ice across the southern section of Lake Ladoga. Until the major Soviet offensive on 14 January 1944 pushed back the German troops, including the *III. (germ.) SS-Panzer-Korps*, to Lake Peipus, at least one million of Leningrad's inhabitants died from starvation, cold, sickness, bombs or shelling. Today in the West, this remains a largely forgotten crime and a tragedy on an enormous scale.[13] In case the Nazis had taken Leningrad in 1941–42, Hitler had ordered the complete and brutal destruction of the city as the "origin of Bolshevism": a fate like that of ancient Carthage.

In a recent interview with the author (LW), the *volksdeutsche* (ethnic German) from Rumania, Karl B. (formerly serving in the *SS-Division "Nordland"*), said retrospectively: "If I had known of the horrible mass starvations caused by the Germans during the siege of Leningrad, I would have never volunteered for the *Waffen-SS* from Rumania in 1943."

The genocide of the Baltic Jews

The annihilation of the European Jews also included the Baltic States. Around 300,000 Jews, or nearly the whole Jewish population in the Baltic countries, were murdered by the Nazis. The Nazis also found willing domestic helpers in the Holocaust from Baltic volunteer personnel, organized in the late summer of 1941 in police or security units. Especially in Latvia, the *SS* and *SD* could essentially rely on Latvian units for the mass shootings of Latvian Jews, including Latvian *Hilfsmannschaften*, guarding the Riga ghetto and participating in the liquidation of Jewish ghettos as far east as Borisow.[14] In the period between 4 June and 28 November 1941, *SS-Standartenführer* Karl Jäger and his *Einsatzkommando 3* murdered 137,346 Jewish men, women and children in Lithuania alone; in total, 195,000 Lithuanian Jews were killed in the Holocaust. Of Estonia's Jewish population, 75 percent succeeded in fleeing to the Soviet Union before the German occupation in 1941. Of the remaining Estonian Jews, according to most recent calculation, all were killed – a total of 929 people – by the *Einsatzkommando 1A* under *SS-Obersturmbannführer* Martin Sandberger. Estonia was declared *"Judenfrei"* at the Wannsee Conference in early 1942. In Estonia, the Germans also murdered 5001,000 Roma and Sinti.

The Baltic States were chosen to serve as a killing ground for deported European Jews. Some 10,000 Jews from other European countries were killed in Estonia after having been deported to camps there from Eastern Europe. The Nazi governmental agencies established 22 concentration camps in occupied Estonian territory for using European Jews as slave labourers. The largest camp was erected in the Estonian city of Vaivara, which served as a transit camp for 20,000 Jews from Lithuania and Latvia, with associate minor camps (*Aussenlager*) in nearby Klooga, Narva, Hungerburg, Wiwikond, Reval, Auvere, Lagedi, Kalevi-Liva, Jagala, Jöwi and Kiviöli. Deportation trains, consisting of European Jews from the occupied countries, were in mid-1943 directed to Estonia in order to supply the oil shist mines with compulsory labour. As the Red Army advanced deeper into Estonia from mid-1944, at least 1,800 Jewish inmates were massacred in the autumn of 1944 in Klooga and Lagedi.[15]

The Nazis also killed around 6,000 ethnic Estonians and 1,000 ethnic Russians, accused of being communist sympathizers. Additionally, around 25,000 Soviet POWs, held by the *Wehrmacht* in Estonia, did not survive German captivity. LW

The Estonian governmental Meri Commission established in 2001 that Estonian citizens and agencies cooperated towards *SS* mass-murders during the German occupation from 1941–44. The Estonian police and security forces had a considerable self-governed status under German rule and were directly involved in the murders and deportations of Baltic Jews. The Meri Commission surmised that out of 10,000 members of the Estonian Home Guard, the *Omakaitse*, 1,000–1,200 persons were directly involved in crimes against humanity in the form of murders of alleged or suspected communists and Estonian Jews from the late summer of 1941. Personnel from the Estonian Legion and the respective brigade in the *Waffen-SS*, together with Estonian police battalions, escorted as guards on deportation trains and served as camp guards in Estonia and Poland. Such personnel also contributed to deportations of civilians from Poland and White Russia to Germany. Other Estonian police battalions are mentioned by the Meri Commission as active in other mass crimes under German command. Many of these Estonian police, military and paramilitary units were later merged into the 20th Estonian *SS*-Division that fought at Narva in 1944 within the *III. (germ.) SS-Panzer-Korps*. The Meri Commission wrote as a summary in its report:

> It is unjust that an entire nation should be criminalized because of the actions of some of its citizens: but it is equally unjust that its criminals should be able to shelter behind a cloak of victimhood. In that light we might see today's international and Baltic debate on the existence of various Estonian national veteran units from the former *Waffen-SS* in present Estonia and Latvia.[16]

Notes

1 Bernd Wegner, *Auf dem Wege zur pangermanischen Armee*, p.111.

2 From 1941, the CO of Army Group North, Georg von Kuechler, supported National Socialistic politics in the East (e.g. immediate executions of the Red Army´s political commissars). On the other hand, during the campaign against Poland in 1939, Kuechler expressed the outmost criticism against *SS* mass murders, calling *SS*-units in the Polish campaign "a disgrace to the German armed forces" (*ein Schandfleck der Armee*); Jörgen Förster, *The German Military Image of Russia*, in: Mark Ericson, *Russia´s War* (London, Weidenfeld & Nicolson), p. 125.

3 Already in the Finnish-Soviet Winter War of 1939–40, 727 Norwegian volunteers served at the Finnish Front within the Swedish Volunteer Corps; Gyllenhaal & Westberg, *Swedes at War*, p.219. For a brilliant and pioneering study of the partly opposing "Germanic" politics between Quisling, the *SS* and the *Reichskommissariat* in terms of volunteers to the *Waffen-SS* in occupied Norway, see the recent book in German of Sigurd Sörlie´s Norwegian dissertation: "Sonnenrad oder Hakenkreuz. Norweger in der Waffen-SS 1941-1945" (Schöningh Verlag, Paderborn, 2019).

4 Neulen, *An deutscher Seite*, p.153.

5 Dr Riedweg's speech in Bad Tölz: BA NS 24/II. "The first intention was to send me to the *SS-Totenkopf-Division* as punishment, but

Steiner intervened and altered my transfer to his *III. (germ.) SS-Panzer-Korps*"; Dr Franz Rieweg to LW in letter of 24.8.1979.

6 Marco Wyss, *Un Suisse au Service de la SS – Franz Riedweg 1907–2005* ("A Swiss serving in the SS") (Edition Alphil-Presses Universitaires Suisses Neuenberg, 2011).

7 SWI SwissInfo.ch, 4 February 2011.

8 A parallel being Nazi-occupied Hungary from March until October 1944.

9 In the 1943 parliamentary election, the *DNSAP* got 43,000 votes (2.1 percent and three MPs).

10 Bundgård Christensen, Poulsen & Scharff Smith, *Under hagekors og Dannebrog*, p.39.

11 See also the chapter in this volume, "From Legions to *SS-Panzergrenadier* Regiments", on the political disputes in the summer of 1943 about this "national" Danish Legion being integrated into a multinational "Germanic" regiment, led by a German regimental commander.

12 Neulen, *An deutscher Seite*, p.60.

13 Robert Gellately, *Lenin, Stalin and Hitler. The Age of Social Catastrophe*, p.491.

14 Helmut Krausnick & Hans-Heinrich Wilhelm, *Die Truppe des Weltanschauungskrieges. Die Einsatzgruppen der Sicherheitspolizei und des SD 1938–1942* (Stuttgart: 1981), p.597.

15 Krausnick & Wilhelm, *ibid.*, p.612.

16 *Estonia, 1940–1945: Reports of the Estonian International Commission for the Investigation of Crimes Against Humanity*; edited by Toomas Hiio, Meelis Maripuu and Indrek Paavel (Tallinn: 2005).

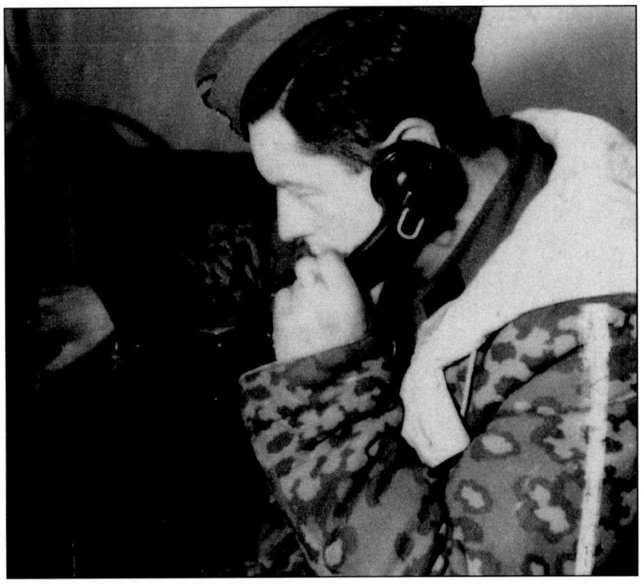

An *SS* signal man at his switchboard in a staff field HQ. The signal field combat arm consisted of various personnel, such as telephone line-men, radio-men, drivers, clerks, mechanics and the supply, cable construction and radio NCOs and officers, of whom many lost their lives under enemy fire.

An elderly *SS* supply NCO paints a number of *SS* steel helmets in winter camouflage white.

Above: an *SS-Panzergrenadier* in his trench in Ingria. Below are two *SS* men collecting a Christmas tree from the Ingrian woods.

An *SS* half-track from "*Nordland*" in Ingria with counter-attacking *SS-Panzergrenadiers* during the retreat westwards to Narva. (NARA)

SS-Panzergrenadiers, armed with Mauser rifles 98K, MP–40 sub-machine guns and *Panzerfausts*, trying to block the Soviet advance through Ingria in January 1944. (NARA)

Some of the surviving German or Nordic soldiers from the *7. Kompanie* of *SS-Regiment "Norge"* that on 26 January 1944 was completely cut off from their battalion, and for 16 days and nights had to march through wooded swamps to reach the German lines on 10 February.

Knut Bakken from Oslo was a member of the *NS* and studied at a business school before he joined the *Regiment "Nordland"* in late 1941. He fought in the East in the Artillery Regiment of *SS-Division "Wiking"*. Qualifying from *Junkerschule* Bad Tölz in March 1944, he served as an artillery officer in the *SS-Division "Nordland"* from Narva to Berlin from 1944–45, and was promoted to *SS-Untersturmführer* in June 1944. Bakken was captured by the Red Army during the battle for Berlin in 1945 and returned to Norway in 1947. He was sentenced to seven months in jail, and later worked as a cafe manager in Oslo.

Olaf Lindvig fought against the German invaders as an officer in 1940 but joined the *NS* in the autumn of that year. Becoming an instructor with the *Norges-SS* in 1940–41 in Elverum and Kongsvinger, he was wounded with the *Legion Norwegen* in 1942 and became Chief of Staff for *Germanske SS Norge*. In January 1944, Lindvig was wounded as *SS-Hauptsturmführer* and CO of the *1./SS-Regiment "Norge"*, and took up a senior position in the Norwegian State Police. After the war, he was sentenced to 12 years' imprisonment. He died in 2007 at the age of 89, in his native town of Fåvang, after a successful career as CEO of a concrete firm and a consultant with Securitas in Oslo.

Assault guns (*Sturmgeschütze*) from the *SS-Sturmgeschützabteilung 11 "Nordland"* at the Oranienbaum Front in Ingria, between December 1943 and January 1944. The *Sturmgeschütz III* (*StuG III.*was the most-produced armoured vehicle in the Third *Reich*, its concept going back to the First World War when the German infantry lacked the means of cracking enemy fortifications on

the Western Front. In 1935, the "father" of German assault artillery (*Sturmartillerie*), Erich von Manstein, proposed such units be established in a direct-fire support role for the infantry. This concept materialized in the *StuG III* during the Second World War.

Assault guns from the "*Nordland*" in Ingria between December 1943 and February 1944. These *Sturmgeschütze III Ausführung G* are partly painted in white winter camouflage, but not fitted with skirts to protect the transmission against Soviet anti-tank rifles and light weapons.

Continued below

One photo shows the repair of the main spring of a *StuG III*.The "*Nordland*" assault guns pictured are equipped with the 7.5cm *StuK 40 L/48* gun. Partly visible are the 7.92mm MG 34 machine guns, mounted on a shield on top of the superstructure for additional anti-infantry protection. The "*Nordland*" assault guns are of the type G (*Ausführung G; SdKfz 142/1*), of which 8,423 were produced between December 1942 and April 1945, representing the final and by far most common *StuG* of the Second World War.

A *Sturmgeschütz III Ausführung G* in winter camouflage in Ingria, during January 1944.

Officers from the *SS-Sturmgeschützabteilung "Nordland"* in a bunker or block-house at the Oranienbaum Front in Ingria. Sitting far right is the CO of this battalion, *SS-Hauptsturmführer* Ernst Roentsch (who was killed in action on 21 January 1944), and to the left is Carlotto von Renteln, CO of the battalion's *1. Kompanie*.

4

THE DEFENCE OF THE NARVA BRIDGEHEAD AND THE BATTLE FOR DORPAT AND THE BLUE HILLS (FEBRUARY–SEPTEMBER 1944) UNTIL THE GERMAN RETREAT OUT OF ESTONIA

In early March 1944, the Red Army's ground offensive against the Narva bridgehead paused and the Soviets instead subjected it to intense artillery and aerial bombardment. On 6–7 March, the old baroque city of Narva was almost completely destroyed by massive bombing raids. After two further major assaults by the Soviets on the lines east of the city, held by the units from the *Brigade "Nederland"*, and north-west of Narva, held by mixed "*Nordland*"-"*Nederland*" units, the mobile actions came to a halt in the Narva sector. The fighting focused on artillery and sniper duels for quite some time.

Erik Laerum: note the wings on his *SS* uniform as a former Captain in the Danish Flying Forces.

Erik Laerum, Danish/Norwegian artillery officer in the *SS-Panzergrenadier Regiment "Danmark"*

During the night our column continued its retreat to Narva. The wind blew hard and it was bitterly cold. We reached Narva immediately after midnight on 29 January 1944, and our arrival filled the peaceful city with misgivings of future ill fortune, misgivings which would soon prove justified. I got lodgings in the city with an elderly Estonian farmer who lived in the western outskirts of the city. As with most Estonians, he was no friend of the Germans, but when he heard that I came from Denmark, he became friendly and helpful.

Within two or three days after our troops had reached Narva, our commanders distributed the obligatory order that the city was to be held to the last man. This had on the Eastern Front been a current phrase which the soldiers did not pay any attention to. But for the regrettable inhabitants it was a deadly serious issue. They got orders to evacuate the city within three weeks and the evacuation began almost immediately. It was the saddest sight imaginable: women, children and elderly were in [the] majority but there were also men in their prime. The Russians had decimated the population when they occupied the city in 1940. Three thousand men with intellectual professions were brought "for questioning" and they were never seen again. It was 10 percent of the city's population of 30,000 inhabitants. The rest left in March 1944 and they never saw their ancient city again.

Otto Carius, company commander in the heavy *Armee Tiger-bataillon 502*

On 16 February 1944, I was transferred with two Tiger tanks to the area held by forces under *Oberst* Wengler, at

Otto Carius

Aerial photo of Narva, taken in 1940, from the north-west of the city. Before its destruction by Soviet aerial bombardment on 6–7 March 1944, the historic city of Narva was considered the most beautiful baroque city in Northern Europe. Narva (like Tallinn) was founded by Danish traders in the 13th century, who built a fortress on the west bank of the Narva River. From 1595-1704, Narva was in the possession of the Swedish Empire and heavily fortified under the warrior kings Charles X Gustav, Gustav II Adolf and Charles X. On the eastern shore of the Narva River, we see the Russian border fortress from the 14th century, Ivangorod, and directly opposite, on the southern shore, lies the fortress and tower of Hermansborg. The civilian population of Narva was, with short notice, evacuated from the city in February 1944. As the front line again approached the Baltic States, their population, disillusioned with German administration but on the other hand frightened of the Soviets' return, could only look on helplessly at what the near future would bring courtesy of their mighty neighbours. A soldier in the Latvian Legion wrote in early 1944: "We have no friends either in the east or the west. They all want to rule and be overlords."

Hermansborg before its destruction in 1944. Unfortunately for German forces, the east bank downstream of Narva rises rapidly, in comparison to the flat land on the western shore, which enabled the Soviets to direct artillery and mortar fire upon the German positions. Soviet snipers were also a plague for this reason.

Riigi between Narva and the Finnish Gulf. The purpose was to ward off Soviet attacks over the frozen Narva river. When I arrived, together with Wengler, at the command place of one of his battalion commanders, a Soviet attack was just being launched. Although "Ivan" had severe casualties, as he attacked over the river without cover, it was dangerous when the Soviets got hold of our shore and dug into our trenches. In that case they could only be thrown out by rapid counter-attacks.

Our Tigers supported our infantry during the counter-attack. But this must be done with the utmost care and precision in our firing to avoid bringing casualties into our own ranks. We drove our tanks 50 metres before the trenches, which mainly went zig-zag. From here we watched our infantry's counter-attack. When the soldiers had taken the first trench, the soldier in at the top waved at us and then we fired at the second trench, where the Russians sat, with our 8.8cm cannons and our machine guns. Thereafter, our infantry worked themselves forward and threw out the enemy.

At this point, the Soviet artillery interfered and made themselves present in an unpleasant way with heavy shelling. The eastern side of the Narva river was steep and from the heights, the Soviets could watch us like on a chess board. It often only lasted three minutes from the point our Tigers went forward, until we noticed the first firing from the Soviet anti-tank guns. Only by driving forward and backward, could we avoid being hit.

The *SS-Panzer-Abteilung "Hermann von Salza"*

The *SS-Panzer-Abteilung 11 "Hermann von Salza"* of the *11. SS-Freiwilligen-Panzergrenadier-Division "Nordland"* was originally planned as a regiment and began forming in early June 1943 at the Grafenwöhr training area in Upper Franconia. The *I. Abteilung* always remained with the division but, for various reasons, never reached the status of a fully equipped "classic" *Panzer-Abteilung*. The *II. Abteilung* formally existed with the division until the end of 1943, but was then detached to the Netherlands (Kampen) as a nucleus to form the heavy *SS-Panzer-Abteilung 103/503*, which in 1945 was attached to the *III. (germ.) SS-Panzer-Korps*. The remaining *I. Abteilung* was supplied with small arms, *Kübelwagen* and lorries etc., but with no tanks. The *SS-Panzer-Abteilung 11 "Hermann von Salza"* was the only *Waffen-SS* tank unit that was given an honorific title, reflected in a specific cuff-name.[3] On 1 May 1943, the *SS-Personalhauptamt* appointed *SS-Sturmbannführer* Paul-Albert Kausch as battalion commander for *"Hermann von Salza"*. Obersturmführer Rudolf Rott was battalion adjutant from June 1943 to January 1944.[4] Kausch attended a course in Paris and at Wünsdorf for battalion commanders of armoured and reconnaissance units. The battalion was supposed to be

Photo taken in the late Thirties from downstream Narva. To the left lies the fortress of Hermansborg, founded by the Danish in the 13th century and completed with its tower (*Hermannsfeste*) by the German Order and its *Ordenmeister* Hermann von Brüggenau-Hasenkamps. To the right is the Russian fortress of Ivangorod, initially erected in 1492 by the Grand Duke Ivan III. During the fighting for the Narva bridgehead, the western tower of Ivangorod housed parts of the brigade staff of *SS "Nederland"* (the Intelligence Section under *SS-Hauptsturmführer* Horst-Henning Kühn).

A street in central Narva with *SS* vehicles, probably close to one of the regimental staff from the *III. (Germ.) SS-Panzer Korps*. During the Soviet aerial bombardment on 6–7 March 1944, the *Regiment "Denmark"* alone lost 34 vehicles.

A unique photo from the eastern shore of the Narva River, taken at the same moment as multiple rockets from a Propagandawerfer 41 are launched by a German crew of *SS* War Correspondents. Each rocket weighed 3.3 kg and, instead of explosives, the rocket contained 0.5 kg of 250 propaganda leaflets to spread over Soviet trenches. This action was part of Operation "Wintermärchen" (Winter Tales) by the *SS-Standarte* "Kurt Eggers" in the Narva area. In the background are both the Russian Castle of Ivangorod and the ruined tower of Hermansborg.

The western part of Ivangorod was pulverized by Soviet aerial forces and artillery.

A street in Narva with typical baroque architecture, destroyed by the Soviet bombardment in March 1944.

Waffen-SS trenches south-east of Ivangorod, in the defence sector of the *SS-Panzergrenadier-Regiment 24 "Danmark"*, in spring 1944. Although the predominantly marshy or otherwise inaccessible Ingrian landscape around Narva favoured defensive warfare, a great handicap for the Germans was the lack of armour. The total tank strength of Army Group North was only 146 *panzers*, while the Soviet Marshals Govorov and Meretskov, commanding the attacking Leningrad and Volkhov Fronts (Army Groups), had a strength of 650 tanks.

The destruction caused in Hermansborg after Soviet shellings in March 1944.

Two partly destroyed famous buildings in central Narva in March 1944: on the left the "*Vana Apteek*" (Old Pharmacy) and immediately behind to the right the *Hotel du Nord*, which even after the Soviet bombing hosted many events for the *Waffen-SS* and *Wehrmacht*. The photograph was taken by the Swedish *SS* war correspondent Gösta Borg after the debris on the road had been partly cleared.

a *panzer* unit equipped with *Panzer IVs*, but it was never intended to deliver *Panzer Vs* (Panther tanks) to the unit.[5] The cadre of experienced officers and NCOs had previously mainly served in the *SS-Division "Wiking"*. The majority of the soldiers in the battalion were ethnic Germans from Rumania (Siebenbürgen and the Banat). Different courses took place for drivers, *Panzerkommandanten*, mechanics, etc., mainly at the *panzer* and mechanized schools of the German Army (*Panzer-Lehrabteilung* in Erlangen and Nürnberg, *Panzerttruppenschule* in Wünsdorf and *Panzer-Schiessschule* in Putlos).

On 30 August 1943, the battalion was transported by train to Croatia and the area around Agram. The "*Hermann von Salza*" was placed under the supervision of the *Panzer-Regiment "Wiking"* commander, Hannes Mühlenkamp.[6] The battalion's personnel, around 800 men, were located in the town of Samobor. A few *Panzer IVs* and assault guns arrived from Grafenwöhr. Originally, the staff, Staff Company and 1st, 2nd, 3rd and 4th companies were located in former factory buildings on the outskirts of Samobor in the mountains. Due to attacks by partisans, some with mortars against the staff company's quarters at night, the "*Hermann von Salza*" troops were withdrawn into the town, some with quarters in a monastery (Josch de Braska).

During its time in Croatia, the "*Hermann von Salza*" was frequently activated in the anti-partisan war and also disarmed Italian units in Croatia after Italy's defection from the Axis pact. The battalion subsequently took over a number

Demolition teams from the pioneer battalion of the *4. SS-Brigade "Nederland"* prepare to blow up the Russian castle and medieval fortifications, known as Ivangorod, on the eastern shore of the Narva River, in order to prevent the Red Army from taking advantage of it, in February 1944. (NARA)

Ivangorod castle is blown up in February 1944.

A unique photo from the eastern shore of the Narva River, taken at the same moment as a multiple rockets from a *Propagandawerfer* 41 are launched by a German crew of *SS* War Correspondents. Each rocket weighed 3.3 kg and, instead of explosives, the rocket contained 0.5 kg of 250 propaganda leaflets to be spread over the Soviet trenches. This action was part of Operation "Wintermärchen" (Winter Tales) by the *SS-Standarte* "Kurt Eggers" in the Narva area. The Russian castle of Ivangorod and the ruined tower of Hermansborg can both be seen in the background.

Hermansborg, top and Ivangorod,below, before their respective destruction in 1944. The other photo shows both castles after their renovation today.

The fortress of Ivangorod (top) is blown up by the *SS* in early 1944 (Hermansborg is to the right). The second photo is of the renovated castles today, with the Narva River in between.

The Mayor's Office (*Rathaus*) of Narva after its destruction in early 1944, and today after renovation.

The burial place, south of the Hermansborg, for *SS*-soldiers from the *Brigade "Nederland"*.

The Danish *SS-Brigadeführer*, Christian Peter Kryssing, was the highest-ranking foreigner in the *Waffen-SS* in the Second World War. Born in 1891 in Kolding, Kryssing advanced before 1940 to be a lieutenant colonel in the Danish artillery. He was an ardent anti-communist but never became a member of the Danish Nazi Party. Being the first commander of the Danish Free Corps in 1941, backed by the Danish government, he was in early 1942 relieved of command due to clashes with other Danish officers who were more dedicated pro-Nazis. Thereafter, Kryssing served in the *SS-Divisions "Totenkopf"* and *"Wiking"* until February 1944, when he became CO of *"Kampfgruppe Küste"* on the Estonian side of the Gulf of Finland, continuing until July 1944. Kryssing got the most severe penalty of all Danish *SS*-volunteers before a Danish post-war court: eight years in prison. According to the Danish writer Tomas Harder, the sentence was a "necessary injustice", being founded on retroactive law. "But it was a political and moral necessity to convict Kryssing after 1945," Harden states. Relieved of his pre-war Danish officer's pension, Kryssing and his wife lived in poverty. Kryssing's two sons served in the *Waffen-SS* and both were killed in action. His wife was severely wounded in 1944 during a Soviet bomb attack on Tallin, where she served as a volunteer nurse.

The Hermansborg (top) and the Ivangorod (bottom) before their respective destruction in 1944.

The fortress of Hermansborg (left) under Soviet artillery fire in the early spring of 1944. The remains of Ivangorod (blown up by the SS in early 1944) are to the right. The second view shows the renovated castles today, with the Narva River in between.

The reality behind the suggestive *Waffen-SS* recruting brochures: a row of dead *SS* soldiers, some of them from Scandinavia, lie in the snow behind a wooden shed on the outskirts of Narva. The bodies await identification and a summary burial. The time is February 1944 after the Red Army's major offensive through Ingria toward the Narva River, where entire companies and even battalions from the *III. (Germ.) SS-Panzer-Korps* were wiped out.

Siivertsi-Vepsküla, north of Narva, in March 1944, a collection point for dead soldiers from the *III. (Germ.) SS-Panzer-Korps* for identification and burial.

German pioneers from the *Waffen-SS* or Army laying mines and constructing barbed wire obstacles on the shore of the Finnish Gulf north of Narva. Due to the catastrophic outcome of the Russian-Japanese War in 1905 (the destruction of the Russian Fleet at Tsushima), the Tsarist Army had in 1905–08 constructed a number of coastal artillery concrete positions along the southern shore of the Gulf of Finland to protect their capital, St Petersburg. These were taken over by the Estonian National Army in around 1920, and by the Germans from 1941.

Dead Soviet marine soldiers on the shore at Mereküla on the Gulf of Finland, on 14 February 1944. A Soviet amphibious assault was repelled by units from the Germanic *SS-Panzer-Korps* and the Army, with great losses for the Russian forces.

The site of the Soviet amphibious landing on 13–14 February 1944 at Mereküla today.

An anti-aircraft gun from the *SS-Kampfgruppe "Küste"* at Mummasaare, during the spring of 1944.

An army anti-aircraft gun from the *Heeres-Flak-Abteilung 292* at Mummasaare during spring 1944. The German *Luftwaffe* had long lost air superiority on the Eastern Front: the Eighteenth Army of Army Group North had less than 150 planes available, while the Soviets' Volkhov Front alone fielded nearly 600 aircraft in early 1944.

German or Estonian infantry under inspection at the HQ of *SS-Brigadeführer* Christian Peter Kryssing, CO of *Kampfgruppe "Küste"*.

The photo shows the Casino of the *"Kampfgruppe Kueste"* and its desolated condition today in Hungerburg, the famous pre-war seaside resort where the Narva River meets the Gulf of Finland.

The burial place at Kreenholm in Narva for the Norwegian *SS-Obersturmführer* Kristian Prytz, CO of *7. Kompanie* of the *SS-Panzergrenadier-Regiment 23 "Norge"*, who was killed in action on 13 February 1944.

From the private photo album of *SS-Obersturmbannführer* Ulrich Dümichen

Obersturmbannführer Ulrich Dümichen was Chief Field Judge of the *III. (Germ.) SS-Panzer-Korps* from the summer of 1943 until the war's end. Dümichen had served at the *SS-und Polizeigericht* (Police Court) *III* in Berlin before the war and held both Prussian judicial state exams. The dubious reputation for brutality of other *SS*-field courts seems eventually not to have been the custom in the *III. (Germ.) SS-Panzer-Korps*, probably due to the personality of the Commanding General, Felix Steiner. Heinrich Himmler had also ordered that the "Germanic", and especially the Scandinavian, *SS* volunteers were to be punished with more lenience than other *Waffen-SS* field courts. Steiner's official judgement of his corps judge to the *SS* Personnel Agency in Berlin from 3 June 1944 does not mention the obligatory laudation of strong beliefs in the Nazi ideology, but emphasizes instead other qualities: "A soldier's judge of the best style, that the field units can only wish to have. A skillful psychologist, who understands the field soldiers and has their full confidence."[1]

In 1980–81, Assistant judge Ulrich Dümichen answered, via letters, some questions from the author (LW): The criminality within the *III. (Germ.) SS-Panzer-Korps* mirrored the history of this unit. Apart from crimes, that necessarily appear in every human society, there were quite some crimes that accelerated in certain situations. E.g. there were many desertions by Dutch *SS*-volunteers during the establishment of the *III. (Germ.) SS-Panzer-Korps* in Franconia [in] 1943. These were often half-kids and simply ran away, bored and disillusioned of the German military, in the direction they thought the Netherlands were situated. As they were brought back by the local police after a couple of hours, they would normally have been tried [and found] guilty of desertion with [a] minimum one year of hard labour. This would have been intolerable and with some judicial manipulation, they were only sentenced to one week in the stockade. ... At the Front, we avoided sending the delinquents to the *SS-Strafvollzugslager Danzig-Matzkau* [the *SS*-Punishment Camp of Danzig-Matzkau], but instead they had to serve more briefly in punishment units of the *III. (Germ.) SS-Panzer-Korps*, such as pioneer or assault platoons. As with Steiner, I was lucky to have the reasonable *SS*-Field Judge, my colleague in the *SS-Freiwilligen-Panzergrenadier-Division "Nordland"*. But both the CO of the *SS-Freiwilligen-Panzergrenadier-Brigade "Nederland"*, *Brigadeführer* Jürgen Wagner, and his *SS*-Field Judge, acted with, for us, unwanted and unnuanced harshness with their sentences; this normally led to corrections in the sentences by me and Felix Steiner.[2]

Before his death, Ulrich Dümichen donated his private photo albums from 1943–45 to LW. These are published for the first time in this volume:

Left: Wooden barracks near the Gulf of Finland, used by units of the III. (germ.) SS-Panzer-Korps, May 1944.

Below: Burning houses during the retreat from Ingria, January 1944. (Images from the private photo albums of Ulrich Dümichen)

Personnel from *SS-Obersturmbannfuehrer* Ulrich Duemichen´s Judicial Section at the *Generalkommando III (germ.) SS-Panzer-Korps*, February 1944.

Left: Dead Soviet Marines after the failed amphibious landing at Merekuela during the night of 13/14 February 1944.

Below left: *SS-Obergruppenfuehrer* Felix Steiner after a staff meeting with the *Wehrmacht*, March 1944.

Below right: Staff officers from the logistic section of the *Generalkommando III. (germ.) SS-Panzer-Korps*, March-April 1944. In the background railway fuel wagons. (Images from the private photo albums of Ulrich Dümichen)

SS-Obergruppenfuehrer Matthias Kleinheisterkampf as acting CO of *III. (germ.) SS-Panzer-Korps* (during Felix Steiner´s sick leave) outside Corps HQ at Sillamäe, March 1945.

Standing to the right is *SS-Oberfuehrer* Joachim Ziegler, Chief-of-Staff *III. (germ.) SS-Panzer-Korps*, talking with an unknown General from the *Wehrmacht*, outside Corps HQ at Sillamäe, March 1944. (Images from the private photo albums of Ulrich Dümichen)

of Italian tanks, so-called "Badoglio-coffins", for training exercise and due to a lack of its own regular *panzers*.[7]

Paul-Albert Kausch commented in 1976:

> In this context, it seems necessary to look upon the dilemma of being supplied with tanks, from another perspective. In the 1943 equipment directives, a *Panzergrenadier-Division* was supposed to have a *Panzer* battalion, but in our case we should be supplied only with *Sturmgeschütze* for supportive tasks to the *Grenadiere*. However, *SS-Obergruppenführer* Steiner and I had other ideas: we wanted a *Panzer-Abteilung* that was able to accomplish independent tactical missions within an armoured corps. Therefore tanks and no *Sturmgeschütze*! But the tanks did not arrive and those *Sturmgeschütze* that were delievered to our corps, were attached to the *SS-Panzerjäger-Abteilung 11* (later *SS-Sturmgeschützabteilung 11*) under *Hauptmann* Dr Karlheinz Schulz-Streeck. After the battles at the *Kinderheimhöhe*, the *SS-Panzerjäger-Abteilung 11* was re-equipped, I think in the *Reich* with [a] *Flak-Kompanie*, *Panzerjäger-Kompanie* and *Sturmgeschütz-Kompanie*, and we ["*Hermann von Salza*"] got the remaining *Sturmgeschütze* (3rd and 4th Companies).[8]

The former *SS-Oberscharführer* Max Stöckle commented in 1993:

> The staff company (including our reconnaissance platoon) was in Croatia equipped with VW *Schwimmwagen*, motorcycles, four 2cm anti-aircraft guns, supply vans for weapons, payment and administration, uniforms etc, including a VW-*Kübelwagen* for the company CO. After the disarmament of the Italian troops in Croatia, we got light Italian tanks (without radio, signalling had to be done with flags) and Italian leather jackets. From Germany we also got a few *Sturmgeschütze* and Panzer IV.

The "*Hermann von Salza*" was transported to the North-eastern Front at Narva, still without *panzers*, on 22 December 1943, and was for a short time partly located at Hungerburg on the River Narva, then transported to Jamburg in Ingria. Max Stöckle stated:

> In our front-line, near the *Regiments "Norge"* and *"Danmark"*, we found around fifteen *Panzer V*s (Panther), which were dug-in (without motors and radios). According to P.A. Kausch these tanks belonged to a Null-serial that were not useful for front-[line] service. We hungered for "real" tanks, and organized within a few days supply parts from Riga and other depots, thereby making around eight of these tanks serviceable, and under all circumstances and at any time kept in use. With these wrecks we later operated successfully, [mainly] due to our formidable tank crews and the maintenance staff.[9]

In the course of the major Soviet offensive through Ingria from 14 January 1944, some companies from the "*Hermann von Salza*" had to hand over their various vehicles to other divisional units; hence their retreat from Jamburg back to Narva was immobile, hazardous and improvised to save the tank crews and the other battalion personnel. Stöckle added: "The anti-aircraft platoon from the staff company had to pull their 2cm-guns by hand back to Narva. The battalion also brought back 6–8 of the repaired Panthers from Ingria to Narva." The first men of the "*Hermann von Salza*" killed in action were the CO of the 1st Company, *SS-Hauptsturmführer* Paul Holtkampf, who was killed on 27 January 1944 at Sarinekoja (Jamburg) by a direct hit during a reconnaissance mission, and *SS-Untersturmführer* Herbert Schmidichen, who was killed on 22 January 1944 at Biegunitzy.

During February 1944, the personnel from 1st, 2nd, 3rd and 4th Companies of the "*Hermann von Salza*" were deployed between Kudruküla and the graveyard of Hungerburg as infantry in trenches on the western side of the River Narva against the Red Army. The anti-aircraft guns were positioned along the front line, bolstered with some 8cm mortars under the command of *SS-Hauptscharführer* Schramm. After the war, Paul-Albert Kausch related the following interesting episode:

> During this time as *Panzer-Infanterie* [at the River Narva] we tried to persuade *Oberst* Wengler to hand over the 6–8 *Panzer VI* (Tiger) from the Army, which were operating in the area of "*Nordland*" and *Kampfgruppe Wengler*. Sorry to say, these suggestions were put aside by *Oberst* Wengler, who in the prevailing critical situation did not want to take any risks by changing the existing crews of the Tiger tanks, although the exchange *Panzer* crews from our 2nd company, if I remember correctly, were at hand.[10]

The restored Panther tanks from Ingria were deployed in various places in the Narva bridgehead, some in Hungerburg and others in the area of the *20. Estonian SS-Division*. The training of tank crews continued during the spring of 1944 in the rear area of the "*Hermann von Salza*" (2nd Company under *SS-Untersturmführer* Artur Grathwol and later 1st Company under *SS-Obersturmführer* Rudolf Rott).

Deployed with his staff company of the "*Hermann von Salza*" in the infantry trenches at the River Narva, Max Stöckle recorded in his diary in February 1944:

> This blasted sand! Our weapons are full of [it], even the food. For days there are fallen Russians lying on the icy river. Some wounded try to creep back. Terribly tough guys! One soldier comes running over the ice from the opposite river bank, shouting: *Kameraden! Nicht schiessen!* ["Comrades! Do not shoot!"] But our MG 34 was too quick and did not hear my order to cease fire. Shortly before our river bank the man is shot dead! One of our own *SS* men, escaping Soviet captivity and killed

SS-Hauptscharführer Willi Fleck in Croatia in 1943. Later an *SS-Obersturmführer* in the *SS "Hermann von Salza"*, Fleck died in the Soviet POW camp at Rüdersdorf in East Berlin on 16 September 1945.

SS-Oberscharführer Max Stöckle from the staff company of *SS-Panzer-Abteilung "Hermann von Salza"*, showing the strain after weeks of trench warfare against the Red Army around the bridgehead at Narva.

SS-Unterscharführer Max Stöckle from the staff company of *SS-Panzer-Abteilung "Hermann von Salza"* in trenches at the River Narva in February 1944.

A Panther of the *SS-Panzer-Abteilung 11 "Hermann von Salza"* near Narva in early 1944. In the turret stands *SS-Obersturmführer* Nöthe and, on the left, *SS-Hauptscharführer* Nissen, an ethnic German from the Danish town of Padborg. This *panzer* was of an early production with defective motors, which at the Oranienbaum Front had been made operative and mobile in 1943–44 by crews from the *I./Panzer-Regiment 29* (Army), and which in February 1944 were handed over to *panzer* crews from the *SS "Hermann von Salza"*.

> by his own comrades! ... *SS-Unterscharführer* Franz Moser is killed by a direct hit from a Russian anti-tank gun! *SS-Unterscharführer* Sepp Schulz is killed by a shot in his head. These damned snipers! We are receiving direct hits into our trenches from Soviet mortars. They are shooting damned good! ... The Russian break-through to the right was cleared up. Hundreds of fallen Soviet soldiers on the ground. An Estonian *SS*-battalion mastered this operation, really brave men.

On 7 June 1944, the companies were moved from the front line to Mummassaare for resting and protection of the coastline. At the same time, *SS-Untersturmführer* Grathwol's 2nd Company was bolstered with some *Panzer IV*s and assault guns. It was directly subordinated to the *Armeeabteilung "Narva"* and deployed near *SS-Obergruppenführer* Steiner's corps HQ at Sillamäe. This unit, together with the remnants of the *SS-Sturmgeschützabteilung 11*, was later, in July 1944, put under the command of Paul-Albert Kausch as *Panzerkampfgruppe "Kausch"*.[11]

After the Soviet air bombardment of Narva on 6–7 March 1944, the Red Army broke through the lines of the *Brigade "Nederland"* north-west of Narva, near the strongpoint of Lilienbach (Popovka), and the Soviets advanced with 12 tanks 500 metres deep into the German lines. At that moment, *SS-Oberscharführer* Philipp Wild from the 1st Company of the *"Hermann von Salza"*, who was positioned with his Panther tank near the Jamburg road, stepped into action and destroyed seven of the Soviet tanks with only 11 shots. The other Soviet tanks retreated, and Wild managed to destroy three more enemy tanks a couple of hours later, accompanied by grenadiers from the *SS-Panzergrenadier-Regiment 48 "General Seyffardt"*. For this action, Wild was decorated with the Knight's Cross.[12]

During the battles for the Tannenbergline (Blue Hills) in July-August 1944, a decisive counter-attack by *Panzerkampfgruppe "Kausch"*, a combined armoured force consisting of the 2nd Company of the *"Hermann von Salza"* under *SS-Untersturmführer* Artur Grathwol and parts of the *SS-Sturmgeschützabteilung 11*, managed to stem the forceful offensive of the Red Army in this area. On the evening of 29 July, they made it possible to retake the tactically important Grenadier Hill.

Artur Grathwol's *SS* personnel file contains a short description of this action: "The immediate counter-attack under the command of *SS-Untersturmführer* Grathwol developed into a successful action. The Russian *panzer* attack by 40–50 tanks was beaten off: two 'Josef Stalin' and fifteen T-34 tanks were destroyed and the Russian infantry sustained heavy losses."[13]

On 26 July, the *Standarten-Oberjunker* and platoon leader in the 4th Company, Georg Wille, succeeded with his *Panzer IV*, 500 metres east of the Blue Hills, to block an attack of 16 Soviet tanks, among them some "Josef Stalins", and was decorated with the German Cross in Gold.[14] Also under Grathwol's command were assault guns from the *SS-Panzerjäger-Abteilung 54 "Nederland"*, and for his actions eastwards from the Blue Hills on 26 July, the Knight's Cross was bestowed on the Dutch *SS-Unterscharführer* Derk-Elsko Bruins.[15]

The Norwegian volunteers, *SS-Untersturmführer* Per Kjölner (left) and *SS-Untersturmführer* Thomas Hvistendahl, in 1944. Kjölner was examined as top of his officer's course at Bad Tölz in 1943 and served with distinction in the *Division "Nordland"* until both he and Hvistendahl returned to Norway in the autumn of 1944 on recommendation of the Chief of Staff for the *Germanic SS-Panzer-Korps*, Helmut von Bockelberg, who instead wanted them to serve politically on the home front. Kjölner became Staff Inspector for *Germanske SS Norge* and was condemned to five-and-a-half year in prison in Oslo in 1946. After his release, Kjölner was owner and CEO of the clothing firm Adelsten, with 100 shops in Norway and Sweden and 1,500 employees. Hvistendahl served both in the *SS-Panzer-Abteilung "Hermann von Salza"* and the *SS-Panzergrenadier-Regiment "Norge"*, and was severly wounded on 29 July 1944 at the Tannenberg defence line in Estonia. He was a member of the *NS*, Hirden and *Germanske SS* in Norway, was condemned to four years of hard labour in Norway after 1945 and later worked as a painter. He died in Oslo 1992.

SS-Oberscharführer Philipp Wild, decorated with the Knight's Cross, sitting on the hull of a Soviet T-34 that served the *"Herman von Salza"* as a breakdown lorry in Narva for damaged German *panzers*. The *"Herman von Salza"* was never, as originally intended in 1943, equipped with Panther tanks but instead got assault guns (*Sturmgeschütze*). In November 1943, however, Hitler had ordered that 60 of the Panthers from the mechanically defective 0-series were to be transported to the Oranienbaum Front in the north and dug in as anti-tank defences there. In December 1943, the *III. [Germ.] SS-Panzer Korps* arrived at the front line at Oranienbaum from Croatia, and took over responsibility for some of these static *panzers*. Most were lost during the Soviet offensive in January 1944, but skilled crews and mechanics from the *"Hermann von Salza"* succeeded in bringing back 14 of these Panthers to the new front line at Narva. These were to be the only Panthers that the *"Hermann von Salza"* were ever to be (unofficially) equipped with. A few Panthers even survived to take part in the final battles for Brandenburg-Berlin in 1945.

Officers from the *"Hermann von Salza"* near the Gulf of Finland, north of Narva, in the spring of 1944. To the right stands the battalion commander, *SS-Sturmbannführer* Paul-Albert Kausch. His black leather coat originates either from captured Italian clothing stocks in Croatia in 1943 or from German U-boat leather coats that were redirected to *panzer* units of the *Waffen-SS*.

An unknown *SS-Standarten-Oberjunker* from the *"Hermann von Salza"*, wearing the EK I and II, the *Panzerkampfabzeichen*, the *Infanteriesturmabzeichen* and the Close Combat Clasp.

A Panther tank from the *"Hermann von Salza"* under repair in woods near Hungerburg, downstream of the Narva.

A Panther tank from the *"Hermann von Salza"* is taken in tow in Narva by a German *Bergepanzer*, a former Soviet T-34 without a turret.

A Panther from the first 0-series of Model D. during rearming in Narva, in the early spring of 1944. To the right, in black *panzer* jacket and white trousers, stands the commander of *1. Kompanie* of the *"Hermann von Salza"*, the Austrian *SS-Obersturmführer* Rudolf Rott (killed in action on 12 February 1945 in Pomerania), and behind him is *SS-Hauptscharführer* Trautmann.

SS-Hauptscharführer Richard Braunstein from the staff company of the *"Hermann von Salza"* sitting on his *panzer* or *StuG III* in Narva, during the summer of 1944. He was later promoted to officer rank and decorated with the German Cross in Gold in October 1944. Braunstein was captured by Soviet troops in 1945 and held prisoner until 1955. He died in 1987.

One of the few Panther tank of the *"Hermann von Salza"*, in the fortress of Hermansborg in Narva, during the spring of 1944.

Unknown panzer soldiers, probably from the *SS-Sturmgeschuetzabteilung* "Nederland", near Narva in the spring of 1944.

SS-Sturmbannführer Paul-Albert Kausch, CO of the *"Hermann von Salza"* in Narva, in early spring 1944, with his adjutant, *SS-Untersturmführer* Hansjoachim Bleise, and Kausch's pet dogs.

In April 1944, the Tigers at Narva were forced to operate in swampy areas where the heavy *panzer* vehicles inevitably were stuck and became easy targets for Soviet anti-tank weapons. On 9 July 1944, Carius' battalion was ordered to undertake a 31-mile motorized march with its Tigers between two villages in intense summer heat. The result was that up to 64 percent of the total force (14 out of 22 tanks) was immobilized due to defects in their engines or tracks, and hence could not participate in the following battles, although the specialized officers in the Tiger battalion had pointed out just such a risk to their superiors.

The original tactical concept of the Tiger tank was, during a German offensive, to break through the enemy's defence and especially destroy his armoured forces. Instead, the Tigers got an almost exclusive defensive role to prevent or beat off the Red Army's or Western Allies' attacks against German infantry units.

Every construction of a tank is a combination of fire power, mobility and the design of the armour. The 88mm cannon of the Tiger, with its precision and capability to penetrate enemy armour, was constructed at the expense of a suitable engine and transmission, which often overheated or broke down. Adding to this, the Tiger's high use of fuel meant a limited area of action. Despite these facts, the Tiger had an impressive kill-ratio in battles against enemy tanks: for every destroyed Tiger, this formidable *panzer* destroyed

Phillip Wild, a *panzer* commandant in the *"Hermann von Salza"*, who was awarded the Knight's Cross on 21 March 1944 for decisive tactical action and outstanding bravery during the initial battles for the Narva bridgehead. Wild was severely wounded during the rescue action by the *SS-Division "Nordland"* and other units from the *11. SS-Panzer-Armee* to relieve the encircled German garrison in the Pomeranian town of Arnswalde during Operation *"Sonnenwende"* in February 1945. Wild was born in 1921 near Darmstadt and died in 1999. On the right, Wild receives the Knight's Cross in March 1944 from the CO of *III. (Germ) SS-Panzer Korps*, *SS-Obergruppenführer* Mathias Kleinheisterkamp.

Kurt Tebring, Philipp Wild's Danish driver, in his Panther tank. Tebring has here received his Iron Cross 1st Class for his achievements in the Narva bridgehead that resulted in Wild receiving the Knight's Cross. Tebring survived the war and lived quietly in Copenhagen until his death.

A Panther of the first defective series at the Oranienburg Front, here in posession of the *"Hermann von Salza"* near Narva in mid-1944. In the turret stands *SS-Oberschaführer* Prendka, killed in action near Marquardt, west of Berlin, in May 1945. Some of the casualties among *panzer* officers and other tank commanders were due to their habit of exposing their heads in an open hatch of the tank to observe the terrain. The extensive losses among both German and Soviet tank personnel bear witness to this fact. "The personal aggressiveness of the commander while observing was decisive for success against vastly superior numbers of enemy formations. The lack of good observation by the Russians often resulted in the defeat of large units. Tank commanders who slam their hatches shut at the beginning of an attack and don't open them again until the objective has been reached are useless, or at least second rate." (Otto Carius)

German troops examining a number of killed Soviet Navy riflemen on the shore of the Finnish Gulf near the village of Mereküla, after the failed amphibious landing by the Red Banner Fleet on 13–14 February 1944, where 350 Soviet soldiers were killed or drowned and 200 captured as prisoners of war. The Soviet naval soldiers succeeded in reaching Mereküla and surrounded the HQ of *Kampfgruppe "Berlin"*, the force responsible for defending this coastal section. On the morning of 14 February, a German counter-attack consisting of a group of Tiger tanks from the Heavy *Panzer Abteilung 503*, parts of the *SS*-Reconnaissance Battalion "*Nordland*", and Estonian and German troops supported by coastal artillery, smashed the landing attempt.

Civilian Estonian refugees leaving Narva on German orders towards the end of February 1944. Nearly all of them, if they survived, would never see their hometown again. The Danish *SS-Hauptsturmführer* and artillery officer Erik Laerum wrote in his diary: "A few days after our arrival in Narva [29 January], orders got through that all Estonian civilians had three weeks to completely evacuate Narva. It was the saddest sight you could see. Women, children and elderly people were in the majority. They drove out of Narva in mostly horse-driven carriages with the childen sitting on top of their meagre possessions. These civilians never saw their home town again. After the Soviet annexation of Estonia in 1940, 3,000 men from the intellectual classes in Narva were apprehended for 'questioning' and had thereafter never been seen again."

Panzer soldiers from the *SS-Panzer-Abteilung "Hermann von Salza"* near Udria in the Gulf of Finland, in June 1944. These men belonged to various tank crews (signalmen, drivers, etc).

Panzer officers and NCOs from the *SS-Panzer-Abteilung "Hermann von Salza"* near Udria in the Gulf of Finland, in June 1944. From the left, *Oberjunker* Kurt Brehmer, *SS-Hauptscharführer* Werner Bürger, *SS-Unterscharführer* Rudi Bachmann, *Oberjunker* Adalbert Brandner and *Oberjunker* Hans Henseler.

Josef Fitzthum photographed in the mosquito-infested marshes in northern Russia in the spring of 1942, as commander of the *Legion Vlaandern* (the Flemish Legion). He war an active pre-war Austrian Nazi who was expatriated from Austria in 1936, and until the *Anschluss* in 1938 was involved in German *SD*-activities against Austria. In July 1942, Fitzthum took command of the *Legion Nederland*. From October 1943 until January 1945, he led a remarkable political career as Himmler's personal plenipotentiary in Albania, where he usurped nearly total power, including the recruitment of the 21st *Waffen-SS* Mountain Division of the *SS "Skanderbeg"*. After being promoted *SS-Gruppenführer* and *Generalleutnant der Waffen-SS* in August 1944, Fitzthum served as CO of the *18. SS-Panzergrenadier-Division "Horst Wessel"*. He was killed in a car accident in Vienna on 10 May 1945.

Other sections of the "*Hermann von Salza*", among them the 1st Company (Rott), were from 19 July, without armour, in action as infantry before and during the retreat to the Tannenberg line:

> During the time of 9–26 July 1944, *SS-Obersturmführer* Rott was attached with four companies to the *Kampfgruppe "Bunse"* to fight off enemy attacks in the flanks along Lipsu Street. Although Rott's force was without *Panzers*, he showed himself to be an exemplary officer. The Russian major attack along Lipsu Street, which threatened the right wing of his unit, was quickly eliminated by counter-attacks. The positions were held for as long [as] it took to protect the retreat [of the main forces] to the Tannenberg line.[16]

SS-Hauptscharführer Rudi Chairsell from the *SS-Panzer-Abteilung "Hermann von Salza"* in 1944.

On 25 July, the staff company of "*Hermann von Salza*", marching on foot from Mummassaare, reached their new quarters in a forestry camp behind the Blue Hills, north-west from the Waivara railway station.

During the battles for Dorpat and south-eastern Estonia in August-September 1944, the 3rd Company and parts of the 4th Company, together with assault guns from the *SS-Sturmgeschützabteilung 11* – in total 13–15 *Sturmgeschütze* – under the command of *SS-Hauptsturmführer* Ernst-Richard Stübben, were attached to *Kampfgruppe "Wagner"*. This unit suffered heavy losses; on 17 September 1944 alone, seven *Sturmgeschütze* were lost and only one-and-a-half crew were saved from being killed or captured.

On 14 September 1944, the commander of *Heeresgruppe Nord, Generaloberst* Ferdinand Schörner, made the decision to initiate the evacuation of *Arméeabteilung "Narva"* and the *III. ("Germ.") SS-Panzer-Korps* from Estonia. Further major Soviet offensives could no longer be repelled by the weakened German defences. The German retreat out of Estonia, under the codename Operation Tree Bough (*Unternehmen Aster*), was accomplished from 15 September (for support and rear units) and during the night of 17–18 September (for fighting units). Parts of the "*Hermann von Salza*" were at this time located in Voka-Toila. The Staff Company (with its supply and repair platoons) was issued with half-tracks (RSO; *Raupenschlepper Ost*).[17]

The 2nd Company (Grathwol), with intact tanks and assault guns, acted as rearguard during the retreat from Estonia. All companies of the "*Hermann von Salza*", including

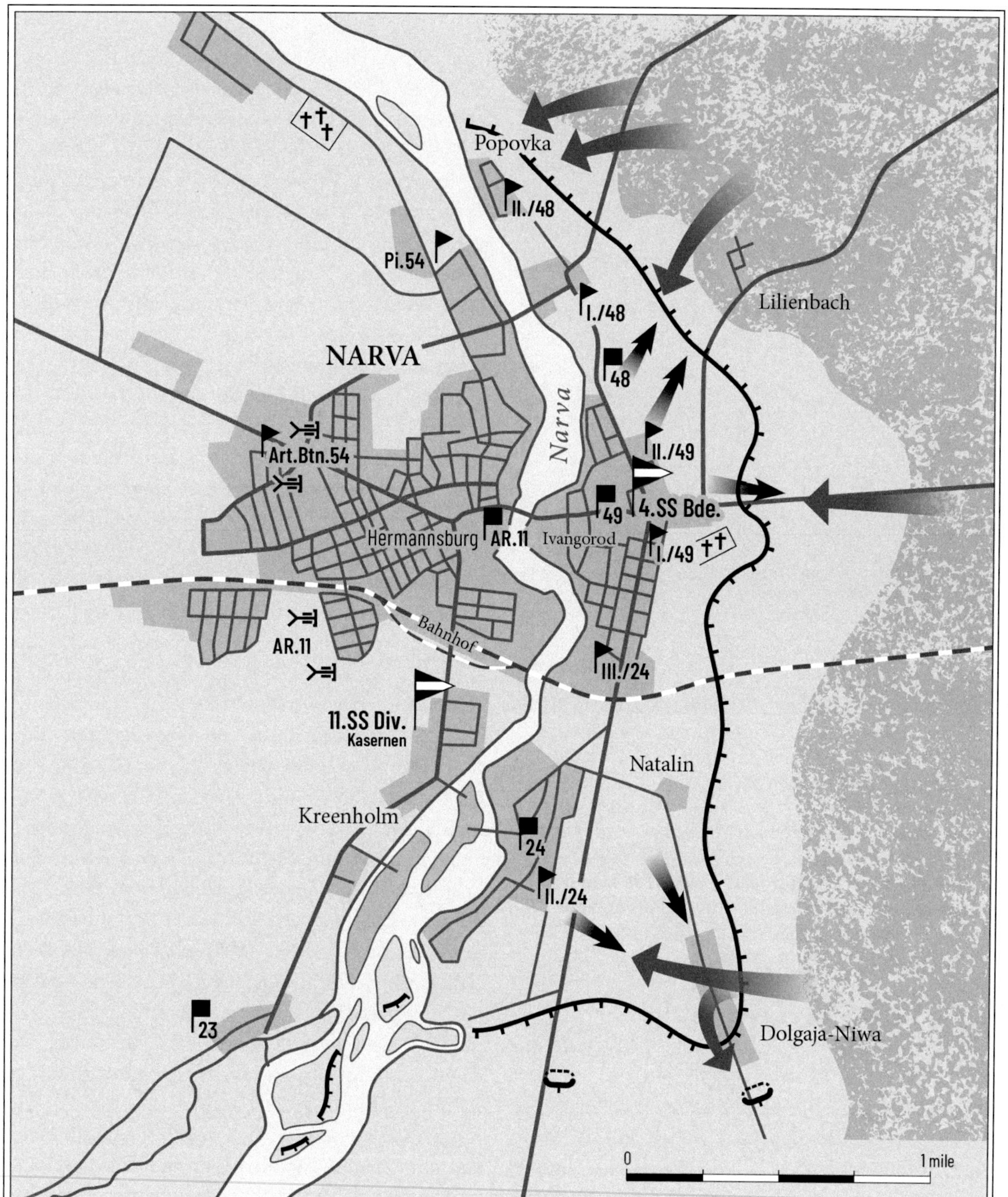

Narva Bridgehead.

the *Panzer-Infanteristen* without armoured vehicles, retreated via Jöwe-Wesenberg-Pernau-Riga-Tuckums-Preekuln-Libau into Latvia. At the beginning of November, the battalion was evacuated across the sea from Courland to Germany. The 1st Company (Rott) took over the rest of the *panzers* and remained in the Courland pocket until January 1945 with the *SS-Division "Nordland"*.

Summing up, the *"Hermann von Salza"*, far from reaching the status of a *Panzer IV* armoured battalion, instead had to use a a stop-gap solution in Ingria by repairing a number of totally out-dated and immobile Panther tanks for acute use. In the end, it was converted into a combined *Panzer-Sturmgeschützabteilung* in late 1944. The *"Hermann von Salza"* almost never had more than a company and a half actually equipped with tanks and assault guns. The remaining *panzer* crews were condemned to serve as infantry from January-November 1944 during the campaigns in the Baltic countries.[18]

LW

The Estonian 20. *SS-Division* at the Narva front

In February 1944, the *20. Estonian SS-Division* arrived in Narva from its former battle positions on the River Nevel, and was attached to the *III. (germ.) SS-Panzer-Korps* as reinforcements after the German retreat from Ingria to the Narva bridgehead.[19] The *Estonian SS-Division* was formed around a cadre from the *3. Estonian SS-Freiwillige Brigade*, which previously fought on the Eastern Front. The Estonian

Paul Maitla was a very well-qualified Estonian officer in the *20. Waffen-Grenadier-Division der SS* (*estnische Nr.1*) within the *III. (Germ.) SS-Panzer-Korps*. Maitla won the Knight's Cross after saving the front from collapsing by leading a daring counter-attack, during which he not only retook the *Grenadierhöhe*, but also parts of the *Kinderheimhöhe* on 29 July 1944. Maitla was for many years counted as missing in Bohemia in 1945, until it was recently revealed that he and a group of other Estonian officers were murdered by Czech partisans during the night of 9-10 May 1945.

SS-soldiers were thrown into a series of incredibly violent battles around the threatening Soviet bridgeheads along the Narva River at Riigiküla, Wasa, Wepsküla and Siivertsi. The fighting raged for two weeks, and all the Soviet strongpoints were eliminated by the Estonians by 7 March and the front line restored, although with heavy losses, especially among officers and NCOs in the *Estonian SS-Division*. Division losses between 17 February and 9 March 1944 were 147 dead, 710 wounded, and 47 missing in action.[20]

During the following lull in fighting at Narva, the *Estonian SS-Division* was reinforced by three Estonian *Ostbatallione* and the general conscription of recruits by the Estonian authorities. A further reinforcement arrived to Narva in March 1944 in the form of the *SS-Panzergrenadier-Bataillon "Narva"*, which had spent a year attached to the *SS-Division "Wiking"* on the southern section of the Eastern Front.[21]

In mid July, the *III. (germ.) SS-Panzer-Korps* was ordered to abandon its positions at Narva and instead establish a new defensive line between the Gulf of Finland and Lake Peipus at the Blue Hills. The Soviets realized what was happening, and on 24 July, the Leningrad Front attacked at Auvere, south-west of Narva, in a bid to cut off and encircle the units of the *III. (germ.) SS-Panzer-Korps* before it had started to retreat from Narva. The Soviet offensive failed due to the stubborn resistance of *Waffen-Grenadier-Regiment der SS 45* under the leadership of *Waffen-SS-Sturmbannführer* Harald Riipalu.[22]

On 25 July, the battalions of the *Waffen-Grenadier-Regiment der SS 46* and *II./Waffen-Grenadier-Regiment der SS 47*, which were located north of Narva to protect the retreat from the city, were attacked by strong Soviet units. Soviet infantry , after heavy artillery fire, penetrated the Estonian defensive lines and established footholds, from which it continued westwards. To avoid annihilation, the Estonian battalions fell back west towards the Tannenberg line, which was reached on 26 July.[23]

The Tannenberg line was immediately exposed to heavy attacks by strong Soviet infantry and armoured units, which with artillery support took the *Kinderheimhöhe*. To take the hill back, a counter-attack was organized during the evening of 27 July, during which *I./Waffen-Grenadier-Regiment der SS 47*, under the leadership of *Waffen-SS-Sturmbannführer* Georg Sooden, succeeded in retaking some parts of the hill, but was thrown back by heavy Soviet attacks. The heaviest Soviet attacks were conducted on 29 July, when the Red Army almost gained control of the central Tannenberg position by deep penetrations of the German front line. During a successful counter-attack by the *I./Waffen-Grenadier-Regiment der SS 45* under *Waffen-SS-Hauptsturmführer* Paul Maitla, the Estonians retook both the tactically important high grounds of the *Grenadierhöhe* and the *Kinderheimhöhe*, in spite of severe Soviet resistance from tanks, artillery and infantry. The Estonian commander of the *Waffen-Grenadier-Regiment der SS 45*, *SS-Sturmbannführer* Harald Riipalu, as well as Paul Maitla, were decorated with the Knight's Cross on 23 August 1944 for these achievements.[24]

The successful German and Estonian warding-off defence during the battle of the Tannenberg line is considered a strategic victory against a superior opponent. The German forces used a system of systematically coordinating all heavy weapons (mainly artillery) in the defensive lines, which enabled the defenders to coordinate fire from two or even three directions, hitting those Soviet forces that managed to break thorugh at different places along the front line. The effective German fire-control of artillery was crucial in destroying the bulk of the Soviet tank forces and also hitting the Red Army infantry hard. The total losses in the Estonian combat units from the *20. SS-Division* at Tannenberg were considerable.

During the whole period from February-August 1944, the various battalions from the *20. EstonianSS-Division* were attached to either the *11. SS-Freiwilligen-Panzergrenadier-Division "Nordland"* or the *4. SS-Freiwilligen-Panzergrenadier-Brigade "Nederland"*. Thus, the *Estonian SS-Division* almost never appeared fighting as a whole division at the front during this period.

In the middle of August 1944, *II./Waffen-Grenadier-Regiment der SS 47*, *I./Waffen-Grenadier-Regiment der SS*

Estonians of the *20. Waffen-Grenadier-Division der SS* (*estnische Nr.1*) at the Narva Front.

***SS-Obersturmbannführer* Arnold Stoffers was buried at the cemetery at Maarjamäe (Reval-Marienberg) on 29 February, just four days after being killed in combat at the Narva Front on 25 February. He was regimental commander of *SS-Panzergrenadier-Regiment 23 "Norge"*. (Courtesy of Björn Leo)**

The cemetery at Maarjamäe today, where 2,156 fallen soldiers rest. (Courtesy of Björn Leo)

45 and *Waffen-Grenadier-Regiment der SS 46* were sent as reinforcements to *Kampfgruppe "Wagner"* to defend the German positions near Dorpat (Tartu) in south-eastern Estonia, where the Soviet 3rd Baltic Front attacked south of Lake Peipus at Pskov, with the aim of capturing Dorpat and to link-up with the major Soviet offensive against the Tannenberg-line. PK

The *Waffen-SS* Cemetery at Maarjamäe, 1944–2018

To bury the many German soldiers who died during the combat in Estonia in 1941, and especially during the fighting at Narva in the spring and summer of 1944, several German cemeteries were erected in Estonia. One of them, Reval-Marienberg (today Tallinn-Maarjamäe), was built in 1941 on the shore of the Finnish Gulf, just east of Tallinn. This cemetery was to become the final resting place for many superior officers of the *III. (Germ.) SS-Panzer-Korps*, such as *SS-Obersturmbannführer* Arnold Stoffers, *SS -Obersturmbannführer* Hermenegild Graf von Westphalen and *SS-Gruppenführer* Fritz von Scholz. After the final evacuation of the German forces in Estonia during September 1944, the war cemetery of Reval-Marienberg was destroyed by the Soviets, and in 1980 was replaced by a Soviet memorial. After Estonia became independent, the German *Volksbund* was able to conclude an agreement with the Estonian City Administration in 1997 to create a commemorative place to honour the fallen. In addition to a 5.5-metre-high stone cross, 24 lying tablets were erected with the names and dates of birth and death of 2,156 German soldiers, in alphabetical order. The burial grounds were marked with 25 cross groups made of natural stone. BL, PK, LW

The German *Schützenpanzerwagen* (half-track)

The half-track in the picture is the famous versatile light version, used by the Army and *Waffen-SS* in their *Panzer-* and *Panzergrenadier-Divisionen*, and *Aufklärungs-Abteilungen* (normally requiring 55 of these half-tracks in each battalion) between 1943 and 1945. This light-armoured personnel-carrier (*leichte Schützenpanzerwagen*; *Sonderkraftfahrzeug 250/1, neu*) entered production in October 1943 and replaced an older version that was complex in shape and required considerable man-hours for manufacturing. Pehrsson's new version has a simplified body, using as many flat armour plates as possible. It was a multi-functional battle vehicle, designed either for protected transport of riflemen or mounted, mobile combat. The crew consisted of a commander, driver and four *Panzergrenadiers*. The half-track *250/1 neu* weighed 5.38 tons, was 1.66 metres high, had a top speed of 60km/h and was armed with two MG 42 with frontal and rear mounting. The *Waffen-SS* and the German Army used half-tracked vehicles in many roles. In the seven *SS-Panzer-Divisionen*, armoured half-tracks were used from mid-1942 for one of six *Panzergrenadier-Bataillonen* as well as in the divisional armoured engineer and armoured reconnaissance battalions. The *SS-Panzergrenadier-Divisionen* had armoured half-tracks only in the divisional armoured reconaissance battalions.

An 8cm *Raketen-Vielfachwerfer* (80mm multiple rocket-launcher) at the Narva Front in February-March 1944. Impressed by the simplicity (and thereby the possibility of relatively cheap mass-production) of captured examples of the Soviet 82mm M–8 Katyusha Rocket Launcher, the Germans copied it as the *Vielfachwerfer*. This version held 24 projectiles, supported by a rail-assembly, mounted on the half-track *SdKfz 4/1* (*"Maultier"*; *gep Zgkw S305*) with a crew of six men and a firing range of 6,000 metres. It was smaller than its Soviet counterpart and had a higher rate of fire and better mobility. Both the Katyusha and the *Vielfachwerfer* were insruments of a new tactical concept: a "high density of fire in a short period of time" (Horst Scheibert). The man in white camouflage dress to the right is *SS-Gruppenführer* Mattias Kleinheisterkamp, acting commander of the *III. (Germ.) SS-Panzer-Korps*.

SS-Obergruppenfuehrer Matthias Kleinheisterkamp.

The *Panzergrenadier-* and *Aufklärungs-Abteilungs* equipped platoon and company commanders with the *SdKfz 251/10* modification, which mounted a PaK 36 anti-tank gun. The heavy companies of the *Aufklärungs-Abteilungen* were equipped with a platoon of *SdKfz 251/9 "Stummel"* models, which were provided with a short-barrelled 75mm gun.

The heavy armoured personnel carrier (*schwere Schützenpanzer-wagen*; *Sonderkraftfahrzeug 251, neu*) could carry up to ten men, as well as its driver and commander). It was also used as a mobile mount for anti-tank or anti-aircraft guns or rockets. LW

Odd Angelsen, Norwegian volunteer in the *SS-Panzergrenadier Regiment "Norge"* (Tommy Natedal's archive)

I was now transferred to the 11. Company in "*Norge*" and in the *Kampfgruppe "Thöny"* we attacked Siivertsi on 11 February 1944, together with artillery men from the *Kriegsmarine* and soldiers from the *Luftwaffe*. We had no support from *Panzers* and we came slowly forward. Many were killed from our battle group here and on 20 February our strength had been reduced from 250 to 80 men. By then we had advanced four kilometres into the village of Siivertsi and its old church from the 16th century. There was also a monument, in the form of a pyramid, to the Swedish King Charles XII and the battle in 1700. At the church some of the King's brave soldiers were buried. The Russian bridgehead had by now been reduced to a pocket of 500 metres on the western shore of the Narva river. The

A multiple rocket-launcher *Werfer* under immediate fire of a projectile.

The strategically important bridge between the eastern and western shores of the Narva River (Narova) in central Narva was reconstructed and reinforced by engineers and soldiers from the *SS-Panzer-Engineering-Batallion 11 "Nordland"* after it was damaged during the Soviet air bombardment which totally destroyed the inner city of Narva in early March 1944. This unit was commanded by *SS-Sturmbannfuehrer* Fritz Bunse and consequently the bridge was baptized "The Buense-Bridge". It crossed the Narova between the fortresses of Ivangorod and Hermannborg.

This four-page series of photographs depicts the protection of the bridge and the practice of creating artificial fog around it. The "Buense-Bridge" was finally blown-up by German forces in June 1944 when the Narva Bridgehead was abandoned and all *Wehrmacht-* and *Waffen-SS* units were redeployed at the "Tannenberg-Line" west of Narva. (Photos courtesy of NARA)

Odd Angelsen

Two *SS* grenadiers take a rest from battle. The grenadier on the left, drinking from a bottle, is armed with a *Panzerfaust* and a *Mauser* carbine 98. The other soldier is carrying ammunition crates. The photo was taken by the Swedish *SS* war correspondent, Gösta Borg.

SS-Unterscharführer Berthold Behnke was decorated with the Iron Cross 2nd Class on 7 February 1944. He was chief of an anti-tank cannon waggon from the *5./SS-Pz. Aufklärungsabteilung 11* and wounded in Ingria on 24 February 1944. The photo is taken near the Gulf of Finland outside Narva in March-April 1944 after Behnke was released from hospital. (Courtesy of Predrag Blanusa & Björn Leo)

The Swedish *SS* war correspondent, *SS-Untersturmführer* Gösta Borg, from Stockholm, takes cover in trenches at a civilian burial place near Narva, eventually the Jaani cemetery, in the summer of 1944.

The front of a *Sd.Kfz 251/9* (with a towed 7.5cm anti-tank cannon) in February 1944. The waggon commandant, *SS-Unterscharführer* Dietrich Vogel, is sitting to the right at the front of the vehicle. (Courtesy of Predrag Blanusa & Björn Leo)

The same *SPW* with the towed 7.5cm anti-tank gun visible behind the vehicle. The photo is probably from the so-called "*Bunkerstrasse*" along the Gulf of Finland near Hungerburg. Eventually this *SPW* participated in or around the ceremony on 19 March 1944 when *SS-Gruppenführer* Matthias Kleinheisterkamp decorated the CO of this anti-tank platoon, *SS-Untersturmführer* Georg Langendorf, with the Knight's Cross. The buffer-stops at the end of the barrel are needed to stop it from recoiling. (Courtesy of Predrag Blanusa & Björn Leo)

SS-Unterscharführer Dietrich Vogel standing in front of a 7.5cm anti-tank gun in Sinimone in the Gulf of Finland, north of Narva, in February 1944. The gun has four white rings painted, symbolizing four destroyed Soviet *panzers*, probably during the fighting around the Ingrian village of Gubanizy on 26 January 1944, where mixed German forces destroyed the bulk of a Soviet tank brigade (consisting of 54 tanks). Fur caps and *Walinkis* (felt boots) are now a natural part of the combat troop-equipment. (Courtesy of Predrag Blanusa & Björn Leo)

SS-Unterscharführer Dietrich Vogel in February 1944, near Hungerburg. He is deorated with the Iron Cross 1st and 2nd class. (Courtesy of Predrag Blanusa & Björn Leo)

The HQ in Narva of the *11. SS-Freiwilligen-Panzergrenadier-Division "Nordland"*, some time in February 1944. Pictured are, from the left: an unknown officer, *SS-Obesturmbannführer* Helmut von Bockelberg (Ia, operations officer, of the *"Nordland"*), *SS-Brigadeführer* Fritz von Scholz (CO of the *"Nordland"*) and *SS-Obersturmführer* Otto Bothe (O1, orderly officer, of the *"Nordland"*). Von Bockelberg was an Army general staff officer who was transferred to the Germanic *SS-Panzer-Korps* in June 1943. The Army lieutenant, Otto Carius, from the Heavy *Panzer-Bataillon 502*, cooperated with his Tiger tanks with the *SS-Division "Nordland"* in early February 1944 against the Soviet bridgeheads of Sivertsi and Riigi. Carius wrote after a visit to Fritz von Scholz at his HQ: "During the whole war, his divisional HQ was the *only one* that was closer to the Front than the regimental HQs!" After the war, von Bockelberg was a member of the West German parliament in Bonn from 1969–76 for the CDU party. Von Scholz was mortally wounded on 27 July 1944 and died of his wounds the following day. Otto Bothe was declared missing in action after the battle for Berlin in April-May 1945.

Russians had focused their mortars and cannons on our lines around this bridgehead and their effect was terrible. Both sides sent out scout and storm troops, which resulted in bloody close combat-fighting which reduced our ranks even further.

Leon Degrelle and Walloons in the *Waffen-SS*

Both in the French- and Dutch-speaking parts of Belgium, fascism was not an unusual phenomenon before the Second World War. The Walloon Belgian Leon Degrelle (1906–94) was educated at a Jesuit College and successfully studied for a law doctorate, before he became a journalist for the conservative Roman Catholic paper *Christus Rex*. Degrelle founded the right-wing Rexist party in 1935, based on fascism, corporatism and later adding Nazi-inspired anti-Semitism into its ideology. After remarkable successes in elections, with a peak in 1936 reaching nearly 20 percent of the vote, the party fell into decline. After the German invasion of Belgium in May 1940, Degrelle was immediately arrested by the Belgian authorities. Freed by the German occupation forces, he re-established his Rexist party and founded a militia, known as the *Formations de Combat*. At the outbreak of the German attack on the Soviet Union in the summer of 1941, Hitler ordered the *Wehrmacht* (the *SS* considered the Walloons to be "Gallic" rather than "Germanic") to set up a Walloon Legion for the Eastern Front, partly consisting of the paramilitary arm of the Rexist Party, the *Formations de Combat*, as well as other Walloon volunteers. In August 1941, the Walloon Legion contained 860 men and was incorporated into the German Army as the *373. (Walloon) Infanterie-Bataillon*.

In 1942, Degrelle met Felix Steiner during the fighting in the Caucasus. They got along well, and Degrelle was impressed by the fighting spirit of the *Waffen-SS* and its ideology. He believed that the *Waffen-SS* held a greater prestige than the German Army. The head of the *SS* recruting branch, *SS-Gruppenführer* Gottlob Berger, always searching for recruiting potential for the *Waffen-SS*, succeeded in getting the battle-experienced Walloon Legion volunteers on the Eastern Front transferred from the German Army on 1 June 1943 and incorporated into the *Waffen-SS*, with Degrelle's strong support. In October 1943 it was redesignated as the *5. SS-Freiwilligen-Sturmbrigade "Wallonien"*, with Degrelle as second-in-command, and consisted in late 1943 of about 1,600 veterans from the Eastern Front and the former Belgian Army, with an additional 600 recruits on the Wildflecken Training Grounds. At the turn of the year 1943–44, the Walloons fought west of the Dniepr River with the "*Wiking*" along with the German *1. Panzer-Armee*, followed by the disastrous encirclement and battle for the Korsun-Cherkassy pocket, from which *the Walloon SS-Brigade* only got out with 632 surviving soldiers from 2,000 men. For mainly propaganda reasons, Degrelle, who led the brigade with skill during the breakout from the Korsun-Cherkassy pocket and was personally decorated by Hitler with the Knight's Cross, was promoted to *SS-Sturmbannführer* on 20 April 1944, and the remnants of the brigade was sent to Wildflecken for rest and recreation.

Degrelle as *SS-Hauptsturmführer* in the *Waffen-SS*, talking with an unknown soldier to the right.

A recruitment poster for the Walloon Legion that took shape as an infantry battalion for the Eastern Front, organized by the German Army. The SS did not consider the Walloon volunteers to be Germanic, but instead more Gallic, and initially, like the French volunteers for "Barbarossa", the Walloon Legion was raised by the Wehrmacht and not the Waffen-SS.

In July 1944, the weakened and retreating German front at the new Tannenberg defensive line, west of Narva, was reinforced by the *Walloon SS-Brigade* with a battalion-sized battlegroup of 452 officers, NCOs and men, against the advancing Red Army. *SS-Hauptsturmführer* Jules Mathieu was in the first instance commissioned to command this weak battalion, for the greater part consisting of fresh recruits.[25] At the time of the battalion's disembarkation at Johvi, 45km west of Narva, on 25 July 1944, Mathieu had been replaced as commander by *SS-Obersturmführer* Georges Ruelle, and the battalion was subsequently named *Kampfgruppe "Ruelle"*.

Degrelle, although not formally in charge of the battalion (he was ordered to avoid front-line duties, as his death would be a disaster for German propaganda), did make his way to Narva on 8 August, where he sought contact with his old aquintance *SS-Obergruppenführer* Felix Steiner at his Corps HQ. Although the Walloon *Kampfgruppe* was a much-reduced battalion, with only one rifle company and insufficient numerical strength, Degrelle personally guaranteed the combat value of the battalion, and they were attached to the ad hoc *Kampfgruppe "Wagner"* from the *III. (germ.) SS-Panzer-Korps* on 10 August, taking up positions

Leon Degrelle distributing medals during a parade in Brussels in 1944, with *SS-Obergruppenführer* Sepp Dietrich in the background.

south of Dorpat (Tartu) on the line Elva-Liiva-Patska, to block a threatening Soviet advance from the south end of Lake Peipus.

The Walloons fought in this area for three weeks and suffered severe losses: only 200 men survived. The Walloon *SS-Untersturmführer* and leader of the battalion's anti-tank platoon, Leon Gillis, was afterwards decorated with the Knight's Cross for the actions of his platoon, which consisted of three guns and himself single-handedly destroying between 15 and 19 Soviet T-34 tanks on 22–23 August 1944. Degrelle himself succeeded on 23 August in blocking a Soviet breakthrough in the area of Lemmatsi with a handful of Walloons, Germans and weak units of Estonian border guards. His intervention with a determined command saved the day, and probably saved Dorpat from being taken the same day. Degrelle was awarded the Oakleaves to his Knight's Cross on 27 August 1944. After severe fighting on 24–25 August around Nöela, the original battle-strength of 452 men had shrunk to just 90 Walloons fit for battle. Degrelle and his *SS* Walloons would, in early 1945, fight again with the *III. (germ.) SS-Panzer-Korps*, this time in Pomerania.

During the final phase of the war, Degrelle managed to get to Denmark and from there fled to Norway, where he succeeded in escaping in a *Heinkel* 111, making a forced landing on a beach near San Sebastian in northern Spain. Degrelle received Spanish citizenship and escaped extradition to Belgium, where the authorities condemned him to death *in absentia*. During his exile in Spain, Degrelle remained the eternal Fascist, and made himself notorious for denying the Holocaust and upholding contacts with European neo-Fascist parties and factions. Degrelle died in 1994 in a hospital in Málaga.

LW

Ivar Skarlo, Norwegian volunteer in the *SS-Panzergrenadier Regiment "Norge"* (Tommy Natedal's archive)

In the morning on February 19 1944, the Red Army discharged an inferno of grenades to prepare a storm assault on our positions at the Narva river near Siivertsi. They shot with everything from 23cm artillery to 8cm mortars. We who were in the forward trenches had not corresponding fire power, and all over the line lay comrades shot to pieces in the trenches. The Soviet snipers hit one after the other. All were hit in the head and the Russians used explosive ammunition. To get some cover against the snipers I had to barricade myself behind the corpses of my comrades, laying them on the top of the trench. The dead become a protection against a sniper that was positioned in a church tower.

I was wounded immediately afterwards by splinters from a grenade. It was urgent to get medical care and I crawled backwards towards our command place with grenades detonating all around me. I drew myself to the rear without knowing into what, but I followed blood stains in the snow and got right [away]. A Norwegian

SS-Obersturmbannführer Wolfgang Joerchel in April 1944 after receiving the Knight's Cross for his leadership of the *SS-Panzer-Grenadier-Regiment 48 "General Seyffardt"* in the defence of Narva. Joerchel was born in 1907 in Silesia and studied Russian at the University of Breslau before joining the *SA* and in 1935 the *Verfügungstruppe*. He was an officer in various positions under Felix Steiner in the *Regiment "Deutschland"* and *Division "Wiking"* before assuming command of the *"General Seyffardt"* in January 1944. At the end of the war he was CO of the *Junkerschule* in Prague, and mystery surrounds his death on 12 May 1945, when it was reported that he was either murdered by a Czech mob or committed suicide.

At the HQ of the *III. (Germ.) SS-Panzer-Korps* in Sillamäe, in March 1944. To the left stands the Chief of Staff, *SS-Oberführer* Joachim Ziegler, who was regarded as an exceptionally talented general staff officer in various positions on the Eastern Front in the German Army fromn 1941–43. By request of Felix Steiner, Zielger was transferred to the *Waffen-SS* on 23 June 1943 as Chief of Staff for the new Germanic *SS-Panzer-Korps*. To the right stands *SS-Obergruppenführer* Felix Steiner, discussing the tactical situation in Narva in the map room with Ziegler.

Albrecht Krügel, Fritz von Scholz and Fritz Knöchlein at the Narva Front.

SS-Sturmbannführer Hans-Heinrich Lohmann joind the *SS* in 1935 and held various positions in the *SS-Regiment "Deutschland"* under Felix Steiner and later in the *SS-Division "Wiking"* in the war against the USSR. After the creation of the *III. (Germ.) SS-Panzer-Korps*, Lohmann was appointed battalion commander in the *SS-Panzergrenadier-Regiment 23 "Norge"*, with whom he was severely wounded in January 1944 during the retreat out of Ingrid; it was here that Lohmann earned the Knight's Cross for his skillful rearguard actions. After returning to the front in Courland in October 1944, Lohmann was designated to relieve the unpopular Fritz Knöchlein as CO of *Regiment "Norge"*, but instead took command of the *Regiment 49 "De Ruyter"* until the end of the war. When Lohmann's regiment was evacuated from Courland to Pomerania on 30 January 1945, it counted just 80 men. Lohmann said: "With such pitiful remnants of our former *SS*-units, we were supposed to throw back the Red Army out of Pomerania! Sheer madness!"

Ivar Skarlo

doctor from Halden operated [on] me and took away all the splinters, some twenty of them, out of my body.

Odd Angelsen, Norwegian volunteer in the *SS-Panzergrenadier Regiment "Norge"* (Tommy Natedal's archive)

On the night [of] February 24, the Russians infiltrated our trenches and killed 12 of our Norwegian comrades who were on guard; they had probably fallen asleep. Not one of us had slept more than one hour after the counter-attack started. We were so tired that no one even had the energy to move an arm or a leg. Furthermore it was so cold that our uniforms were frozen stiff on our bodies. All were dirty and unwashed and no one had changed underwear for a long time. Shirts and pullovers were full of lice. I had gone without socks in my leather boots for 14 days and had no feeling in my legs. And here we were, standing guard night after night without relief.

Every night we sent out scout patrols. In the days we could count on uninterrupted Russian fire from mortars and artillery for hours. There were no bunkers to take cover inside and conditions were harder than anyone can imagine without having experienced this himself. On February 26 our battle group had shrunk down to 56 men, and the same night Russian bombers killed another nine men. Our mortar position was hit by a Russian grenade which made our *SS-Unterscharführer* blind and killed one man. Finally, a Russian storm troop succeeded in infiltrating the trenches of the *4. "Danmark"*, taking the CO and eight men prisoners. We made three counter-attacks without result. On March 15, units from *"Danmark"* succeeded in penetrating the Russian units. As an example of the severe fighting, 20 Soviet tanks were destroyed just on March 17. We had by now been supplied with a new anti-tank weapon, the later so famous *Panzerfaust*.

SS-Oberscharführer Fritz Höpfinger from the *"Nordland"*, who was severely wounded in January 1944, photographed in late 1944 in Baden, Germany.

Odd Angelsen, Norwegian volunteer in the *SS-Panzergrenadier Regiment "Norge"* (Tommy Natedal's archive)

On March 6, 1944, we attacked the Russian bridgehead at Siivertsi. At 6 pm our artillery fired for one hour against the Russian positions. Immediately afterwards, orders came for a frontal attack and we ran against the graveyard over a field. The cemetery was surrounded by a stone wall, one metre high, which was reinforced with Russian barbed wire and mines. We ran and shot all we could at the same time. We were opposed by a murderous fire from machine guns and mortars. We were thrown back twice. At the end, there were more corpses outside the cemetery of Sivertsii than the number of those buried inside, although the graveyard had been used for several hundred years. Now our artillery opened fire and our tanks fired against the stone wall, which enabled us to break through. I was head of a group of eight infantrymen with a machine gun and the rest with machine pistols. I ran across the field and succeeded in reaching the inside of the cemetery. I took cover behind a gravestone and waited for the others. The machine-gunner came after me but went hanging in the barbed wire and was mortally wounded.

An NCO awaiting decoration with the Iron Cross 1st Class at Narva, March 1944. He already carries the *Infanteriesturmabzeichen* and the Iron Cross 2nd Class. (Courtesy of Björn Leo)

Peter Puhm, *SS-Unterscharfuehrer* in the signals battalion *"Nordland"* (Lennart Westberg's archive)

I was responsible for an 80-Watt radio transmission group from the *Nachrichten-Abteilung "Nordland"*. In March 1944 I was detached with my group to the artillery regimental chief [of the] *"Nordland"*, *SS-Obersturmbannführer* Karl, who had his command post in the fortress of Hermansborg. The night before, material and vehicles were destroyed during the Soviet bomb attack on March 6–7,. [When] a signal vehicle got a direct hit by a bomb, we were put in as reserve signal personnel. Our duty was to coordinate the communications of this artillery detachment for collective fire control. Around 5 April the Russians tried to destroy the tower of Hermansborg with artillery, probably to prevent it from being used as an observation point. But they succeeded only in shooting down the lantern in the tower. On May 5 the Red Army put in heavy artillery, probably 30cm, and destroyed the upper part of the tower.

SS-Haupsturmführer Günther Wanhöfer.

The Battle of the Narva Bridgehead

Soviet troops crossed the old Polish-Soviet border at Zjitomir on 4 January 1944. To the north, the Red Army executed its great offensive from Leningrad and Oranienbaum westwards through Ingria against Narva and Novogord on 14 January. The strategic goal was to crush *Heeresgruppe Nord* and take the German-occupied Estonia, which in its turn had been annexed by the USSR in 1940. Through this, Stalin wanted to get access to the Baltic ports and get the Red Fleet into the Baltic Sea after it had been shut up in the Finnish Gulf

The burial place for *SS-Division "Nordland"* at Kreenholm in 1944 and today. The graves of these *SS* soldiers were dug up by German prisoners in the autumn of 1944 and moved to a typical Soviet mass grave. Only after Estonia regained its independence in 1990 were all these war graves reconstructed by the Federal German Wargraves Agencies.

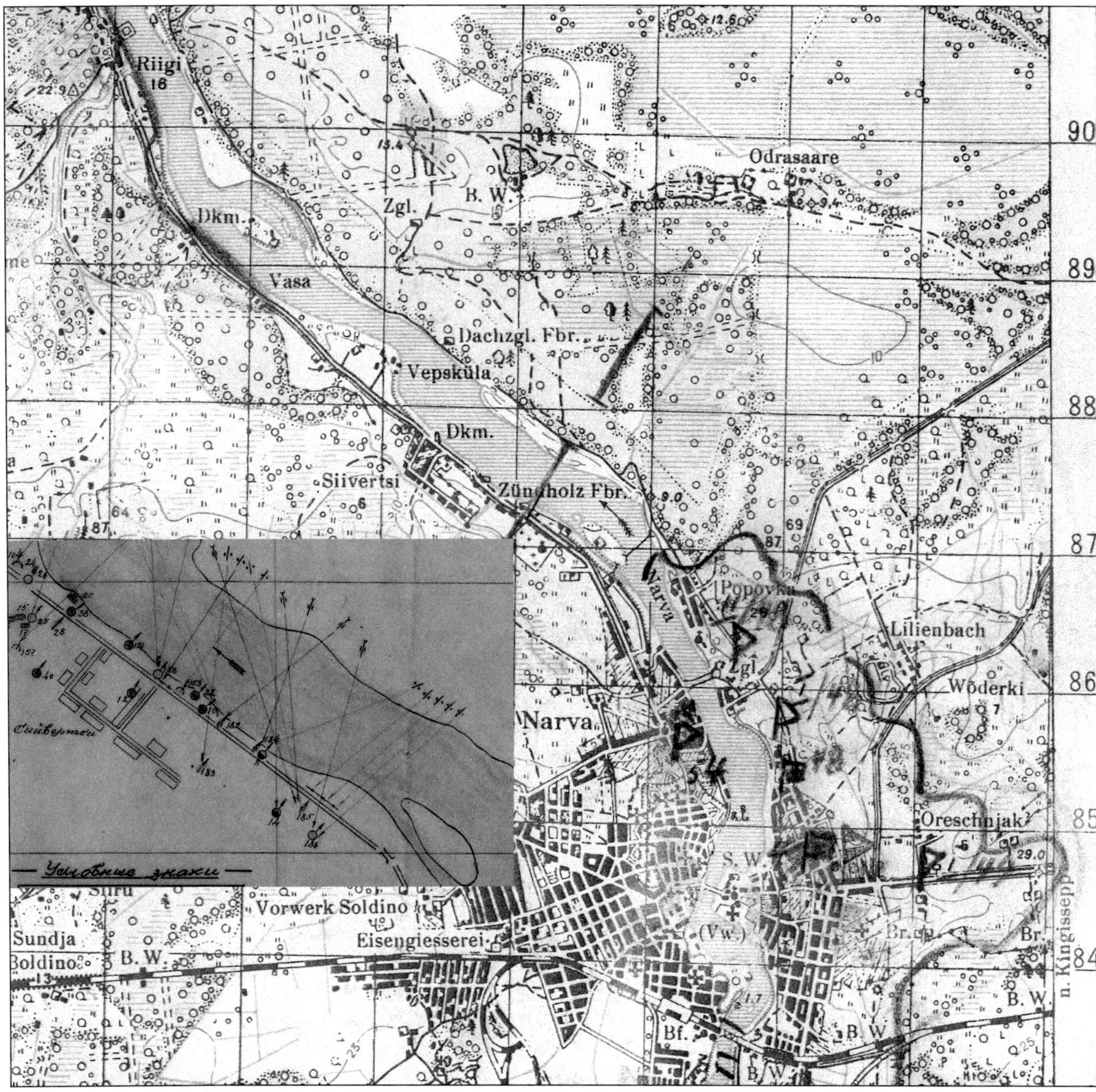

The Soviets attacked the German positions at Siivertsi repeatedly, and the *SS-Pionier-Bataillon 54*, under the leadership of *SS-Hauptstumführer* Günther Wanhöfer, was thrown into action and, with heavy losses, blocked the Soviet advance at the *Zündholzfabrik*. Wanhöfer was wounded in both of his eyes during the combat. (Courtesy of Björn Leo)

since the late summer of 1941. Another of Stalin's goals was, by occupying Estonia, to create the necessary conditions for a Soviet offensive from the Baltic States against East Prussia and the *Reich* mainland. By occupying Estonia, Stalin aimed to force Hitler's brother-in-arms, Finland, to capitulate or make peace under the imminent threat of Soviet aerial and amphibious attacks from Estonia.

But the plans of Stalin and the *Stavka* were thwarted. The Germans fortified themselves in the Narva bridgehead for nearly six months and blocked all Soviet offensives into the Estonian mainland during the hard battles of the spring and summer 1944. Consequently, the Finns pushed aside all Soviet proposals for peace in April 1944.

The Red Army suffered from logistic supply problems at Narva due to the useless roads and the German destruction carried out during their retreat through Ingermanland. Another big handicap was the Red Army's poor intelligence organization during the battles for Narva, as well as a lack of anti aircraft, reconnaissance and engineering capacities in the Red Army units. The greatest threat from the Soviets was the deep thrust in February 1944 over the Narva River at the Krivasso marshes, 10km south of the city. The Soviet 314th Rifle Division reached Auvere, 10km west of Narva, and threatened to cut off the railroad between Tallinn and Narva. This Soviet bridgehead was partly destroyed by operations conducted by *"Der Panzergraf"* (the *Panzer* count), *Generalleutnant* von Strachwitz, in March 1944.

For the Germans, another dangerous bridgehead at Riigikuela was liquidated in early March 1944 by units from the *20. Estonian SS-Division* and companies from *"Norge"* and *"Danmark"*. At Narva, Estonians also fought against Estonians: the German *20. SS-Division* and the Soviet 8th Estonian Rifle Corps. After repeated Soviet offensives against the Narva bridgehead (including bomber attacks against Narva and Tallinn) failed, the fighting petered out and was replaced by artillery assaults, sniper activities and recce operations. After the Soviet failure at Narva, the *Stavka* moved its focus against the central Eastern front and the German *Heeresgruppe Mitte*. On 22 June 1944, the Red Army attacked in force the Finnish front at Viborg on the Karelian

SS-soldiers in a trench taking cover from a Soviet air attack. The soldier in the foreground is probably the group leader, carrying the new *SturmGewehr* 44.

A ceremony in the Estonian former recreation resort of Hungerburg on the shores of the Gulf of Finland, downstream from Narva, in February-March 1944: officers from the *SS-Sturmgeschütz Bataillon 11* decorate men from their unit with the Iron Cross 1st and 2nd Class.

Two Danish volunteers from the *SS-Panzer-Grenadier-Regiment 24 "Danmark"* ride a motorcycle on Joala Street in southern Narva in the spring of 1944. In the background lies the Kreenholm manufacturing plant. This complex served as HQ for the Norwegian-Danish *SS-Hauptsturmführer* Erik Laerum, a skilled artillery officer from the pre-war Danish Army who was also a dedicated National Socialist in Denmark. In March 1944, Laerum organized and synchronized all artillery and mortar pieces in the *SS-Regiment "Danmark"* into a deadly effective system, which enabled the fire control to open precise fire, day or night and in all weathers, giving cover and protection for the "*Danmark*" infantry units of.

Thanks to the Swedish Narva-expert Björn Leo, the wounded man can be identified as *SS-Haupsturmführer* Günther Wanhöfer from the *SS-Pioneer Bataillon 54 "Nederland"*. He has been wounded and bandaged over his eyes in the bridgehead of Sivertsii, just north of central Narva along the Narva River, and is being escorted to the nearest field hospital by *SS-Untersturmführer* Horwarth and other *SS* soldiers. A German and Soviet map show the exact position of Wanhöfer when being wounded, probably by shrapnel from 7.62cm Soviet anti-tank guns on the opposite bank of the river. The *SS-Pionier Bataillon 54* succeeded in blocking the Soviet advance at the *Zündholzfabrik* (match factory) with heavy losses. The bridgehead was annihilated mainly by the efforts of the Estonian *SS-Grenadier Regiments 45* and *46*. (Courtesy of Björn Leo)

SS-Obersturmführer Fritz Sidon from Lichtenstein commanded the *9./SS-Regiment "Danmark"*. He successfully covered the retreat for elements of the Germanic *SS-Panzer-Korps* at Witvino in January 1944. From early 1945, Sidon served as adjutant to the CO of *SS-Panzer-Abteilung "Hermann von Salza"*, *SS-Obersturmbannführer* Paul-Albert Kausch. Sidon belonged to a famous family of politicans and senior civil servants (de la Fontaine) in Lichtenstein and died in 1996.

Himmler's ambition was to strengthen the influence of the *SS* in, for example, occupied Norway, by establishing a Norwegian branch of the *Allgemeine SS*: *Germanske SS Norge* (*GSSN*). One of its aims was to convert former *SS* volunteers into service in the *NS*-party, the police and the civil service in Norway. This poster announces "*SS*-Day" in Oslo, 14–15 August 1943.

German propaganda poster for service in the *Waffen-SS*. The ideology of the *SS* was of a notably reactionary and anti-modern, almost archaic character in its "bizarre Romanticism, which in its substance distinguished itself from Hitler's own modern personal philosophy" (Bernd Wegner). The complex expansion of the *SS* in diversified security, political and economic matters during the Thirties threatened Himmler's central control over his new empire. Only the perspectives of war and thereby territorial expansion in the East opened up new potentials and possibilities to mastermind the expansion of the *SS* on a much larger and controlled scale.

Isthmus, causing the Finns to retreat. However, by putting up an impressive defence with the assistance of German heavy weapons and a squadron of *Stukas*, the Finns succeeded in stabilizing the front until August.

The CO of *Armeeabteilung "Narva"* in 1944, the German infantry general Anton Grasser, wrote in a study for the US Army in 1948:

> Until the evacuation of the country [Estonia], the actual combat terrain was located east of the Mustvee-Lohusuu-Iisaku-Johvi highway. The ground was swampy, with the exception of a strip of land along the Finnish Gulf. In addition to the Mustvee-Johvi highway, there remained only the Johvi-Narva highway; both could only be considered as firm roads in the summer. During the muddy period both highways had to be closed to all motor traffic. All other roads lacked a firm base and could not be used even by horse-drawn vehicles during spring and [autumn]. With the exception of the sandy banks of the Narva River and the Front north of the Johvi-Narva railroad, it was impossible to dig into the ground to any great depth.
>
> Artillery emplacements could not be constructed in the swampy woods. If small sand dunes could not be found, the guns were emplaced on corduroy [log] roads. The infantry positions consisted of abatis which were connected with barbed wire. Shelters consisted merely of underground huts.
>
> At the outset neither side employed tanks. Only in the course of later fighting were tanks committed, initially by the Russians. With each commitment of armor losses were incurred, as tanks bogged down in the mud. Subsequently, both sides discontinued their employment. Tanks were not used again until the evacuation of the country.
>
> In July 1944, after the withdrawal of Army Group Center, the staff of XXVI and the XLIII Corps were withdrawn from the Narva Front. Only the *III. (germ.) SS-Panzer-Korps* remained with the *Armeeabteilung Narva* ... The continuous threat from the south to the rear of the *III. (germ.) SS-Panzer-Korps* at Narva forced the German command to take back and straighten its Narva line at the end of July 1944. The city of Narva was abandoned. The Russians greatly exploited this withdrawal through their propaganda organs. The old gateway to the Baltic countries was once again in their possession. The yielding of Narva to the Russians was a heavy blow to the Estonian population.
>
> Even before the beginning of the Russian offensive at Army Group Center, the idea of evacuating the Baltic countries, withdrawing to the Dvina, and maintaining the Riga bridgehead had gained ground. *Armeeabteilung Narva* took the following steps in preparation for the evacuation of Estonia:
>
> 1. The operation was assigned the code name "*Entrümpelung*" [meaning] house cleaning. All equipment not absolutely needed was moved to Germany.
> 2. A small group of officers, sworn to absolute secrecy, conducted a dry run of the planned operation under the code name "Tannenbaum I". Direction of withdrawal and lines of resistance were established on the maps and were reconnoitred on the ground inconspicuously.
> 3. *Armeeabteilung Narva* designated highways for motorized and horse-drawn vehicles. Bridges were reinforced.
>
> A withdrawal directly west toward Reval and the Island of Oesel would have been the least difficult for *Armeeabteilung Narva*. The overall situation however necessitated a southwesterly and ultimately southern direction toward Riga.[26]

The battles around the Narva bridgehead were costy for both parties. From February to June 1944, the Red Army lost 65,000 dead or missing, with 235,000 wounded. The German and allied losses at Narva during the same period has been estimated at 12,000 dead or missing and 46,000 wounded. (LW)

Narva – a historical symbol for Himmler and the *SS* in 1944

The main theatre of war for the defensive battles of the *III. (germ.) SS-Panzer-Korps* against the Red Army became, during the whole of 1944, the Baltic countries: Ingria, Estonia, Latvia and Lithuania. These regions were once strongholds for the Teutonic Order and the Swedish Empire. Narva was, during Swedish rule from 1581–1704, an architectural jewel in Carolingian baroque style, formed by the Swedish fortification expert Erik Dahlberg, and considered second only to Stockholm. The city of Narva became the battleground for six months of hard fighting in 1944 and was practically wiped out, especially during the Soviet aerial bombardment on 6–7 March.

During the summer of 1944, the German defensive lines on the Eastern Front had been splintered in different directions by the Red Army. The Narva bridgehead suddenly emerged as the most easterly German position on the Eastern Front and the only place where the Germans and their allies could hold ground against the Soviets. The theatre of war at Narva – in combination with the fact that so many multinational units from the *Waffen-SS* were concentrated in this area within the *III. (germ.) SS-Panzer-Korps* – therefore achieved a high propaganda value and an essential degree of prestige in the eys of Hitler and Himmler.

In the Danish recruiting brochure for the *Waffen-SS*, reproduced here, the *SS* makes a historic, symbolic parallel: in the foreground, "Germanic" *SS*-soldiers from Denmark are marching against a background of the Danish King Valdemar II, who in 1219, with his army of crusaders, defeated the Estonian tribes at the castle of Lyndanise, the site for the

SS-Standartenfuehrer Wolfgang Joerchel was awarded the Knight´s Cross while commanding the *SS-Panzergrenadier-Regiment 48 "General Seyffardt"* in the defence of the Narva Bridgehead. In March 1944, Soviet forces made a faint attack against "Nordland" positions but directed its real blow against the Regiment "General Seyffardt" which was forced out of its positions. Due to a counter-attack led by Wolfgang Joerchel, a Soviet breakthrough was averted. (NARA)

The *SS* crew of a 7.5cm Infantry Gun Model 18 (*leichtes Infanteriegeschütz 18*) take a break after pounding enemy positions around the Narva bridgehead. The roughly 100 used shells in the foreground bear witness to the intensity of the shelling. Some 12,000 examples of this gun were produced by *Rheinmetall* between 1932 and 1945. Its maximum firing range was 3,550 metres (3,880 yards).

A group of NCOs from the *SS-Panzer-Pionier-Abteilung 11 "Nordland"*, photographed on 15 May 1944 outside their HQ at Kreenholm. The island of Kreenholm (German for "Crow Isles") divided the Narva River waterfalls. In 1856 the German cotton merchant, Ludwig Knoop, built Europe´s largest cotton spinning mill on Kreenholm and a part of its old brick wall is visible behind the SS-soldiers (courtesy of Björn Leo).

Soviet prisoners of war laying mines on the shore of the Gulf of Finland at Mummassare, where the "Swedish platoon" of the *SS-Panzer-Aufklärungsabteilung "Nordland"* was located in the spring of 1944.

A half-track *SdKfz 250/7* from the "*Nordland*" in the swamps of Auwere during the spring of 1944. This *SPW* belonged to the "Swedish platoon" of the *SS-Panzer-Aufklärungsabteilung "Nordland"* and carried an 8cm mortar with 12 grenades and two MG 42s.

Senior officers in the *4. SS-Freiwilligen-Panzergrenadier-Brigade "Nederland"* in the spring of 1944 in Narva. From the left are: Lothar Hofer (CO *II./SS-Artillerie-Regiment 53*), Carl-Heinz Frühauf (CO *II./De Ruyter*), Dietrich Ziemssen (operations officer), Jürgen Wagner (CO *Brigade "Nederland"*), Christian Steenholdt-Schütt (brigade-adjutant), Hans Meyer (CO *II./General Seyffardt*), Hans Collani (CO *De Ruyter*) and Wilhelm Schlüter (CO *I./SS-Artillerie-Regiment 54*). Hofer came as a police officer to the *Waffen-SS* and advanced after 1945 to become a colonel in the West German Border Police (*Bundesgrenzschutz*).

future Tallinn (Estonian for "the Danish castle"). In 1256, the Danes founded at Narva a border fortification against the East, which in 1346 came into the possession of the Teutonic Order and was expanded to the stone castle of Hermansborg. In November 1700, the Swedish warrior King Charles XII achieved one of his greatest victories when he defeated a superior Russian army of 40,000 men with a force half that size in the Battle of Narva.

Himmler also made other "Germanic" allusions to the "fateful struggle in the East". He proposed to Hitler in February 1943 that the new *SS-Panzergrenadier-Division* should be named "*Waräger*". This division would partly consist of Scandinavian volunteers and would become an integral part of the new *III. ("Germanic") SS-Panzer-Korps*. Himmler wrote in his memo to Hitler: "*Waräger* will once again become the collective name for Danes, Flemish, Dutch, Norwegians, Swedes and Swiss, as they are all from the same Germanic tribe." *Väringar* were Nordic-Swedish Viking tribes that went on trading or looting expeditions in the East. However, Hitler did not approve of the name "*Waräger*" and the division was instead named "*Nordland*".

In Norwegian pro-Quisling periodicals or in *SS* newspapers from the front, Norwegian volunteers from the *III. (Germ.) SS-Panzer-Korps* in 1944 often scorned "the degenerated Jewish Swedish state" which it was said no longer lived up to its former reputation as a warrior Greater Empire. Instead of Charles XII, Norwegian *SS-Panzer Grenadiers* "defended the West against the barbaric East" in 1944. (LW)

The "*Panzer* Count" Hyazinth Strachwitz

The colourful *Generalleutnant* Graf Strachwitz von Gross-Zauche und Camminetz was born in Gross-Stein, in the Kingdom of Prussia, in 1893 and belonged to old Silesian nobility. After his time in Berlin as a cadet, Strachwitz joined the prestigious cavalry regiment *Garde de Corps* in Potsdam, which dated back to the time of Frederick the Great. During the First World War, the colourful Strachwitz led a cavalry patrol in the form of a deep raid behind the French lines to the outskirts of Paris, being captured and becoming a French POW from October 1914 until 1918. After the war, Strachwitz joined the *Freikorps*, battling Polish insurgents on Germany's eastern borders, before returning to his family estates in Silesia. As a reserve officer, he became thrilled by the new *Panzer Waffe* and re-enlisted in 1934, considering the tanks to be the new cavalry. Although in his later 40s when the Second World War broke out, Strrachwitz became one of the most dashing and capable tank commanders of the war, was wounded 14 times and was the most decorated regimental commander in the *Wehrmacht*, nicknamed *Der Panzergraf* (The Panzer Count). Strachwitz, then commander of a *Panzer-Abteilung* from the *16. Panzer-Division*, was the first German officer to enter the city of Stalingrad in late August 1942, then being one of the few who escaped the abyss as he was flown out, wounded, from the encircled Sixth Army. With his energetic leadership, he participated in the recapture of Kharkov in mid-March 1943, as commander of the prestigious *Grossdeutschland* tank regiment. He joined the Nazi party before the war and held the rank of *SS-Standartenführer* in 1944.

Soldiers from the *Wehrmacht* building bunkers on the outskirts of Narva in February 1944.

In March 1944, Strachwitz was appointed as *Höherer SS-Panzerführer* (Higher Tank Commander) to *Heeresgruppe Nord*, commanding a mixed force of tanks, including Tigers from the *Schwere Panzer-Abteilung 502*. That same month, the German Army High Command and *Armeeabteilung Narwa* commissioned Strachwitz with the task of liquidating the Soviet breakthrough at Krivasso, to the south of Narva. With his staff from the *Grossdeutschland* division and reinforced by *Stukas*, *panzers*, *Nebelwerfer* and infantry, Strachwitz's units splintered the Red Army at Krivasso, and eliminated its 72nd Rifle Corps and parts of its 109th Rifle Corps, with Soviet losses of up to 6,000 men during the period 26–31 March 1944.

Lieutenant Otto Carius, company commander in the heavy *Panzer-Abteilung 502*, witnessed how Strachwitz was careful in details. During an attack, the infantry were more mobile without their winter clothing; these were collected, packaged by infantry groups with name labels and transported by half-track to the units after the breakthrough, in order not to let them freeze. Strachwitz's aide-de-camp calculated beforehand the precise time that permitted exact fire from artillery, *Nebelwerfer* and *panzers*. Five minutes before the overall assault, German artillery had orders to open fire and for every minute moved forwarded its fire at the front. Strachwitz had also acquired anti-aircraft batteries consisting of 20mm, 37mm and 88mm guns.

Additionally, the whole operation was supported by batteries of a *Nebelwerfer* regiment, that first shot with napalm-like grenades and then with percussion shells. The effect on the Red Army was devastating. The German tank commanders had produced their own maps and aerial reconnaissance photos especiallyfor this operation. The ground-to air radio contact with the *Stukas* was handled by a half-track with special radio equipment. Before the attack, the concept had been tested in a similar area of terrain behind the front. Field Marshal Walter Model was personally present and addressed the officers of the operation. The bridgehead of Narva had to be held at all costs as the oil slate in Estonia was of the utmost importance to German submarines.

On 7 April 1944, the Strachwitz battle group again succeeded in breaking the remaining Soviet forces at Krivasso and the Red Army lost 5,700 men. The attempt to liquidate the Soviet pocket at Auvere failed, due to the advent of spring and the thick mud that hindered the use of Tiger tanks. The Soviet General Govorov was upset over the Red Army losses at Krivasso and ordered his units to stay on the defensive. On 15 April 1944, Hitler decorated Strachwitz with diamonds on the Knight's Cross - at that time Germany's highest military decoration - for his successes at Narva.

Strachwitz's youngest son Harti was killed in action on 25 March 1945 near Holstein. As the war drew to a close, Strachwitz's *panzer* brigade was surrounded in Czechoslovakia but managed to break out in April 1945, and he was taken

Martin Gross

An anti-aircraft crew with a 2cm-*Flak* from the *SS-Flakabteilung "Nordland"* at Udria, in the Gulf of Finland, in mid-1944.

A crew of *SS*-gunners around an 8.8cm-*Flak* from the *SS-Flakabteilung "Nordland"* at Udria in Estonia in mid-1944.

prisoner by the US Army. During his captivity, Strachwitz's wife Alda was killed, run over by a US military truck in Velden on 6 January 1946. His Silesian estates were confiscated by the Soviets. In July 1947 he married again, to Nora, *née* von Stumm (1916–2000), and they had four children, born between 1951 and 1960. Hyazinth Strachwitz and his wife went to Syria in 1949, invited by the government, to be an agriculture and military instructor to the Syrian armed forces, but a *coup d'etat* there forced him return to Germany in 1951 via Lebanon and Livorno in Italy, where they ran a winery. The family settled on the Winkl estate in Bavaria, where Strachwitz founded the *Oberschlesisches Hilfswerk* (Upper Silesian Fund) for refugee Silesians in need. Strachwitz lived out his life quietly, and died on 25 April 1968 of lung cancer in a hospital at Trostberg in Bavaria. (LW)

The Tiger tank

Max Hastings writes in his book *Armageddon*: "While all who studies the Second World War should acknowledge that the German army in quality was superior to its opponents, it would be wrong to believe that the *Wehrmacht* at every time fought with skill and inventiveness. Especially during the last months of the war, many German reports from the front witnessed blunders and inefficient conduct from various commanders." The company commander Otto Carius in *Schwere Panzer-Abteilung 502*, who fought against the Red Army at Narva and Daugavpils (Dünaburg), recollects on several occasions his incompetent battalion commander, and how superior German staff too often did not master the tactical principals for using Tiger tanks in battle.

An armoured half-track *Sonderkraftfahrzeug 251/9, Ausführung D*, from the 5th company of *SS-Pz.Aufklärungsabteilung 11*, near Hungerburg in May 1944, with Commandant Uetz. (Courtesy of Predrag Blanusa & Björn Leo)

12 enemy tanks. The Tiger I (*Panzerkampfwagen VI Ausf E/ SdKfz 181*) was equipped with the 88mm *KwK 36*, which was mounted coaxially with a MG 34. The Tiger I was a potent tank offering first-class protection and firepower, but its mobility and mechanical reliability were too limited to allow it to reach and fulfil its true potential. The Tiger I was issued to the heavy tank detachments and heavy tank companies of three *SS* divisions and to the *Grossdeutschland Division*, and remained in service until the end of the war. The Tiger II (*Panzerkampfwagen VI Ausf B/SdKfz 182*) had a new turret large enough to mount the long 88mm L/71 gun. The first such King Tigers (*Königstiger*) were issued to training units in February and May 1944 and were delievered to combat units in June 1944, but insufficient numbers were produced of both the Tiger I and II to arrest the flood of enemy armour. LW

Horst Ernst, grenadier in the SS-*Panzergrenadier-Regiment "Norge"* (Tommy Natedal's archive)

At the beginning of April 1944, I was on guard [from] 04.00 until 08.00 at night, when in the early morning I saw nothing in front of me of the terrain. For the first time I experienced a heavier and more prolonged Soviet artillery assault. It lasted for four hours, the earth shook and erupted. I had an uneasy feeling in my stomach, both of fear and insecurity. At 12 o'clock the artillery barrier moved 100 metres backwards into our lines and when we watched over the top of our trenches, we saw around twenty T-34s and around 100 Russian infantrymen running against us. We immediately shot yellow-red-green signal rockets (signalling "Enemy attacking") and the artillery observers directed our artillery fire against the enemy tanks. The terrain in front of us disappeared in a wall of smoke and earth out of which wild shooting T-34s emerged. Behind the *Panzers* the Russian infantry came running, shooting at us with submachine guns. Our anti-tank guns hit some of the T-34s without being able to stop the rest. I fired mechanically with my MG 42, cartridge-belt after cartridge-belt, the weapons drill from the infantry training now paying-off, as we acted precisely and mechanically in the heat of the battle. We had become machines, freed from personal feelings, acting only with will and muscles. I had no reflection of time, I only felt a cold hatred against those who attacked us. For the first time I experienced that the Russians used the forbidden explosive dum-dum ammunition [which] caused serious damage. Our artillery barrage hit the Russian infantry hard. Some T-34s approached our trenches before our anti-tank guns could fire.

Our greatest fear was that the tanks could climb up on our trenches and then crush or suffocate us to death, which had happened previously. At the end, the Russian assault came to an end and a ghostly stillness emerged, only interrupted by the shrieks of the wounded.

Hans-Gösta Pehrsson, Swedish company commander in the *SS-Panzer-Aufklärung-sabteilung "Nordland"* (from a lecture before Swedish officers in 1952; Lennart Westberg's archive)

The Russian as a tactician was very quick to learn and soon adopted new methods from his opponent, and they probably learnt the most from the great tank battles in the middle sector of the Eastern Front in 1943–44. A Soviet tank assault in 1942 and 1944 were quite different things. Before 1944, the tanks preferred to operate in groups before their infantry and tried to put our machine-gun and anti-tank gun-positions out of action. Later on, their tanks only in exceptional cases drove before but ... level with their infantry. Their tanks shot concentrated breaches in our front and shot [at] everything that moved. At the slightest opposition, their artillery struck. The Russian fire control was either driving in the tanks or among the infantry.

The Soviet weapons developed signifiquently [from] 1941–1944: the salvo rocket weapon, popular[ly] renowned [as] the *Stalin organ*, had during the first two years of war more a psychological then a deadly effect. Later, they developed greater calibres and with far more shrapnel or flame effects. Their 7.62cm anti-tank gun was fantastic ("*ratsch-bom*") with great morale effect. Mortars (8 and 12cm): their tactical use *en masse* was [highly skilled] and devastating. Statistics showed that the Soviet mortars caused more casualties then all other weapons together. The Soviet mass army is not unbeatable if it is opposed by an alert and undaunted opponent that lets the Russians pour its ammunitions into empty terrain and works with ... the terrain as an ally.

Reports from Narva to Stockholm in 1944

The Swedish military attaché in Berlin, Colonel Curt Juhlin-Dannfelt, was extremely well-informed on German military and also political conditions. One of his sources was Swedish volunteers in the *SS-Panzergrenadier- Division "Nordland"*. On 7 June 1944, Juhlin-Dannfelt sent to Stockholm a detailed description on new German secret weapons at the front. This was information that the three Swedish *SS* soldiers Sven Alm, Knut Fagerström and Karl-Erik Pehrsson, during leave in Berlin, had passed on to Captain Sigvard Drake af Hagelsrum, assistant Swedish military attaché.

Erik Laerum, Danish artillery officer in the *SS Panzergrenadier Regiment "Danmark"*

[Re the German salvo-rocket weapon "*Dauerwerfer*"] This was the absolute most dreaded weapon from [a] Russian point of view. The [S]oviets never advanced forward any point where this weapon was known to exist. This fear gave the Germans room to breathe during the retreat on the Eastern front. The grenades['] individual effects [are]

One of the company adjutants from *SS-Sturmgeschützabteilung 11* has arrived in his VW *Schwimmwagen* with food for the crews. The mosquito nets on the men could indicate spring 1944, near one of the marshes around Narva.

NCOs from the *SS*-Assault Gun Battalion "*Nordland*" having fun while trying to open a bottle of wine or schnapps. Two of the men are wearing the camouflage fatigue dress for tank crews with pea-dot pattern.

Assault gun NCOs and men from the "Nordland" near the Gulf of Finland, north of Narva, in spring 1944. The men are, from the left: Beeker, Klösel, Holzinger, Knecht and Brüst.

SS-Unterscharführer Prasse stands in front of his assault gun north of Narva in the Gulf of Finland. Note the unusual painting of a dragon on the 7.5cm L/48 gun.

SS-Hauptscharführer Danneberg with his crew, sitting with foliage on their well-camouflaged *StuG III* near the Gulf of Finland in spring 1944. Their unit is in a *Ruhestellung* (recreation area) after the previous fierce battles in and retreat out of Ingria in January 1944.

SS-Geschützführer (assault gun commandant) *SS-Unterscharführer* Ewald Beeker and men from his crew. Note the timber logs attached to the side of their assault gun, probably as protection against Soviet anti-tank rifles.

In front of an assault gun from the 3rd Company of the *SS-Sturmgeschützabteilung "Nordland"* stand, from the left: *SS-Untersturmführer* Hermann Meyer, *SS-Unterscharführer* Kupka, *SS-Unterscharführer* Prasse and *SS-Untersturmführer* Rudolf Peternell.

Standing with peaked cap before his VW *Kübelwagen* is the CO of the 1st Company of *SS-Sturmgeschützabteilung "Nordland"*, *Obersturmführer* Carlotto von Renteln (1921–77), with *Untersturmführer* Klassen and some NCOs from his unit. Von Renteln's ancestors were Baltic Germans, and his father, Evert von Renteln, was a colonel in the Second World War, serving as liaison officer to the so-called *Osttruppen* in the German Army on the Eastern Front. In May 1945, Evert von Renteln was, together with volunteer Cossack units from the German Army, handed over by the British to the Red Army, after which he was probably murdered by the Soviets in a Gulag camp.

SS-Untersturmführer Rudolf Peternell in front of an assault gun from the "*Nordland*".

Unterscharführer Becker (left) and Knecht with an anonymous NCO from the *SS*-Assault Gun Battalion 11 in the Gulf of Finland, some time in spring 1944. The men are wearing the grey field uniform of the armoured *Sturm Artillerie*.

Soldiers from the *SS-Sturmgeschützabteilung* "Nordland" outside their bunker near the Gulf of Finland, in spring 1944. After three months of continous attacks from Marshal Govorov's armies against Army Group North, the Germans were driven back from Leningrad into Estonia. But the Soviets failed to take Narva, in many ways thanks to the stiff rearguard resistance of the *III. (Germ.) SS-Panzer-Korps* and elite Army units all the way through Ingria to the Narva River. In April 1944, the spring thaw made all movements difficult, and a deadlock ensued for the Red Army until its new major offensive from 26 July 1944 against the German Tannenberg Line at Sinimäed. These pictures show the timber and earth bunkers erected by units of the Germanic *SS-Panzer-Korps* in the early spring of 1944.

SS-Unterscharführer Pfennig (left) and *SS-Rottenführer* Mortens behind their assault gun near Narva. The crews of *panzers* and assault guns would often dig out a small temporary bunker or trench under their armoured vehicle as protection against enemy artillery fire.

A *Sturmgeschütz* from the "*Nordland*" has taken cover between two bomb-damaged wooden houses on the outskirts of Narva.

Men from the *SS-Sturmgeschützabteilung 11* with a destroyed Soviet T-34 tank in the eastern outskirts of Narva. The T-34 had a good aluminium diesel engine and a superior streamlined armour, but its mobility and effectiveness were restrained due to poor transmission and radio equipment. Its battlefield effectiveness was handicapped by the lack of a cupola for the tank commander, who was also forced to be the gunner (the crews of the German *Panzer III* and *IV* consisted of five men with a dedicated commander). The flaws of the T-34 were only corrected from the beginning of 1944 as the T-34/85 emerged.

fantastic and can hardly be described. Even at a distance of 1,500 metres, the earth shakes from the explosions.

[Re the soldierly qualities on the Narva Front] The Germans were elite soldiers but even better were the Norwegians in *Nordland* who all the time fought like lions. Concerning the Russians, I was told that these fought with great bravery and skill and must be considered as an elite. Also the recent Estonian *SS* units are extremely good soldiers. As an example I was told that the Russians had succeeded in establishing a bridgehead at the southeastern riverbank of the Narva river. Against these, Estonian units were put into action. These were only equipped with fifteen rounds per rifle, some hand grenades and knives. The Soviet bridgehead was completely destroyed by the Estonians.

The Russians had captured our strong-point [at] Dolgaja-Niva and penetrated deep into our main defence line. They had used a new tactic which outwitted our defence. The Russians took one week for their advance against our strong-point. Every night they had crawled a bit further forward, and had camouflaged themselves so well before dawn that no one in our unit observed anything in the terrain in front of them. At the end, the Russians had taken cover close to our trenches and waited for the signal to attack. The Russian artillery fired a short but violent shelling that also killed some of their own in their advanced positions. The surviving Russians then stormed forward, without their usual "Urrääh!" and penetrated our trenches.

The Soviet units that attacked us this day, 12 June 1944, consisted of a punishment regiment. They had constantly been marching for one week and during this time they ate what they carried: some bread, a bottle of vodka and a bag of sunflower seed. They were naturally half-insane from hunger when they threw themselves over our positions. However, they endured being shot at by their own artillery and fought us for eight hours before they disappeared. The Russians were incredibly imaginative in their warfare.

Erik Laerum, Danish artillery officer in the *SS-Panzergrenadier Regiment "Danmark"*

The retreat from Narva cost a Dutch *SS* regiment its existence. They were supposed to be a rear guard but were cut off and annihilated. A few men came through and appeared in our lines after a couple of weeks in a miserable condition. We held fast at the Tannenberg Line [with] their beautiful fir trees. The Estonians called it The Blue Hills after the bluish woods. Between the hills went the railway and the main road between Tallinn and Narva. To

Wolfgang Joerchel

Arnold Stoffers

Albrecht Krügel

Fritz Knöchlein

Regimental commanders in the *11. SS-Freiwilligen-Panzergrenadier-Division "Nordland"*. From the left: Wolfgang Joerchel, Arnold Stoffers, Albrecht Krügel and Fritz Knöchlein. None of them survived the Second World War.

Fritz Geiger

Wilhelm Körbel

Richard Spörle

Rudolf Ternedde

Regimental commanders of *SS-Panzer-Grenadier-Regiment "Norge"* of the *SS-Division "Nordland"*.
From the left: Fritz Geiger, Wilhelm Körbel, Rudolf Ternedde and Richard Spörle.

the left our regiment "*Danmark*" had contact with units from the *Wehrmacht* who defended five to six kilometres of low and swampy terrain up to the Finnish Gulf. They were in the marshes but I had happily switched positions with those units as the Russians could not deploy tanks up there. We were on dry land, so they attacked us instead. The Tannenberg Line, between the open sea in the north and the swamps in the south, is the bottle neck of Estonia and here [lay] a Swedish defence position after the Russians conquered Narva in 1704. In our defence lines there were still well preserved trenches from the Swedish struggle for Estonia. The trenches were also well used in our defence system.

Felix Steiner

SS-Obergruppenführer Felix Steiner

Felix Steiner was born in Stallupönen in East Prussia in 1896, the son of a school teacher, and participated as an officer and company commander in the Great War. He was assigned to the elite *Stosstruppen* (Strike Troop) that helped break the deadlock on the Eastern Front during the fighting around Riga in 1917. Steiner also fought on the Western Front as a *Stosstruppen* officer and was convinced that only such highly trained, flexible units would be able to gain success in future campaigns. In 1918–19, he was the leader of a *Freikorps* in Klaipéda (Memel) and joined the regular Army, the *Reichswehr*, in 1920, being promoted to *Hauptmann* in 1927. Steiner's experiences of the great infantry losses on the Western Front contributed to him developing a more flexible assault tactic with well-educated and well-equipped units. In 1935, he left the regular Army, frustrated by what he considered a lack of innovation, and joined Himmler's *SS-Verfügungstruppe*, the predecessor of the *Waffen-SS*, as an *SS-Obersturmbannführer*. He became the first commander of *SS-Regiment "Deutschland"*, stationed in Munich, in 1936. Steiner's assertion that he left the regular Army in protest against conservative tactical mentalities has been questioned by historians, who claim that "personal reasons" were the actual cause for this decision.[27] During manoeuvres in 1938, Hitler was impressed by the educational standard of Steiner's

The crew of a 7.5cm anti-tank gun near Narva in June 1944. The mostly *Volksdeutsche* soldiers lying around the gun are Fielker, Lange, Urbatschka, Gruber, Rothaas and Lauritz. This 7.5cm PaK (*Panzerabwehrkanone*) 40 was the first really effective German anti-tank gun in the Second World War. It was designed and produced by Rheinmetall AG, it weighed 1,425 kilos, its length was 3.45 metres and its maximum range was 7,678 metres. (Courtesy of Predrag Blanusa & Björn Leo)

Soldiers from the signals platoon of the *SS-Aufklärung Bataillon "Nordland"* in the Narva bridgehead in the village of Mummasaare on 7 July 1944. From the left (with a MG 42) are *SS-Unterscharführer* Pollaschek, *Sturmmann* Wimms, *SS-Unterscharführer* Barth, *Sturmmann* Straub, *SS-Rottenführer* Konrad, *Panzergrenadier* Hans Tasch and Kurt Hartig. In the background is a telephone switchboard. Some of the soldiers are carrying the *SS* field cap (*Einheitsfeldmütze* 1943).

SS-Obersturmführer Georg Langendorf with NCOs of his company in Mummasaare, in June 1944. From the left are Alfred Weiss, Karl Gienger, Fien, Georg Langendorf, Sepp Schirmer, Thumser and König.

units. Steiner also favoured the use of a new camouflage smock, which was developed by one of his officers, Dr Wim Brandt. This camouflage clothing later spread to the entire *Waffen-SS*. During the German attack on Poland in 1939, the *Abwehr* officer Helmuth Grosscurth noted in his diary that Steiner's *Regiment "Deutschland"* murdered both civilian Jews and prisoners of war during that campaign.

Steiner participated in the 1940 campaign against France with his *SS-Regiment "Deutschland"*, being decorated with the Knight's Cross, promoted to *SS-Brigadeführer* and on 1 December 1940 commissioned with the formation of the new motorized *SS-Infanterie-Division "Wiking"*, that partly consisted of volunteers from Scandinavia and the Netherlands. While several of his officers and NCOs were sceptical about the value of foreign volunteers, Steiner greeted them into the *Waffen-SS* with enthusiasm. He was known for shaking hands with every man in formations waiting for inspection. During the campaign against the Soviet Union, "*Wiking*" advanced into Galicia, where divisional units committed mass murders of at least 600 Galician Jews near the town of Lviv (Lemberg). Steiner's personal responsibility for this mass crime remained unclear after West German prosecutors' investigations into the matter in the Sixties, but the issue must be considered as a tarnish on Steiner's reputation, especially with his *Regiment "Deutschland"* being active in similar genocidal crimes in Poland in 1939.

The initiative of concentrating all Germanic volunteers, by dissolving the existing legions and unifying them into a Germanic *SS-Panzer-Korps*, clearly derived from Felix Steiner and Dr Franz Riedweg, Chief of Staff of the Germanic Coordination Agency (*Germanische SS-Freiwilligen-Leitstelle*), in September 1942.[28] After heavy fighting with the "*Wiking*" on the German-Soviet front, Steiner was commissioned with the task of creating the *III. (germ.) SS-Panzer-Korps* in 1943. In 1942, Steiner had criticized the chief of the *SS-Hauptamt*, *SS-Gruppenführer* Gottlob Berger, for spreading unrealistic and embellished propaganda to Norwegian *SS* volunteers, and his relationship to Himmler was from time to time strained. Himmler also accused Steiner of building a personal cult of himself in his *Waffen-SS* units. Steiner had a good relationship with his soldiers, and was also successful in transferring competent general staff officers from the Army to his *SS-Panzer-Korps*, such as Joachim Ziegler, Jürgen von Bock and Helmut von Bockelberg. In 1943, Steiner had contact with groups within the *Wehrmacht* that were opposed to the Nazi regime, who in turn had connections to the circles planning the bomb plot against Hitler on 20 July 1944. After the successful and effective defence of Estonia at the Blue Hills line against the superior Red Army in July-August 1944, Steiner was personally presented with his Swords decoration to the Knight's Cross by Hitler, the ceremony taking place in Hitler's HQ at the end of September 1944. In January 1945, Steiner was entrusted with command of the *11. SS-Panzer-Armee*, a grandiose name for a "ghost-army" of scattered units well below army-strength during the fighting for Pomerania and Brandenburg. In contrast to many other senior commanders, Steiner was regarded as a favourite of the Nazi regime during the last months of the war. In March 1945, Joseph Goebbels noted in his diary: "Steiner makes on me an eminent impression. He is energetic and resolute and takes on his mission with great *elan*."[29]

Steiner resumed command of the *III. (germ.) SS-Panzer-Korps* west of the Oder River during April 1945. Disillusioned by the outcome of the war, Steiner refused to carry out Hitler's, Keitel's and Heinrici's orders to attack Berlin-Spandau from his bridgehead at Oranienburg. Steiner's decision probably spared many soldiers' lives in this last phase of the conflict. In April 1945, Steiner also dismissed under-age units from the *Hitler-Jugend* and characterized their engagement at the Oder Front and in Brandenburg as "*Kindermord*" (murder of children). Steiner also described the orders to attack the encircled Berlin with his weak units as "unfeasible and impossible".

Felix Steiner's post-war activities included apologetic and revisionist publications on the *Waffen-SS*, trying to prove the impossible: that the *Waffen-SS* was a purely military phenomenon. Steiner thus proved to be a confirmed Nazi who had learnt nothing from the Nazi era. (LW)

Erik Laerum, Danish artillery officer in the *SS Panzergrenadier Regiment "Danmark"*

At the Blue Hills we waited for the Russians to come. And they came almost immediately. Already the day after we had evacuated Narva they were near us and started a major offensive. If they had realized how weak our position was with a few hundred infantry men in the front line, they could without difficulties have thrown us out. But the hard resistance made them obviously believe that we were far stronger than we actually were. Our defence was based upon artillery units with mixed infantry. The Red attack was initiated with a large-scale air and artillery attack. Near my position some shells exploded in the trees, [and] splinters killed two of our men and wounded two others that stood beside me, and to whom I just had talked. At the same time the Red artillery started to fire air bursts that grew to a hurricane of explosions that I had never experienced before. In my bunker there were two elderly German officers who had experienced the First World War. They said it was worse than Verdun. The Red Army has an exceptionally heavy artillery and when they concentrate their fire, as they did against us, it is not nice to be the target. The bursts hit the terrain like spears.

SS-Obersturmbannführer Paul-Albert Kausch

Paul-Albert Kausch was born in 1911 in Jädersdorf, Pomerania. He was the son of an estate owner, Friedrich Kausch, who was killed in action in the First World War on 27 August 1914. His mother sold the estate in 1919 and moved with her son to Prenzlau. After his high school examinations in Potsdam,

Kausch joined the *Hitler-Jugend* and the *SS* in 1932 and became a member of the Nazi Party on 1 February 1933. On 8 July 1933, at the age of 22, Kausch joined the *Leibstandarte SS "Adolf Hitler"* in Berlin-Lichterfelde, and was promoted to *SS-Untersturmführer* in 1936. Between 1936 and 1939 he served in various *SS-Totenkopf* units – in reality (which is seldom mentioned in his postwar biographies), Kausch served in the notorious concentration camps of Dachau and Buchenwald.[30]

Paul-Albert Kausch

After briefly serving in the Army, Kausch was in 1939 transferred as artillery company commander to the newly formed *SS-Totenkopfdivision* in 1939. Kausch took part in the campaign in the West in 1940 and was transferred to the new *SS-Division "Wiking"* as aide-de-camp to the divisional commander, Felix Steiner. In this position and as artillery unit commander, Kausch took part in the German campaign against the Soviet Union. On the eve of establishing the new *III. (germ.) SS-Panzer-Korps*, Kausch was assigned as commander of the *SS-Panzer-Abteilung 11 "Hermann von Salza"* in the *11. SS-Freiwilligen-Panzergrenadier-Division "Nordland"* on 1 May 1943. Promoted to *SS-Sturmbannführer* in January 1944, Kausch was decorated with the Knight's Cross after the successful defensive battle at the Tannenberg Line near Narva in July-August 1944. After being wounded during the Narva fighting, he took up command of the "*Hermann von Salza*" after it had been evacuated from the Baltic countries to Germany. Kausch commanded his *panzer* units during the battle for Pomerania and the German counter-attack to relieve Arnswalde in February 1945. Kausch was designated as commander of another *SS-panzer-regiment* but Steiner kept him within his corps and trusted him with the command

Danish grenadiers from the *SS-Regiment "Danmark"* in trenches around the Narva bridgehead in June 1944.

A Dutch volunteer from the *4. SS-Frewilligen-Brigade "Nederland"* looks at a poster at the outpost of Lilienbach, in the eastern Narva bridgehead. The "Tourist" poster is humorous and presents "concerts" by "Ivan" (the Red Army) with *Katyusha* rockets and artillery.

The Danish *SS-Obersturmführer* Christen Dall in his Volkswagen in Narva, with his driver. Dall was CO of the *13./SS-Regiment "Norge"* until July 1944, ending the war as an adjutant in the *38. SS -Division "Nibelungen"*. Dall was an ethnic German from the Danish province of Schleswig.

of the new *SS-Panzer-Regiment 11*, which combined the "*Hermann von Salza*" with the *Schwere SS-Panzer-Abteilung 503*. As regimental commander, Kausch took part in the final battles at the Oder-Brandenburg from 16 April 1945 and the battle for Berlin in April-May 1945. Kausch was severly wounded in Berlin on 28 April and taken prisoner by the Red Army. He returned to Germany and his wife Erika on 16 January 1956, serving as holder of procuration with a world-known pharmaceutical corporation from 1956-76. Paul-Albert Kausch died aged 91 on 27 October 2001 in Ingelheim on the River Rhine. (LW)

The Battle for the Tannenberg Line

After six months of hard battles around the Narva bridgehead, the *Armeeabteilung Narva*, under the command of *Generaloberst* Johannes Friessner, began its planned withdrawal from Narva on the morning of 26 July 1944. This process was essentially motivated by the Red Army's destruction earlier in July of *Heeresgruppe Mitte*, which caused the German Army Command (*OKH*) to detach several units from the weakened Narva Front to the *Heeresgruppe Mitte* area. The Red Army saw its chance, and on 24 July fiercely attacked the four Estonian rifle battalions from the *20. SS-Division*, who were deployed around Auvere, south-west of Narva. Despite an enormous artillery bombardment and mass attacks from Soviet tanks and infantry, the Estonians held their line in close combat. This Estonian defensive success saved the Germans' general withdrawal from Narva,

Thomas Sandborg took a law degree in Norway in 1936 and served as a judge before he volunteered for the *Waffen-SS* in 1943. He was also active in the *Germanske SS Norge*. As *SS-Obersturmführer*, Sandborg served as CO of the *11. Kompanie* in the *SS-Panzergrenadier-Regiment 23 "Norge"* in 1944. During fierce fighting around Baldone in Latvia on 23 September 1944, Sandborg was killed by a shot to the head during an attack by his company near the village of Dekmeri-Silisi. Sandborg was married at the time of his death and had several children. He was buried in Riga. The swift and tactically successful redeployment of the *III. (Germ.) SS-Panzer-Korps* out of Estonia (Operation *Aster*) to the Riga area, probably saved the German Sixteenth and Eighteenth Armies from encirclement and destruction by General Ivan Bagramyan's advancing troops. The blocking of these Soviet forces was terribly costly for the Germanic *SS-Panzer-Korps*: the *SS-Regiment "Danmark"* alone lost nearly 300 men.

and earned *SS-Sturmbannführer* Harald Riipalu the Knight's Cross.

The German units in the Narva bridgehead retreated and took up new positions at the so-called Tannenberg Line, 20km west of Narva. The line was 20km long and guarded the densely populated north-western Estonia and its capital Tallinn. The Tannenberg Line ran in a north-south direction and its northern part to the coast of the Gulf of Finland was marked by a wide stretch of fairly high ground, among these the so-called "Sweden Wall", dating from the time of Charles XII and Peter the Great in 1704. The central part was dominated by three tactically important hills that overlooked the landscape: the Blue Hills (*Vaivara Sinimäed* in Estonian; *Blaue Bergen* in German). These were (running west to east): Hill 69.9, Grenadier Hill and Orphanage Hill. The southern part of the Tannenberg Line was dominated by swampy marshlands.

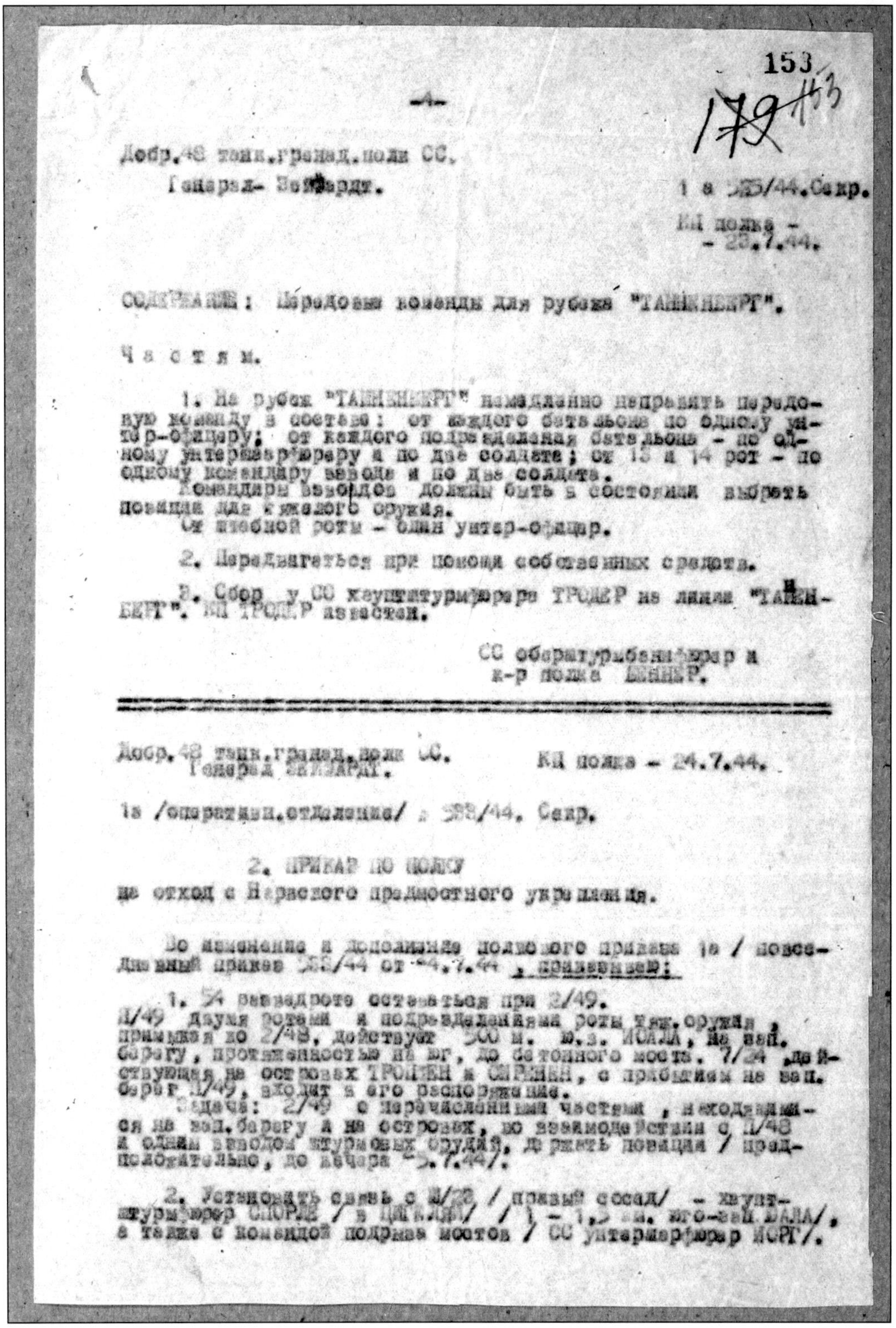
153

-4-

179 153

Добр. 48 танк. гренад. полк СС.
Генерал- Зейфардт.

1 а [illegible]/44. Секр.

КП полка -
- 23.7.44.

СОДЕРЖАНИЕ: Передовые команды для рубежа "ТАННЕНБЕРГ".

Ч а с т я м.

1. На рубеж "ТАННЕНБЕРГ" немедленно направить передовую команду в составе: от каждого батальона по одному унтер-офицеру; от каждого подразделения батальона - по одному унтершарфюреру и по два солдата; от 13 и 14 рот - по одному командиру взвода и по два солдата.
Командиры взводов должны быть в состоянии выбрать позиции для тяжелого оружия.
От штабной роты - один унтер-офицер.

2. Передвигаться при помощи собственных средств.

3. Сбор у СС хауптштурмфюрера ТРОДЕР на линии "ТАННЕНБЕРГ". КП ТРОДЕР известен.

СС оберштурмбанфюрер и
к-р полка [illegible].

Добр. 48 танк. гренад. полк СС.
Генерал Зейфардт.

КП полка - 24.7.44.

1а /оперативн. отделение/ [illegible]/44. Секр.

2. ПРИКАЗ ПО ПОЛКУ
на отход с Нарвского предмостного укрепления.

Во изменение и дополнение полкового приказа 1а / повседневный приказ [illegible]/44 от [illegible].7.44, приказываю:

1. [illegible] взводроте оставаться при 2/49.
II/49 двумя ротами и подразделениями роты тяж. оружия, примыкая ко 2/48, действует 500 м. ю.з. [illegible], на зап. берегу, протяженностью на юг, до бетонного моста. 7/[illegible], действующая на островах [illegible] и [illegible], с прибытием на зап. берег II/49, входит в его распоряжение.
Задача: 2/49 с перечисленными частями, находящимися на зап. берегу и на островах, во взаимодействии с II/48 и одним взводом штурмовых орудий, держать позиции / предположительно, до вечера [illegible].7.44/.

2. Установить связь с [illegible] / правый сосед/ - хауптштурмфюрер [illegible] / в [illegible]/ / [illegible] - 1,5 км. юго-зап. [illegible]/, а также с командой подрыва мостов / СС унтершарфюрер [illegible]/.

An *SS*-document from Russian military archives in Moscow: a captured order from the Dutch *SS-Regiment 48 "General Seyffardt"*, that was destroyed by units of the Red Army near Repniku during the German retreat from Narva to the Tannenberg Line. (Courtesy of Petter Kjellander)

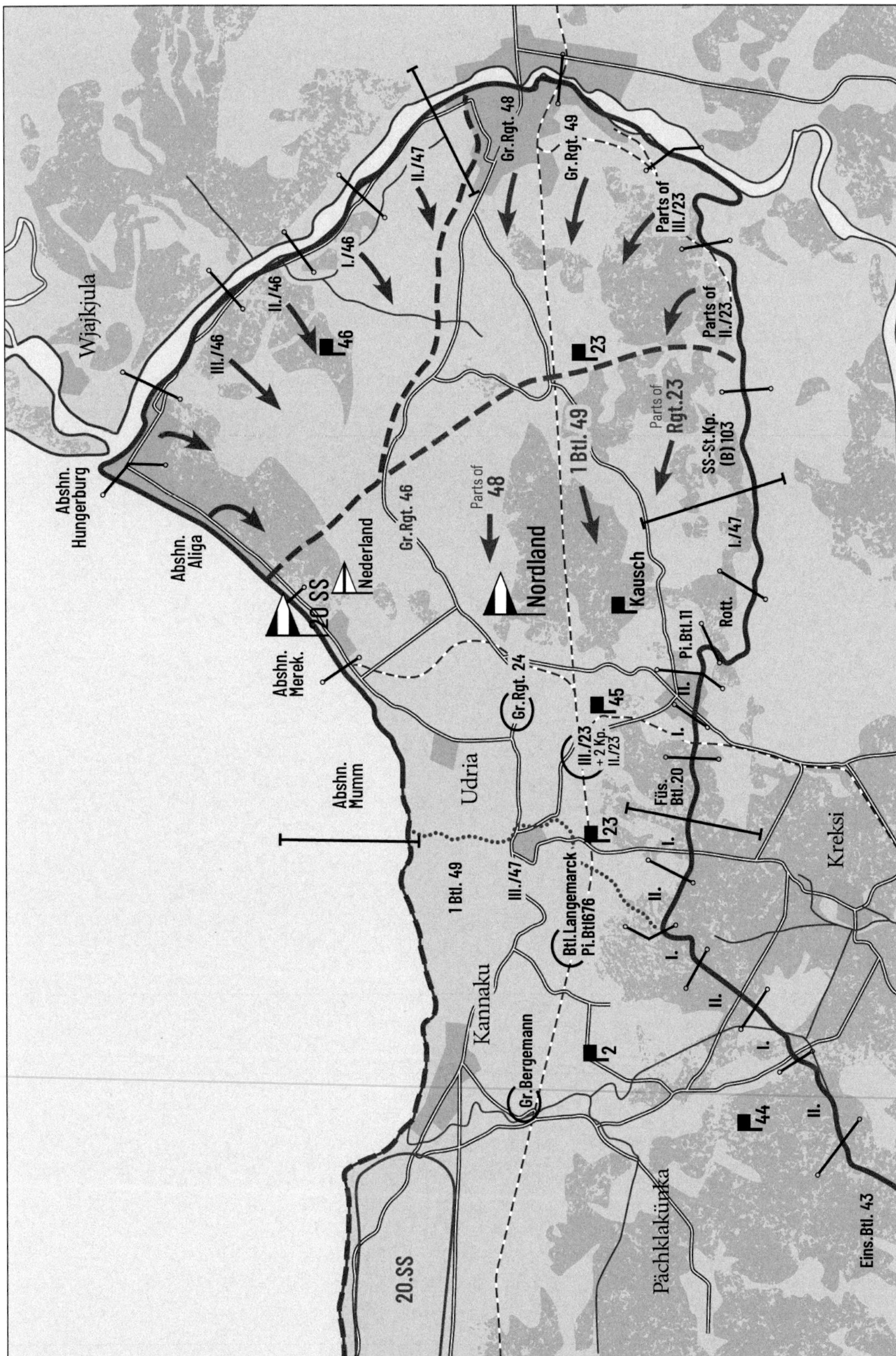

The retreat from the Narva River to the Tannenbergstellung.

SS-Obersturmbannführer Richard Benner, CO of the fatal *SS-Regiment 48 "General Seyffardt"*, that during the retreat from Narva westwards to the new positions of the Tannenberg Line on 25–26 July 1944 was destroyed by the Red Army. Benner was killed during this rearguard action. He was previously a regimental commander in the *6. SS-Gebirgs-Division "Nord"* on the Arctic Finnish-Soviet Front.

SS-Obergruppenführer Felix Steiner with officers from his staff at the Corps HQ at Sillamäe in August 1944.

A destroyed *Pz IV* at the former Blue Hills battlefield after the war. The photograph was taken in 1949 at the *Kinderheimhöhe*. The area is today still full of unexploded shells and mines, and the remains of fallen German and Soviet soldiers.

On 25 July, units from the Red Army succeeded in crossing the Narva River between Hunberburg and Narva and proceeded westwards towards the Tannenberg Line.

The Key to the Baltic States

The Soviet Leningrad Front (the Red Army "Front" was the equivalent of a German Army Group) under Marshal Leonid Govorov looked upon the Blue Hills as a key strategic position for their German counterparts and deployed their best formations to attack the Tannenberg Line. Govorov's aim was a quick breakthrough to Tallinn and the occupation of northern Estonia as a base for further operations against the rest of Estonia, Riga and Courland. Furthermore, the Soviets wanted to launch actions against Germany's ally of Finland from aerial and naval bases on Estonian soil.

During the period of 26 July to 8 August 1944, the Blue Hills were the scene of fierce battles. The troops under Marshall Govorov had at the beginning of the offensive a strength of 136,830 men, with 150 armoured vehicles, 1,680 assault guns and 546 aeroplanes. Opposing them, *Generaloberst* Friessner had at his disposal 22,250 men, just seven tanks, 70–80 assault guns and 48 aircraft. Besides 24

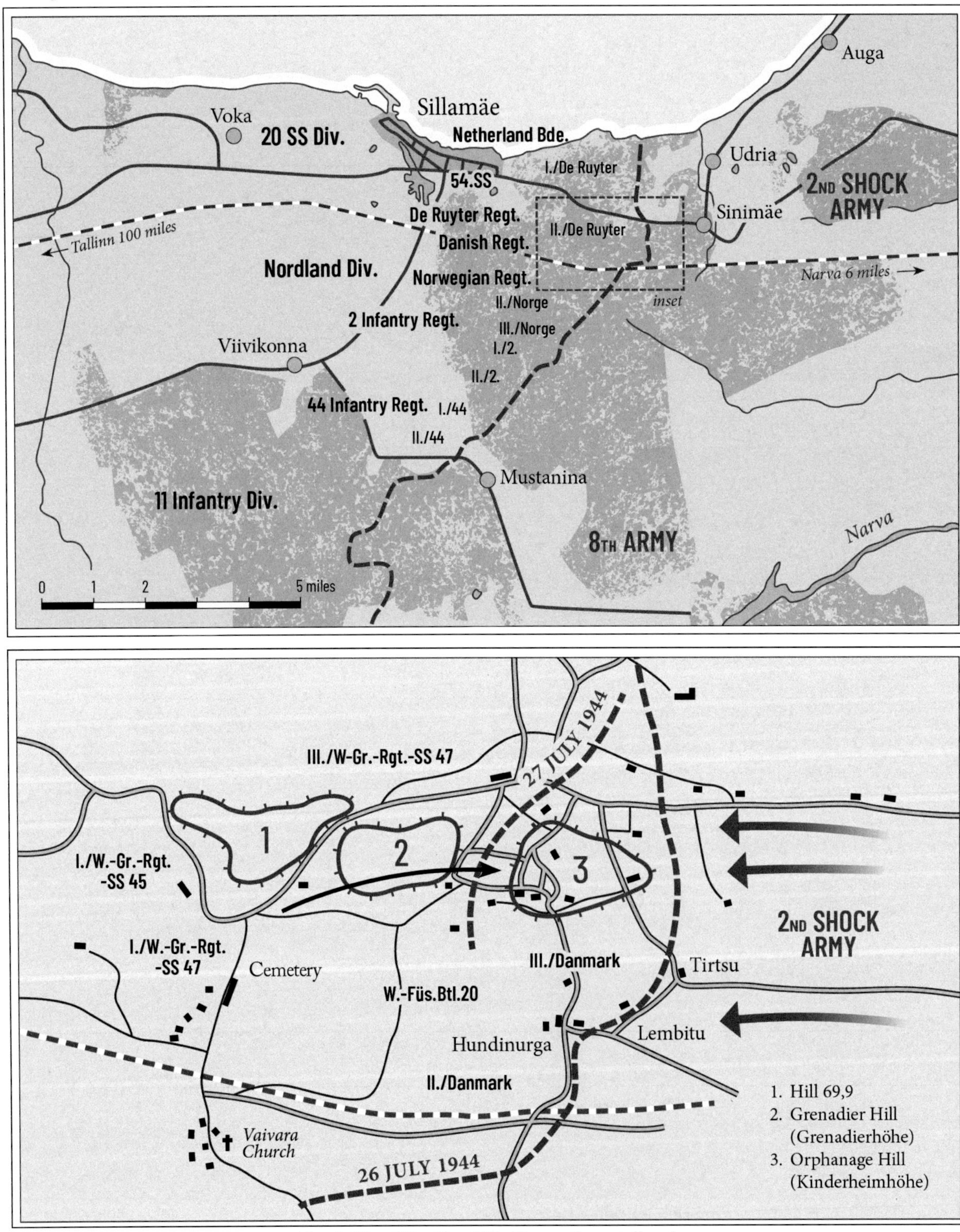

The Battle of the Blue Hills (*Tannenbergstellung*).

German battalions from the *Wehrmacht*, 24 mixed German, Estonian, Netherlandic, Danish, Flemish, Norwegian and Walloon Waffen-SS battalions of various strength participated in the battle for the Tannenberg Line.

Breakthrough at any Cost

The Germans deployed their units in the Tannenberg Line, from north to south, as follows: Estonian *II./SS-Waffen-Grenadier-Regiment 47*; *SS-Pioneer-Bataillon 54 "Nederland"*; *SS-Panzergrenadier-Regiment 49 "De Ruyter"*; *SS-Kampfgruppe "Rehmann"*; *III.* and *II./SS-Panzergrenadier-Regiment 24 "Danmark"*; *II./SS-Panzergrenadier-Regiment 23 "Norge"*; parts of the *11. Infanterie-Division* (Army); and *300. Infanterie-Division z.b.V.*[31]

Before the Tannenberg Line was occupied by the retreating German units from the Narva bridgehead, the *III. (germ.) SS-Panzer-Korps* had ordered army pioneer units to construct connecting trenches and defence lines around the Blue Hills. These trenches were, however, incomplete, and obsolete in their construction. The following intense Soviet artillery fire, beginning with the Red Army's initial attack on 26 July, caused considerable casualties among the deployed German infantry units on Orphanage Hill, due to these poorly prepared trenches and other defences. This hill was taken by the attacking Soviets after the Estonian and Flemish *SS* units were decimated by artillery fire and forced to retreat westwards. Notwithstanding local Soviet penetration by tanks, the other German defensive positions held for the time being, but radio and telephone communications had broken down due to the intense firing.[32]

The following days saw intense Soviet artillery barrages on all three hills in the Tannenberg Line, with massive infantry and tank assaults including some deep penetrations into the German lines which caused acute crises for the defenders. However, the line held due to the skilled, well-prepared and coordinated German fire from all heavy weapons, combined with decisive and successful counter-attacks by, above all, Estonian units, together with a tactically important counter-attack with tanks and assault-guns from the combined unit of *SS-Panzer-Abteilung 11 "Hermann von Salza"* and the *SS-Sturmgeschütz-Abteilung 11* under *SS-Obersturmbannführer* Kausch.[33]

Despite repeated daily offensives and overwhelming forces, the Red Army was incapable of making any significant progress at the Blue Hills. After Stalin sent Govorov a personal and sharply worded order at the beginning of August to break through the German lines, the Soviet forces received further reinforcements and repeated their attacks over the following days. Once again the German lines held, and on 10 August, Govorov decided to cancel his offensive. No further major actions were taken along this front line until the Germans began evacuating Estonia in mid-September 1944.[34]

The German losses on the Tannenberg Line are well-documented in the archives, while those of the Red Army were never mentioned during the Soviet era. More recently, however, Russian and Estonian researchers have concluded that the losses of the Red Army between 24 July and 10 August were 8,000 killed or missing, with another 27,000–28,000 wounded. The total German losses between 23 July and 7 August were 1,291 killed in action, 5,834 wounded and 2,022 missing.[35] After the fighting on 29 July, there were only 225 soldiers left alive in the Soviet 109th Rifle Guards Corps, which bore the burnt of the combat that day, while the other deployed units from the Red Army lost their ability to attack due to high losses.

Armistice between Finland and the USSR

The German-Soviet front line at Narva and the Blue Hills was directly connected to developments on the Finnish-Soviet front north of the Gulf of Finland at the Karelian Isthmus, both politically and strategically. During the Battle of Tali-Ihantala, near Viborg, that took place between 25 June and 9 July 1944, Finnish forces succeeded in blocking the major Soviet offensive in that area. Due to skilled concentrations of artillery, deciphering of Soviet codes, a stable defence and energetic counter-attacks, the Finnish defence (reinforced by German *Stuka* and assault gun units) broke the edge of the Soviet thrust. The Soviets lost around 5,000 killed, 14,000 wounded and 300 tanks destroyed at Tali-Ihantala. On 12 July, Stalin decided to break off the offensive due to the Soviet losses on the Karelian Isthmus. Instead, the focus of the Red Army was shifted to the Estonian theatre of war and the Tannenberg Line on 24 July. After the Finnish and German successes at Tali-Ihantala and the Blue Hills, the Soviet Union mitigated their demands on an unconditional Finnish surrender as their terms for peace and Finland escaped the fate of being taken over by the Soviets. On 4 September 1944 an armistice came into effect between Finland and the USSR. Hitler in turn withdraw his forces out of Estonia from mid-September and into positions in the so-called Courland pocket in Latvia, where they would remain until the end of the war. PK, LW

Knights' Crosses at Sillamäe HQ

The HQ for the *III. (Germ.) SS-Panzer-Korps* was established in Sillamäe from February 1944 until the evacuation of Estonia in September 1944.

This was a small Estonian fishing village on the coast of the Gulf of Finland. Here, commanding general *SS-Oberrgruppenführer* Felix Steiner, with his closest staff of operational officers, oversaw the tactical and strategic actions and movements of the various units of the corps. Further parts of the corps staff consisted of logistics, personnel, signals, military police, courts-martial, etc. The staff were protected by a staff company. One of the junior members was *SS-Obersturmführer* Günther Mierwald, who was born in Berlin and served as orderly officer (OO). Mierwald had his camera at hand during the awards ceremony for *SS-Hauptsturmführer* Karl-Heinz Ertel, *Waffen-SS-Obersturmbannführer* Harald Riipalu, *SS-Obersturmbannführer* Paul-Albert Kausch and

A recruitment poster in Denmark for volunteer service in the *Waffen-SS*. The allusion to ancient *Wiking* sagas of conquering the East is apparent.

Norwegian poster for volunteer service in the *Legion Norwegen*, with references to the *Wiking* war expeditions to the East. More than 12,000 Danes sought to enlist with the *Waffen-SS* during the Second World War. Of these, 6,000 were accepted, of whom a third were killed at the Front. "The largest group of the Danish volunteers, by far, were Nazis, mostly from organized groups, who often came from a Nazi family or environment. Nevertheless, like the majority of the other Danish volunteers, they represented a broad cross-section of the Danish population. The Danish volunteers were not to any special degree criminals or mentally backward, as many Danes claimed in the years immediately following the war. However, for some volunteers, socialization difficulties and a warped view of authority were, apparently, significant for their attraction to the *Waffen-SS*." (Niels Bo Poulsen *et al.*, *Under Hagekors of Dannebrog*)

On 23 August 1944, the Estonian regimental commander in the *20. Waffen-Grenadier-Division der SS*, Harald Riipalu, receives the Knightss Cross from Felix Steiner at the corps HQ in Sillamäe. Riipalu was recognized for his tactical ability and personal bravery in the battles around Auvere and the Blue Hills. Riipalu, who was a supporter of the *SS* and its "European order", was, as a candidate for *SS* membership (*SS-Bewerber*), entitled to wear the *SS*-runes on his breastpocket. In May 1945, he succeeded in escaping to Denmark, and lived in England from 1948 until his death of heart failure in 1961. Due to his intimate knowledge of the Soviet Union and the Red Army, Riipalu was a consultant to the British Intelligence Service, SIS.

After the ceremony of awarding Knight's Crosses at the HQ of the *III. (Germ.) SS-Panzer-Korps* on 23 August 1944. The recipents are, from the left: Harald Riipalu (CO *45. Estonian SS-Regiment*); Paul-Albert Kausch (CO of *Panzer Batallion 11 "Hermann von Salza"*); Wilhelm Schlüter (CO *SS-Artillerie-Regiment 54 "Nederland"*); and Karl-Heinz Ertel (Adjutant *SS-Panzergrenadier-Regiment 49 "de Ruyter"*).

A photo from Felix Steiner's corps HQ at Sillamäe in September 1944. *SS-Brigadeführer* Joachim Ziegler (right) is congratulated by the Chief of Staff of the *III. (Germ.) SS-Panzer Korps*, *SS-Obersturmbannführer* Helmut von Bockelberg (left), after Ziegler had received the Knight's Cross for his recent tactical command of the *11. SS-Freiwilligen-Panzergrenadier-Division "Nordland"* during the last phase of the battle for the Blue Hills in the Tannenberg Line.

SS-Brigadeführer Joachim Ziegler.

The German *SS-Untersturmführer* Willi Hund, CO of *7. Kompanie* of *SS-Regiment "Norge"* in 1944–45.

SS-Sturmbannführer Wilhelm Schlüter, and took a series of unique photos at the corps HQ which are presented here.

During the 1990s, Gunther Mierwald revisited Estonia and Sillamäe. He tried to locate the former HQ buildings, which were all wooden summer cottages, but the old buildings were gone, and instead he found new Soviet concrete vacation buldings for workers.

Marshal Leonid Govorov

Leonid Govorov was born 1897 in Butyrki, near Kirov, the son of an office worker. He became an artillery officer in 1917, and from 1920 participated on the Red side during the Russian Revolution, after having fought for the Whites for a short time. For the latter reason Govorov was nearly executed during Stalin's purge of the officer corps in 1938. He was examined at the Frunze Academy in 1933 and the General Staff Academy in 1938. During the Finnish Winter War, Govorov was chief of artillery in the Seventh Army, where, with skill, he created the penetration of the Mannerheim Line in 1940.

During his service as artillery commander in the German-Soviet war in 1941, Govorov got the attention of Zhukov and became his protégé. Govorov broke the Finnish-German blockade of Leningrad in 1943, and was promoted to Marshal of the Soviet Union in June 1944. He was chief of the Leningrad Front from 1942–44, and therefore served as the opponent of Walter Model (and Felix Steiner) during the battles for Narva and the Tannenberg Line in 1944. While still commander of the Leningrad Front, Govorov simultaneously directed and coordinated the operations by the 2nd and 3rd Baltic Fronts in October 1944.

Marshal Leonid Govorov

From February 1945, Govorov was commander of the 2nd Baltic Front in the struggle against the Germans in Latvia and Poland. After he war, he became Vice Minister of Defence in 1952 and modernized the Soviet Air Force into the jet- and atomic bomb-age. Govorov died in Moscow in 1955 of heart disease. LW

Ago Loorpärg, Estonian company commander in the 20. SS-Division (Petter Kjellander's archives)

The Blue Hills were shot at with all kind of weapons. The impression was even more extraordinary during sunset. The Russians used *Katyushas* (Stalin-Organs) and artillery. Our side answered with *Nebelwerfers*, artillery and rocket-driven bombs that we called "cows" because of the sounds they gave. They had long white tails behind them when they were fired and they all landed at Sinimäed. Red and blue shadows blistered on the Grenadier Hill like Nordic light due to the explosions. The sky was red during the sunset and the clouds and the smoke were also red. All of this was incredibly beautiful and very frightening at the same time. It gave us an impression of a true hell."

Anonymous Norwegian volunteer in the *SS -Panzergrenadier Regiment "Norge"* (Tommy Natedal's archive)

A couple of days earlier, the luxuriant vegetation on the wooded Blue Hills was green and beautiful. Now the terrain more looked like a gravel-pit. The craters from bombs and artillery were frequent. We met wounded who were hardly able to stand on their own legs. They tried to go backwards for help. We found a demolished trench. The smoke had still not vanished from the hill. We heard noises from the wounded. They also awaited the Soviet assault and thought perhaps that there were not too many prisoners to be taken during the fighting around the Blue Hills, and hoped to get away in time. We also found many killed but no one had the time to bury them yet. Those who were not attending to the wounded were busy improving their trenches with materials they found. A Soviet assault was already under way. The Red [Army] troops attacked in force, close together, and right on up the south-eastern parts of the hills. Furious machine-gun series went into the ranks of the Russians. The soldiers shrieked and tumbled over each other but they were driven forward and could not be stopped. The first of our trenches were taken and the Russians stormed on to the top. We blocked the two sides of the break-in and shot with everything we could. Our positions on the top, where our battalion commander had his command post, now intervened and the Russians were forced to take shelter in the bomb craters. Some of them had advanced wide to the western side. Beneath us, between the hill and the railroad, there was a heavy combat up the hill and past us. The tension [grew]. How should this end? Killed and wounded covered the ground. Many cried for help in vain.

Helmut Rand, Estonian grenadier in the *20. SS-Division* (Petter Kjellander's archive)

The Red Army fired upon the hill with heavy artillery and soon an attack followed. We held our positions in [the] following days and rejected all the enemy attacks. Especially difficult was the 29 July. We were constantly under enemy artillery fire. The air was filled with smoke from explosions; dust and earth flew everywhere around. All the burning tanks also produced heavy smoke. Russian air planes attacked us at low level as there were no trees to hinder them from flying low to the ground. We could see the faces of the pilots. In this rain of bullets and steel, we had the feeling that life was at its end. *SS-Sturmbannführer* Maitla left five of us with three MG 42s to defend the hill, and took the others to attack the adjoining hill. There emerged more and more Soviet tanks in the valley between the two hills. Several of them were stopped and started to burn where they stood. Maitla's attack was successful and soon all hills were in our possession. This was followed by a third sleepless night. The enemy artillery never stopped bombarding us. I felt hunger, we had eaten all our food and started to smoke to minimize our hunger.

Colonel General Ferdinand Schörner (1892–1973) was commander of Army Group North (renamed Army Group Courland) from July 1944 until January 1945. A veteran of the First World War, Schörner was awarded the exclusive *Pour le Mérite* military order in 1917 after the battle at Caporetto. Pretty much like Walter Model, Schörner could convince Hitler to endorse withdrawals that would have made the *Führer* sack any other commander that had proposed them. Schörner and his skilled general staff officers succeeded, with short notice, in September 1944 in executing a strategically brilliant withdrawal of Army Group North out of Estonia, Operation *Aster*, via Riga into the Courland pocket. After his return in 1958 to West Germany from the Soviet Union and East Germany, Schörner was sentenced to four-and-a-half years in jail for illegal executions of German soldiers accused of desertion. In 2011, British historian Ian Kershaw described Ferdinand Schörner as "extraordinarily brutal". Before his death in Munich in 1973, Schörner had been the last living German field marshal.

The strategic situation in 1944

On 1 June 1944, the German forces on the Eastern Front numbered 2,460,000 troops, supplemented by 550,000 allied forces. These troops were supported by 2,608 tanks and assault guns and 7,080 pieces of artillery. On 2 March 1944, the Red Army's strength was 6,394,500 men, with an additional 727,000 hospitalized. The Soviet armoured strength was 7,753 tanks and self-propelled guns, and over 100,000 guns and mortars. In June 1944, the Red Army completely crushed *Heeresgruppe Mitte*, which suffered losses of 200,000 German troops. At the end of July, Soviet armoured wedges forced their way straight up between Vilnius and Dünaburg towards the Riga area, in order to cut off *Heeresgruppe Mitte* and *Nord* from one another. On 1 August, the Red Army reached the Baltic Sea near the Latvian city of Tukkums on the southern Riga Gulf. After new Soviet offensives in September against Dorpat, Hitler evacuated Estonia, creating a bridgehead in Courland which would remain until the end of the war. In September, Helsinki entered into a ceasefire with Moscow and even undertook to drive German troops out of Lapland.

The allied landing in Sicily in July 1943 had been a shock that rattled all of Germany's allies, not only Italy, but also Hungary, Romania and Bulgaria. These countries carried out clandestine contacts with the Allies in an effort to reach separate agreements. This led to German countermeasures, including the occupation of Hungary in October 1944 when faced with the threat presented by the Red Army on the Carpathian Front. In Yugoslavia, in addition to an ongoing partisan war against Italian-German occupation, a bloody civil war was under way between the pro-Nazi Croatian *Ustasha* movement and the Serbian *Chetniks*, including Tito's partisans.

Men from the "*Nordland*" around a VW *Schwimmwagen* Type 166, in the mud of the bridgehead of Narva, some time in spring 1944.

SS-panzer crews in Estonia in 1944. Sitting in front is *SS-Obersturmführer* Heinz Stamm, later transferred to the *SS-Panzer-Aufklärungsabteilung "Nordland"*, who went missing in action on 7 March 1945 at Speck, near the Order River, after he crossed the German-Soviet front line by mistake.

A *Sd.Kfz. 231* in March 1944, in the Narva bridgehead, with its German-Rumanian crew: sitting on the *SPW* is *SS-Rottenführer* Seiler, while standing are *SS*-grenadiers Depner and Metschulat.

In one fell sweep, the Balkans became the focus of a relentless Soviet offensive between 20 August1944 - when the Red Army attacked Romania - and 4 September, when they crossed over the Danube towards Belgrade and Budapest, and reached Lake Balaton in Hungary. On 5 September 5, Bulgaria was forced to turn its weapons on its former German allies. The Germans evacuated their troops from the Balkans, and on 14 October British forces landed in Athens to protect, among other objectives, the political power structure in the country against the threat of communist partisan forces. Italy became the backdrop for a series of drawn-out and successful German defensive engagements against Allied forces invading from Sicily, striving to push north into central Italy. The Germans, under *Generalfeldmarschall* Albert Kesselring, managed to hold the fortified Gothic Line throughout the winter of 1943–44. Considering the advantage of Allied access to Ultra, the invaluable decoding of German tactical ciphers, Kesselring's defence in Italy appears in retrospect as brilliant. The result was a nightmarish campaign for the Allied infantry in Italy, with the German defenders aided by the terrain and winter weather. Between September 1943 and April 1945, the Allies lost 60,000 dead (the Germans 50,000) in Italy, total Allied losses in the peninsula being 320,000. No campaign in the West (Middle East, Mediterranean and Western Fronts) cost more in terms of dead and wounded Allied infantry soldiers than the Italian campaign.

The disintegration of the *Luftwaffe* also resulted in the loss of airborne photographic reconnaissance for the *Fremde Heeres Ost*, the German Intelligence on the Eastern Front. The few air reconnaissance missions carried out in the East by the new German jet planes could not compensate for this lack of intelligence for the *OKH*. (LW)

Erik Laerum, Danish artillery officer in the SS *Panzergrenadier Regiment "Danmark"*

[At] eight o'clock on 28 July 1944, the Russian artillery started their prolonged fire and from the Finnish Gulf a swarm of bombers emerged [at] low altitude along our artillery positions. We had not one fighter to put against them. When the enemy artillery fire suddenly stopped over the whole perimeter, the surprise of the day appeared: a Soviet tank formation of a couple of hundred *Panzers* thundered on against our batteries. One must personally have experienced such a tank assault to realize its impact. Our infantry in the first line let the tanks roll over them and fired their *Panzerfausts* against their unprotected back while we sent barrage fire against them. The attack lasted for five hours and at two o'clock in the afternoon it looked threatening. But all of our dispensable men were assembled for a counter-attack against the Russian infantry which had broken through with the *Panzers*. At around four o'clock, the Russians withdrew. They left 72 shot-up tanks. I had followed the battle from the cemetery stone wall at Vaivara and I was not surprised that the Russian losses were so high since our barrage fire was so compact. The Russian attacks were repeated every day, up to 4 August. By then the Red Army had consumed their *panzer* corps and six rifle divisions were annhiliated.

The myth of Narva, 1944

Apart from the iconization by Himmler and the *SS* propaganda apparatus in 1944 of the battles for the Narva bridgehead by the *Waffen-SS*, its mythologization has continued into modern time. Above all, a cadre of post-war apologist writers have glorified the role of the *Waffen-SS* at the Battle of Narva. The book *Tragedy of the Faithful* (*Tragödie um die Treue*) by the *Waffen-SS* veteran historian Wilhelm Tieke describes the Battle of Narva in 1944 as mainly executed by the *III. (Germ.) SS-Panzer-Korps*. This book was for many years, and is still today, the only work covering the fighting at Narva. Tieke's focus on the *Waffen-SS* has contributed to the myth that Narva was exclusively defended by *Waffen-SS* units.[36] Besides politically glorifying the defensive struggles of the *III. (Germ.) SS-Panzer-Korps* at Narva, such accounts try to monopolize the military's remarkable success in blocking the Red Army for six months at Narva, solely on behalf of the *III. (Germ.) SS-Panzer-Korps*. In reality, the units of the *Waffen-SS* represented a clear minority of all German defensive forces in and around Narva, at least during the first half of 1944.

On 25 March 1944, the strength of the *Heer* divisions in and around Narva amounted to 84,128 soldiers. These Army units were the 11th, 58th, 61st, 114th, 122nd, 127th, 170th and 225th Infantry Divisions, and the *Division "Feldherrnhalle"*. The units from the *Waffen-SS* (*"Nordland"*, *"Nederland"* and the Estonian 20th *SS*-Division) had at the same time a total strength of just 20,425 men.

It was only in July 1944, after the majority of the Army divisions had been relocated from Narva – mainly to the severely threatened *Heeresgruppe Mitte* – that the fighting developed into some form of "Battle of the Germanic *Waffen-SS*". On 24 July, *"Nordland"*, *"Nederland"* and the Estonian *20. Waffen-Grenadier-Division der SS* had a respective strength of 10,827, 6,998 and 15,682 men: a total strength of 33,507 soldiers. This should be compared with the *11. Infanterie-Division* from the *Heer* with only 715 men. At this time the Flemish battalion (*SS-Kampfgruppe "Rehmann"*), consisting of 450 men, arrived at the Narva Front, which not only strengthened the number of *SS* soldiers, but also those of Germanic extraction.

Total losses for the *Waffen-SS* and *Heer* during the Battle of the Blue Mountains between 23 July and 7 August 1944 amounted to 9,147 dead, wounded and missing. PK & LW

The Flemish in the III. (germ.) SS-Panzer-Korps

After the Nazi occupation of Belgium in 1940, collaboration with Germany began from various Flemish right-wing and fascist parties and fractions. The most dominant was the VNV (Vlaams Nationaal Verbond), the Flemish National Union, founded in 1933 by Staf de Clercq, known as

The tragedy of war in plastic

The *Waffen-SS* has, since the end of the Second World War, not only been portrayed in books and films, but also in professional re-enactment shows and plastic models. As a complement to the vast amount of photographs presented in this volume, the following four dioramas contribute another perspective to the realities for soldiers on the front line. The excellent model builder, Johan Fohlin, from Stockholm has, for the last 20 years, built models, mainly focusing on the Second World War. He has a vast interest in the combat actions that took place in the Baltic countries and Pomerania during 1944 and 1945. Johan explains his techniques to create the utmost realism in his diorama scenes: "When designing the dioramas I have used model kits in 1/35th scale as a starting point. All of the models are modified to the specific needs, with photo-etched and plastic parts for the vehicles, and scratch-built parts for the figures. Each component on the dioramas is then painted and weathered with acrylic and enamel-based paints."

The feeling of humanity in the midst of adversity, the compassion and brotherhood between soldiers where each day could be their very last.

The crew of the *Schützenpanzerwagen* "214" - Commander Fritz Ehle, driver Valentin Rether and gunner Georg Bodendorfs - during the hectic summer months of 1944, when contact was lost between Army Group North and Army Group Centre.

Estonian volunteers during a dramatic moment, right before they emerge from their cover in an attempt to knock out a Soviet tank. To help them they have several Tellermine 43, *Gaballte ladung* (bundled grenades) and a *Hafthohlladung/Panzerknacker* magnetic mine.

The reality of war: a group of soldiers from the "*Nordland*", with the help of a horse and cart, transport two fallen soldiers and comrades in arms to their final resting place.

Remi Schrijnen was the only Flemish volunteer in the *Waffen-SS* to receive the Knight's Cross. Schrijnen was a dedicated pre-war Flemish nationalist in Belgium and joined the fascist *Vlaams Nationaal Verbond* (*VNV*) before the Second World War. During the Battle of the Blue Hills, Schrijnen single-handedly destroyed at least seven Soviet tanks with his 7.5cm *PAK 40*, as *SS-Unterscharführer* in the *SS-Kampfgruppe "Langemarck"*. Returning to Belgium in 1945, Schrijnen was arrested and condemned to death, a sentence that was commuted to life imprisonment. After frequent discrimination by the Belgian authorities, due to Schrijnen's demands for amnesty for other Flemish *SS* volunteers to the Eastern Front, Schrijnen emigrated to West Germany, where he died in 2006.

den Leider (the Leader). In pre-war Belgium, the Dutch-speaking Flemings felt themselves socially and economically discriminated against by the French-speaking Walloons. The VNV advocated a pan-Dutch state, called Dietsland, a sort of Greater Netherlands based around Flanders, the Netherlands and French Flanders (a coastal border region of France, which belonged to France but was culturally Flemish). After the German occupation, all right-wing factions were forced to merge into the VNV. This did not inclue not Jef van de Wiele's movement, De Vlag, which was in favour of the incorporation of Flanders into the German Reich. To the SS, the idea of a separate Dietsland was a dangerous rival to the concept of a Greater Germanic Reich. Himmler and the SS began, in late 1940, to recruit "Germanic" Flemings to the Waffen-SS. These 600 Flemish volunteers formed the cadre for the Flemish Legion, designed for the Eastern Front after Hitler's attack on the USSR in June 1941, which attracted further Flemish volunteers due to its anti-Bolshevist propaganda. The Flemish Legion saw action in the Volkhov-Leningrad

Flemish veterans parading in Antwerp on 8 June 1943, serving as recruiting propaganda ro raise volunteers for establishing the new *SS-Sturmbrigade "Langemarck"*. At the front of the parade marches the colour guard for the Flemish Lion flag of the then recently dissolved *Legion Vlaanderen*. For historic and political reasons, no Flemish *SS*-unit was ever fully integrated in the *III. (Germ.) SS-Panzer-Korps*. In July 1944, a reinforced Flemish battalion from the "*Langemarck*" was *ad hoc* sent to reinforce the Narva Front alongside the Germanic *SS-Panzer-Korps*. During only six days of intense fighting around the Blue Hills, the Flemings suffered 90 percent losses. The recruitment of Flemish *SS*-volunteers reflected the disrupted factions of domestic Flemish National Socialism: the *VNV* (deClercq and Dr Elias) and *DeVlag* (van de Wiele) navigated between a more nationalistic form of National Socialistic ideology and an *SS*-inspired "Greater Germanic" conception.

The MP 40 submachine gun

The MP 40 (*Maschinenpistole*; submachine gun) is probably, together with the Thompson gun, the most popular known submachine gun from the Second World War. The MP 40 is often named the *Schmeisser*, although the weapons engineer Hugo Schmeisser, who in the Great War constructed the MP 18 (the world's first mass-produced submachine gun) and later developed the *Maschinenkarabiner* 36, was never involved in the construction of the MP 40. Its predecessor, the MP 38, was developed by Heinrich Vollmeer at the request of the German Army after the lessons of the Spanish Civil War. Immediately after the beginning of the Second World War, the German Army required a cheaper and more simplified version of the MP 38, and the Erma factory's answer was the MP 40. Its manufacturing process made extensive use of pressing, spot-welding and brazing. This weapon was primarily issued to *panzer* and *Fallschirmjäger* (paratrooper) soldiers, as well to Army squad and platoon leaders. The ordinary German infantry was mainly armed with the *Mauser* carbine 98k. Only after the Germans experienced Soviet superiority in house-to-house and short-range urban fighting in Stalingrad in 1942–43, where entire Red Army units were equipped with submachine guns, did the German Army develop the system of assault platoons (*Sturmzüge*) armed with the MP 40 or the *Sturmgewehr* 44. Around a million MP 40s were manufactured in the Second World War. LW

area in 1942–43. In May 1943, the Legion was dissolved and reformed as the SS-Freiwilligen-Sturmbrigade "Langemarck". In December 1943, the brigade, with a total unit strength of 2,022 men, was sent to the Ukraine as part of Heeresgruppe Süd. After suffering heavy losses in the Zhitomir pocket in January 1944, the brigade was refitted in Bohemia and raised up to strength with 1,700 new Flemish recruits. In July 1944, a battalion of the Sturmbrigade "Langemarck" was formed into the Kampfgruppe "Rehmann" and on 25 July arrived at the Baltic Front as a part of Felix Steiner's III. (germ.) SS-Panzer-Korps, which had taken up new defensive positions in the Tannenberg Line, west of Narva. Alongside the 11. SS-Panzergrenadier-Division "Nordland" and Estonian SS-units, the "Langemarck" suffered heavy losses against the Red Army in the battles for the Tannenberg Line. Renamed the Kampfgruppe D'Haese (after their new commander), the Flemish defended the strategically important Orphanage Hill within the Tannenberg position but were eventually forced to fall back to the Grenadier Hill with heavy losses. On 26 and 27 July, the Flemish anti-tank NCO Remi Schrijnen knocked out numerous Soviet tanks at Tannenberg, for which he was decorated with the Knight's Cross. During the following German general retreat out of Estonia, the Flemish Kampfgruppe executed a fighting withdrawal alongside the III. (germ.) SS-Panzer-Korps into the Courland pocket. In September, the remaining 130 Flemings were evacuated from the Baltic battlefield over the sea to Germany to join the rest of the SS-"Langemarck" Brigade. Like the SS-Brigade "Wallonien", the Flemish SS volunteers were to see action

Soviet submachine guns

The Soviet expert on automatic weapons, Vasily Degtyaryev, designed the first pioneering Soviet submachine gun: the PPD 34/38 ("PP" standing for *Pistolet-Pulemyot*, the Russian term for a submachine gun, and "D" being the initial of the designer), which appeared in 1934 for the Soviet Army. From 1942, the PPD was replaced by the PPSh submachine gun, designed by Georgii Shpagin (the "Sh" being his initials). The Soviet PPSh submachine gun was a robust, reliable weapon of pressed steel, which retained the old-fashioned wooden butt. It fired the standard pistol cartridge of 7.62mm, held in either a 71-round drum or a 35-round box. The rate of fire was 700 rounds per minute. The Red Army favoured the submachine gun, and whole battalions were frequently armed with it. The total number manufactured exceeded five million. (LW)

Anonymous Estonian grenadier in the *20. SS-Division* (Petter Kjellander's archive)

Our Company were put in action in the trenches at Mummasaare on the night of 27 July. We positioned ourselves when units from the Soviet 8th Army and the 2nd [Shock] Army attacked us. The first attack was done with tanks, of course with artillery support and air attacks. The ground shook. When the enemy's strong fire started, we withdrew and when the fire was moved to the front we ran to our trenches to confront the enemy attack. As always, we let the Russians come to a distance of about 30 to 50 metres before we met them with heavy machine-gun fire, but also with mortars and anti tank-guns. Most of the Soviet armour ran into mines. The Soviet infantry was met with hand-weapon fire and it is possible that none of them survived. The next attack came on 29 July and the third on 30 July. With these three attacks, all trees on the Blue Hills were shot to pieces. No one could imagine that the landscape would look like that. But it was also a mass grave for Soviet tanks. On the night, our pioneers set out new tank and infantry mines as well as barbed wire.

again with the III. (germ.) SS-Panzer-Korps during the battle for Pomerania in early 1945. (LW)

The harsh and brutal lives of Soviet soldiers

Between 1941 and 1945, 30 million Soviet soldiers served in the Red Army. Initially facing certain defeat and death, they finally advanced to victory in Berlin. Their bloody toll was enormous, the numbers hard to believe: more than eight million Red Army soldiers killed at the war's end, too often driven to needless sacrifices by Stalin and his entourage in the Communist system. The *Wehrmacht*, on the other hand, deliberately killed Soviet prisoners of war or let them systematically starve to death: out of 5.7 million Soviet POWs, some 3.3 million (57 percent) died in Nazi custody by summary execution, exposure or starvation.[37] For 60 years the Soviet Union hid and suppressed their soldiers' experiences in the Second World War, replacing it with propaganda about Soviet victory being achieved in the name of Stalin, the Motherland or the Communist Party. In 2006, the British historian Catherine Merridale, with her brilliant book *Ivan's War*, was the first researcher to reveal the real, and horrifying, lives of the ordinary men in the Red Army.[38]

From the very beginning of the Nazi invasion of the Soviet Union in 1941, the Red Army soldiers were badly trained and poorly equipped. Stalin refused to put the troops in suitable defensive positions and hence contributed to the horrifying number of Soviets killed, wounded or taken prisoner during the initial German attacks. During all the campaigns on the Eastern Front, most Red Army soldiers were either killed or wounded within three months of their arrival on the front line. The German (and US) system of keeping platoons together by letting wounded men return to their original front units, thereby creating an atmosphere of collective friendship and solidarity, did not exist in the Red Army; there, mistrust and terror were the ordinary management methods, enforced by the *NKVD* security troops who were so well equipped, even with tanks, that they represented an army within the Soviet Army.[39] Soviet reports from the critical period of 1941–42 give the number of Soviet death sentences at 790,000, with nearly 200,000 executed. Another report from Stalingrad gives the number of Red Army soldiers shot by the *NKVD* as 15,000. The British historian, Norman Davies, estimates that the total losses of the Red Army by internal executions may well exeed the total numbers of British and US soldiers killed in action in the Second World War.

The medical care in the Red Army was insufficient and catastrophic. Davies writes:

> The descriptions of Soviet field hospitals are horrifying to read. Piles of multilated corpses were transported on open lorries, dumped in a heap on the ground and rinsed with cold water to separate the dead from the still living. The surgeons had not time for long operations and only seconds to judge the injuries. Men with several or internal injuries were laid outside to die in agony, while commandeered peasants dragged the corpses to a mass grave in the nearby woods.[40]

"The Russians" or "Ivan", which were the common names of the Red Army outside the Soviet Union, consisted of 70 official nationalities. The non-Russians constituted 40–45 percent of the Soviet citizens, the Ukrainians being the largest ethnic group (around18 percent). Nazi racial propaganda symbolized the campaigns on the Eastern Front with ancient struggles against "the Asian hordes" and "Djingis Kahn". These phrases became ironically more and more true, as heavy Russian casualties, combined with the mobilization of recruits from Soviet Central Asian republics, resulted in the Red Army, during the final phase of the war, being, in reality, Eurasia on the march. Recent Russian research has also revealed that at least a million Soviet citizens served in German uniform as *Hiwis* (*Hilfswillige*), as armed infantry in the *Wehrmacht* or in German police and security forces.[41]

The Stalinistic pre-war terror, which had permeated almost all parts of life in the Soviet Union and had killed millions of citizens during the Twenties and Thirties, remained intact in the Second World War (90 percent of Soviet territory remained unoccupied by the Nazis). The

Joachim Zigler

Communist terror modified some aspects to satisfy the needs of war, but Stalinist terror never changed.The number of Soviet citizens liquidated by Communist terror remained very much the same in the Forties compared with the Thirties.

However, although the Red Army soldier was poorly led, poorly trained and poorly equipped in the first phases of the German-Soviet war, the Soviet infantryman of 1944 was an altogether much more formidable soldier of remarkably improved fighting qualities.

Catherine Merridale describes the Soviet advance into Germany as an army "fueled by rage and vodka, whipped into a frenzy by its political officers ... The Russian soldier's 'rage in battle must be terrible', a slogan at the time said. In practice, this meant rape, pillage and plunder on a scale that has yet to be recognized." The Red Army, Merridale writes, embarked "on an orgy of war crimes".[42]

The new qualities of the Red Army were noted by the Swedish war correspondent in the *Waffen-SS*, *Untersturmführer* Gösta Borg:

> The massive assault-technique was developed between 1944–1945. The fighting in 1941 was idyllic in comparison with the earthquakes that smashed the German Eastern Front during the summer and autumn of 1944. The difference between an earthquake and the modern battlefield – massive assault – "annihilating combat at a distance" – is essentially this: Natural force never seeks out a specific group of individuals, never seeks them out with a raging will to kill – the massive assault's overwhelming characteristic is the presence of a fanatical will: this incredible force strikes out to annihilate, "to blow to bits the faces of each and every one of them".[43]

Borg was unusually qualified to analyze the Red Army, as he was examined as the top student at the Swedish officer's school of Karlberg in Stockholm and served in the *Waffen-SS* in 1941 and 1943–45. Borg described the efficiency of the offensives launched by the modernized Red Army in 1944–45 as "earthquakes of TNT and masses of tanks that smashed apart everything in the way: terrain, weapons and people". (LW)

General staff officers from the Army in the *III. (Germ.)* SS-Panzer-Korps: Joachim Ziegler

A somewhat neglected factor for the actual or propagandistically alleged elite military character of certain units within the *Waffen-SS* is the standard of their general staff officers. Without an experienced, intelligent and tactically flexible higher command of the subordinated troops on the battlefield, the courage and motivation of the individual soldiers and officers is almost meaningless.

The *Waffen-SS* had no general staff education of their own and were dependent on the education of suitable staff officers at the Army's *Kriegsakademie* (War Academy). From the spring of 1943, in line with Hitler's wish and permission to erect more new *SS*-divisions, qualified general staff officers from the Army were transferred to corresponding positions in divisional or corps staffs of the *Waffen-SS*. This arrangement and its transfers were made in consultation between *Generaloberst* Kurt Zeitzler, the Army's Chief of Staff, and *SS-Gruppenführer* Hans Jüttner, Chief of Staff of the *SS-Führungshauptamt*. The transfer was voluntary and the Army officers were given the status and ranks of officers in the *Waffen-SS*, often at the same time being promoted one rank.

The *III. (germ.) SS-Panzer-Korps* seem to have been fortunate to receive especially skilled general staff officers from the Army, particularly in the persons of *Oberstleutnant im Generalstab* Joachim Ziegler, *Major im Generalstab* Helmut von Bockelberg and *Hauptmann im Generalstab* Jürgen von Bock.

Joachim Ziegler was born in Hanau am Main, near Frankfurt, in 1904. His father was a cavalry officer who was killed at Verdun in September 1914. The family were originally French protestant Huguenots, fleeing Catholic oppression in France for Prussia in the eighteenth century. After passing the Gymnasium in Darmstadt, Ziegler's interest in nature tended toward a career in forestry, but he chose to join the cavalry, *Reiter-Regiment 16*, in 1923, being promoted to *Leutnant* in 1926 after war school. Ziegler was also interested in the humanities, musically gifted and talented in sports.

Even as a young officer, Ziegler was conspicuous for his independent thinking and objectivity. He was posted as company commander to the newly created German *Panzerwaffe*, the Regiment 6 in Neu-Ruppin in 1935, experienced the conversion of the cavalry to tanks and served with the *Legion Condor* in the Spanish Civil War, for which he was decorated with the Spanish Cross in Gold. In January 1935, Ziegler was promoted to *Hauptmann* and remained with the *panzer* troops as adjutant to the *3. Panzer-Brigade* in Berlin. As a *Major im Generalstab*, Ziegler served as Intelligence officer (Ic) of the *7. Panzer-Division*, led by Erwin Rommel in the offensive against France in the summer of 1940, where Ziegler earned his Iron Cross, 1st Class. Considered an outstanding officer, Ziegler was promoted to major in 1940 and transferred permanently to the General Staff.[44]

In the campaign against the Soviet Union, Ziegler served as operations officer and Chief of Staff in various motorized and armoured divisions and panzer corps, promoted to full *Oberst* and awarded the German Cross in Gold in March 1943. Since 1937, Ziegler had enjoyed a "picture-book career" in the *Wehrmacht*.

As a result of high losses and the great expansion of the field formations of the *Waffen-SS* from 1943, there was a chronic shortage of both field and general staff officers in the *Waffen-SS*. Despite its own shortage of personnel, the *OKH* transferred 25 General Staff officers from the Army to the *Waffen-SS* in mid-1943. Such a transfer from the Army to the *Waffen-SS* could only be done if the officer in question voluntarily and willingly did so. Joachim Ziegler was transferred to *Waffen-SS* service as a specialized *Generalstabsoffizier* on 15. June 1943, and was at the same time assigned to the new *III. (germ.) SS-Panzer-Korps* as Chief of Staff under *SS-Obergruppenführer* Felix Steiner. Ziegler and Steiner had met in the summer of 1942, during the German campaign in the Caucasus when Steiner commanded the *SS-Division "Wiking"* and Ziegler was Chief of Staff of the *LVII. Panzer-Korps*.

The motivation for Ziegler to join the *III. (Germ.) SS-Panzer-Korps* has been described by his sister:

> I know almost with certainty when the strong influence from Felix Steiner with my brother started: in the Caucasus [in] 1943–1943 as 'Jochen' was operations officer and Steiner's *SS-Division "Wiking"* marched beside him. The critical point occurred during the hasty retreat [out of the Caucasus] as my brother's weak army divisional commander left the wounded behind, who finally were rescued by Steiner's *SS*-division. During a leave, my brother told me about these events, still boiling with anger ... However, it was no easy decision for him to change side; to shortly summarize: during a struggle for life and death he preferred to fight with a sharp blade than with a corroded [one].[45]

From July 1943 to July 1944, Joachim Ziegler was Chief of Staff of *III. (Germ.) SS-Panzer-Korps* under Steiner. During the brutal anti-partisan actions of the *SS-Panzer-Korps* in Croatia during the autumn of 1943, the Third *Reich*'s Plenipotentiary in Croatia, General Edmund Glaise von Horstenau, was notified by the Foreign Minister of the Croatian *Ustascha*, Mladen Lorkovic, about the *SS-Panzer'Korps*' "dirty filth" (*namenlose Schweinerei*) while burning and plundering Croatian villages during that October. General Horste von Gleisenau, as representative for the *Wehrmacht* in Croatia, became upset and immediately telephoned the staff of the *SS-Panzer-Korps* in Zagreb. He spoke to Ziegler, who referred to "general orders".[46]

After Fritz von Scholz was killed in action as divisional commander of the "*Nordland*" during the Battle of the Blue Hills in July 1944, Ziegler was appointed as his successor as full commander of the division on 1 August and promoted to *SS-Brigadeführer*. His successor as Chief of Staff of *III. (germ.) SS-Panzer-Korps* was *SS-Obersturmbannführer* Helmut von Bockelberg. Ziegler was noted not only for his outstanding professional capabilities, but also as a humane and understanding commander who led the division with circumspection and a calm disposition. He was obviously a man who followed the dictates of his own conscience and was no rigid follower of orders. In particular, he resisted the senseless squandering of his division, because it consisted to a certain extent of foreign volunteers. That is illustrated primarily by his uncompromising attitude toward the senseless Battle of Berlin in 1945. Ziegler won the Knight's

Crew members from a "*Nordland*" reconnaissance *SPW*, probably in the autumn of 1944 near Paplaken in Latvia (Courland).

Cross in September 1944 for his command of the division on the Baltic Front and continued as a skillful divisional commander of the "*Nordland*" until the final battle for Berlin. For his successful leadership of the "*Nordland*" during the battles in Pomerania in January-March 1945, Ziegler was awarded the Oak Leaves to the Knight's Cross. When the foreign volunteers of the "*Nederland*" and "*Nordland*" were scattered to the winds during the fighting on the Oder, Felix Steiner emphatically advised Ziegler to avoid being drawn into the city of Berlin under any circumstances; that would mean the end of the division. As later events proved, Zeigler kept Steiner's advice constantly in mind. After the "*Nordland*" was transferred from the *III. (germ.) SS-Panzer-Korps* to the *LVI. Panzer-Korps*, Steiner and Ziegler remained in contact through a radio relay. Both pinned their final hopes on the advance of the Western Allies and held to the opinion that the foreign volunteers should be spared the final battle.

The Red Army closed the circle around Berlin on 25 April 1945. The commanding general of the *LVI. Panzer-Korps* and Ziegler's immediate superior, *General der Artillerie* Helmuth Weidling, ordered the "*Nordland*" to take part in the direct defence of the capital. Zielger wanted to prevent his division from being sacrificed in Berlin and argued with Weidling's operations order, doing his best to obstruct its execution. Ziegler apparently transferred important elements of his division, including essential parts of the signals battalion, to the western section of Berlin. His intention was, in part, to raise questions about the combat power of the division, but also to have the "*Nordland*" positioned for a breakout from Berlin to the west. When Ziegler refused Weidling's questionable order on 25 April to attack with the "*Nordland*" to reach the eastern outskirts of Berlin and, instead, ordered the division's radio net to go to radio silence, Weidling removed Ziegler from command of the division, his place being taken by *SS-Brigadeführer* Dr Gustav Krukenberg, who had entered the city with a battle group of fanatic French *SS* volunteers from the *SS-Division "Charlemagne"*. Ziegler was thereafter kept in custody in the *Reich* Chancellery and was killed on the night of 2 May by Russian artillery while trying to break out of Berlin in the *Freidrichstrasse* near the *Weidendammer Brücke*. (LW)

The battlefield at the Blue Hills today

Around 40,000 soldiers, of them 35,000 from the Red Army, were killed during the battles at the Tannenberg Line from 26 July to 8 August 1944. Nearly all soldiers were buried where they fell, and they lie there still. In a letter in 1991, the Swedish-Estonian writer and film producer Peeter Puide, from Stockholm, described the landscape at the Blue Hills at the beginning of the 1990s:

> Nowadays the landscape is covered with leaf trees, mostly ash, as the pine forests were totally shot down during the fighting in 1944. Some new houses have been built but most of the landscape is untouched. If you bring a field shovel you can uncover a lot of war memories. These are not entirely un-dangerous. I dug up ammunition, splinters from air bombs, and parts of grenades and skeleton parts after digging by chance east of the Orphanage Hill. I was told that one could find helmets and weapons in the bushes – and even mines! The fire trenches are still there, including three or four big artillery bunkers in the hills. The churchyard at Vaivara is flattened. Many of the gravestones bear marks of bullets and splinters. The infantry trenches east of the church yard [are] now grown for potatoes. There must have been [an] enormous amount of war materials that was found by the local *kolchose* during all the years after the Second World War. The offensive was moved to the area of Tartu in August 1944 and no one cared for the area around the Blue Hills afterwards. Still the remains of the fallen Soviet soldiers may be counted in the earth in the thousands.

SS-Oberscharführer Walter Schwarck as platoon leader, sitting at the front of a camouflaged *SPW "Stummel"*, *Sd.Kfz. 251/9*, with a 7.5cm *StuK 37 L/24*, near Narva in February-March 1944. In total, 1,141 *SPW 251/9*s of this type were produced, and there were still 582 in active service on 1 March 1945.

Panzergruppe "Saalbach"

Operation "Bagration", the long-awaited Soviet summer offensive, was launched against *Heeresgruppe Mitte* on 22 June 1944. The Red Army rapidly tore a 400km gap in the German lines and overwhelmed *Heeresgruppe Mitte*. A deep and fast Soviet *panzer* penetration emerged between *Heeresgruppe Nord* and *Mitte* along the Düna River (Daugava). With a rapidly moving armoured column, the Soviets stormed

SS-Hauptsturmführer Rudolf Saalbach immediately after receiving the Knight's Cross at Hungerburg in March 1944.

A photograph taken by the Swedish *SS*-volunteer Markus Ledin, from Stockholm, of a Soviet plane attacking his train travelling from Narva to Riga in 1944.

forward along the Lithuanian-Latvian border area between Vilnius and Daugavpils (Dünaburg) against the Gulf of Riga.

Among the few motorized and partly armoured units that the Germans could assign to the south from the Narva Front was *SS-Aufklärungs-Abteilung 11 "Nordland"* under *SS-Sturmbannführer* Rudolf Saalbach. Embarkation took place on 11–12 July at the railway stations in Vaivara and Kothla-Jövi, and via express train the armoured companies of this battalion reached the Dünaburg area 800km away in Latvia. On 10 July, Saalbach's battalion took up positions in Jakobstadt and prepared for action. Together with elements from the *61.* and *225. Infanterie-Divisionen*, the *SS-Panzer-Aufklärungsabteilung "Nordland"* constituted a task force under *General der Kavallerie* Philipp Kleffel. The mission of this task force was to close the gap between the two army groups as fast as possible by serving as blocking units (*Sperrverbände*) against the advancing Red Army, but also to discover the tactical direction of the armoured Soviet column.

Panzergruppe "Saalbach" consequently carried out a number of scouting missions in combination with counter-attacks to delay the Soviet advance. The different companies of Saalbach's battalion were split up, and it was not unusual for these armoured scouting elements to drive up to 70 miles in one night. The CO of the *1. Kompanie*, *SS-Obersturmführer* Siegfried Lorenz, recalled:

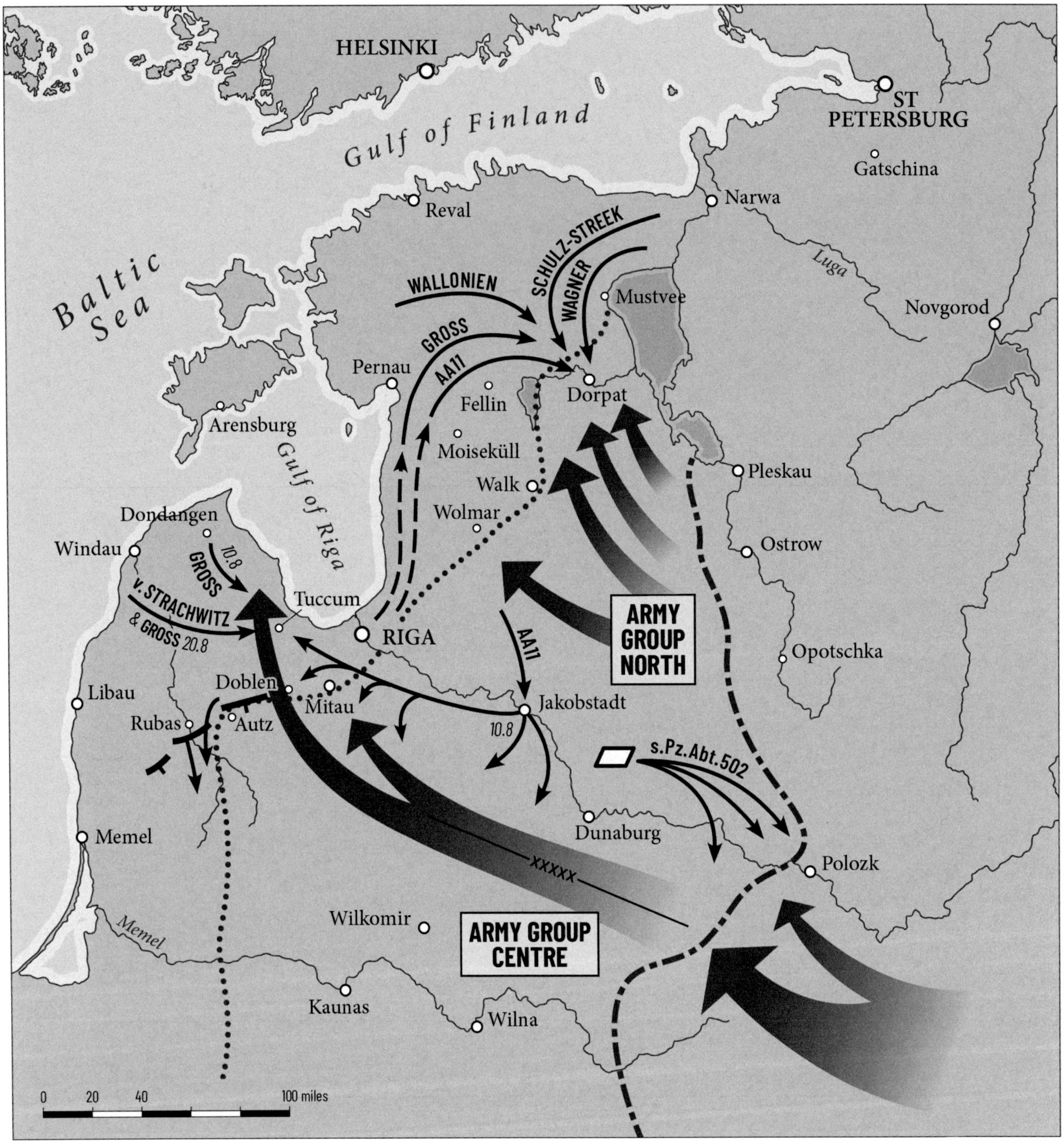

The Battle of the Baltics, summer 1944.

I drove there through an area which was entirely empty of Germans and Russians, and after many kilometres, I approached onto a main road leading to Riga in an east by southeast direction. There, I met the General of the corps (Kleffel) and en route made several eastward thrusts into the forest area to see if they contained Russian units, but found nothing. Unfortunately, at that time our radio only had a range of 10 to 20 miles. Consequently, I was not successful in making contact with battalion HQ from there. Later, however, via a priest's telephone which was still functioning, I succeeded in calling a house which stood directly across from the battalion's HQ. Thus I was able to report over the phone. This was only one example of how one could, at that time, work out a solution by improvising. I got the opportunity to talk at length with the General. In the course of which he told me that in his view, and as confirmed by my reconnaissance results, the Russian build-up was aimed at Riga. Until then the German side had always assumed that the enemy would be swinging off to the north to begin with, from Dünaburg. This was the so-called operative-result of my reconnaissance, which I could then further confirm, by making my way back quite close to the length of the Russian front line. It took me some time to find the way back to the battalion.

Sten Eriksson

Somewhat later, *SS-Sturmbannführer* Saalbach summarized the tactical importance of Lorenz's mission in his recommendation for the German Cross in Gold for Lorenz:

> On 17 July, *SS-Obersturmführer* Lorenz was instructed to lead a *Kampfgruppe*, comprised of parts of the *SS-Panzer-Auklärungsabteilung "Nordland"*, and form a defensive line northwest of Lake Scolly by Komai, and defend it against any and all enemy attacks. Immediately upon his men having taken up defensive positions, the enemy in force tried to break through and make a flanking attack against Komai. *SS-Obersturmführer* Lorenz has, by always placing himself in the centre of the battle, even after the enemy having blocked off the retreat road, until the very last moment, held the defence of this retreat route over Komai, so vital to the division, thereby staving off an extremely dangerous threat on the divison's flank.

In his justification for the awarding of the German Cross in Gold to *SS-Obersturmführer* Georg Langendorf, CO of the *5. Kompanie*, Saalbach described some other performances during the Latvian campaign:

> During the battalion's operations that were connected with the retreat carried out in the area of Dünaburg-Birsen, *SS-Obersturmführer* Langendorf received orders at Alisovo to watch over the retreat and prevent the enemy following up too soon. Langendorf has, in addition to fulfilling a remarkable consolidation of his heavy weapons, personally led his motorized weaponry on situations that were critically decisive for the battalion, and thereby two times prevented threatening breakthroughs by the superior enemy.
>
> During rearguard delaying operations, the enemy succeeded in cutting off the battalion's connection with the commanding army corps in the area of Dünaburg-Birsen by Kupreliskis, and, additionally, they blocked the path of retreat from the flank. Langendorf immediately took command over a small *Kampfgruppe*, made up of heavy and medium-heavy weaponry, with the purpose of eliminating this Soviet threat. With great personal bravery and incredible focus, Langendorf not only succeeded in holding off enemy forces, but also destroyed them, partially accomplished in close-combat performance, and thereby opening the only path of retreat for the battalion.
>
> On 1 August 1944, during the fighting around Biest, the battalion received orders to carry out a night-attack against superior Russian forces in the village of Gujanay, [and were] ordered to take the village and succeed with an attack in the northwest direction. This difficult night attack, which was accomplished by the 3. and 4. rifle Companies on foot, was brilliantly supported by Langendorf with his heavy weaponry. Without any regard to his own personal safety, he was always present on the front-line with the infantry companies leading the operations of his motorized weapons thus giving the grenadiers the possibility to advance quickly without respite.

The successful performance of *Panzergruppe "Saalbach"* (*SS–Panzer Aufklärungsabteiling "Nordland"*) during these blocking and reconnaissance actions within *Kampfgruppe "Kleffel"*, contributed to the Soviet collapse of operations during July 1944 in these areas around the River Düna and the borders between Latvia and Lithuania; and Riga was, for the time being, saved. Also crucial for these both strategical and tactical successes for the Germans were the skilled operations performed by the *schwere Panzer-Abteilung 502* around Dünaburg (Daugavpils) in July, blocking the Soviet advance. After completing its mission in Latvia and Lithuania, the *SS-Aufklärungs-Abteilung 11 "Nordland"* was transported by train back to the area west of Narva. LW

Sten Eriksson – Swedish *SS* war correspondent in Narva

Sten Eriksson from Ängelholm arrived at the Narva Front in April 1944 as a Swedish volunteer. He had been assigned to a student company in the Swedish Army and joined the *Waffen-SS* in Oslo in 1942 after crossing the Swedish-Norwegian border. After serving with the *SS-Division "Wiking"* in the Caucasus, Eriksson was during the spring of 1944 transferred to Narva as a war correspondent and joined the Estonian units there, where he felt there was a good comradeship:

> During the battles at Narva, I experienced for the first time a Soviet tank assault. At that moment, I served at the front with a Danish *SS* company. We correspondents had orders

> not to expose ourselves unnecessarily. I had the chance to retreat but felt that I ought not. Some T-34s were hit but a couple broke through and were shot up with *Panzerfaust.* At that moment Russian infantry had also started to roll up our trenches. Most of the Danish soldiers succeeded in retreating over the road. Some were hit by panic and ran but they did not [go] far.

Eriksson also participated in the hard battles around Sinimäe (Blaue Bergen) in July-August 1944: "It looked like a gigantic [pile of] rubble. There lay all dead, I think it was soldiers from Langemarck. It looked unnatural and it was curiously peaceful at [that] place." After having been wounded near Narva in late summer 1944, Eriksson returned to the front in Courland in the autumn and was once again wounded at Christmas 1944. In March 1945, Eriksson participated in the battle for Pomerania with the *11. SS-Panzergrenadier-Division "Nordland"*, and he also took part in the final battle for Berlin in April and May. Eriksson returner to Sweden in the summer of 1945 and was for many years a cultural journalist for the *Borås Tidning* newspaper. He died in Borås in 2006. LW

SS-Panzer-Brigade "Gross"

The overwhelming Soviet summer offensive of 1944 had swept through Belorussia and soon reached the borders of Poland and the Baltic countries. At the end of July, the situation was most criticial for the Germans. Between the thereatened fronts of *Heeresgruppen Mitte* and *Nord*, the successful performance of *Kampfgruppe "Kleffel"* in July 1944 around the River Düna in Latvia prevented the Red Army from reaching its primary goal of Riga, forcing the Soviets to drive further to the west towards Tukkums on the Baltic Sea.

On 1 August 1944, a Soviet forward force from the 3rd Soviet Mechanized Corps broke through between Autz and Mitau near Tuckum in Latvia, a few kilometres from the Gulf of Riga on the Baltic Sea, thereby threatening to completely cut off *Heeresgruppe Nord* from the rest of the German Army on the Eastern Front. Reinforcements to the practically annihilated *Heeresgruppe Mitte* had drained the reserves of the German High Command, so the Germans had to hastily improvise. The new commander of *Heeresgruppe Nord* (as of 25 July 1944), *Generaloberst* Ferdinand Schörner, ordered the formation of *ad hoc* emergency *Kampfgruppen* in order to conduct a counter-attack to restore land contact between the two army groups. Some of these battlegroups would also include replacement units and soldiers from the *III. (germ.) SS-Panzer-Korps.*

There were various *Waffen-SS* and Army training centres and schools in Latvia, having been set up since 1941–42 in the conquered Eastern territories. One of the combat groups there was *SS-Panzer-Brigade "Gross"*, formed from the *SS-Panzer-Ausbildungs-und Ersatz-Regiment* that was located at Seelager, near Dondangen (Dundaga), in the northern part of the Lavian peninsula of Courland. Following common practice in the *Waffen-SS*, this *Kampfgruppe* was named after its commander, *SS-Obersturmbannführer* Martin Gross, who had been a long-time officer in the *Leibstandarte SS "Adolf Hitler"* and distinguished himself during the operation to retake Kharkov in March 1943. After the failed Kursk offensive, Gross was transferred as commander of the *SS panzer* training regiment at Dondangen, and was also appointed commander of the battlegroup after his unit was mobilized for the front.[47]

The *SS-Führungshauptamt* in Berlin, seeing a threat of their central armoured education depots for all *Waffen-SS panzer* divisons being drained for *ad hoc* purposes, ordered the immediate transfer on 27 July 1944 of the *SS-Panzer-Ausbildungs-und Ersatz-Regiment* (around 8,000 men) in Dondangen via Libau to Germany. Due to the immediate Soviet threats against the Baltic countries, *Heeresgruppe Nord*, however, got permission to extract 2,000 men to form the *SS-Panzer-Brigade "Gross"*, while the remaining 6,000 recruits and specialist officers from the Dondangen armoured centre were evacuated to the *Reich*.

Martin Gross' weak brigade, initially consisting of only 10–15 outdated *Panzer III* and *Panzer IV* tanks, was bolstered with two *Panzergrenadier-Bataillonen* and the 1st and 2nd *SS*-Armoured Reconnaissance Training and Replacement Battalions from Riga-Strand. The brigade also consisted of a pioneer company, an assault gun company and an anti-aircraft company. *SS-Hauptsturmführer* Fritz Herzig, previously sub-commander at Seelager, was on 4 August appointed as operations officer (Ia) in the brigade staff. On 5 August, *Brigade "Gross"* was committed with a thrust towards Tuckum in order to make contact with *Heeresgruppe Nord.* The brigade advanced with a handful *panzers* within 3km of Tuckum but failed to move futher due to strong Soviet resistance. A new attempt by the brigade on 8 August to

Martin Gross

reach *Kampfgruppe "Kleffel"* also failed. Therefore, "*Gross*" (which by 16 August had a strength of 2,500 men) was attached to the *ad hoc Panzer-Divison "Strachwitz"* which had been formed from various units: *Brigade "Gross", 101. Panzer-Brigade* (Army), *337. Nachrichten-Abteilung, III. SS-Artillerie-Regiment, SS-Kampfgruppe "Hierthes"* (both from the *19. Latvian Waffen-Grenadier-Division der SS*) and the divisional staff of the *337. Infanterie-Division*. The plan made by *Generalmajor* Hyacinth Graf von Strachwitz was to make a major coordinated armoured attack in force against the Red Army and break through to *Heeresgruppe Nord* in Riga.[48]

On 19 August, *SS-Panzer-Brigade "Gross"* received orders, together with the assembled forces under Strachwitz, to attack Tuckum and restore the German front between the two army groups. At 4:00 a.m. on 20 August, *Panzer-Division "Strachwitz"* attacked and achieved total surprise over the Red Army, reaching Tuckums by 5:00 a.m. With a small armoured group, Strachwitz continued the attack and made a successful link-up with German units in the Riga area. *SS-Panzer-Brigade "Gross"* moved eastwards and reached the Doblen-Autz road on 26 August. In coordination with *Korps "Kleffel"*, Strachwitz had been successful in breaking the Soviet encirclement of Riga from the German forces in Courland.

Meanwhile, a new Soviet armoured thrust, executed by 30 divisions of the 3rd Baltic Front, threatened Heeresgruppe Nord in south-eastern Estonia between Lake Wirz and Lake Peipus, near the university town of Dorpat (Tartu). The *SS-Panzer-Brigade "Gross"* was detached from *Panzergruppe "Strachwitz"* and directed to the Dorpat (Tartu) area, arriving at Elva, south-west of Dorpat, on 25 August. Its mission was to establish a stronger connection between the Eighteenth Army and *Armeeabteilung "Narva"*. The brigade was somewhat weakened by having to leave some units back in the Tuckums area. *Kampfgruppe "Strachwitz"* could not prevent Dorpat from falling into the hands of the Red Army. With supporting fire, the tanks from "*Strachwitz*" attacked eastwards from Elva along the road towards Tamsa. The *Kampfgruppe* was ambushed by Soviet anti-tank weapons near the village of Uhuta, but continued to press forward. Meanwhile, Soviet forces took Elva and thereby threatened the flanks of "*Strachwitz*", forcing it to break off its advance eastwards and retreat to Elva. This was accomplished under covering fire from the *I. SS-Panzergrenadier-Bataillon*[49] (*SS-Sturmbannführer* Alfred Arnold), which acted as rearguard.

By 12 September, Gross' brigade's armoured strength amounted to eight *Panzer III*s, one *Panzer IV*, three Panthers, one assault gun and 17 half-tracks (*SdKfz 251*). As the German positions around the bridgehead of Narva, being for some time the most easterly part of the German Eastern Front, was threatened with being outflanked by the Red Army, Narva had been abandoned at the end of July and German forces fell back to the new Tannenberg Line west of Narva. During the general German retreat out of Estonia in September, the brigade performed rearguard actions on the border of Estonia and Latvia and withdrew past Riga into Courland. On 4 October, the *SS-Infanterie-Bataillon "Runge"* was transferred from *Brigade "Gross"* and attached to the *11. SS-Freiwilligen-Panzergrenadier-Divison "Nordland"*. Around 20 October, the remainder of *SS-Panzer-Brigade "Gross"* was evacuated to the *Reich* and the *SS Panzer* training grounds at Sennelager near Paderborn in Westphalia, where the brigade was dismantled and the personnel distributed as replacements to various *SS-panzer divisions*. (LW)

SS-Obersturmbannführer Martin Gross

Martin Gross was born in 1911 in Frankfurt am Main, the son of a railway secretary. He joined the *Hitler-Jugend* in 1928 and the *SA* in 1929, and participated in the street fighting between the Nazis and communists. Due to his active Nazi commitment, he lost his job and was also imprisoned during the Weimar Republic. Gross entered the *SS* in 1931, and from May 1933 belonged to the *Leibstandarte SS "Adolf Hitler"*. As well as taking part in all Germany's pre-war actions (the re-entrance of the Saar, the annexation of the Sudetenland, the *Anschluss* of Austria and the occupation of Czechoslovakia), he participated in the campaigns against Poland, France, Greece and the Soviet Union, and from 1 June 1942 was unit commander within the *SS-Panzer-Regiment 1* of the *Leibstandarte*. He served with distinction during the *I. SS-Panzer-Korps*' recapture of Kharkov in February-March 1943 and in the summer 1943 offensive at Kursk (he earned the Knight's Cross on 22 July). On 8 March 1944, Gross was assigned command of *SS-Panzer-Asubildungs- und Ersatz-Regiment "Seelager"* in Dondangen, Latvia.[50] After serving as CO of *SS-Panzer-Brigade "Gross"* in the Baltic countries from July-November 1944, he succeeded *SS-Obersturmbannführer* Herbert Kuhlmann as commander of *SS-Panzer-Regiment 12 "Hitler-Jugend"* in March 1945. He participated in the defensive battles out of Hungary and into Austria in April-May and was taken prisoner by the US Army near the city of Enns on 8 May. Martin Gross passed away on 1 March 1984. (LW)

The *Sturmgewehr 44*

The *Sturmgewehr 44* (*StG 44*) is considered to be the world's first automatic carbine and the ancestor of all modern automatic carbines, including the Soviet post-war AK-47 (Kalashnikov). The *Sturmgewehr 44* offered a high rate of fire, high precision and a good range, superior to both the German MP 40 submachine gun and the standard *Mauser Gewehr 98K* rifle. The *StG 44* had as high precision as the 98K at distances up to 300 metres and just slightly inferior at up to 600 metres. The *StG 44* made the German infantry and *Panzergrenadier* units less dependent on the MG 4 machine gun. Units from the *III SS-Panzer-Korps* in Estonia were equipped with the *StG 44* during August-September 1944. The *StG 44* was produced in 425,977 units and was used at the front from July 1944 until May 1945. It weighed 5.22kg, the magazine contained 30 7.92 x 33mm cartridges and the rate of fire was

500 rounds per minute. After the Second World War, surplus *StG 44*s were used by the *DDR Volksarmee* (East German National People's Army). NATO's G 3 automatic carbine and the Swedish AK 4 are reminiscent of the *StG 44* as they were developed by the same German engineers and technicians. (LW)

Kurt Müller, signals NCO in the *SS-Korpsnachrichtenabteilung 503* (Lennart Westberg's archive)

The task of our corps signal battalion was to transmit and receive orders and information to and from the staff of the *III. (germ.) SS-Panzer-Korps* to subordinated divisions and brigades or directly attached units. To the corps artillery commander, *Oberst* Kresin and to artillery commanders from the *Wehrmacht* we established special communications. We also had radio contact with the reconnaissance planes from the *Luftwaffe* and their air field. Without our communications unit, any proper transfer of tactical orders from our corps HQ was not possible. We worked with wire telephones, teleprinters and radio as means of communication. The closer our net to subordinated units and to our neighbour units (corps and divisions) was, the more secure were our communications. If the telephone cables were shot up or if the corps staff regrouped, we established temporary radio communications. Wires and cables were, unlike radio, not possible for the enemy to intercept or to disturb. A radio station could both be located and disturbed and consequently become a target of pinpointed artillery assaults to knock out the command place in question. Our radio messages were coded with our Enigma cipher machines. We also had teleprinter communication with our superior army staff.

The war archives of the *Waffen-SS* and their fate

The archives (war diaries, correspondence, situation maps etc.) of the different *Waffen-SS* units and their predecessor, the *SS-Verfügungstruppe*, were already splintered and divided during the Second World War. The various training and recruitment depots in Berlin, Graz, Vienna, Ellwangen etc. collected and filed the various field unit archives while they in the end were deposited in the *Kriegsgeschichtliche Abteilung der Waffen-SS* (the War Historical Department of the *Waffen-SS*) in Oranienburg, just north of Berlin, others being kept in the *SS* recruiting depots. The archival organization of the *Waffen-SS* was expanded after the German attack on the Soviet Union in June 1941, which from 1942–43 led to a substantial increase in the field units of the *Waffen-SS*.

Due to the intensive Allied bombing of Berlin in late 1943, the War Historical Department of the *Waffen-SS* moved from Oranienburg to the castle of Zasmuk in Bohemia, where the new War Historical Archive of the *Waffen-SS* (*Kriegsarchiv der Waffen-SS*) was established until the end of the war. In late April 1945, the voluminous archival holdings of this main depot were evacuated by trucks due to the Red Army advancing into Bohemia. This motorized *SS*-column made its way to the West, aiming for Bavaria. In the Bavarian Forest (Böhmerwald), the *SS* personnel, however, for various reasons, set fire to the evacuated war archives of the *Waffen-SS* and destroyed them. An affidavit from one of the members of this *SS*-column states that he observed the name "*Wiking*" among those records to be destroyed. Luckily, some files were left at the castle of Zasmuk, seized by the Russians and are now deposited in the Czech Military Archive in Prague. The most well-known of these surviving archives are the war diaries of the *SS-Kavalleriebrigade* and *SS-Infanteriebrigade*, under the *Kommandostab der Waffen-SS* from 1941–42. These units were operating as combined anti-partisan units, which at the same time had the mission to commit mass murder on Soviet citizens of Jewish ancestry in White Russia.

The fate of the various local war archival holdings of the *Waffen-SS* in the recruiting and training depots at the very end of the war remains uncertain. They were probably in most cases burnt by remaining *SS* units, but they could also have been seized by the Red Army in 1945 and taken to Moscow, remaining inaccessable for Western historians ever since. The training depot for the *11. SS-Freiwilligen-Panzergrenadier-Division "Nordland"* was situated in the barracks of Graz-Wetzelsdorf in Austria, which were captured by the Red Army in May 1945. The fate of the deposited "*Nordland*" archives in these barracks remains unknown.

Regarding the *III. (Germ.) SS-Panzer-Korps*, some records were destroyed and others survived. Unfortunately, the complete war diary of the *11. SS-Freiwilligen-Panzergrenadier-Division "Nordland"*, from the summer of 1943 to the end of April 1945, was burnt by its permanent stenographer at the divisional staff since Narva, *SS-Unterscharführer* Wolfgang Venghaus, on 25 April 1945, at Charlottenburg castle in Berlin. Parts of the war diary belonging to the signals battalions of the "*Nordland*" and the corps staff did, however, survive the war. Miraculously, the complete war diary (with appendixes) of the *4. SS-Freiwilligen-Panzergrenadier-Brigade "Nederland"* survived the war and is now in the custody of the German *Bundesarchiv*. These "*Nederland*" files were probably brought to the Western Allies' lines when *SS-Brigadeführer* Jürgen Wagner and his staff crossed the Elbe at Tangermünde in early May 1945. Some parts of the war diary from 1943 and early 1944 belonging to the *Generalkommando III. (germ.) SS-Panzer-Korps* also survived the war; among them files from the signals battalion of the corps staff. Most of the remaining files of the corps staff were destroyed in April 1945 in Mecklenburg, shortly before the German capitulation.
LW

The war correspondents of the *Waffen-SS*

During the Second World War, the German War Propaganda (*Wehrmacht* and *Waffen-SS*) produced 80,000 written articles and two million photographs from the different front-line

Gunter d'Alquen (1910–98) was chief editor of the *SS* weekly *Das Schwarze Korps* (The Black Corps), the official newspaper of the *SS*. Commander of the *SS-Standarte "Kurt Eggers"*, he was the son of a Catholic businessman in Essen. In 1926, d'Alquen joined the *SA*, and as a 17-year-old joined the National Socialist Party.

An *SS* field correspondent exercises enemy-directed propaganda via a megaphone from his trench, probably in a bid to convince Red Army soldiers to defect. On the trench lies a Soviet submachine-gun PPd–34/38 (*Pistolet-Pulemet-Degtyaryova*), a favoured captured weapon among the German troops due to its reliability during icy and snowy conditions in contrast to some German machine pistols.

The wartime HQ of the *SS-Standarte "Kurt Eggers"* photographed today. It was situated in Berlin-Zehlendorf, Heimat 27, from 1942 until the end of the war, and accommodated the staff, laboratories, archives, etc.

units of the Third *Reich*. In the last year of the war, at least 20,000 metres of film were produced every week.

The war propaganda of the *Waffen-SS* was, in terms of organization and purpose, fully integrated in the National Socialist ideological system, aimed for both internal indoctrination and external propagandistic use. Central elements were the hatred for everything Jewish, the disgust for Parliamentarism and the glorification and justification of the expansionist-aggressive war aims of the Third *Reich*. The Second World War was predominently a conflict between ideologies, and well-suited for propagandistic, psychological indoctrination and persuasion. Hitler's and Goebbels' minds were still spooked by the German defeat in the Great War, and especially the fact that the *Kaiserreich* so quickly ceased to exist in 1918 like a house of cards, being replaced by the democratic Weimar Republic. The new totalitarian Nazi *Reich* was determined to suppress all internal opposition from the start, and through massive propaganda and indoctrination ensure a final struggle for Nazi victory – or death.

The Nazi propaganda had both internal and external-international duties.The traditional acitivites of war correspondents at the front were combined with other German propaganda activities, aimed for the public abroad. Within neutral Sweden, Germany distributed throughout the war large numbers of German magazines, ahead of its time in terms of professional layout, photo quality, etc. The picture magazine *Signal* was distributed in 20 languages, including Swedish, every second week from 1941 until March 1945. Other periodicals included *Tyska Röster* (German Voices), with a monthly edition of 60,0000. These weres on sale in every Swedish tobacco kiosk from the Arctic Circle to southern Sweden throughout the war. The Swedish volunteer in the *Waffen-SS* from 1943–45 (and future journalist), Sten Eriksson, commented retrospectively in 1986:

> As in all that man was doing, it was naturally a big proportion of the irrational that played a role. All we that were to be volunteers [in the *Waffen-SS*], had surely seen the German propaganda films during the first years of war, and strongly been influenced by the suggestive expressions for faithful drama. There were films that with enormous power corresponded with something elementary in mankind, and that especially can worry young men: these deep rooted needs of forming rites and original male ideals.

The Germans learned from their propaganda experiences and mistakes in the First World War, substantially increasing their propaganda efforts after 1940 . The war correspondent units of the *Waffen-SS*, although in the beginning as small as the armed *SS* (*Verfügungstruppe*) itself, grew as fast as the *Waffen-SS* expanded during the war. From just the strength of a company in March 1940, it expanded to regiment size in 1943: the *SS-Standarte "Kurt Eggers"* under its CO, *SS-Hauptsturmführer* Gunter d'Alquen. He was previously Editor-in Chief for *The Black Corps,* the *SS*'s own paper, and considered a "coming man" in the *SS*, with many good connections to its internal hierarchy. Actually, the "*Kurt Eggers*" propaganda organization of the *Waffen-SS* succeeded in expanding very fast, often at the expense of the *Wehrmacht*, and its presence in German, occupied and international press and radio rapidly grew from 1941. Dr Jochen Lehnhardt also points out that as a parallel phenomenon to this remarkable expansion, the ideological essence and tone of the war correspondents from the *Waffen-SS* was unmistakably radical.[51] The image created by this wartime *SS* propaganda did not only influence the Third *Reich* but also, due to Dr Lehnhardt's conclusions, had an impact into the present time.

In December 1942, the *Waffen-SS* consisted of 246,717 men and 334 war correspondents; by June 1944, it had a strength of 594,443 men and 1,180 war correspondents. As of 1 January 1942, the *Waffen-SS* counted 25 "Germanic" war correspondents, and up to December 1942 their number rose to 85. Due to an internal memo by the *SS-Standarte "Kurt Eggers"* in early 1943, the purpose of the *SS* war correspondents was not only to depict the battles at the front and emphasize the role of the *Waffen-SS*, but also "to impart the Germanic people with the struggle for the New Europe, and especially illustrate the dedication of their sons in the *Waffen-SS* and the Volunteer Legions".

After making the new soldiering of the *Waffen-SS* known to the German public in 1940–42, the traditional activities of *SS* war correspondents were substituted by so-called "*Aktivpropaganda*"; i.e., forms of psychological agitative warfare aimed at the enemy at the front, or at their own troops through indoctrination. But it was not until the defeats at the Volga and in Tunisia that the active psychological warfare began. The first test was organized in the winter of 1943, by despatching a special unit of the "*Kurt Eggers*" to the north-west of the Eastern Front: the Oranienbaum pocket near Leningrad. Here, *Obergruppenfuhrer* Felix Steiner was in charge, commanding the new *III. SS-Panzer Korps*. The propaganda operation was nicknamed *Wintermärchen* (Winter Saga). All German intelligence during the turn of the year 1943–44 pointed to a major Soviet offensive against the German front in the Oranienbaum pocket. Logically, a soldier who is preparing to attack is especially immune to enemy propaganda, but Gunter d'Alquen still orderered operation "Winter Saga" to continue as planned. In the end, four million leaflets were distributed by special air artillery (*Propagandawerfer*) or by planes over the Soviet trenches. The result, in terms of Soviet deserters, was characterized by d'Alquen as "considerable" (*beachtlich*), but no records have survived from "Winter Saga". After the Soviet offensive of 15 January 1944, the special "*Kurt Eggers*" units were evacuated to the Estonian town of Narva and then to Wesenberg. Operation "Winter Saga" continued against the Red Army at the Narva Front and, although very much on the defensive, the *SS* could record some success in terms of Soviet deserters, even during January-April 1944.

The bridgehead at Narva in 1944 wasd of special propagandist importance, as a symbol for "a great historic past in the struggle between the West and the East". It was the ground where, in 1700, the Swedish warrior king Charles XII destroyed a superior Russian army. In mid-1944, after the Red Army had forced the *Wehrmacht* into substantial retreats along the whole Eastern Front, Narva also became the vital most easterly part of the German-Soviet front, where the multinational *III. (Germ.) SS-Panzer-Korps* played a substantial role. This was heavily underlined by the war correspondent units of the *Waffen-SS* in Narva in their dispatches and propaganda. *SS*-articles from the Narva Front often quoted Norwegian (Quisling) *SS*-volunteers from the *SS-Panzergrenadier-Regiment "Norge"*, who looked with contempt upon the "degenerated Jewish-Democratic Sweden", which as a nation had lost its former "glorious past in the East under Charles XII". Hence, the propaganda of the *SS-Standarte "Kurt Eggers"* also politically supported, for example, Quisling's Norway – the "new Sparta of Scandinavia" – as being predestined to take over Sweden's formerly dominating role in the northern hemisphere, after the Nazis' final victory.

As the Nazi war efforts, after the German defeats at Stalingrad and Tunis, were reinforced into a "total war" (*Der totale Krieg*), the new paradigm of "*Aktivpropaganda*" and its psychological methods of war propaganda fitted well into the activities of the *SS-Standarte "Kurt Eggers"*. After the failed bomb plot and intended *coup d'état* of 20 July 1944, the volume of agressive propaganda, mobilization and tightened repressive control over the civil population, new recruits for the front and the existing German forces at the various fronts was massive.

After the July bomb plot, Himmler was appointed new Commander in Chief of the Reserve Army, and thereby the *SS* vastly increased its influence within the German Army. Although Goebbels, as *Reich* Plenipotentiary for the Total War Effort, succeeded in sending a million men to the front between August and December 1944, German losses in the first three of these months numbered 1,189,000 dead and wounded. In reality, the Nazis were scraping the bottom of the barrel, thereby multiplying the need for additional aggressive propaganda.

Dr Jochen Lehnhardt has shown how long-lived the wartime propaganda for the *Waffen-SS* has been, casting its successful shadow into West Germany and up to this day.[52] Dr Lehnhardt points out the reasons for Himmler and the *SS* to intensify the propaganda in favour of the *Waffen-SS* in the Second World War: to heighten its status due to future functions as an internal Imperial Guard, as the nucleus of the Third *Reich*'s "People's Army" and to facilitate the recruitment of "Germanic", ethnic German and domestic volunteers to the *Waffen-SS*.[53]

Within the polycratic system of the Third *Reich*, in 1945 the war correspondent organization of the *Waffen-SS* under Gunter d'Alquen succeeded in merging the whole *Wehrmacht* war propaganda apparatus with the *SS*. By that time, the swift ride of the Third *Reich* into the abyss was, however, inevitable.

With his exemplary analysis of the peace-time *Junkerschulen*, the officer schools of the *Waffen-SS* in Brunswick and Bad Tölz, Dr Jens Westemeier has shown how effectively post-war propaganda activities by former high-ranking *SS*-officers within the HIAG formed the myth and self-image of these *Junkerschulen* as elite military institutions.[54] Dr Westemeier's research proves convincingly the opposite: the quality of the *SS* teachers was highly unsatisfactory, the standard of education was clearly below the standards of the German Army's officer schools and the standard of the majority of the *SS* cadets was also dubious.[55] But due to the energetic post-war propaganda books in the Fifties and Sixties by former *SS Junkers*, a long-lived myth was created, accepted even by strong critics of the *Waffen-SS*, that the *Junkerschulen* impersonated elite military institutions, even international ones. As Dr Westemeier points out, the standards of the *Junkerschulen* were only improved during the Second World War as teachers, cadets and the educational methods were influenced by practical experiences and modern methods at the front. LW

The Finns in the *Waffen-SS*

After the Winter War between Finland and the Soviet Union in 1939–40, the continued communist threat against the Finnish state caused the Finnish government to gradually orientate its country towards Nazi Germany. This pro-German tradition had existed in influential Finnish circles since 1919, as Finland gained independence from the previously Tsarist and then Bolshevik Russia, partly with German military assistance. During the German planning for Operation "Barbarossa" in 1940–41, the Finnish armed forces gained a role in Hitler's campaign in the East. By the late Thirties, Heinrich Himmler considered most Finns (not only the Finno-Swedes) as Germanic by race and hence racial kinsmen, worthy to join the *Waffen-SS*.

As the only allied country not occupied by Nazi Germany, Finland recruited a battalion of 1,400 Finns in the spring of 1941 to serve in the *Waffen-SS*. These Finnish volunteers were mainly integrated in the *SS-Division "Wiking"* during the German offensives through Galicia in the summer of 1941 and into the Caucasus mountains in late 1942. For political reasons (so as not to alienate the Western Allies), the Finnish *SS*-battalion was called back to Finland in the early summer 1943 by the commander in chief of the nation's forces, Field Marshal Gustaf Mannerheim, and dissolved on 11 July 1943, after suffering losses of 256 men on the Eastern Front.

Hitler and Himmler growlingly accepted this dissolution, although Hitler never quite lost hope of establishing some new Finnish *SS*-unit. Himmler had planned to raise a regiment of Finnish *SS* volunteers within the *III. (Germ) SS-Panzer-Korps* in 1942–43, to be named after Finland's nationel literary epic: *Kalevala*. However, in line with hardening Finnish-German relations, these plans had to be dissolved. (LW)

SS-Fallschirmjäger-Bataillon 500/600 in Estonia in 1944

After participating in Operation "*Rösselsprung*" – the partly airborne assault on the Yugoslav partisan leader Josip Broz Tito and his HQ, in the Bosnian village of Drvar, from 25 May to 4 June 1944 – the *SS-Fallschirmjäger-Bataillon 500/600* was transported to Estonia. At the end of June 1944, the battalion (with 196 men, 81 NCOs and 15 officers) was stationed in Wesenberg (Rakvere) between Narva and Tallin. It was during this time subordinated to the *III. (Germ) SS-Panzer-Korps*. The *SS-Fallschirmjäger-Bataillon 500/600* was held in reserve for "*Fall Tanne Ost*", the planned airborne occupation of the strategically situated Finnish island of Hogland (Suursaari), which controlled the Gulf of Finland. Also planned at this time was Operation "*Tanne West*": the German occupation of the Finnish Aaland islands. Both eventualities were planned due to the expected Finnish intention to separately conclude peace with the Sovet Union, and in turn to prevent the Soviets from occupying these islands.

Instead, at the end of July 1944, the *SS-Fallschirmjäger-Bataillon 500/600* was heavily engaged in defending against penetrating Red Army forces in Lithuania near Wilna and Kauen. (LW)

The Swedes in the *III. (germ.) SS-Panzer-Korps*

A total of some 180 Swedes joined the *Waffen-SS* between 1940 and 1945. From this number, it is estimated that only around 100 Swedes finally reached the front lines with weapons in hand, the rest being earlier discharged, successfully applying to leave the *Waffen-SS* or simply deserting, disillusioned with the reality of the *Waffen-SS*. Additionally, around 15–20 Swedes served in the *Wehrmacht* or the *Wehrmachtgefolge* (e.g. the Organization Todt). Around 30 Swedes were killed during the fighting in the Soviet Union, the Baltic lands, Hungary, Pomerania and Berlin. Until 1943, the Swedes in the *SS* were scattered throughout various units, although most of them served in the *5. SS-Panzer-Division "Wiking"*. The Swedes in the *SS* participated, from a military point of view, in the most severe battles that Swedes had ever experienced. Several of them also witnessed the Holocaust.

After the Nazi invasion of the Soviet Union on 22 June 1941, the Swedish government was flooded with German requests to join or support Hitler's war against the USSR. In the German propaganda for the anti-Bolshevist crusade in the East, the Nazis were also well aware of emphasizing that the choice was between Berlin and Moscow, not between Berlin and London. Through a flexible propaganda programme, Berlin attempted to attract support from all factions of the Swedish extreme right, the parliamentary conservatives and traditional German-friendly circles. In Himmler's staff, *SS-Gruppenführer* Gottlob Berger and his chief of recruitment to the *Waffen-SS*, *SS-Sturmbannführer* Dr Franz Riedweg, were both enthusiastic and optimistic in their hopes of raising considerable numbers of Swedish volunteers in the *Waffen-SS* for the Eastern campaign.

On 4 and 5 July 1941, a special German emissary to Sweden, Karl Schnurre, presented new and radical proposals in conversations with Swedish Foreign Minister Christian Günther. Berlin wanted Sweden to join with the Axis Powers

SS-Obersturmführer Hans-Gösta Pehrsson was the most high-ranking and decorated Swedish volunteer in the *Waffen-SS*. Living as an engineer in Copenhagen before the war, he joined the *Freikorps "Danmark"* in 1941 and was promoted to NCO. Pehrsson passed exams at the *Junkerschule* Bad Tölz in 1943 and became a platoon leader and *SS-Untersturmführer* in the *SS*-Reconnaissance Battalion "*Nordland*" in 1943, advancing to CO of its third company in early 1944 until the war's end. Between 17 and 25 April, Pehrsson served as Ic on the divisional staff of the "*Nordland*", under *SS-Brigadeführer* Joachim Ziegler. During the last days of the battle for Berlin, he took command of his old company and took part in the distrous attempt to break out of Berlin at the *Weidendammer Brücke* and along the northern *Friedrichstrasse*. Pehrsson escaped Soviet captivity in Berlin and returned through Germany to Sweden. After the war he was a successful technical engineer in Stockholm, and died in 1974 of cancer. Pehrsson was a pre-war member of the Danish Nazi Party *DNSAP*.

The Swedish volunteer Heino Meyer, from Stockholm, as *SS-Untersturmführer* in the *"Germanic" SS-Panzer-Korps* in 1944. Meyer fought in the *SS-Division "Wiking"* in 1942–43 and graduated from the *Junkerschule* Bad Tölz in 1943. He was severely wounded during fighting around the Pomeranian village of Vossberg on 1 March 1945. Meyer's father was German and a speech trainer in Stockholm before the war, and the son belonged to those not so few Swedes whose motivation for joining the *Waffen-SS* was a combination of German relationship on their father's or mother's side and a positive opinion of Nazism and the Third *Reich*.

Swedes and ethnic Germans from Rumania in the command-*SPW* (*Sd.Kfz. 250/1*) of the Swedish *SS-Untersturmführer* Hans-Gösta Pehrsson (standing in white camouflage jacket with cap and binoculars) on the shore of the Gulf of Finland at Mummasaare. Pehrsson's crew is practising and coordinating the *SPW*'s MG 42. Sitting behind the MG is the ethnic German Muzzi Emmerich from Rumania.

Half-tracks (*SPW Sd.Kfz. 250/1*) with Swedish *SS*-volunteers on their railway transport from Wesenberg in Estonia to Jakobstadt-Dünaburg in Latvia. The photograph is from a stop at the main railway station in Riga on 12 July 1944. Closest to the camera without shirt sits the Swedish *Sturmmann* Karl-Erik Pehrsson from Härnösand, who only five days afterwards was killed during a reconnaissance mission near the village of Kunigisy in Latvia. Sitting against the back of the next *SPW* is the CO of the 3rd *SS*-Reconnaissance Battalion "*Nordland*", *SS-Obesturmführer* Hans-Gösta Pehrsson. Due to the annihilation of the German Army Group Centre in June-July 1944, Soviet forces broke through into Latvia along the Düna River. The *Armee-Abteilung "Narva"* therefore sent *ad hoc* units to Latvia to block these Soviet penetrations.

Swedish volunteers around a destroyed Soviet T-34 in Latvia in July 1944, during fighting against strong Soviet forces breaking through the German lines near Dünaburg after the collapse of the German Army Group Centre the previous month.

Wolfang Eldh-Albietz

Carl Svensson

Markus Ledin and Erik Wallin

Bo Wikström

Sigurd Baecklund

Count Knut Posse

Marcus Ledin

Swedish *SS*-volunteers

Photographs from the operations of the "Swedish Platoon" (mortar section) of the *SS-Panzer-Aufklärungs-Abteilung "Nordland"* against the advancing Red Army through Latvia, heading for Riga, after the destruction of *Heeresgruppe Mitte* in June-July 1944. The top photograph shows a group of Swedish, Estonian-Swedish-German and ethnic-German *SS-Panzer-Grenadiers* during a pause in the fightings.

(Germany, Italy and Japan) and energetically marketed the Nazis' desire that Swedish volunteers, preferably in the form of a volunteer corps, be allowed to fight in the German armed forces in the East, like the Spanish volunteer "Blue Division". Günther explained to Schnurre that both actions were completely incompatible with Swedish neutrality and bluntly rejected the German proposals. Günther explained that Swedish volunteers would be allowed only to serve in the Finnish armed forces against the Soviet Union. The negative Swedish reaction regarding volunteers for the East was strongly criticized by the Nazi Foreign Minister, von Ribbentrop, in a conversation at the end of September 1941 with the chief of the Swedish diplomatic mission in Berlin, Arvid Richert, as "a completely incomprehensible position with respect to Europe's struggle with destiny".

The meagre number of Swedish volunteers in the *Waffen-SS* was considered a recruiting fiasco in Berlin, and even Adolf Hitler, at a conference at his HQ on 16 July 1941, was most critical:

> The *Führer* voiced harsh criticism of the Swedes for the very meagre volunteer contingent they had provided for the struggle against Communism in the East, and even *Reichsmarschall* Göring described the Swedes as decadent. The Finns on the other hand earned broad praise for their pluck.[56]

When the *"Germanic" SS-Panzer-Korps* was established in the summer of 1943, Heinrich Himmler and the *SS-Führungshauptamt* decided to concentrate all surviving Swedish *SS* volunteers in this corps. Hence the remaining Swedes, a little over 20 men with an additional 18 Estonian-Swedes, were transferred to the *SS-Panzer-Aufklärungs-Abteilung 11 "Nordland"*. The latter was organized in two reconnaissance companies (armoured cars with 2cm guns), two half-track companies (*Panzergrenadiere* in armoured personnel carriers) and one heavy company (including an anti-tank platoon armed with the short-barrelled 7.5cm cannon). The Swedes and the Estonian ethnic Swedes formed a platoon in the battalion's *3. Kompanie* (called the "Swedish Company"). The three other rifle platoons were composed of ethnic Germans from Rumania.The total strength of the battalion was about 800 men. From April 1944 until the final battle in Berlin, the company was commanded by the Swedish *SS-Obersturmführer* Hans-Gösta Pehrsson from Karlskrona, who since the late summer of 1941 had served in the *Waffen-SS*. In a letter to the Swedish Defence Staff in 1946, Pehrsson summarized:

> I was wounded between Leningrad and Narva. Thereafter I was without pause in battle at different critical points of the Baltic Front, until division *"Nordland"* was avacuated at sea from Courland to Pomerania. About the Baltic operations can be mentioned: recce missions to a depth of 30 (Swedish) miles in Latvia and Lithuania, with combined motorized missions or as infantry. Flanking rearguard battles from Narva over Tartu (Dorpat) and Riga to Preekuln in Courland and trench warfare.

The "Swedish Company" was a fully motorized *Panzergrenadier* (rifle) company, equipped with half-tracks, armed with 7.92cm machine guns, MG 42 and 8cm mortars. In the *SS* reconnaissance battalion *"Nordland"* were officers from Germany, Sweden, Norway, Switzerland, Denmark and the Netherlands.

Apart from Hans-Gösta Pehrsson, the following Swedish officers and NCOs served as platoon commanders in the *SS-Panzer-Aufklärungs-Abteilung 11 "Nordland"*: Walter Nilsson from Boden (KIA 20 January 1944 at Volosovo in Ingria); Rune Ahlgren from Rosersberg (who volunteered directly from the Swedish officers' school of Karlberg and was killed on 30 October 1944 at Preekuln in Courland); Gunnar Eklöf from Malmberget (wounded on 17 July 1944 at Daugavpils (Dünaburg) in Latvia); Sigurd Baecklund from Gävle (who survived the war); and Heino Meyer from Stockholm (who was seriously wounded on 3 March 1945 at Vossberg, Pomerania).

A battle-hardened *SS*-unit

The *SS-Panzer-Aufklärungs-Abteilung 11* was a highly mobile unit that was weak in personnel but strong in firepower thanks to its vehicles. Considering the firepower of the battalion, the assistant Swedish military attaché in Berlin, Captain Sigvard Drake af Hagelsrum, noted in June 1944 in a report to the Swedish Defence Staff, after a conversation with Swedish *SS* volunteers Sven Alm, Kurt Fagerström and Karl-Erik Pehrsson in Berlin:

> Within a *Panzer-Aufklärungsabteilung* there are 300 active machine guns (MG 42). In each half-track there are two active MGs and two in reserve, plus seven reserve barrels to each MG. The theoretical fire intensity of each MG is told to be around 3,000 rounds per minute. In reality, it was only 1,500 rounds per minute as the barrel had to be replaced after each 250 rounds. This is done with a swift manoeuvre in less than four seconds. As an example of the fire power of this *SS* recce battalion, the following was told to me: during the fighting on the Eastern Front, a village had to be retaken from the Russians. The whole *Abteilung* was used for the attack. In less than five minutes the whole village was completely put on fire.

The battalion's later employment in Estonia, Courland and Pomerania was in decidedly mobile combat – flank security, immediate counter-attacks and fighting retreat – so the strengths of the unit could be utilized. As one of the best units in the *"Nordland"* division, it was seen as a "fire brigade" and was infrequently employed as an entire battalion. It was instead mostly engaged as separate companies and with other units, even outside the *III. (germ.) SS-Panzer-Korps*. Although the number of Swedish and Estonian-Swedish soldiers was only minimal, their fate is presumably representative of that of most of the Scandinavian volunteers in the *"Germanic" SS-Panzer-Korps*.

Idealists or adventurers?

A majority of the 180 Swedish *SS* volunteers in the Second World War (apart from the ethnic Estonian-Swedes) were, according to the files of the Swedish Security Police, already organized Nazis or Nazism sympathizers. Others were traditionally pro-German by upbringing, while several Swedes in the *SS* had German family ties or were pure adventurers. A striking number of Swedes, around 50 men, deserted or asked to be dismissed from duty in advance from their contracts with the *SS*, and returned home to Sweden. The low number of Swedes in the *Waffen-SS* on the Eastern Front was a huge disappointment for Berlin.

Siren calls from Germany

Sten Eriksson, who after the war became a cultural journalist in Sweden and from 1944–45 was an *SS* war correspondent, made the following conclusion of the ideology of the *SS*-Swedes:

> We who came to active service in the *Waffen-SS*, did have with certainty a clear and positive view of the German National Socialism. The comments I heard from Swedes were more directed against the German mentality and not against the political ideology. To seek excuses afterwards that we entirely and only should have stood as fighters against the Soviet [Union], seems to me as doubtful and not credible as to claim that we in the *Waffen-SS* were never objects of political education. It was in fact the high ideals that permeated the whole of the *Waffen-SS* that made its units so powerful.
>
> Distinctive for young men in every generation are a shifting degree of lust for adventures and special experiences, combined with the feeling of frustration or even alienation in present society. It is then easy to be carried away by the German people's enthusiasm over the miraculous upsurge following the Nazi take-over of power. We were many young Swedes who visited Germany in the Thirties in the summers. With that I will not propose that pro-German sympathies swept over Sweden like a mild spring breeze. Very often one had to fight for one's political opinions. It was actually after the German occupation of Denmark and Norway that the climate hardened, even in my Swedish southern province.

From Leningrad to Berlin

The *SS-Aufklärungs-Abteilung* with its "Swedish Company" belonged to the most mobile and battle-hardened units within the *SS-Panzer-Korps*. When the Red Army crushed Army Group Centre in White Russia in June-July 1944 with its major Operation "Bagration" offensive and threatened the German flank in the Baltic countries with armoureds

Matthias Kleinheisterkamp

formations focusing on Riga via Dünaburg (Daugavpils), it was the *SS-Panzer-Aufklärungs-Abteilung "Nordland"* that in mid-July was sent as a blocking and reconnaissance unit (*Sperrverband*) to this area between Latvia and Lithuania. The battalion could, due to its mobile and flexible tactics and in coordination with Army units, delay the Soviets from taking Riga for some time. At the same time the battalion could deliver tactically valuable information to *Heeresgruppe Nord*. The batallion's operations at the River Düna in the summer of 1944 were actually the first and last occasion that this reconnaissance detachment was operating in its intended way. It was usually split up in a counter-productive manner and was misused as a tactical arm.

Between Leningrad and Narva, in the Narva bridgehead, at Dorpat-Tartu and later in Courland and Pomerania, the *SS-Panzer-Aufklärungs-Abteilung "Nordland"* was never used for its actual reconnaissance purposes, but was sent to fulfil tasks for which it was neither properly trained nor equipped. This detachment, in whiche most *SS* Swedes served, was mostly split up, being consumed and misused as an armed and motorized infantry battalion on foot and trifled away as an *ad-hoc* unit in different acute crises. The apocalyptic battle for Berlin finally sealed its fate. LW

Erik Laerum, Danish artillery officer in the *SS Panzergrenadier-Regiment "Danmark"*

For some time there had been talks that our *Panzer-Korps* should be relocated to the Karelian Isthmus where the Russians focused on a decisive assault on the Finns. But it was not easy to find out if this was true. It was, however, quite clear that the Red Army's assaults on both sides of the Finnish Gulf were dependant and linked together.

Georg Keppler

Martin Unrein

When it was quiet at the Finnish side, we were attacked, and when we were left in peace, the Finns were in turn attacked. One day the news reached us about the fall of Viborg and that the Finns sought peace with Moscow. One night at the beginning of September 1944, when it was very quite at our Front in northern Estonia, I was awakened by eruptions under the earth and the noise of heavy, distant explosions. When I came out from my bunker, I saw how the dark September sky quivered at strange lights from the Finnish Gulf, the earth shivered and the air brought with it the sound of vast explosions out at sea. From all bunkers and trenches soldiers emerged to watch this phenomena. It was the Finns who blew up their fortresses, ammunition stores and depots on the island of Hogland, so as to not let them fall into the hands of the Soviets.

Commanders of the *III. (germ.) SS-Panzer-Korps*

The founder and first commanding officer of the *III. (germ.) SS-Panzer-Korps*, *SS-Obergruppenführer* Felix Steiner, was followed by several other corps commanders after he had been in charge of the corps from 1 May 1943 until 25 February 1944. Steiner's absence as corps commander was partly due to being in disfavour with Himmler over various matters, "and Steiner, informally relieved from his position as corps commander for disciplinary reasons, was formally hidden in terms of 'sick-leave'".[57]

Mathias Kleinheisterkamp (1893–1945) replaced Steiner from 25 February until 16 April 1944, before the former returned until 30 October 1944. Kleinheisterkamp was born in Wuppertal, the son of a railway secretary, and served with distinction in the First World War as a *Leutnant* both on the Western and Eastern Front. In 1918, Kleinheisterkamp joined the *Freikorps* and in the Twenties served in the *Reichswehr* until he joined the *Allgemeine-SS* in 1933 and the *SS-Verfügungstruppe* in 1935. During the war, he became a regimental commander in the *SS-Division "Totenkopf"*, briefly became divisional commander of "*Totenkopf*" in 1941 (although he experienced grave friction with the notorious Theodor Eicke, the unit's previous commander and one of the founders of the *Waffen-SS*) and *SS-Division "Das Reich"* on the Eastern Front, as well as commander of the *SS-Gebirgs-Division "Nord"* in Finland in 1942–43 (enjoying an excellent relationship with Eduard Dietl, commander of the *20. Gebirgs-Armee*). After his time with the *III. (germ.) SS-Panzer-Korps* in the spring of 1944, Kleinheisterkamp commanded the *VII. SS-Panzer-Korps* and the *XI. SS-Armee-Korps*. In the final phase of the war, he was taken prisoner by the Red Army during the night of 29–30 April in the Halbe pocket south-east of Berlin, and committed suicide as a POW the following week.

Georg Keppler (1894–1966) commanded the corps from 30 October 1944 to 4 February 1945. Being somewhat anonymous, Keppler held more senior commands than any other *Waffen-SS* commander and was internally valued as a brilliant divisional and corps commander. Keppler was born in Mainz, the son of a colonel, and earned the Iron Cross, both classes, in the First World War. After the war he spent 14 years as a police commander, joined the Greman Army in 1934 and the *SS-Verfügungstruppe* in 1935, serving as battalion commander under Felix Steiner in the *SS-Regiment "Deutschland"* in Munich. Keppler acted as commander of the *SS-Regiment "Der Führer"* in France in 1940 and in Russia in 1941, briefly taking command of the *SS-Divisions "Totenkopf"* and *"Nord"*. After being seriously ill with a brain tumour in

The Dutch *SS-Unterscharführer* Caspar Sporck from *SS-Panzer-Aufklärungsabteilung 11* was decorated with the Knight's Cross on 23 October 1944 after his successful actions defending Dorpat in Estonia as part of *SS-Kampfgruppe "Wagner"* in late August 1944. Sporck was commander of a *SPW "Stummel" Sd.Kfz. 251/9* with a mounted 7.5cm cannon. Sporck had already earned the Iron Cross 1st and 2nd class in Ingria after destroying 11 Soviet tanks at Gubanizy. On 6 March 1945, Sporck was severely wounded in the bridgehead at Altdamm near Stettin, and died on 8 April at a hospital in Bayreuth, where he is buried.

Sitting during a rest for a meal near Lake Peipus in August 1944 are, from the left, *SS-Kampfgruppe "Wagner"* soldiers Fritz Ihle, Valentin Rether and Heinz Glaucke, all wearing the 1944 camouflage fatigues (pea-dot pattern). After the Red Army had experienced a serious setback while trying to battle its way into Estonia by way of the Narva bridgehead and the Tannenberg positions, the Soviets tried to outflank the German forces south of Lake Peipus, heading for the old Estonian-Swedish university town of Dorpat. Here the Soviets "outnumbered the Germans over 4:1 in terms of men and armour, and over 14:1 in terms of artillery" (Prit Buttar).

A *SPW* from the *"Nordland"*, mounted with a *Pak 36* 3.7cm anti-tank cannon, during fighting with *SS-Kampfgruppe "Wagner"* at Lake Peipus in late August 1944. This vehicle was often used by platoon commanders to give fire support for the grenadiers.

1941–42, he commanded the *2. SS-Panzer-Division "Das Reich"*, *I. SS-Panzer-Korps*, *III. (germ.) SS-Panzer-Korps* and *XVIII. SS-Armee-Korps*, surrendering US Army forces in May 1945. From 1948 until his retirement, Keppler ran a chemist shop in Hamburg.

Martin Unrein (1901–72) commanded the corps from 4 February 1945 until early April 1945. Unrein was a most unusual successor for Keppler, being *Generalleutnant* in the German Army, previously (and briefly) commander of the *6. Panzer-Division* during the Battle of Kursk and later commanding the *14. Panzer-Division*. After his time with the *III. (germ.) SS-Panzer-Korps*, Unrein led the *Panzer-Division "Clausewitz"* (as part of General Walter Wencks' relief force for Berlin in April 1945) and was taken as a POW by the US Army on 24 April. After the war, Unrein served as a lieutenant colonel and commander of the 3836th Labor Service Center of the US Army in Esslingen, West Germany.

SS-Kampfgruppe "Wagner"

On 12 August 1944, the 3rd Baltic Front attacked and broke through the German positions 30 miles west of Pleskau and threatened south-eastern Estonia. The Soviet tactical aim was to defeat the German Eighteenth Army and take the important city of Dorpat (Tartu) on Lake Peipus. Strategically, the Soviet *Stavka* had also planned the swift occupation of Estonia, thereby trapping the whole of *Armeeabteilung "Narva"* by reaching the Gulf of Finland behind the German forces. *Armeeabteilung "Narva"* and the *III. (germ.) SS-Panzer-Korps* responded by composing a task force to be sent south to defend Dorpat and hold the tactically important line between Lake Wirtz and Lake Peipus. This emergency *Kampfgruppe* would be named after its commander, *SS-Brigadeführer* Jürgen Wagner (CO of the *SS-Brigade "Nederland"*) and was composed of the following elements: *23. Grenadier-Regiment* of the *11. Infantry Division*, a battalion from the *5. SS-Freiwilligen-Sturmbrigade "Wallonien"*, *SS-Panzer-Aufklärungsabteilung 11 "Nordland"*, *SS-Sturmgeschützabteilung 11*, *II. SS-Artillerie-Regiment 54* and various battalions from Army artillery and rocket artillery units with signals and pioneer companies attached. On the night of 13–14 August, this *ad hoc* battle group left the Narva sector and deployed along a line south of Dorpat. As it turned out, *Kampfgruppe "Wagner"* was too weak to effectively block the massive Soviet offensive from the Pskov area, and on 23 August, *Panzergruppe "Strachwitz"* arrived at the front near Dorpat from Riga. Around 19–21 August, three Estonian battalions - *I./Waffen-Grenadier-Regiment 45 der SS* and the two battalions of *Waffen-Grenadier-Regiment 46 der SS* - arrived around Dorpat. Formed into a *Kampfgruppe* under *Waffen-SS-Sturmbannführer* Paul Vent, the battalions were, together with Leon Degrelle's *SS-Sturmbrigade "Wallonien"*, immediately deployed against the Red Army south-west of Dorpat. During incredibly fierce battles, the weak Estonian and German battalions were pushed northwards by the numerically superior Soviet forces.[58]

A platoon leader (sitting to the left) from the *"Nordland"* gives orders during the combined reconnasissance and fighting-blocking operations of *SS-Kampfgruppe "Wagner"* in north-east Estonia near Dorpat and Lake Peipus in August 1944. The *SPW* is a *SdKfz 250/1 (neu)*, followed by a motorcycle messenger. *SS-Kampfgruppe "Wagner"* consisted of the mobile *SS-Panzer-Aufklärungsabteilung "Nordland"*, a battalion of the 5th *SS* Volunteer Assault Brigade *"Wallonien"*, an infantry regiment from the 11th Infantry Division and artillery and *Sturmgeschütze* from the *"Nordland"* and *"Nederland"*. On 24 August, *SS-Panzer-Brigade "Gross"* and *Panzer-Brigade 101* (*Heer*) joined *SS-Kampfgruppe "Wagner"* at the villages of Elva and Noo. At the end of August, Wagner's units managed to establish a stable defensive line and block further Soviet advances north of Dorpat along the River Embach.

A *SPW SdKfz 251/5* from the pioneer platoon in *SS-Panzer-Auflärungsabteilung "Nordland"* in August 1944 near Lake Peipus. To the right stands the ethnic German Horst Borger from Rumania. This *SPW* was able to carry elements of light bridges. After the Red Army, in an outflanking manoeuvre, had taken the Estonian town of Voru on 13 August, and Ivan Maslennikov's 3rd Baltic Front threatened the town of Dorpat, Colonel General Hans Friessner, CO of *Armee-Abteilung "Narwa"*, dispatched *SS-Brigadeführer* Jürgen Wagner from *SS-Division "Nederland"* to take command of the *ad hoc* battlegroup *SS-Kampfgruppe "Wagner"*, designed to block the Red Army along Lake Vörtsjärv and the Embach River.

A *Sd.Kfz. 250/1* half-track, part of *SS-Kampfgruppe "Wagner"*, during a pause in the fighting around Dorpat in August 1944. An exhausted member of its crew is sleeping on the bonnet of the *SPW*, which is hidden in a shelter. The *SPW* is of the new type *Leichter Schützenpanzerwagen* (*neuer Art*), which from the autumn of 1943 was of a simplified manufacture. Until production ceased at the end of 1944, a total of 6,800 half-tracks of this new 250-type were made. Hanging on the driver's mirror is the jacket of an *SS-Hauptscharführer*.

On 24 August, the (heavy) 5th Company was engaged in close-combat at Räni, south-west of Dorpat. On 25 August, the battle for the town itself started, *SS-Unterscharführer* Berthold Behnke with his 7.5cm anti-tank gun from the 5th Company being the last to defend the airfield there. The battalion commander, *SS-Sturmbannführer* Rudolf Saalbach, wrote in his recommendation for awarding the German Cross in Gold to *SS-Obersturmführer* Siegfred Lorenz, CO of the 1st Company:

> In connection with the enemy's breakthrough in the east, the battalion was defensively grouped along a 15 kilometre broad front. The battalion's left flank fought, under the leadership of the 5th company's CO, in Mustvee against a forceful enemy. The only link-up road was cut off by Russian infantry units and the only suitable detour route was 30km long. Radio communication was cut off. Due to the mission's critical importance, *SS-Obersturmführer* Lorenz, commanding a company on the right flank, was forced to attempt fighting his way through to the left flank, in order to free the independently fighting *Kampfgruppe* located on the eastern flank from imminent encirclement, and directed it to a new area. *SS-Obersturmführer* Lorenz succeeded with this objective by dint of his courage and competence, and he thereby made it possible for the battalion to launch its forces against the flanks of the Soviet *Panzer* attack. While carrying out this mission, Lorenz was wounded by fire from enemy planes.

The *SS-Panzer-Aufklärungsabteilung "Nordland"* acted during the operations around Dorpat partly in its role as reconnaissance battalion. But too often, this specialized unit was split up and misused as a tactical weapon, and was seldom, if ever, deployed as a unified entity. As Eike Middeldorf, tactical officer in the OKH in 1944–45, wrote in 1952 about the misuse of German reconnaissance battalions during the Second World War: "Their fighting units were augmented with other units, or alternatively, were put at the disposal of other units, and their reconnaissance sections were ordered to attach themselves to the Divisional staff. As a rule, this generally meant the beginning of the end for the batallion as a whole."[59]

Dorpat fell to the Red Army on 25 August. At the beginning of September 1944, from a German perspective, the situation and the front north of Dorpat and the Embach River miraculously stabilized until the general German retreat out of Estonia later that month. During the course of intense combat actions, *Kampfgruppe "Wagner"* successfully prevented the Soviets' northward advance, establishing a new line of defence north of Dorpat and along the Embach River. Soviet attempts to cross the river were prevented in hard defensive battles and counter-attacks. The Red Army was unable to exploit its initial progess at Lake Peipus due to effective stop-gap measures by the combined German forces sent to the Dorpat area. PK, LW

A private *SS*-man (Schütze) with the submachine-gun MPi 40 on his back, dressed in the *Waffen-SS* uniform/44 and the mountain cap (*Bergmütze*) with the Death´s Head emblem. In the belt the carries two cases of ammunition and two hand grenades.

Soviet marshals

Long before the Nazi invasion of the USSR, Josef Stalin had within the borders of the Soviet Union created an incomparable system of mass murder and suppression.[60] Stalin had destroyed the trust between people, and Soviet society was ruled by permanent paranoia, fear and arbitrary justice. Not even devoted loyalty was a guarantee against execution and death. Nearly all of his political comrades from the past were gone: Stalin had murdered them all. All that remained was his entourage of flunkeys and henchmen: Beria ("our Himmler", as Stalin presented him), Voroshilov, Molotov and others. The Red Army marshals lived, and died, in Josef Stalin's shadow, in some sense like their German counterparts and Adolf Hitler, but in essential issues very different than the German marshals. The half-hearted effort by German officers to assassinate Hitler on 20 July 1944 had no parallel in the USSR. Soviet marshals lived in a terrifying world of constant terror and potential death. Military failure could, under Stalin, easily mean demotion, torture and death. Stalin's purge and mass murder of Red Army officers in 1938 decimated its officer corps on the eve of the Second World War. Although during the apocalyptic battles on the Eastern Front, Stalin was smart enough, unlike Hitler, not to interfere with the brilliancy in the field of his top marshals, he was always jealous about their revenue and glory, demoting some of his top generals into obscurity after 1945.

Two star Soviet marshals rose above all others in military excellence, due to their capacity as both commanders and coordinators of multi-front campaigns in the field and as General Staff officers: Georgy Zhukov, Deputy Supreme Commander in the Second World War, and Aleksandr Vasilevsky, the Chief of the General Staff and *Stavka* representative. Below are short biographies of leading Soviet commanders whose activities in some parts affected the *III. (germ.) SS-Panzer-Korps* in 1944–45.

Aleksandr Vasilevsky (1895–1977) was the son of a Russian Orthodox priest, enlisted in the Tsarist Army in January 1915 and did not join the Communist Party until Stalin's mass purge in 1938. Vasilevsky graduated from the General Staff Academy in 1937 and proved himself an extraordinarily reliable staff officer. In May 1942, he was promoted to Chief of the Red Army's General Staff, the *Stavka*. Vasilevsky influenced the course and outcome of the war on the Eastern Front in a way that no other Soviet general officer can match. In cooperation with Georgy Zhukov, he was the brain behind the successful operations at Stalingrad and Kursk, and for Operation "Bagration" against the German *Heeresgruppe Mitte*. As field commander, he led the 3rd and 4th Ukrainian Fronts in January and February 1944 in the Nikopol-Krivoi Rog operation, on the Baltic Front in the winter of 1944–45, and in August 1945 was appointed commander of Soviet forces who fought Imperial Japan in the Far East, where he executed the Manchurian Offensive. He made significant contributions to the remarkable evolution of the Red Army during the war, combined with the planning and conduct of multi-front campaigns. After 1945, Vasilevsky served as Chief of the General Staff, and from 1949–53 was Minister of the Armed Forces.

Konstantin Rokossovsky (1896–1968) was the son of a Polish rail road machinist and a Russian mother. He grew up in Warsaw, becoming fluent in Polish. Joining the Red Army in 1918, he was classmate and friend with Zhukov at the Soviet Cavalry Academy in the 1920s and Soviet military attaché with Chiang Kai-Shek. Stalin's paranoia was not lessened by Rokossovsky's service abroad, and it was probably only his good relations with Zhukov that saved him from being murdered when he was deported to the *Gulag* camp of Norilsk. During interrogation and torture, the *NKVD* smashed nine of Rokossovsky's teeth. Zhukov got him out of the *Gulag*, he was reinstated in the Red Army 1940 and promoted to lieutenant general during the crisis of 1941. His star rose during his performance on the important Don Front, at Kursk and during Operation "Bagration" in 1944, smashing the German *Heeresgruppe Mitte*. Although protesting against Stalin's tactics three times during the same conference, he was, to everybody's surprise, not shot but promoted to Marshal of the Soviet Union on 29 June 1944. He played a major role in the East Prussian and East Pomeranian offensive campaigns, but Rokossovsky was not appointed as commander of the final attack against Berlin in 1945. Instead, he commanded the 2nd Belorussian Front on the Baltic coast, stormed Mecklenburg and linked up with British forces at Wismar. After the war, he was appointed Polish Ministry of Defence from 1949–56 and served from 1958–62 as Vice Minister of Defence of the Soviet Union.

Georgy Zhukov (1896–1974) had an impressively broad capacity, with a brilliant career as Front commander and as a staff officer at the highest level. "Where Zhukov is, there is victory" was a saying in the Red Army. The son of a shoemaker from Strelkovka, east of Moscow, Zhukov was a devoted reader of Alan Pinkerston and Arthur Conan Doyle, studying mathematics and geography. When assuming command at critical times and places in desperate defensive battles, Zhukov also had a stroke of luck in his career, as he seemed to stop the German advance against Leiningrad in the autumn of 1941, although the Germans themselves decided to make a halt outside the city. A parallel process was the sudden winter cold which blocked the German conquest of Moscow in the autumn of 1941 and gave Zhukov the necessary time to prepare for the decisive counter-attack with fresh Siberian troops around the capital and save the city. Zhukov was also the brain behind the successful Soviet offensives during the latter phase of the war. His ruthless mass execution of soldiers who were suspected of cowardice or desertion did not weaken his position with the murderous Stalin. Zhukov commanded large armies during a more prolonged time than any other Allied commander: when Zhukov led the defence of Leningrad in 1941, Eisenhower was still chief of staff for the Third Army in Louisiana. Zhukov's tactical conduct during Operation "Berlin", the final offensive at the Oder (the Seelow bridgehead) against the *Reich* capital, was not Zhukov's finest hour, making decisive tactical errors in planning and execution of the initial phase of the attack. But the final victory made him world-famous – particularly when Zhukov in person received the surrender of German forces on 8 May 1945 in Berlin-Karlshorst – although after the war he fell into disfavour with the jealous Stalin. Zhukov came to power again under Nikita Khrushchev's regime after 1953, and belonged to the group of officers who in 1953 arrested and shot the Chief of the Soviet Security forces, Laurent Beria. Zhukov was appointed Minister of Defence in 1955 but was forced to resign two years later.

Ivan Konev (1897–1973) was born into a peasant family and became a veteran in the Great War and the Russian Civil War. Joining the Red Army in 1918, he was a graduate of the Frunze Military Academy in 1934. He played a key role in the defence of Moscow and the following Soviet counter-attacks in the winter of 1941–42, thereafter being promoted by Stalin to colonel-general. During the Battle of Kursk, Konev proved an expert in camouflage and deception, making the Germans seriously underestimate his forces on the southern sector of the battlefield. For his following successful operations in the Ukraine, Stalin promoted Konev to Marshal of the Soviet Union in February 1944. After advancing from the Vistula to the Oder River in January 1945, Konev attacked at the Oder-Neisse Front south of Berlin in April, some of his troops joining up with Zhukov's armies for the final battle for Berlin and other units advancing to Prague. After Second World War, Konev was appointed Commander of the Soviet Occupation Forces in East Germany and Allied High Commissioner in Austria. From 1946-50, Konev served as Commander of Soviet ground forces, until Stalin demoted him to an obscure command post in the Carpathians, clearly in line with Stalin's habit and policy of relegating popular wartime commanders into the shadows. (LW)

The slaughterhouse: the Eastern Front

It is worth recalling that the majority of German combat forces were concentrated on the German-Soviet front, and it was consequently on the Eastern Front where the major portion of *Wehrmacht* and *Waffen-SS* forces were destroyed. Eighty percent of Germany's permanent personnel losses took place in the East. The combined invasion forces during "Barbarossa" included units from Germany, Hungary, Slovakia, Romania, Italy, Finland, Spain, Croatia and Vichy France. In September 1941, more Frenchmen fought for Germany on the Eastern Front than did so for the Western Allies. Behind the Nazi propaganda facade of the armoured German *blitzkrieg* hid the fact that the *Wehrmacht* depended on more than a million horses for its mobility (with one horse consuming 5kg of oats and wheat a day). In July 1943, the *Wehrmacht* and *Waffen-SS* had at their disposal over 3.1 million men, as well as 2,500 tanks and self-propelled guns, on the Eastern Front; the Red Army at this time had at their disposal 7 million men, with 12,700 tanks and self-propelled artillery pieces.

The Red Army had learned a great deal from their tactical mistakes of 1941–42, becoming a more dangerous and flexible opponent in subsequent engagements. By means of its numerical advantage in personnel and materiel, the Soviet forces were also able to vary the main focal point of their attacks on various fronts, thereby keeping the Germans uncertain as to their primary objective. The Soviet superior commanders (army and corps level) had an average age of 44 years; their German equivalents had an average age of 55–58. On 16 April 1945, the Red Army counted 2.5 millions soldiers on the Eastern Front while the Germans had 750,000. The Red Army lost 96,500 tanks and assault guns here (36 percent of total stocks), and 72,000 anti-tank guns (51 percent of total stocks) during the 46-month period of the conflict from 1941–45,[61] along with an estimated 10 million soldiers killed.

Notes

1 Personnel file of Ulrich Dümichen, SSO Bundesarchiv Berlin-Lichterfelde (former US Berlin Document Center).

2 Letter from Ulrich Dümichen to the author (LW), 15 September 1980.

3 Hermann von Salza (1170-1239) was a Grand Master of the Teutonic Order.

4 Rudolf Rott was successor to *SS-Hauptsturmführer* Holtkamp (who was killed in action in January 1944 near Jamburg) as CO of the 1st company of the *"Hermann von Salza"*. Rott was killed on 10 February 1945 in Pomerania, being posthumously awarded the Knight's Cross.

5 This was "in accordance with the KstN 1175a of 25 January 1943 (*Kriegsstärkenachweis* for all *Panzergrenadier* divisions), as once again ordered by the *SS-Führungshauptamt* in the reorganization order for the *Division "Nordland"* from 30 October 1943 (Martin Block on Axis History Forum, 17 April 2005).

6 *SS-Standartenführer* Johannes-Rudolf Mühlenkamp joined the *SS VT* (*Regiment Germania*) in 1934 and served for a while as adjutant to Paul Hausser. Transferred from *"Das Reich"* to *"Wiking"*, he commanded the *SS-Panzer-Regiment 5* and won his Knight's Cross as its commander. As commander of the *5. SS-Panzer-Division "Wiking"*, he won the oakleaves to his Knight's Cross and ended his service as General Inspector of the *Waffen-SS Panzer* troops.

7 In a letter to Paul-Albert Kausch from Günter Dickten (previous *SS-Untersturmführer* in the 3rd company of the *"Hermann von Salza"* from 1943-45) of 25 January 1979 (copy in the archives of LW), Dickten gives the number of Italian tanks used by the battalion in Croatia as 18-20 and the type as "LTM 35".

8 Kausch is hereafter, if not otherwise mentioned, cited in the personal annotations by Max Stöckle, former *SS-Oberscharführer* of the *"Hermann von Salza"* from 1943--45: *Ehemalige SS-Panzerabteilung "Hermann von Salza"; versuchter Nachweis der damaligen Kriegsausrüstung* (copy in the archives of LW).

9 These Panther tanks were of the type *Panzerkampfwagen V Ausf. D* (*Sd Kfz 171*), and belonged to the first series of Panthers, with production starting in January 1943. The first vehicles were issued during February 1943, although recalled in April 1943 for major modifications. Those Panthers thereafter issued were primarily sent to the 51st and 52nd *Panzerabteilungen* (Army), going into action at Kursk in July 1943 (nearly all 60 of these Panthers were suffering from overheating). Further Panthers from this first series were also delievered to the 23rd and 26th independent *Panzer Regiments*, and the *Panzer Regiments "Das Reich"* and *Leibstandarte SS "Adolf Hitler"*. These Panthers are mainly identified by the "old-style" cupola for the commander in the turret (without a mounted machine gun): a new cupola was introduced for the further series (*Ausf A, G* and *F*) from 1943-45. Those Panthers from the first series that were found unfit for front-line service were sent back to the *panzer* depots, and 60 of these were delivered to the *Panzerabteilung "Nord"* of Army Group North (with personnel from

I./Panzer-Regiment 29). This special tank unit was dissolved by Army orders of 13 February 1944, and 13 of these immobilized and dug-in Panthers were made serviceable by the mechanical staff of the *"Hermann von Salza"*. At least one of these Panthers even remained with the *"Hermann von Salza"* until the final battle of Berlin from 16 April 1945, and was engaged in a Panzer battle at Prötzel on 19 April 1945 (to be described in volume 2 of this book)! (The facts in this footnote have partly been collected from a letter by Jürgen Wilhelm to Max Stöckle from 12 May 1994.)

10 These Tiger tanks belonged to the *502. Heavy Tank Batallion* (*schwere Panzer Abteilung 502*), which defended the Narva bridgehead between 28 January and 28 April 1944 (among the company commanders of this overall successful battalion was *Oberleutnant* Otto Carius). *Oberst* Maximilian Wengler (1890-1945) commanded the *Grenadier-Regiment 366* in Ingria and in Narva, later being promoted to *Generalmajor der Reserve* and killed in action on 27 March 1945 in East Prussia.

11 Facts on the *Panzerkampfgruppe "Kausch"* given during an interview (by LW) with Paul-Albert Kausch at his home in Ingelheim, 25 May 1991.

12 Wild's *panzer* driver during the mission at Lilienbach-Popovka was the Danish *SS-Oberscharführer* Kurt Tebring from Copenhagen (personal information from Petter Kjellander).

13 *SS*-personnel file of Artur Grathwol (US Berlin Document Center); proposal for the German Cross in Gold.

14 *SS*-personnel file of Georg Wille (US Berlin Document Center); proposal for the German Cross in Gold.

15 Bruins was born in 1923 at Vlagtwedde in the Dutch province of Groningen, and died in 1986 as a successful businessman in Gerolstein, West Germany.

16 *SS*-personnel file of Rudolf Rott (US Berlin Document Center); motivation for the German Cross in Gold for Rott, dated 4 November 1944. As Kausch was wounded during the fighting at the Tannenberg line, Rott was acting battalion commander in his absence.

17 Max Stöckle said, on 16 September 1993, that the clothing squad (*Bekleidungskammer*) was shipped off directly from Reval (Tallinn) to Gotenhafen in Germany and then to the training area of Hammerstein.

18 Paul-Albert Kausch described "this misuse of specialist *Panzer* personnel as infantry" as "idiotic and insane" during the author's (LW) interview with Kausch at his home in Ingelheim on 25 May 1991.

19 This section is founded on the pioneering research by the Swedish expert on Estonian forces in the *Wehrmacht* and the *Waffen-SS* from 1941--45, Petter Kjellander, of Stockholm.

20 KTB *Armee-Abteilung "Narwa"*, BA-MA RH 24-54 / 116 / 69-178; Viis Kibedat Rünnakupäeva, Karl Gailit, Eesti Sõna 11.03.44; Kui võideldi kodupinna eest – Mälestuskilde sõja-aastatest 1944, Harald Riipalu, 2005, s. 75-91; letter to the author (PK) from former *Hstuf.* Rudolf Bruus, Estonia, 23 November 2004; Ümbersünd tules. Ühest terastihedast päevast Narva jõe ääres, Jüri Remmelgas, Eesti Sõna 17/3 1944; Viis Kibedat Rünnakupäeva, Karl Gailit, Eesti Sõna 11/3 1944; Katkestatud lahing, Ain Mere, Eesti Hääl 8/7 1960; letter to the author (PK) from former *SS-Unterscharführer* Harald Nugiseks, Estonia, 7 November 2005; TsAMO 2303 / 1 / 370; Verlustmeldung von 10/3 1944, BA-MA RH 24-54 / 125 / 56; Verlustmeldung vom 15/3 1944 mit Nachmeldung, BA-MA RH 24-54 / 125 / 62.

21 Stammtafel der Einheiten der *20. Estn. SS-Frw.Div*, BA-MA RS 3-20 / 1; Fahrt des Herrn Oberbefehlshabers zur *Armeegruppe Narwa* mit XXVI., XXXXIII.AK. und *III.SS.Pz.Korps* mit allen Divisionen vom 16. bis 17.4.44, NARA T-311 / 70 / 10191297-10191298.

22 Riipalu, pp.115-17; "Auvere", unpublished manuscript by Harald Riipalu, Kindral Laidoner Museum, ART 140 F.20 1:26; KTB "Narwa", BA-MA RH 24-54 / 153 / 135-142; TsAMO 1109 / 1 / 23.

23 Uno Kooks memoirs, Sõjaveteranide arhiiv, Tartu Institute, Canada; letter to the author (PK) from former *SS-Untersturmführer* Olaf Tammark, USA, 19 April 2006; KTB *"Nederland"*, BA-MA RS 3 / 23 / 6.

24 Truppengliederung, BA-MA RS 3-23 / 7 / 214; Brigade-Befehl Nr.8 für die Verteidigung in der Tannenbergstellung, 28.7.44, BA-MA RS 3-23 / 7; KTB "Narwa", BA-MA RH 24-54 / 153 / 158-179; Alfred Põldma koostatud konspekt võitlustest Sinimägedes 1944., ERA 4996 / 1 / 232; KTB "Narwa", BA-MA RH 24-54 / 156 / 4-16; Lahingud Idarindel ja Sinimägedes Soodeni pataljonis ja hiljem 47. rügemendis. A. Toomsalu, KLM ET 283 Ar F.10 143; Mina olen kompanii ülem, Hando Ruus, Varemetest tõuseb kättemaks, 8. augustil 1944; Vallutasime Grenaderimäe, Jakob Uudevald, Võitluse Teedel Nr. 3, 2000; Ilo Hindreuse mälestused: Vabatahtlikuna idarindel. Minu sõjateekond 1941-1944 ja vangipõlv 1944-1956, ERA 4996 / 1 / 115; letter to author (PK) from former *SS-Untersturmführer* Heino Reigo, Estonia, 9 March 2007; TsAMO 309 / 4073 / 561; letter to author (PK) from former Grenadier Alexander Alas, Estonia, 30 April 2009; letter to author (PK) from former *SS-Unterscharführer* Edgar Võsu, Estonia, 18 April 2012.

25 Eddy de Bruyne & Marc Rikmenspoel, *For Rex and for Belgium. Léon Degrelle and Walloon Political & Military Collaboration 1940-45* (Solihull: Helion, 2004), p.129.

26 Anton Grasser, *Fighting on the Narva Front. The Evacuation of Estonia and the Withdrawal to the Dvina*; Department of the Army, Office of the Chief of Military History; MS D-151, Record Group 338; National Archives, Washington DC.

27 Bernd Wegner, *Hitler's Politische Soldaten. Die Waffen-SS 1933-1945* (Paderborn: 1999), p.175, note 214.

28 Bernd Wegner, *Auf dem Wege zur pangermanischen Armee. Dokumente zur Entstehungsgeschichte des III. ("germanischen") SS-Panzerkorps*; in *Militärgeschichtliche Mitteilungen* 2/1980, pp.101-36.

29 Elke Fröhlich (ed.), *Die Tagebücher von Joseph Goebbels, Teil II* (Munich: 1995), p.395.

30 Jens Westmeier, *Die Junkerschulgeneration*, in Schulte, Lieb & Wegner, *Die Waffen-SS. Neue Forschungen* (Schöning, Paderborn: 2014), p.272. A classic example of an apologetic biography is Franz Kurowski's *SS-Obersturmbannführer Paul-Albert Kausch* (Wuerzburg: Flechsig Verlag, 2013).

31 "z.b.V." (German: *zur besonderer Verwendung*; for special purposes). The *300. Infanterie-Division z.b.V.* consisted of four Estonian border guards regiments. The Estonian *20. SS-Division* was during this period placed as corps reserve and was resting in the area Waka-Künnapuu, due to its previous heavy losses. Vorbefehl für die Verteidigung in der Tannenbergstellung, *SS- Pz.Gren.Brig. Nederland*, 26.7.44, BA-MA RS 3-23 / 7 / 227; Truppengliederung,

BA-MA RS 3-23 / 7 / 214; Brigade-Befehl Nr.8 für die Verteidigung in der Tannenbergstellung, 28.7.44, BA-MA RS 3-23 / 7.

32 *The Last Knight of Flanders*, Allen Brandt, 1998, s. 123-26; Lahingud Idarindel ja Sinimägedes Soodeni pataljonis ja hiljem 47. rügemendis. A. Toomsalu, KLM ET 283 Ar F.10 143; Petter Kjellanders interview with former *SS-Hauptsturmführer Ellef Rasmussen*, 26 July 2008; KTB "Narwa", BA-MA RH 24-54 / 153 / 152-154.

33 Vorschlag Ritterkreuz Karl-Heinz Ertel, NARA AA3343 SSO / 191; Lennart Westbergs interview with Paul Albert Kausch, 22 May 1991; KTB "Narwa", BA-MA RH 24-54 / 153 / 158-180; Deutschen Kreuzes im Gold Vorschlag Artur Grathwol, NARA AA3343 SSO / 029A; KTB SS-Pz.Gr.Brig. "Nederland", BA-MA RS 3-23 / 6; Minu Söjamälestused, Richard Säägi, 2007, pp.42-47.

34 TsAMO 217 / 1221 / 4959; KTB "Narwa", BA-MA RH 24-54 / 156 / 2-61.

35 Casualties from 23 July to 7 August 1944, NARA T-312 / 1635 / 000086; Vastaspoolte inimkaotustest Narva rindel 1944. aasta 24. juulist kuni 7. augustini (Narva ja Sinimägede lahingud), Artjom Astafjev, Andrus Kütt & Reigo Rosenthal, Tuna Nr 4, 2015, s. 67-72.

36 A more extreme example is the US publisher and writer Richard Landwehr and his publication *Narva 1944: The Waffen-SS and the Battle for Europe* (Silver Springs, Maryland: Bibliophile Legion Books, 1981): "Perhaps someday, we too – those of us who live comfortably in the 'free' West – will realize the great debt that we owe to the Narva Front soliders. They were fighting *our battle* as well!"; *ibid.*, p.164.

37 In the autumn of 1944, 11.4 million men and women served in the Soviet forces (6.7 million belonged to active troops at the front). A plausible estimation and recent research suggests that the USSR lost 8.7 million soldiers dead, with 22 million wounded or sick. Additionally, the Soviet Union lost at least 18 million dead civilians. The Soviet figures and statistics do not separate losses caused by actual fighting at the front, those who were executed or starved to death by the Nazis, losses caused by the Soviet security forces, such as the NKVD, or through summary executions;Max Hastings: *Armageddon. The Battle for Germany 1944-45* (London: MacMillan, 2004), p.148.

38 Catherine Merridale, *Ivan's War. The Red Army 1939-45* (London: Faber & Faber, 2006).

39 One of the first army leaders in history to explore collective solidarity within his regiments and companies was the reformative Swedish King Gustav II Adolf (1594-1632), who drafted his units out of the same native villages and landscapes, thus shaping an important spirit of affinity and recognition within his troops.

40 Davies, *Europe at War*, p.253.

41 During the nationalist Polish uprising in Warsaw in August 1944, the Polish fought primarily not against Germans but Russians, White Russians (not Ukrainians as believed) and the largest infantry group being Azerians in the RONA and *Dirlewanger* brigades under the *SS*, as the *Wehrmacht* were unwilling to withdraw combat units from the front; Davies, *Europe at War*, p.205.

42 *New York Times*, 15 February 2006.

43 Gösta Borg, *Det röda massanfallet* (Stockholm: Fahlcrantz & Gumaelius, 1951).

44 *SS* personnel file of Joachim Ziegler (SSO), US Berlin Document Center/Bundesarchiv Berlin-Lichterfelde.

45 Letter to LW, 25 January 1983, from Alice von W. (Ziegler's sister was at that time secretary to the colonel in the General Staff, Claus von Stauffenberg, of 20 July bomb plot fame, in the Berlin HQ of the Reserve Army, *Oberkommando des Heeres*).

46 After this conversation, Horste von Gleisenau described, in his diary, Ziegler as "disgusting"; Jens Westemeier, *Jugend, Krieg und Internierung. Hans Robert Jauss. Wissenschaftliche Dokumentation.* The author (LW) is thankful for Dr Jens Westemeier's kind access to his unpublished manuscript of this documentation and for his permission to quote from it.

47 The author (LW) wishes to thank Roland Pfeiffer and Uwe Kuppen for sharing their great expertise on *SS-Panzerbrigade "Gross"*.

48 Roland Pfeiffer, *Zur Geschichte der SS-Panzer-Brigade "Gross"* (memo, 2005). Personal information from Uwe Kuppen to author (LW).

49 Also known as *Gruppe "Arnold"* after its commander. The other regiment was known as *Gruppe "Runge"*.

50 SS personnel dossier of Martin Gross; US Berlin Document Center; copy in author´s (LW) private archives.

51 Lehnhardt, *ibid.*, p.388.

52 Jochen Lehnhardt, *Die Inszenierung des nationalsozialistischen Soldaten: Die Waffen-SS in der NS-Propaganda*, in Jan Erik Schulte, Peter Lieb & Bernd Wegner (eds), *Die Waffen-SS. Neue Forschungen.* (Paderborn: 2014), pp.377-91.

53 Lehnhardt, *ibid.*, p.379.

54 Jens Westemeier, *Die Junkerschulgeneration*, in Jan Erik Schulte, Peter Lieb & Bernd Wegner (eds), *Die Waffen-SS. Neue Forschungen* (Paderborn: 2014), pp.269-85. HIAG was the post-war West German association for former veterans of the *Waffen-SS*.

55 Dr Westemeier points out that in 1935, a regular personnel commission (*Heerespruefstelle*) of psychologists, doctors and officers from the German Army tested 86 *SS* cadets from the *Junkerschule* in Brunswick over two days for their officer potential, according to the standards of the Army: 50 percent of these *SS* cadets would not have been accepted by the Army in 1935. Westemeier, *ibid.*, p.273.

56 Gyllenhaal & Westberg, *Swedes at War*, p.257. Hitler's remark on the Swedish *SS* was written down by Otto Bräutigam, army liason officer for *Reichsminister* Alfred Rosenberg at Hitler's HQ, in his diary entry of 16 July 1941 (Library of Congress Archives). In contrast, 9,000 Swedish citizens volunteered for Allied service against Hitler in the Second World War; Gyllenhaal & Westberg, *Swedes at War*, p.153.

57 Personal information 4 March 1993, given to LW by Günther Mierwald, former *SS-Obersturmführer* and *Ordonnanzoffizier* with the staff of the *III. (germ.) SS-Panzer-Korps* (author's archives).

58 *Aufstellung Kampfgruppe Wagner*, NARA T-312 / 1633 / 000848-000849; KTB *Kampfgruppe Wagner*, BA-MA RS 2-3 / 6; KTB Narwa, BA-MA RH 24–54 / 156 / 109-120.

59 Eike Middeldorf, *Taktik på östfronten* (Stockholm: SMB, 2002).

60 Max Hastings, *Armageddon*, p.145.

61 Niklas Zetterling & Anders Frankson, *Kursk 1943: a statistical analysis* (London: Frank Cass, 2000).

BIBLIOGRAPHY

ARCHIVAL DOCUMENTS & OTHER SOURCES

Bundesarchiv (BA), Berlin-Lichterfelde
NS 19 – Persönlicher Stab Reichsführer-SS
NS 21 – SS-Hauptamt
NS 33 – SS-Führungshauptamt
SSO – SS-Führerpersonalakten
PK - Parteikarte NSDAP
RuS - Rasse- und Siedlungsakten

Bundesarchiv-Militärarchiv (BAMA), Freiburg im Breisgau
Nachlass Wolfgang Vopersal, NS 756
Nachlass Gotthard Heinrici, N 265/134
Tätigkeitsbericht des Generalkommandos III. (germ.) SS-Panzer-Korps, IIa, 26.5.1943 – 31.3.1944, RS 2-3/2
War Diary of SS-Kampfgruppe "Wagner", RS 2-3/6
War Diary of 4. SS-Freiwilligen-Panzergrenadier-Brigade "Nederland"

Czech State Military Archives (Vojenski ustredni archiv), Prague
Fragments of the Waffen-SS War Archives in Sasmuk, Bohemia (Castle Zasmuky)

Deutsche Dienststelle (Wehrmachtauskunftstelle; WASt), Berlin
Personnel, deaths and list of graves for military personnel in the Wehrmacht and Waffen-SS 1939-45

Imperial War Museum (IWM), London
Various captured German documents

Institut für Zeitgeschichte (IfZ), Munich
ZS 521-6 Interview with Werner Grothmann
ZS 0111 Interview with Oldwig von Natzmer
ZS 669 Interview with Dr. Franz Riedweg
ZS 2165 Interrview with Melitta Wiedemann

Norges Hjemmefrontsmuseum (Norwegian Resistance Museum), Oslo
Prisoner-of –War-report (PWIS/Norway)
No 36: Interrogation of Karl Leib
No 38: Interrogation of Karl Leib

Ohio University Libraries, Athens, Ohio
Mahn Center, Alden Library
Cornelius Ryan Collection of World War II Papers
German Forces

To centralize the vast amount of captured Nazi documents in US custody, the US Berlin Document Center was established in West Berlin after 1945. This archive contained e.g. the central index of the National Socialist Party with 10.5 Million party member cards, 600,000 personnel files of the *Waffen-SS, SS* and *Gestapo*, as well as information on 2.5 million *Volksdeutsche*. The photo shows the entrance and administration building of the US Berlin Document Center in Berlin-Grunewald, at Wasserkäfersteig 1, in 1980.

Roman Burghart
Theodor Busse
Theodor von Dufving
Ernst Gross
Gotthard Heinrici
Hans Henseler
Gunnar Illum
Gustav Krukenberg
Hanns-Heinrich Lohmann
Hasso von Manteuffel
Hans Refior
Julius Schaub
Walter Timm
Hans-Oskar Wöhlermann

Swedish National Archives (Riksarkivet), Stockholm
Files of the Swedish Security Police 1938-47
Personal dossiers of Swedish Volunteers in the Waffen-SS 1940-45
Files on Swedish and German National Socialism
Files of the Swedish Foreign Ministry and the Swedish Legation in Berlin 1940-46

Swedish War Archives (Krigsarkivet), Stockholm
Reports from the Swedish Military Attache in Berlin 1940-45
Reports from the Intelligence Section of the Swedish Defense Staff 1940-45

Swedish Defence Forces & Army HQ, Stockholm
Archives of the Military Intelligence and Security Services (MUST)

Swiss National Archives, Bern
Urteil des Bundesstrafgerichts gegen u.a. Franz Riedweg, Heinrich, Bueler und Paul Benz, BStr 10/47

Trondheims Rättsmuseum, Trondheim
Misc. SS propaganda leaflets

US Berlin Center (former BDC; today: Bundesarchiv Berlin-Lichterfelde)
Personnel Records of SS officers and members of the NSDAP. Filmed in NARA Record Group 242, microform A3343
Non-Biographic Collection

US National Archives and Records Administration (NARA), College Park, Maryland, US
Military Records Division. Captured German World War II Documents, Record Group 242, Microfilm:
T-77 Armed Forces High Command (OKW)
T-78 Army High Command (OKH)
T-175 Records of the Reich Leader of SS and Chief of German Police
T-311 Army Groups
T-312 Field Armies
T-314 Army Corps
T-315 Army Divisions
T-354 Waffen-SS units
T-580 Berlin Document Center (Hoover Film Project)

Bundesarchiv - Aussenstelle Ludwigsburg (BAL)
Records of the *Zentrale Stelle der Landesjustizverwaltungen zur Verfolgung von Nationalsozialistischen Gewaltverbrechen* (Federal German Judicial Commission for the Investigation of Nazi Genozide Crimes), Ludwigsburg
Interrogations, trial records, copies of Soviet and other East European captured German records etc. from investigations and trials in German courts concerning Nazi mass crimes before West-German and Federal German courts

Manuscripts
Paul Dahm (*former SS-Sturmbannführer*; *Germanische Leitstelle* Haag:) Memoirs from World War II
Joachim Engelmann (former officer in the 18. PGD): *Die 18. Panzergrenadier-Division an der Oder bis zum Endkampf um Berlin (1 März 1945 – 2. Mai 1945).*
Helmut Jurisch (1945 NCO in the Panzer-Korps "Grossdeutschland", II.Pz.Rgt. Kurmark): *Meine Fahrradtour nach Neuruppin – Erinnerungen an meine Rekrutenzeit* (1995); *Mein Weg durch den Halbe-Kessel in die Gefangenschaft*
Gustav Krukenberg (former *SS-Brigadeführer* and last CO of the 11. SS-Freiwilligen-Panzergrenadier-Division "Nordland"): *Endkampf um Berlin*
Herbert Kuntze (9. Fallschirmjäger-Division), Dipl.Ing., Oberstleutnant a.D.: *Berlin 24 April bis 2 Mai 1945*
Leib, Karl (former *SS-Standartenführer* and Chief of the *Germanische Leitstelle* in Oslo 1943-45): *Die germanischen bzw. Europäischen Freiwilligen der Waffen-SS, deren Versorgung und die Ziele der deutschen Führung*
Jakob Lobmeyer: *SS-Jagd-Panzer-Abteilung 561 z.b.V. 1944-45*
Mueller, Kurt (SS Panzer Corps Signals Batallion 503): *SS-Panzer-Korps-Nachrichten-Abteilung 503*
Ole Petersen (Danish Volunteer in the Waffen-SS): Memo on SS-*Kampfgruppe* Scheibe and I./Regiment 48 "General Seyffardt" in Pomerania 1945
Weitzdörfer, Rüdiger (former SS-Obersturmbannfüuhrer and CO of the SS-Panzer-Korps-Nachrichten-Abteilung 503): *Meine Soldaten und Militärzeit*
Zuehlke, Gerhard (SS-Panzergrenadier-Regiment 23 "Norge"): *Tatsachenbericht ueber die Erlebnisse im Einsatz und Kampf der SS-Divisionen "Wiking" und "Nordland" 1940-1945* (undated)

Interrrogation of Gottlob Berger at Nuernberg, Germany, 20 April 1948, by Judge Michael A. Musmanno (photocopy in LW:s Archive)

Private Archives

Predrag Blanusa, Stockholm
Paul Dahm, Germany
Alexander Dolezalek, Vlotho
Theodor von Dufving, Germany
Geir Brenden, Oslo
Alvin Carlsson, Sweden
Lars Gyllenhaal, Sweden
Petter Kjellander, Stockholm
Uwe Kuppen, Germany
Lars Larsen, Denmark
Lars T. Larsson, Sweden
Karl Leib, Germany
Siegfried Moritz, Germany
Martin Månsson, Sweden
Tommy Natedal, Norway
Hans Werner Neulen, Germany
Holger Thor Nielsen, Denmark
Jens Pank Bjerregaard, Denmark
Roland Pfeiffer, Germany
Peter Schmitz, Germany
Peter Schöttler, Germany
Richard Schulze-Kossens, Germany
Knut Sivertsen, Norway
Andreas Vogt, Germany
Lennart Westberg, Sundsvall
Weitzdörfer, Rüdiger, Germany
Zuehlke, Gerhard, Germany

Lennart Westberg's archives (correspondence & interviews with former *Volksdeutsche* in the *Waffen-SS*):

Karl Balint
Horst Borger
Hans Hedrich
Peter Jung
Jonel M. Orelt
Hans Stemper
Franz Bereznyak

Lennart Westberg's archive (correspondence & interviews with former German Army commanders):

Erik von Amsberg; Colonel and Chief *Wehrmacht* Adjutant to Hitler, letters 1971
Erich Buschenhagen; General and Chief of Staff in occupied Norway
Theodor Busse; *General der Infanterie*, letters 1974
Heinrich Eberbach; *General der Panzertruppen*, letters 1974
Friedrich Foertsch; *General der Bundeswehr*, letter 1975
Reinhard Gehlen; Chief *Fremde Heere Ost* and the *Bundesnachrichtendienst*, letter 1975
Franz Halder; *Generaloberst* and Chief of the German General Staff, letters 1972
Adolf Heusinger; *General der Bundeswehr*, letter 1971
Cord von Hobe; *Generalleutnant a.D.*, letter 1973
Karl Hollidt; General, letter 1974
Friedrich Hossbach; *General der Infanterie*; letter 1978
Hubert Lanz; *General der Gebirgstruppen a.D.*, letter 1974
Erich von Manstein; *Generalfeldmarschall a.D.*, letter 1973
Hasso von Manteuffel; *General der Panzergruppen a.D.*, letter 1974
Gerhard Matzky; *General a.D.*, letter 1975
Ulrich de Mazière; *Generalleutnant der Bundeswehr a.D.*, letter 1975
Burkhardt Mueller-Hildebrandt; *General a.D.*, letter 1975
Udo Ritgen; *Brigadegeneral der Bundeswehr a.D.*, letter 1975
Walther von Seydlitz; *General a.D.*, letters 1972
Heinz Trettner; *General a.D.*, letter 1976
Otto Uechtritz; *General a.D.*, letters 1976
Walther Wenck; *General der Panzertruppen a.D.*, letter 1972
Otto Wöhler; *General a.D.*, letter 1976

Tommy Natedal's archives (quoted letters and interviews)

Odd Angelsen
Horst Ernst
Björn Heisholdt
Erling Schiötz
Ivar Skarlo

Geir Brenden's correspondence & interviews with former members of Waffen-SS from 1991-2005:

Knut Baardseth
Alf Borge
Amund Enger
Audbjörn Fiskum
Fredrik Jensen
Bjørn Lindstad
Olav Lindvig
Trygve Rönning
John Sandstad
Kasper Sivesind
Ivar Skarlo
Karsten Sveen
Lage Sögaard
Häkon Windingstad

Petter Kjellander's archives (letters and interviews):

Alexander Alas
Rudolf Bruus
Robert Helde
Vambola Karro
Robert Kivi
Ants Köverjalg

Lennart Westberg (left) interviewing Paul-Albert Kausch (right) in Walsrode 1984 about his time as CO *SS-Panzer-Abteilung "Hermann von Salza"*. Standing behind is former *SS-Hauptsturmführer* Ellef Rasmussen.

Ago Loopärg
Helmut Rand
Ellef Rasmussen
Arkadi Rei
Heino Reigo
Remy Schrijnen
Ilor Tamm
Olaf Tammark
Edgar Vösu

INTERVIEWS & CORRESPONDENCES (SEE ALSO FOOTNOTES) BY LENNART WESTBERG FOR VOLS I & 2

d'Alquen, Gunter, former SS-Standartenführer and CO of the SS War Correspondent Regiment "Kurt Eggers";
Paul Benz; Swiss SS-Untersturmführer, SS-Hauptamt
Berger, Gottlob; former SS-Obergruppenfihrer and Chief of the SS-Hauptamt;
Best, Werner Dr; former SS-Obergruppenführer and Reich Plenipotentiary in Denmark;
Beerbohm, Hans Heinrich; Dr.rer.Pol, former Kapitänleutnant zur See;
Bock, Jürgen von; former Obersturmbannführer and Operations Officer in the 4. SS-Freiwilligen-Panzergrenadier-Brigade "Nederland";
Borg, Goesta, former SS-Untersturmführer and SS War Correspondent
Bockelberg, Helmut von; former SS-Standartenführer and Chief-of-Staff III. (germ.) SS-Panzer-Korps;
Brunaes, Ole; former SS-Obersturmführer in the Germanischen Leitstelle
Buehler, Heinrich Dr., Swiss SS-Hauptsturmführer, SS-Hauptamt
Burbach, Heinz; former SS-Oberscharführer, SS-Kampfgruppe "Schweitzer";
Carius, Oto; former Oberleutnant, heavy Panzer Batallion 103
Chairsell, Rudolf, former Untersturmfrer, SS-Panzer-Abteilung "Hermann von Salza";
Dahm, Paul; former SS-Standartenführer, SS-Ergänzungsstelle "Nord", Oslo;
Diers, Georg; former SS-Oberscharführer, heavy SS-Panzer Batallion 503;
Dolezalek, Alexander, Dr.; former SS-Hauptsturmführer;Germanische Leitstelle Berlin;
Dufving, Theodor von; former Colonel and Chief-of-Staff 56th Panzer Corps (General Weidling);
Eriksson, Sten; former SS War Corresponent "Nordland";
Falke, Paul; former SS-Sturmbannführer and Operations Officer (Ia) in the III. (germ.) SS-Panzer-Korps;
Feilberg, Kaj; former Untersturmfüher in the SS-Panzer-Aufklärungsabteilung 11 "Nordland";
Fenet, Henri; former SS-Hauptsturmführer and CO French SS-Sturm Batallion "Charlemagne";
Gaul, Günter; former SS-Oberscharführer, SS-Panzer-Batallion "Hermann von Salza";
Genzow, Heinz; former SS-Rottenführer, 11th SS Volunteer Panzer-Grenadier Division "Nordland";
Greef, Günther; former SS-Hauptsturmführer and Intelligence officer in the 11. SS-Freiwilligen-Panzergrenadier-Division "Nordland";

Grothmann, Werner; former SS-Obesturmbannführer and Chief-Adjutant von Heinrich Himmler;
Harmel, Heinz; SS-Brigadeführer and CO of 10. SS-Panzer-Division "Frundsberg"
Herwig, Walter, former SS-Standarten-Junker; SS-Panzergrenadier-Regiment 24 "Danmark"
Hund, Willi; former SS-Obersturmführer and company commander SS-Panzergrenadier-Regiment 23 "Norge";
Jacobsen, Rudolf, Dr.; former SS-Obersturmbannführer, Germanische Leitstelle Berlin;
Jurisch, Helmut; former sergeant; Panzer-Korps "Gross-Deutschland";
Kausch, Paul-Albert; former SS-Obersturmbannführer, CO SS-Panzer-Abteilung "Hermann von Salza";
Knappe, Siegfried; former Hauptmann and Operations Officer (Ia) LVI Panzer Corps (General Weidling);
Koopmann, Paul; former SS-Hauptsturmführer, Germanische Leitstelle Berlin;
Kopp, Erich Dr.; former SS-Hauptsturmführer, Germanische Leitstelle Berlin;
Kormann, Georg; former SS-Obersturmführer and signals officer in the 4. SS-Freiwilligen-Panzergrenadier-Brigade "Nederland";
Krüger, Hans-Caspar; former SS-Untersturmführer and SS War Correspondent;
Kühn, Horst-Henning; former SS-Hauptsturmführer; Germanische Leitstelle Berlin; Intelligence Officer (Ic) SS-Freiwilligen-Panzergrenadier-Brigade "Nederland";
Körner, Karl; former SS-Oberscharführer, heavy SS-Panzer Batallion 503;
Krukenberg, Gustav Dr jur; former SS-Brigadeführer and CO 33.Waffen-Grenadier-Division der SS "Charlemagne" (Französische Nr. 1);
Kuhlmann, Franz; former Kapitänleutnant zur See;
Kuntze, Herbert, former Oberleutnant; 9. Paratroop Division;
Langendorf, Georg; former SS-Obersturmführer; 11. SS-Panzer-Aufklärungsabteilung 11 "Nordland";
Leib, Karl; former SS-Standartenführer; SS-Ergänzungsstelle "Nord", Oslo;
Lohmann, Hanns-Heinrich; former SS-Obersturmbannführer, SS-Panzergrenadier-Regiment 49 "De Ruyter";
Lorenz, Siegfried; former SS-Obersturmführer, SS-Panzer-Aufklärungsabteilung 11 "Nordland";
Loringhoven, Bernd Freiherr von; former Lieutenant Colonel; German Army General Staff (OKH);
Mecklenburg, Firedrich-Franz von, Grossherzog; former SS-Hauptsturmführer in the staff of III. (germ.) SS-Panzer-Korps;
Mueller, Kurt, former SS-Sturmmann in the SS-Panzer-Korps-Nachrichten-Abteilung 103 (503) 1944-45
Nixdorf, Werner; former SS-Obersturmführer and signals officer III. (germ). SS-Panzer-Korps;
Riedweg, Franz Dr; former SS-Obersturmbannführer and Chief of Germanische Leitstelle Berlin, Adjutant to SS-Obergruppenführer Steiner;
Rohr, Robert; former SS-Untersturmführer and signals officer in the heavy SS-Panzer Batallion 503;
Ruoff, Joachim; former SS-Standartenführer and I a respective *Amtschef* in the SS-Führungshauptamt in Berlin
Schenck, Ernst-Günther; former SS-Standartenführer; SS-Wirtschafts- und Verwaltungshauptamt Berlin;
Schlotter, Eugen; former SS-Sturmbannführer, CO SS Signal Batallion 11;
Schulze-Kossens, Richard; former SS-Obersturmbannführer; adjutant to Rudolf von Ribbentrop and Adolf Hitler; last commandant of the SS Cadet School, Bad Tölz
Seidel, Helmut; former SS-Oberscharführer, SS-Panzer-Aufklärungs-Abteilung 11 "Nordland";
Sell, Robert; former SS-Unterscharführer, SS-Kampfgruppe "Voss";
Sidon, Fritz, former SS-Obersturmführer, SS-Panzergrenadier-Regiment 24 "Danmark; Germanische Leitstelle Berlin; Adjutant to CO SS-Panzer-Abteilung "Hermann von Salza";
Sierck, Joachim, Dr.Ing., former Navy Cadet *Kriegsmarine*;
Spaarmann, Erich; former SS-Standartenführer, Germanische Leitstelle Berlin;
Spaeter, Helmuth; former Major (Army), Panzerkorps "Gross-Deutschland";
Stöckle, Max, former SS-Oberscharführer, staff company SS-Panzer-Abteilung "Hermann von Salz";
Ternedde, Rudolf; former SS-Sturmbannführer, CO SS-Panzergrenadier-Regiment 24 "Danmark";
Ulrich, Fritz, former SS-Sturmbannführer, Germanische Leitstelle Berlin;
Venghaus, Wolfgang; former SS-Unterscharführer, staff 11. SS-Freiwilligen-Panzergrenadier-Division "Nordland";
Wallin, Erik, former SS-Unterscharführer, SS-Panzer-Aufklärungsabteilung 11 "Nordland";
Weiss, Alfred, former SS-Hauptscharführer, SS-Panzer-Aufklärungsabteilung 11 "Nordland";
Weitzdörfer, Rüdiger; former SS-Obersturmbannführer and CO of SS-Panzer-Nachrichten-abteilung 103;
Ziegler, H.W. Prof.Dr; former SS-Standartenführer; Germanische Leitstelle Berlin;
Zuehlke, Gerhard; former SS-Untersturmführer, SS-Panzergrenadier-Regiment 23 "Norge" 1944-45

Internet

Estonia, 1940-1945; Reports of the Estonian International Commission for the Investigation of Crimes Against Humanity; Edited by Toomas Hiio, Melis Maripuu and Indrek Paavle, Tallin, 2005

Interrogation 4 September 1947 by the CIC of the former SS-*Obergruppenführer* Maximilian von Herff, Chief of the SS-Pesonnel Main Agency; *Sturmpanzer.com*

Interrogation of the former SS-*Obergruppenführer* Gottlob Berger at Nürnberg, Germany, 20 April 1948, by Judge Michael A. Musmanno (copy in LW:s archives).

PRINTED BOOKS AND JOURNAL ARTICLES

Ailsby, Christopher, *Waffen-SS: The Unpublished Photographs* (London: Brown Packaging, 1998)

Arlt, Kurt (Ed.), *Militärgeschichtliches Handbuch Brandenburg-Berlin* (Potsdam, Militärgeschichtliches Forschungsamt, 2010)

Augstein, Rudolf *"Historikerstreit', die Dokumentation der Kontroverse um die Einzigartigkeit der nationalsocialistischen Judenvernichtung* (Munich, Piper, 1987)

Bartov, Omer, *Hitler's Army: Soldiers, Nazis and War in the Third Reich* (New York: Oxford University Press, 1992)

Bartov, Omer *The Eastern Front 1941--5, German troops and the Barbarisation of Warfare* (London: MacMillan, 2001)

Baxter, Ian, *SS: The Secret Archives – Eastern Front* (London: Amber Books, 2003)

Beevor, Antony, *The Fall of Berlin* (New York: Viking, 2002)

Bjerregaard, Jens Pank: *SS Regiment 24 Danmark I Bataljon. Oprettelsen og undergangen I 1943-1944* (Aarhus, Eget forlag, 2013)

Böhler, Jochen, *Auftakt zum Vernichtungskrieg. Die Wehrmacht in Polen 1939* (Bonn: Fischer, 2006)

Bonn, Keith, *Slaughterhouse: The Encyclopedia of the Eastern* Front (New York: Military Book Club, 2002)

Bonn, Keith E. of the Aberjona Press in: *Slaughterhouse. The Handbook of the Eastern Front*, (Aberjona Press, Bedford, 2005)

Borg, Gösta *Det röda massanfallet* (Stockholm: Fahlcrantz & Gumaelius, 1951)

Brandt, Allen *The Last Knight of Flanders*, (Schiffer Publishing 1998)

Brenden, Geir & Schei, Derek M, *Norske krigsfrivillige på tysk side Nr 2* (Hövedsmannen ANS, 2009)

Brenden, Geir, Natedal, Tommy & Thoresen, Flovik, *Norske offiserer i Waffen-SS* (Oslo: Historie & Kultur, 2013)

Brenden, Geir & Thomassen, Arne Häkon, *Hitlers Norske Skijegere* (Historie & Kultur, 2013)

Brenden, Geir & Natedal, Tommy, *Norwegian volunteers of the Waffen SS* (Solihull: Helion, 2016)

Bruyne, Eddy de & Rikmenspoel, Marc *For Rex and for Belgium. Léon Degrelle and Walloon Political & Military Collaboration 1940-45* (Solihull: Helion, 2004)

Bundgard, Christensen, Poulsen, Niels & Scharff Smith, Peter, *Under hagekors og Dannebrog. Danskere i Waffen-SS* (Copenhagen: Aschehoug, 1998)

Bundgard, Christensen, Poulsen, Niels & Scharff Smith, Peter, *Waffen-SS, Europas nazistiska soldater* (Copenhagen: Gyldendal, 2015)

Burleigh, Michael, *The Third Reich. A New History* (London: PanMacMillan, 2000)

Burleigh, Michael, *Moral Combat. A History of World War II* (London: Harper, 2010)

Buttar, Prit, *Between Giants. The Battle for the Baltics in World War II* (Oxford: Osprey, 2013)

Bøgh, Frank, *Gruppen, Peter. Tysk terror i Danmark* (Copenhagen: Documentas, 2007).

Carius, Otto, *Tiger im Schlamm* (Neckargemund: Vowinckel Verlag, 1960)

Carius, Otto *Tigers in the Mud*, Mechanigsburg, Stackpole, (2003)

Christiansen, Karl O. *Landssvigerkriminaliteten i sociologisk belysning* (Copenhagen: Gads Forlag, 1955)

Christensen, Claus Bundgård, Poulsen, Niels Bo & Smith, Peter Scharff (eds.), *Dagbog fra østfronten. En dansker i Waffen-SS 1941-44* (Copenhagen: Aschehoug, 2005)

Christensen, Claus Bundgård, Lund, Joachim Niels, Olesen, Wium & Sørensen, Jakob *Danmark besat – krig og hverdag 1940-45* (Informations Forlag, 2015)

Colby, William, *Honorable Men: My Life in the CIA* (New York, Simon & Schuster, 1978)

Cüppers, Martin *Wegbereiter ders Shoah. Die Waffen-SS, der Kommandostab Reichsführer-SS und die Judenvernichtung 1939-45*, (Kindle 2005)

Davies, Norman, *Europe at War. No simple Victory* (London PanMacMillan, 2006)

Drobiazko, S.I., *Russkaja osvoboditelnaja armija* (Moscow: Izdatelstvo AST, 1998)

Drobjazko, S.I.: *Vostochnye legiony i kazachi chasti* (Moscow: Izdatelstvo AST, 1999)

Ekdahl, Sven, *The Battle of Grunwald/Tannenberg and its political and symbolic interpretations in Poland and Germany through the Centuries*; in: *New Approaches. Jan Matejko's Battle of Grunwald* (Edited by Katarzyna Murawska-Muthesius), The National Museum of Warsaw, 2010

Ekdahl, Sven *Crusades and Colonization in the Baltic: A Historiographic Analysis*, in Alan V. Murray (ed.), *The North-Eastern Frontiers of Medieval Europe. The Expansion of Latin Europe 1000-1500* (Farnham: Ashgate, 2014)

Emberland, Terje, Religion og rase. Nyhedenskap og nazisme i Norge 1933-1945 (Oslo: Humanist Forlag 2003)

Emberland, Terje & Kott, Matthew, *Himmlers Norge* (Oslo: Aschehoug, 2012)

Engel, Helmut, *Das Kriegsende 1945 im Berliner Südosten*; Friedrichshagener Hefte Nr. 64 (Berlin, Verlag Antiquariat Brandel, 2012)

Estes, Kenneth. W. *An European Anabasis*, (Helion Ltd UK, 2014)

Frankson, Anders & Zetterling, Niklas, *Analysing World War II Eastern Front Battles* in: The Journal of Slavic Military Studies, Vol 11 1998, p. 176-203

Frankson, Anders *Kort historik om Tigerförbanden* i: Otto Carius, *Med Tigern på slagfältet. Otto Carius om pansarkriget på östfronten 1941-45;* SMB Stockholm 2012

Friedrich, Jörg *Die kalte Amnestie. NS-Täter in der Bundesrepublik* (Berlin, Ullstein, 2997)

Fröhlich, Elke (ed.), *Die Tagebücher von Joseph Goebbels, Teil II* (Munich: 1995)

Ganser, Daniele, NATO´s Secret Armies: Operation Gladio and Terrorism in Western Europé (London, Frankc Cass, 2005)

Gebhardt, Mirian, *Als die Soldaten kamen. Die Vergewaltung deutscher Frauen am Ende des zweiten Krieges* (München, Deutsche Verslagsanstalt, 2015)

Gellately, Robert, *Lenin, Stalin and Hitler. The Age of Social Catastrophe* (London: Vintage Books, 2008)

Gentile, Carlo: *'Politische Soldaten. Die 16. SS-Panzergrenadier-Division "Reichsführer-SS' in Italien 1944', Quellen und Forschungen aus italienischen Archiven und Bibliotheken 8* (2001)

Gerald Fleming, *Hitler and the Final solution* (Princeton, University of California Press, 1995)

Gilbert, Martin, *Auschwitz and the Allies* (New York: Holt Rinehart Winston, 1981)

Gyllenhaal, Lars & Westberg, Lennart, *Swedes at War, Willing Warriors from a Neutral Nation, 1914–1945* (Bedford, Pennsylvania: The Aberjona Press, 2010)

Görlitz, Walter, *Die Waffen-SS* (Berlin: Arani, 1960)

Hamilton, A. Stephan *The Oder Front 1945. Generaloberst Gotthard Heinrici, Heeresgruppe Weichsel and Germany's Final Defense in the East, 20 March-3 May* (Solihull: Helion & Company Ltd, 2011)

Harder, Thomas *Kryssing. Manden, der valgte forkert* (Copenhagen: Lindhardt og Ringhof, 2014)

Hastings, Max: *Armageddon. The Battle for Germany 1944-45* (London: MacMillan, 2004)

Hastings, Max, *Armageddon. The Battle for Germany 1944-45* (London, Vintage, 2005).

Hastings, Max *Das Reich. The March of the 2nd SS Panzer-Division through France 1944* (London: Pan Books, 2009)

Herrmann, Gerd-Ulrich *Das Kriegsende 1945*, Culturcon Medien, Berlin 2010

Höhne, Heinz, *The Order of the Death's Head* (New York: Penguin Books, 1971)

Horchem, Hans Josef *Kinder im Krieg, Kindheit und Jugend im Dritten Reich*; Mittler & Sohn, Hamburg 2014

Hördler, Stefan *KZ-System und Waffen-SS. Genese, Interpendenzen und Verbrechen*, in Schulte, Lieb & Wegner, *Die Waffen-SS. Neue Forschungen* (Paderborn: Schöningh, 2014)

Haaest, Erik, *Frontsvin* (Helsinge: Bogan, 1975), *Frostknuder* (Copenhagen: Bogan, 1975) and *Forrædere*, (Copenhagen: Bogan, 1975). The three volumes were later re-edited and published as a one-volume book titled *Frikorpsfolk* (Helsinge: Bogan, 1995)

Haaest, Erik *Intet nyt fra ostfronten*, Viborg 1998

In´t Veld, N.K.C.A. De SS en Nederland: Documenten uit SS-Archieven 1935-1945 (The Hague, Martinus Nijhoff, 1976)

Jokipii, Mauno, *Panttipataljoona. Suomalaisen SSpataljoonan historia* (Helsinki: Veljesapu, 1968)

Jonassen, Lasse Bruun & Lind, Jonas *Schøiler Gruppen. Danske terrorister i tysk tjeneste 1944-45* (Copenhagen: Informations Forlag, 2012).

Jones, Nigel, *The Birth of the Nazis. How the Freikorps blazed a trail for Hitler* (New York: Carroll & Graf, 2004)

Jünger, Ernst *Tagebücher*, Ernst Klett Verlag, Stuttgart, 1975

Kaden, Eric *Das Wort als Waffe. Der Propagandakrieg der Waffen-SS und die SS-Standarte "Kurt Eggers";* Winkelried Verlag, Dresden, 2009

Kaienburg, Hermann *Der Militär- und Witschaftskomplex der SS im KZ-Standort Sachsenhausen-Oranienburg*; Metropol-Verlag, Berlin 2006

Keegan, John, *Waffen-SS, The Asphalt Soldiers* (London: Ballantine, 1970)

Kempner, Robert M.W. *SS im Kreuzverhör* (Nördlingen, Rütten & Löning Verlag, 1964)

Kershaw, Ian *Hitlers Macht, Das Profil der NS-Herrschaft* (Munich: Deutscher Taschenbuchverlag, 2001)

Kirkebæk, Mikkel *Schalburg. En patriotisk landsforræder* (Copenhagen: Gyldendal, 2008)

Kirkebæk, Mikkel & Lauridsen, John T. (eds.), *Et liv uden fædreland. Søren Kams erindringer* (Copenhagen: Lindhardt & Ringhof, 2015)

Kjellander, Petter, *Estniska frontsoldater berättar (20th Estonian Waffen-Grenadier-Division der SS)*, Vol. 1, *Till siste man*; Vol. 2, *Undergången* (Stockholm: Svenskt Militärhistoriskt Bibliotek, 2011)

Klee, Ernst, *Personenlexikon zum Dritten Reich. Wer war was vor und nach 1945* (Augsburg: Weltbild, 2003)

Kleijn, Cees & S.J.P. Reurs: *Report on Dutch sources concerning the involvement of the SS-Division "Wiking" in war crimes and crimes against humanity in Ukraine in the summer of 1941* (Amsterdam, Manuscript, 2018)

Knobloch, Heinz *Der beherzte Reviervorsteher. Ungewöhnliche Zivilcourage am Hackeschen Markt*; Berlin, Morgenbuch Verlag, 1993

Knopp, Guido: *Die SS. Eine Warnung der Geschichte* (Munich, Bertelsmann, 2002

Koehl, Robert L., *The Black Corps, The Structure and Power Struggles of the Nazi SS* (Madison, 1983)

Krabbe, Oluf *Danske soldater i kamp på Østfronten 1941-1945* (Odense: Odense Universitetsforlag, 1976

Krausnick, Wilhelm & Wilhelm, Hans-Heinrich, *Die Truppe des Weltanschauuungskrieges. Die Einsatzgruppen der Sicherheitspolizei und des SD 1938–1942* (Stuttgart: Deutsche Verlagsanstalt, 1981)

Kristensen, Henrik Skov & Tamm, Ditlev *Dødsdømt – Flemming Helweg-Larsens beretning* (Copenhagen: Gyldendal, 2008)

Kristensen, Henrik Skov *Straffelejren: Fårhus, landssvigerne og retsopgøret* (Copenhagen: Gyldendal, 2011)

Krivosheyev, G.F, *Soviet Combat Casualties and Losses in the Twentieth Century* (London, Greenhill Books 1997)

Kühl, Stefan *Ganze normal Organisationen. Zur Soziologie des Holocaust* (Berlin: 2014)

Knopp, Guido *Die SS. Eine Warnung der Geschichte* (Munich: Bertelsmann, 2002),

Knopp, Guido *Geheimnisse des "Dritten Reiches"* (München, Bertelsmann 2011)

Kurowski, Franz, *SS-Obersturmbannführer Paul-Albert Kausch* (Würzburg: Flechsig, 2013)

Kwiet, Konrad (ed.), *Ausbildungsziel Judenmord?* (Frankfurt am Main: Fischer, 2003)

Landwehr, Richard, *Narva 1944: The Waffen-SS and the Battle for Europa* (Silver Spring, Maryland: Bibliophile Legion Books, 1981)

Laerum, Erik *Dansk soldat i krig og fred* (Kultur & Politik, Copenhagen, 1955

Larsen, Dennis *Fortrængt grusomhed. Danske SS-vagter 1941-45*, (Copenhagen: Gyldendal, 2010)

Larsen, Dennis & Stræde, Therkel *En skole i vold. Bobruisk 1941-44* (Copenhagen: Gyldendal, 2014)

Leleu, Jean-Luc *Gründe für die Expansion der Waffen-SS*, in: Schulte, Lieb & Wegner

Longerich, Peter, *Heinrich Himmler. Biographie* (Munich: Siedler, 2009)

Ludeke, Alexander, *Panzer der Wehrmacht* (Stuttgart: Motorbuch Verlag, 2009)

Lundin, Ingvar, *Baltiska judar* (Malmö: Warne, 2000)

Lundtofte, Henrik *Håndlangerne: Schalburgkorpsets Efterretningstjeneste og Hipokorpset 1943-1945* (Copenhagen: Politikens Forlag, 2014)

Maeger, Herbert, *Verlorene Ehre, Verratene Treue* (Rosenheim: Rosenheimer Verlagshaus, 2002)

Marini, A. Marini. A. *Del Caucaso a Leningrado* (Buenos Aires: Circulo Militar Argentino, 1958). The two volumes were later published in Danish under his own name. P.R. Engelhardt, *Fra Kaukasus til Leningrad* (Copenhagen: Forlaget ZAC, 1980);

Matthäus, Jürgen, Kwiet, Konrad, Förster, Jürgen & Breitman, Richard, *Ausbildungsziel Judenmord? "Weltanschauliche Erziehung" von SS, Polizei und Waffen-SS im Rahmen der "Endlösung"* (Frankfurt: Fischer, 2003)

Megargee, Geoffrey, *War of Annihilation: Combat and Genocide on the Eastern Front, 1941* (New York: Bowman & Littlefield, 2006)

Merridale, Catherine, *Ivan's War. The Red Army, 1939–1945* (New York: Picador, 2009)

Messerschmidt, Manfred, *Die Wehrmacht im NS-Staat* (Hamburg: R.V. Decker, 1969)

Middeldorf, Eike *Taktik im Russlandfeldzug*, Koehler, Hamburg, 1956

Middeldorf, Eike, *Taktik på östfronten* (Stockholm, Norstedts Akademiska Förlag, 2005)

Moore, John P., *Signal Officers of the Waffen-SS* (Portland, OR, J P Moore Publishing, 1996)

Mueller, Michael, *Canaris. Hitlers Abwehrchef* (Berlin: List, 2007)

Mühlen, Bengt von zur (Ed.): *Der Todeskampf der Reichshauptstadt* (Berlin, Chronos, 1994)

Murray, Alan V. (ed.): *The North-Eastern Frontiers of Medieval Europe*. The Expansion of Latin Europe 1000-15000 (Farnham, Ashgate, 2014)

Neitzel, Sönke (ed.), *Tapping Hitler's Generals: Transcripts of Secret Conversations 1942–1945* (St Paul, Minn.: Frontline Books, 2007)

Neulen, Hans Werner, *An deutscher Seite. Internationale Frieiwillige von Wehrmacht und Waffen-SS* (Munich: Universitas, 1985)

Neulen, Hans Werner *Am Himmel Europas. Luftstreitkräfte an deutscher Seite 1939-1945* (Munich: Universitas Verlag, 1998)

Nielsen, Holger Thor *Nordic Warriors, SS-Panzergrenadier-Regiment 24 Danmark, Eastern Front, 1943-45*, Shelf Books, Halifax, 1999

Nipe Jr, George *Last victory in Russia. The SS-Panzer-Korps and Manstein's Kharkov Counteroffensive February-March 1943* (Pennsylvania:Schiffer Publishing, 2000)

Oertle, Vincenz, *Schweizer Freiwillige an deutscher Seite 1939–1945* (Zürich: Thesis, 1997)

Paxton, Robert O. *Vichy France: Old Guard and New Order 1940-44*. New York, Knopf 1972

Pedersen, Bjarne Salling *I krig for fjenden, SS-frivillig Georg Rasmussens erindringer* (Copenhagen: Informations Forlag, 2011)

Porter, David *Hitler's Secret Weapons 1933-1945*, Amber Books, London 2010

Poulsen, Henning *Besættelsesmagten og de danske nazister: Det politiske forhold mellem tyske myndigheder og nazistiske kredse i Danmark 1940-43* (Copenhagen: Gyldendal, 1970)

Pringle, Heather, *The Master Plan. Himmler's Scholars and the Holocaust* (London: Harper Collins, 2006)

Ramm, Gerald, *Ein unbekannter Kamerad. Deutsche Kriegsgräberstätten zwischen Oderbruch und Spree* (Woltersdorf, P & R Verlag, 1993)

Rhodes, Richard, *Die Deutschen Mörder. Die SS-Einsatzgruppen und der Holcaust* (Bergisch Gladbach, Bastei-Lübbe, 2002)

Rikmenspoel, Marc J., *Waffen-SS: The Encyclopedia* (New York: Military Book Club, 2002)

Roseman, Mark, *The Villa, the Lake, the Meeting.Wannsee and the Final Solution* (London: Penguin, 2001)
Rohrkamp, René *"Weltanschaulich gefestigte Kämpfer" – Die Soldaten der Waffen-SS 1933-1945* (Ferdinand Schöning, 2010)
Rohrkamp, René *Die Rekrutierungspraxis der Waffen-SS*, p. 57, in: Schulte, Lieb & Wegner
Roslyng-Jensen Palle, *Danskerne og besættelsen. Holdninger og meninger 1939-1945* (Copenhagen: Gads Forlag, 2007
Rueckerl, Adalbert, *NS-Prozesse* (Karlsruhe: C.F. Mueller, 1971)
Schenck, Ernst Günther, *1945. Als Artzt in Hitlers Reichskanzlei* (Stockach, Bavarian Connection, 1986)
Scherzer, Veit, *Sous le Signe SS – Französische Freiwillige in der Waffen-SS*, (Bayreuth: Scherzer, 2018)
Schmalenbach, Paul *Prinz Eugen unter drei Flaggen*, Koehler, Hamburg, 2001
Schuetz, Waldemar (ed.), *General Felix Steiner* (Duesseldorf: Deutsche Verlagsanstalt, 1999)
Schultz-Naumann, Joachim. *Last Thirty Days*, (New York, Madison Books, 1991)
Schulte, Jan Erik, Lieb, Peter & Wegner, Bernd (eds), *Die Waffen-SS. Neue Forschungen* (Paderborn: 2014)
Sierck, Joachim *Der Einsatz von Marineangehörigen aus Stralsund in Berlin*; in: *Der Todeskampf der Reichshauptstadt* (Ed. Bengt von zur Mühlen), Chronos, Berlin, 1994
Smelser, Ronald & Syring, Enrico (Ed.), *Die Militärelite des Dritten Reiches*. Ullstein 1995
Smelser, Ronald & Syring, Enrico, *Die SS. Elite unter dem Totenkopf* (Paderborn: Schöningh, 2000)
Smelser, Ronald and Davies, Edward J. *The Myth of the Eastern Front: the Nazi-Soviet War in American Popular Culture* (Cambridge: 2008)
Snyder, Timothy, *Bloodlands, Eastern Europe Between Hitler and Stalin* (New York: Basic Books, 2019)
Stafford, David *Endgame, 1945. The Missing Final Chapter of World War II*, Back Bay Books, New York 2007
Stenger, Dieter, *Panzers East and West: The German 10th SS Panzer Division from the Eastern Front to Normandy* (London, Rowman & Littlefield, 2017)
Stiglegger, Marcus *Nazi-Chic und Nazi-Trash. Faschistische Ästhetik in der populären Kultur* (Berlin: 2011)
Sørlie, Sigurd, *Solkors eller hakekors. Nordmenn i Waffen-SS 1940–1945* (Oslo: Dreyer, 2015)
Stein, Georg, *The Waffen-SS. Hitler's Elite Guard at War 1939–1945* (New York: Cornell University Press, 1966)
Steinert, Marlies G. *Die 23 Tage der Regierung Dönitz*, Econ Verlag, Düsseldorf, 1967
Sydnor, Charles W., *Soldiers of Destruction: The SS Death's Head Division, 1933–1945* (Princeton: Princeton University Press, 1990)
Tamm, Ditlev *Retsopgøret efter besættelsen* (Copenhagen: Jurist- og Økonomforbundets Forlag, 1985
Tieke, Wilhelm *Das Ende zwischen Oder und Elbe. Der Kampf um Berlin 1945*, Motorbuch Verlag, Stuttgart 1981
Tieke, Wilhelm, *Tragedy of the Faithful. A History of the III. (Germ.) SS-Panzer-Korps* (Winnipeg: Fedorowicz, 2001)
Tissier, Tony Le; Zhukov at the Oder. The Decisive Battle for Berlin (Mechanicsburg, Stackpole, 2009)
Trigg', Jonathan *Hitler's Vikings: The History of the Scandinavian Waffen-SS: The Legions, the SS-Wiking and the SS-Nordland* (Brimscombe Port: The History Press, 2011)
Veum, Erik & Brenden, Geir, *De som falt. Nordmenn drept i tysk krigstjeneste* (Oslo: NRK Activum, 2009)
Veum, Eirik, Brenden, Geir & Torgeir, Lindtvedt Dalen, *Deres aere var Troskap* (Vega, 2016)
Weale, Adrian *Renegades, Hitler's Englishmen*; Warner Books, London, 1994
Weale, Adrian, *The SS. A New Story* (London: Little, Brown, 2013)
Weber, Thomas, *Hitler's First War* (Oxford: Oxford University Press, 2010)
Wegner, Bernd, *Hitlers politische Soldaten: Die Waffen-SS 1933–1945* (Paderborn: Schöning, 1982)
Wegner, Bernd, *Auf dem Wege zur pangermanischen Armee. Dokumente zur Entstehungsgeschichte des III. ("germanischen") SS-Panzerkorps*, in Militärgeschichtliche Mitteilungen, 2/1980 (Freiburg i.Br.)
Wegner, Bernd *The Waffen-SS: Organization, Ideology and Function* (New Jersey: Blackwell, 1990)
Westemeier, Jens, *Hans Robert Jauss. Jugend, Krieg und Internierung* (Konstanz: Konstanz University Press, 2016)
Westerlund, Lars, *Cirkus Collani* (*The Finnish SS-Volunteer Battalion*) (Helsinki: Books on Demand, 2017)
Wilbeck, Christopher W. *Sledgehammers. Strengths and Flaws of Tiger Tank Batallions in World War II*, Aberjona Press, Bedford (US) 2004
Williamson, Gordon, *The SS: Hitler's Instrument of Terror* (London: Brown Packaging, 1994)
Winkler, Heinrich August *Auf ewig in Hitler's Schatten? Über die Deutschen und ihre Geschichte*; C.H. Beck, Munich, 2007
Wolf, Eric *Envisioning Power. Ideologies of Dominance and Crisis*, (Berkeley, University of California Press, 1999)
Zetterling, Niklas & Frankson, Anders, *Kursk 1943: a statistical analysis* (London: Frank Cass, 2000)